5

Story & Art by
Yuki Yoshihara

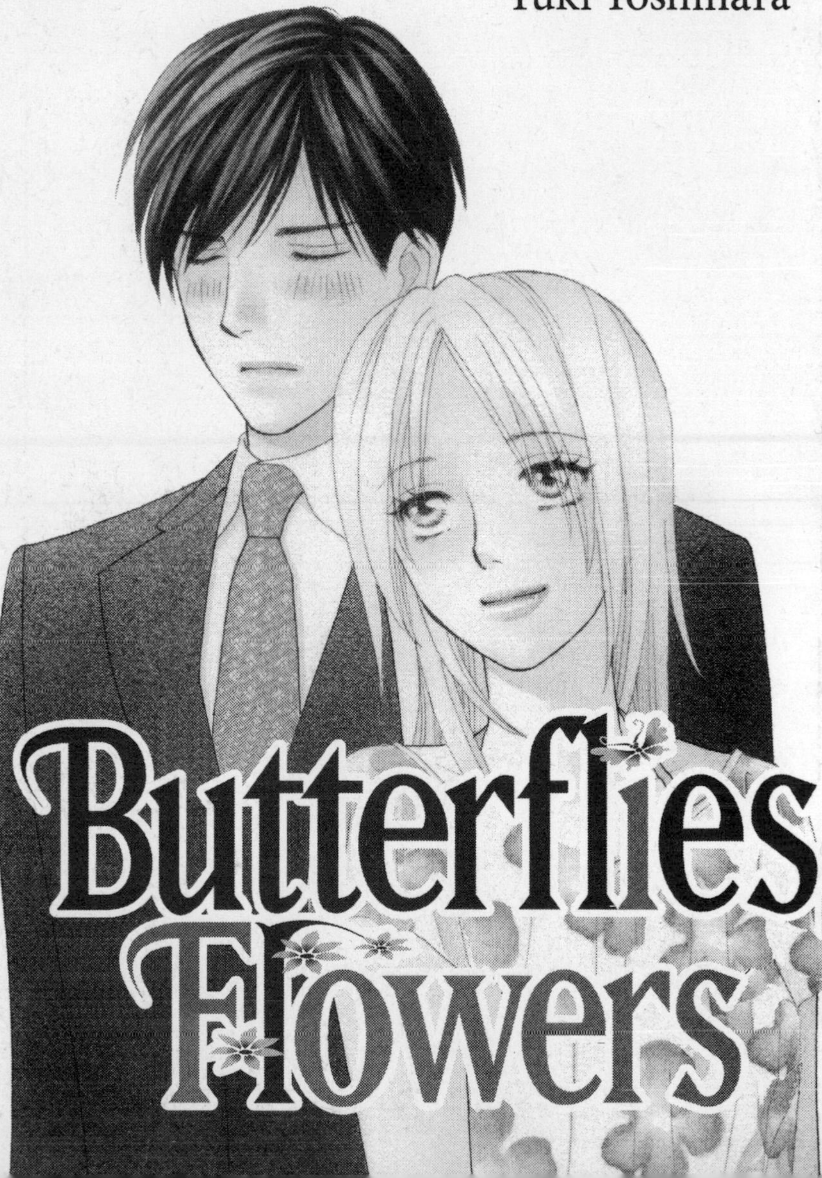

Butterflies Flowers

Butterflies, Flowers 5

Characters

◆Choko Kuze
She's an office worker from an upper-class family who used to be rich. Domoto usually gets the better of her, but at times, she brings out her "aristocratic girl's resolve."

Story Thus Far

◆Choko's family used to be extremely rich until 14 years ago when they went bankrupt. Now they're just a working-class family running a soba shop.

◆Choko starts working in the Administration Department of a real estate company. But being unskilled, Choko finds herself being pushed around by the senior staff and the mean Director Domoto...

◆Domoto's father used to be a servant who worked for the Kuze family. The director is actually "Cha-chan," the boy who looked after Choko when she was small!

◆Masayuki Domoto

The Director whom Choko loves.
He's the son of a former servant
to the Kuze family. He is a rather
high-handed supervisor, but he
supports Choko in her private life.
Her childhood nickname for him
is "Cha-chan."

◆Genzaburo Suou

He's a veteran office worker in the Administration
Department and a good friend of Domoto. He's a
guy, but he usually cross-dresses.

◆Domoto tells Choko that he will protect her with his life. Choko finds
out what it's like to be in love. But Domoto continues to treat her as if she
were a child...

◆Choko gets Domoto to accept her as an adult, and the two start dating.

◆And at long last the two become lovers, strengthening their bond.
Domoto declares he will no longer sexually harass her and even asks if
she wants to live with him...?!

Butterflies, Flowers

Contents

Chapter 21
Breakfast for Two

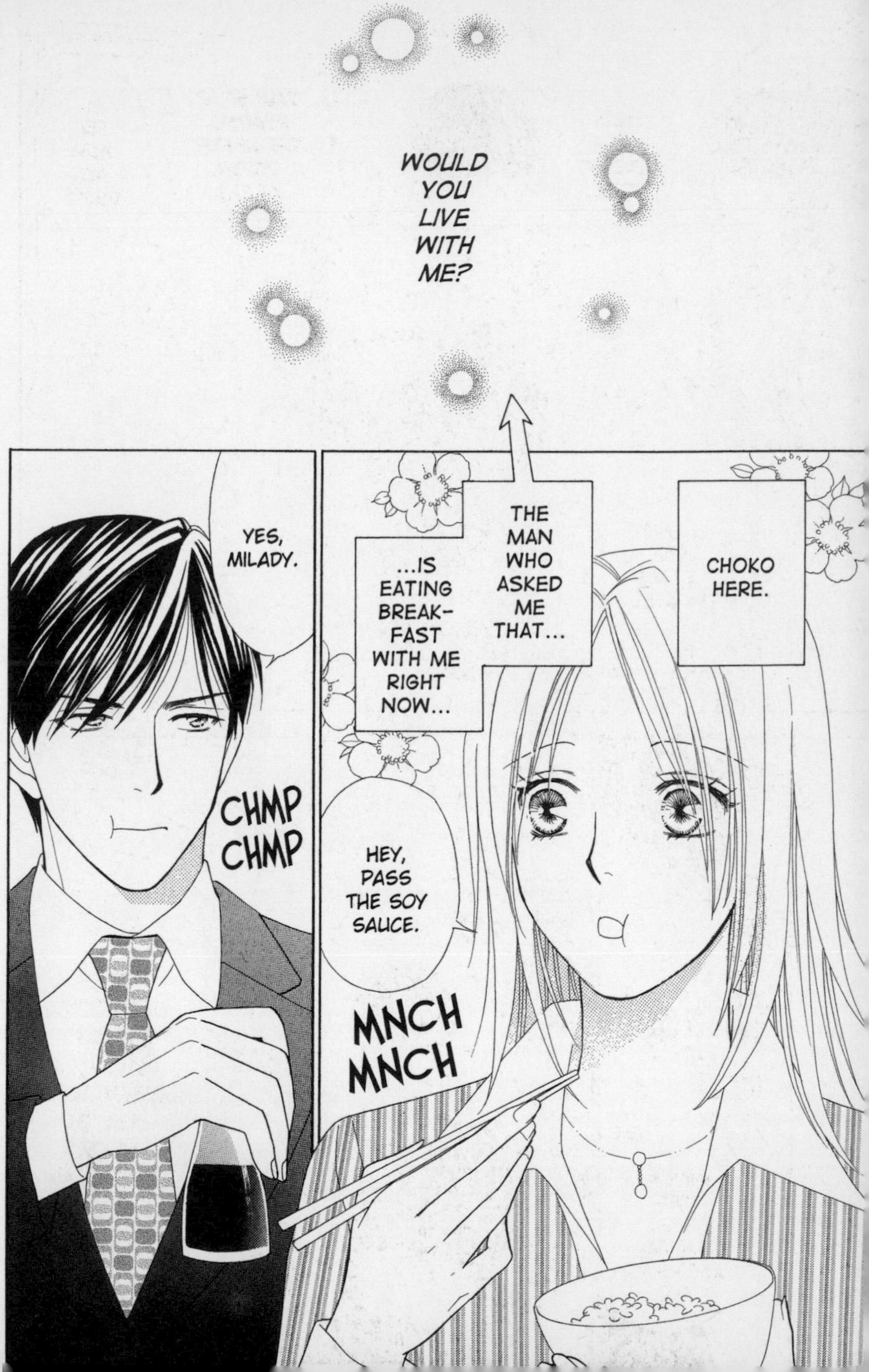
WOULD YOU LIVE WITH ME?
CHOKO HERE.
THE MAN WHO ASKED ME THAT...
...IS EATING BREAK-FAST WITH ME RIGHT NOW...
HEY, PASS THE SOY SAUCE.
MNCH MNCH
YES, MILADY.
CHMP CHMP

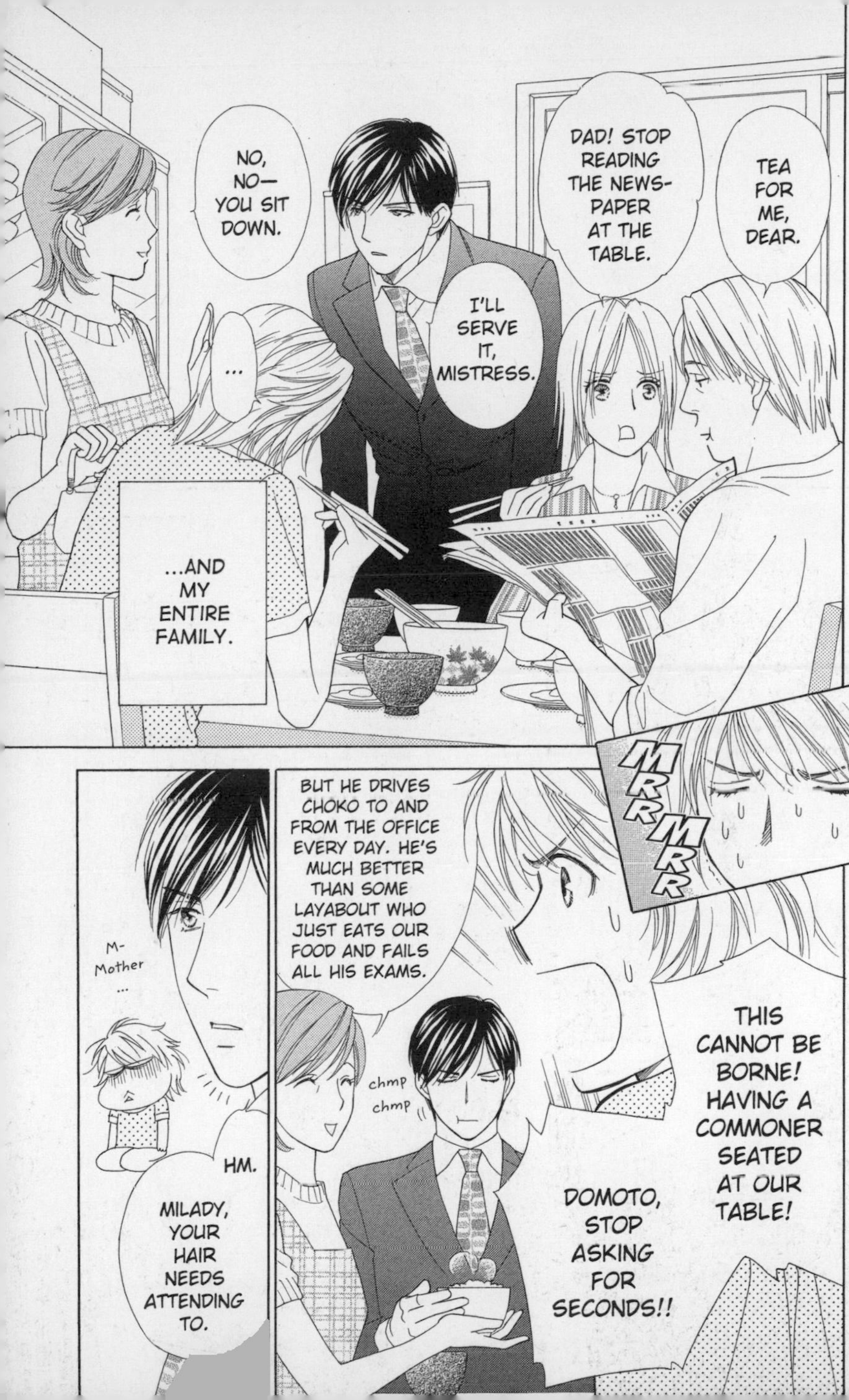
TEA FOR ME, DEAR.
DAD! STOP READING THE NEWS-PAPER AT THE TABLE.
I'LL SERVE IT, MISTRESS.
NO, NO—YOU SIT DOWN.
...
...AND MY ENTIRE FAMILY.
MRR MRR
BUT HE DRIVES CHOKO TO AND FROM THE OFFICE EVERY DAY. HE'S MUCH BETTER THAN SOME LAYABOUT WHO JUST EATS OUR FOOD AND FAILS ALL HIS EXAMS.
THIS CANNOT BE BORNE! HAVING A COMMONER SEATED AT OUR TABLE!
DOMOTO, STOP ASKING FOR SECONDS!!
chmp chmp
M-Mother ...
HM.
MILADY, YOUR HAIR NEEDS ATTENDING TO.

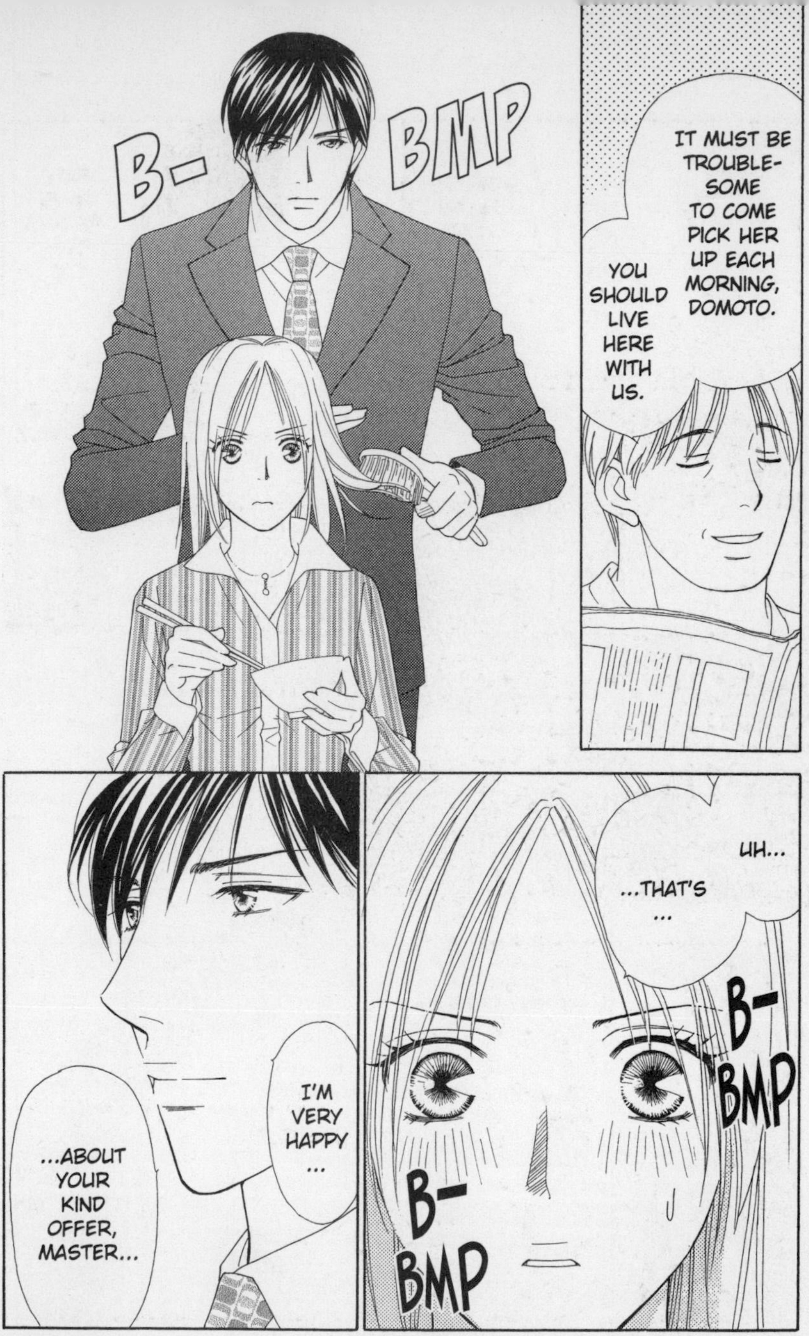
IT MUST BE TROUBLE-SOME TO COME PICK HER UP EACH MORNING, DOMOTO.
YOU SHOULD LIVE HERE WITH US.
B- BMP
UH...
...THAT'S ...
B- BMP
B- BMP
I'M VERY HAPPY ...
...ABOUT YOUR KIND OFFER, MASTER...

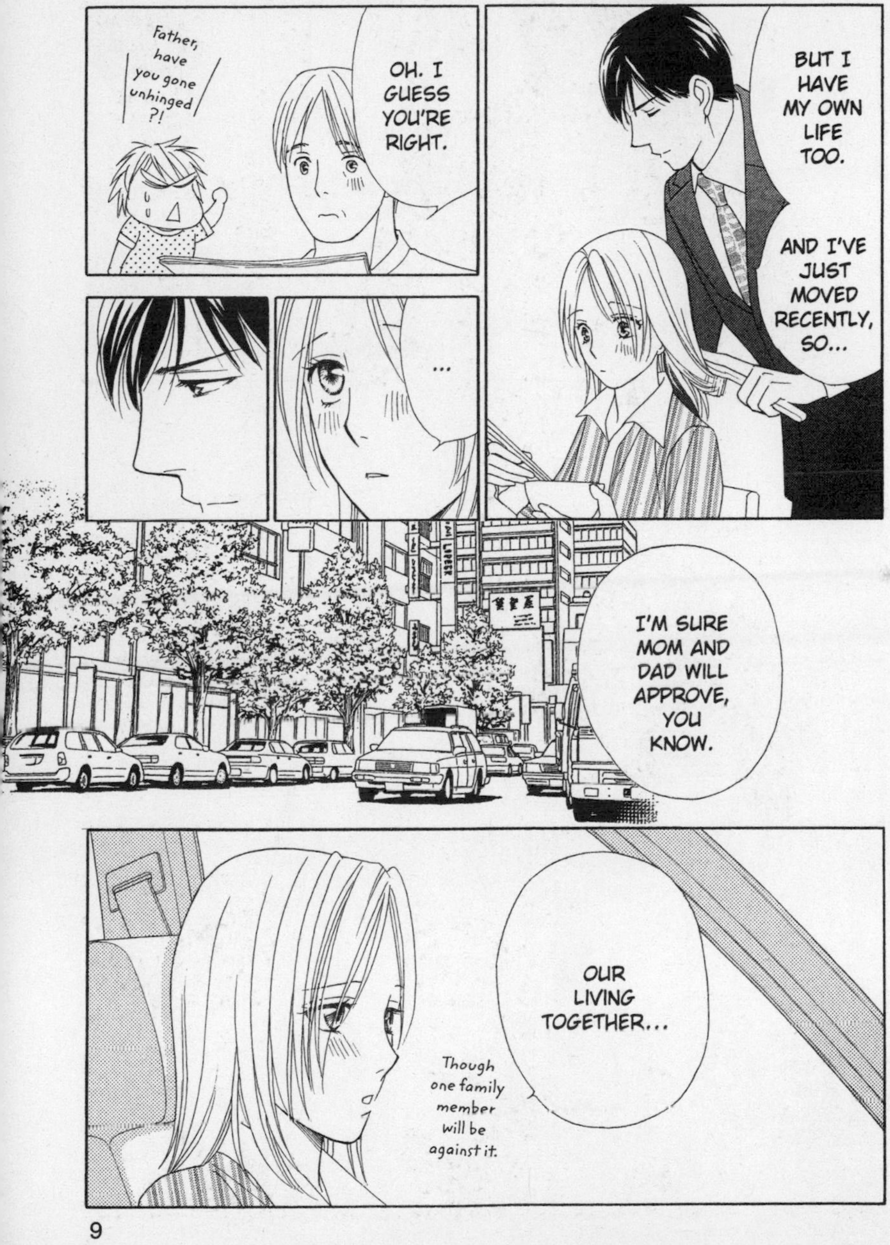
BUT I HAVE MY OWN LIFE TOO.
AND I'VE JUST MOVED RECENTLY, SO...
OH. I GUESS YOU'RE RIGHT.
Father, have you gone unhinged ?!
...
I'M SURE MOM AND DAD WILL APPROVE, YOU KNOW.
OUR LIVING TOGETHER...
Though one family member will be against it.

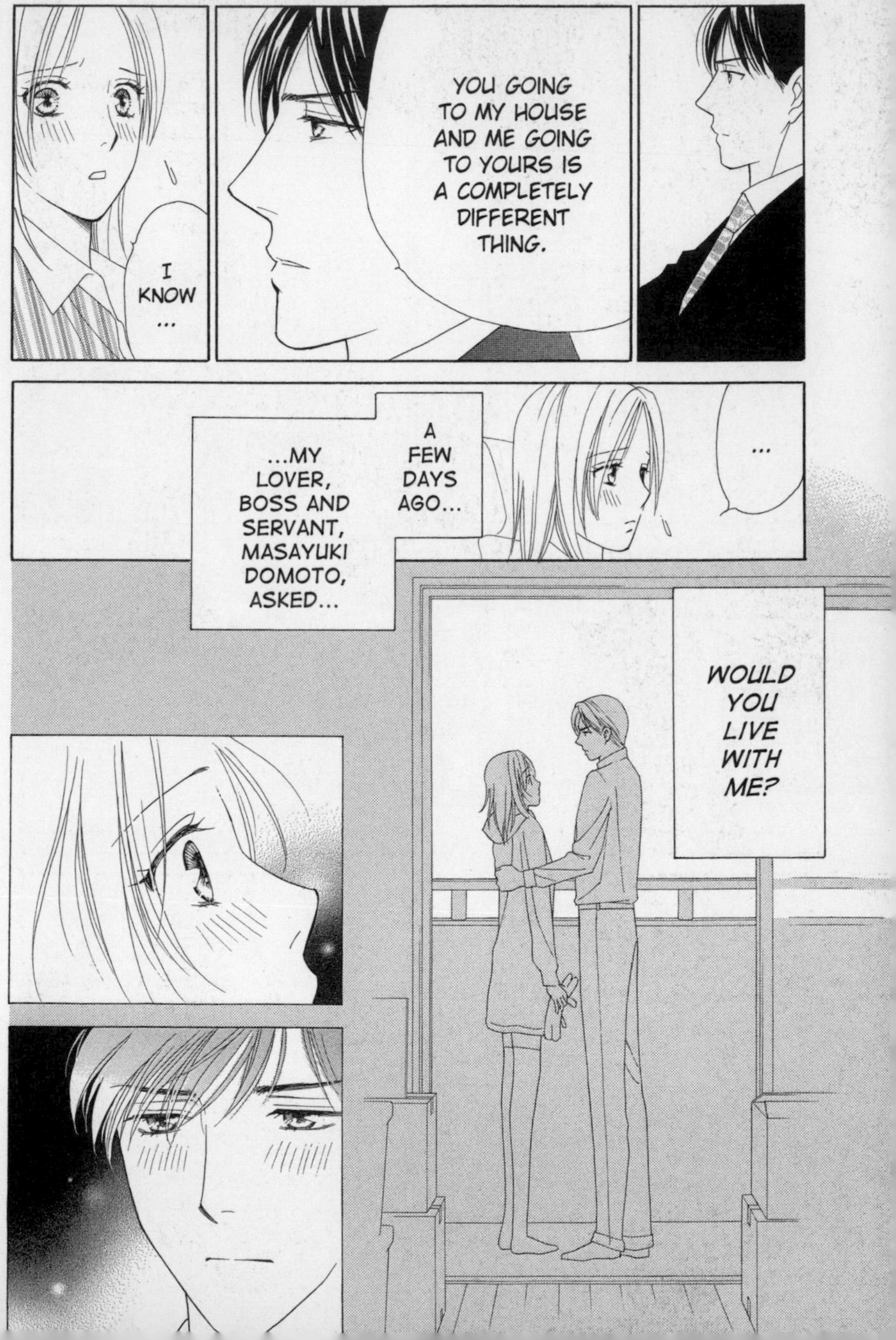
YOU GOING TO MY HOUSE AND ME GOING TO YOURS IS A COMPLETELY DIFFERENT THING.
I KNOW ...
...
A FEW DAYS AGO...
...MY LOVER, BOSS AND SERVANT, MASAYUKI DOMOTO, ASKED...
WOULD YOU LIVE WITH ME?

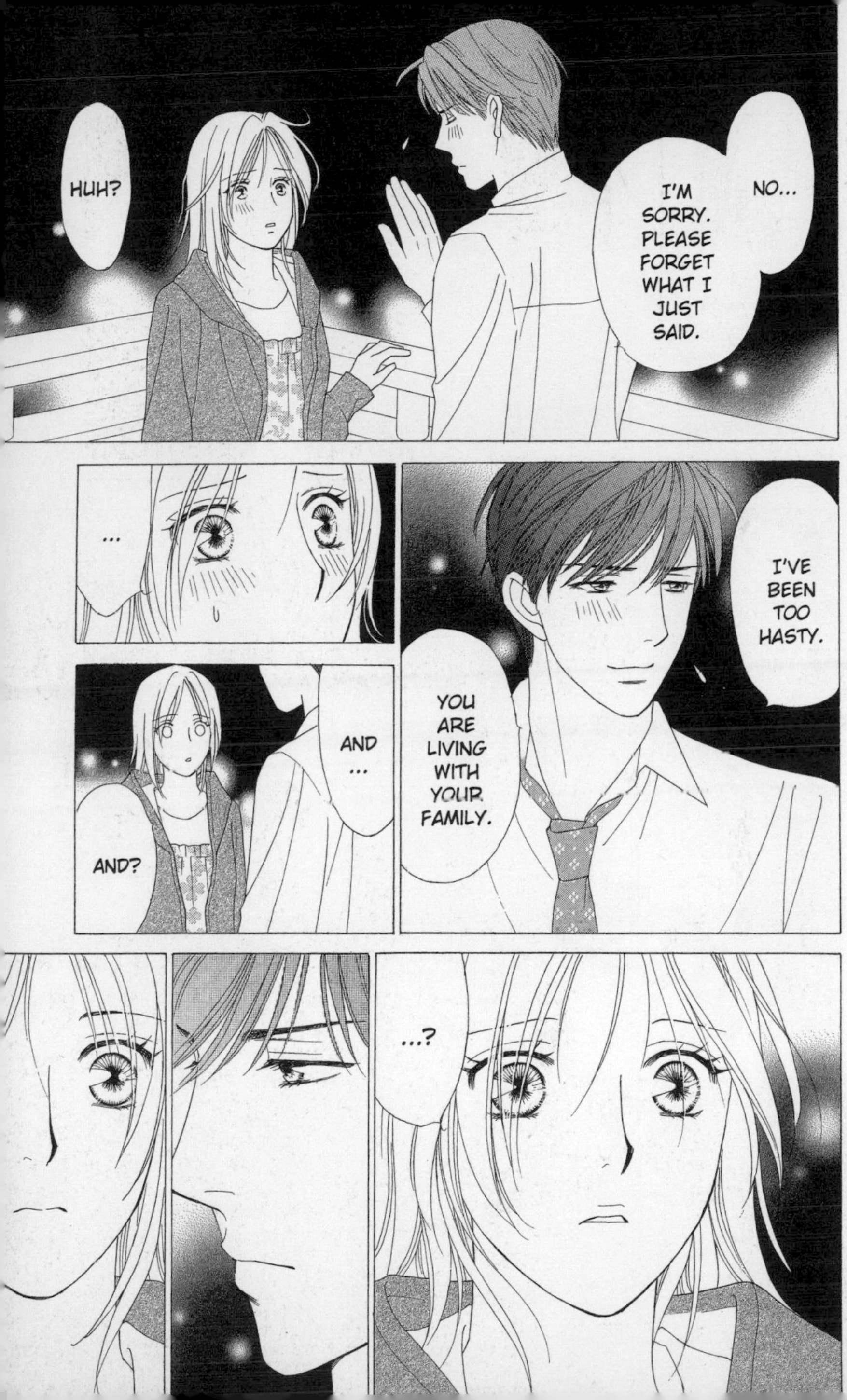
NO...
I'M SORRY. PLEASE FORGET WHAT I JUST SAID.
HUH?
I'VE BEEN TOO HASTY.
YOU ARE LIVING WITH YOUR FAMILY.
...
AND ...
AND?
...?

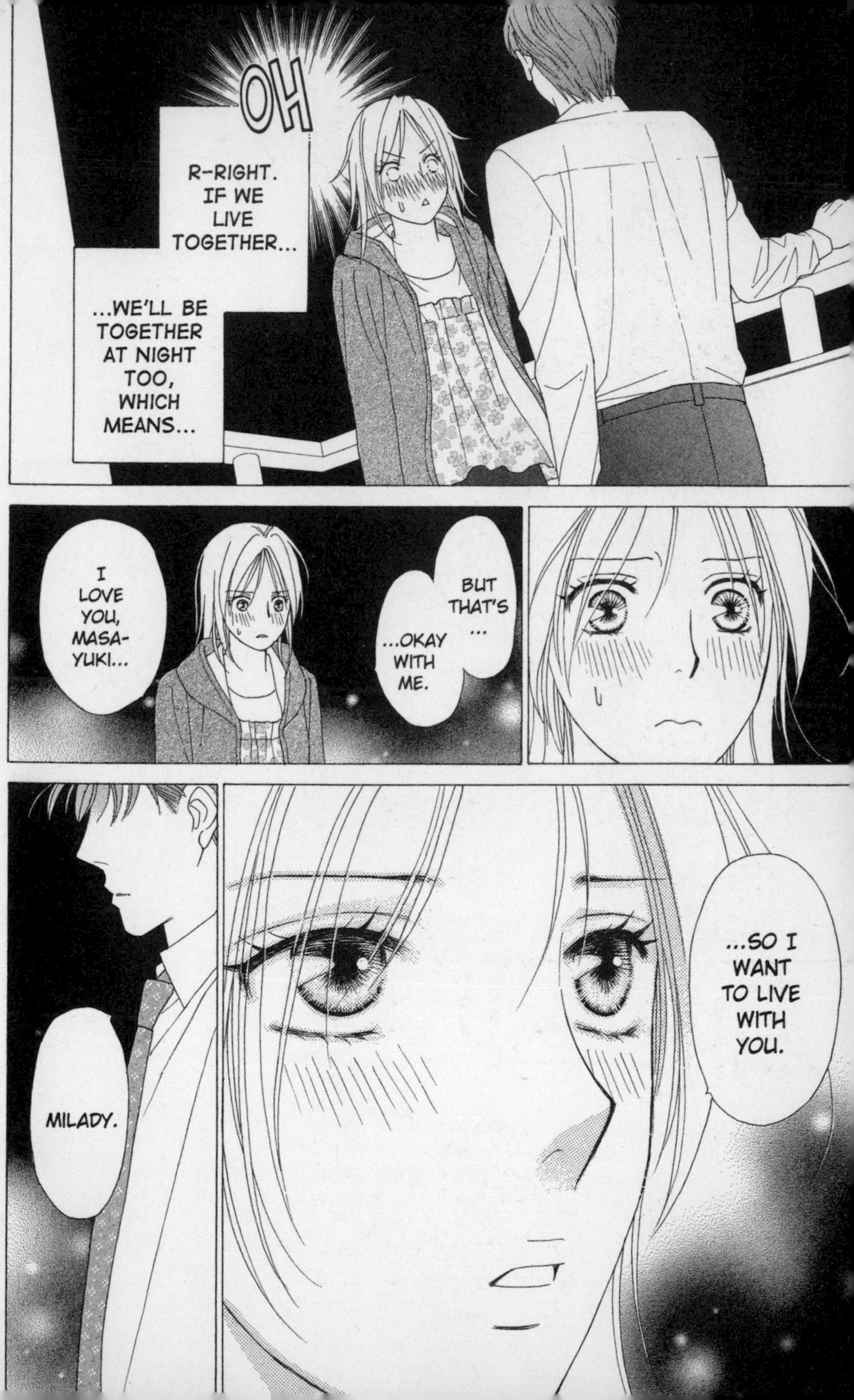
OH
R-RIGHT. IF WE LIVE TOGETHER...
...WE'LL BE TOGETHER AT NIGHT TOO, WHICH MEANS...
BUT THAT'S ...
...OKAY WITH ME.
I LOVE YOU, MASA-YUKI...
...SO I WANT TO LIVE WITH YOU.
MILADY.

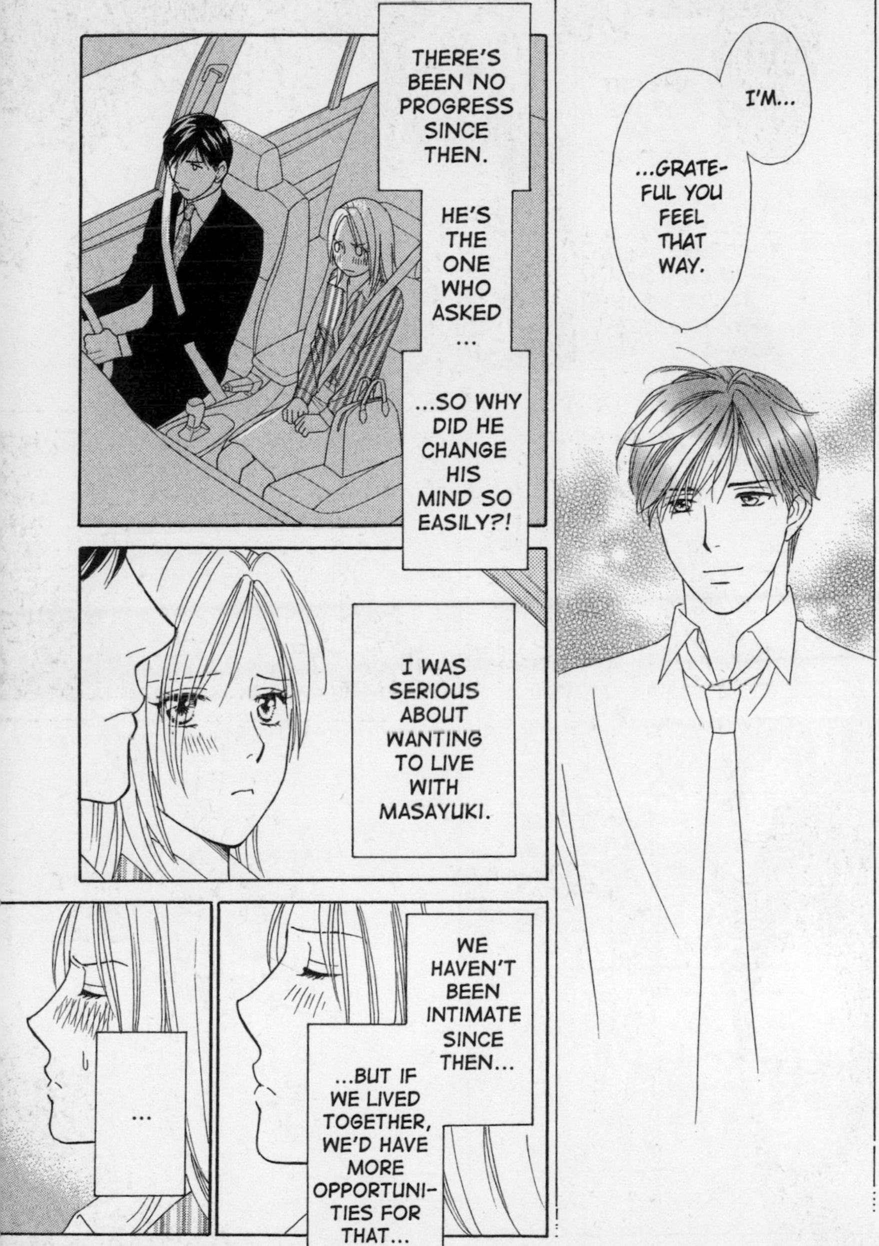
I'M...
...GRATE-FUL YOU FEEL THAT WAY.
THERE'S BEEN NO PROGRESS SINCE THEN.
HE'S THE ONE WHO ASKED...
...SO WHY DID HE CHANGE HIS MIND SO EASILY?!
I WAS SERIOUS ABOUT WANTING TO LIVE WITH MASAYUKI.
WE HAVEN'T BEEN INTIMATE SINCE THEN...
...BUT IF WE LIVED TOGETHER, WE'D HAVE MORE OPPORTUNI-TIES FOR THAT...
...

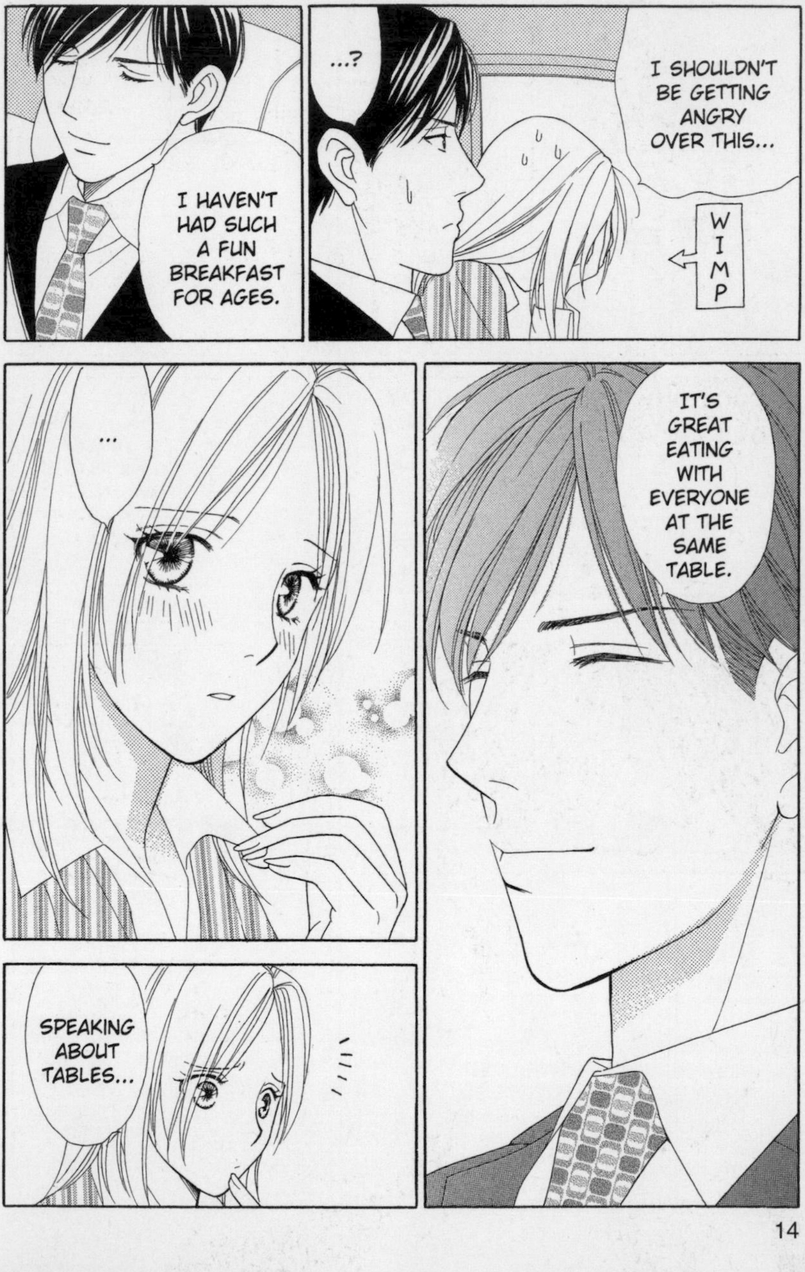
I SHOULDN'T BE GETTING ANGRY OVER THIS...
...?
WIMP
I HAVEN'T HAD SUCH A FUN BREAKFAST FOR AGES.
IT'S GREAT EATING WITH EVERYONE AT THE SAME TABLE.
...
SPEAKING ABOUT TABLES...

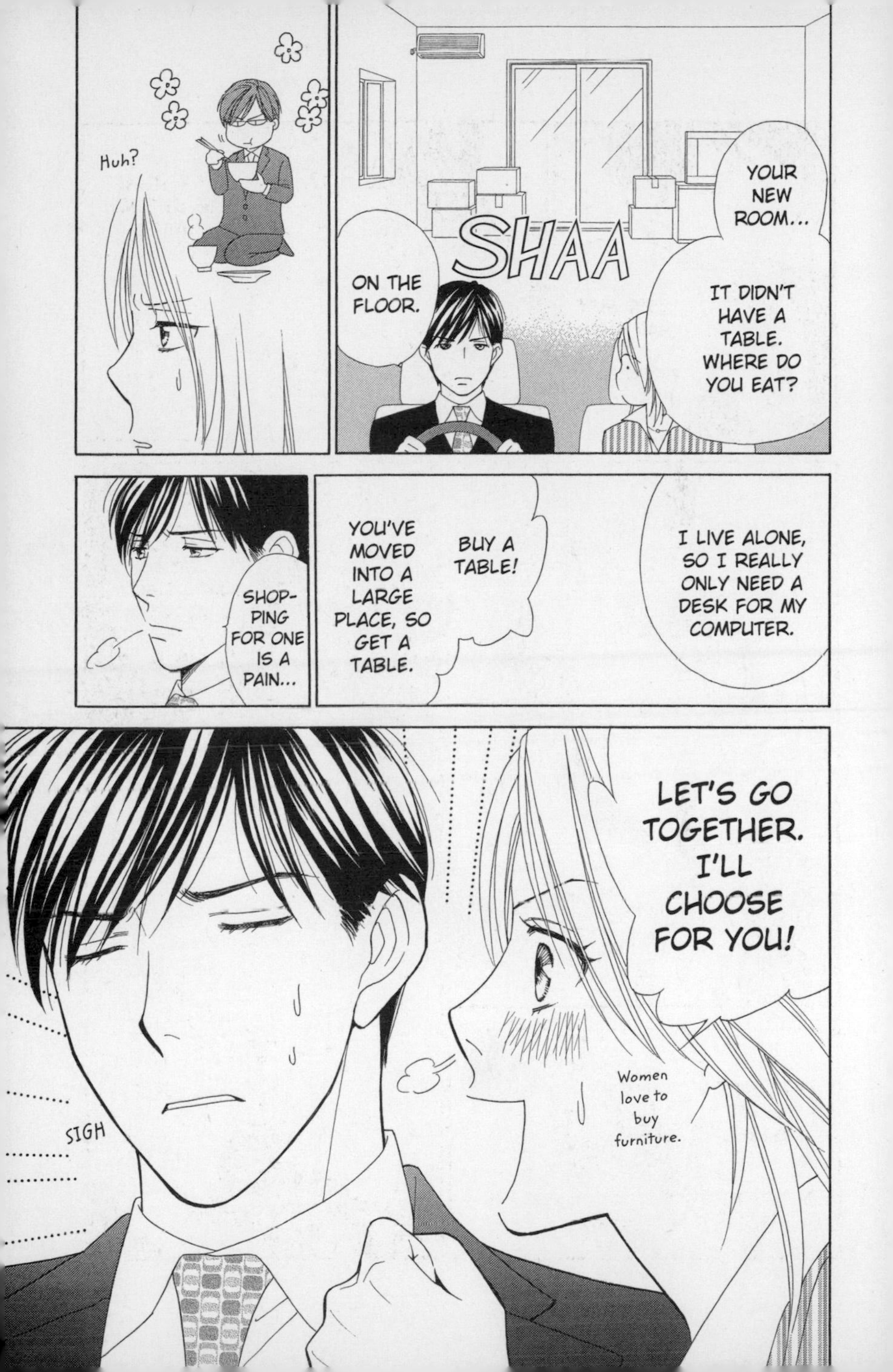
YOUR NEW ROOM...
IT DIDN'T HAVE A TABLE. WHERE DO YOU EAT?
SHAA
ON THE FLOOR.
Huh?
I LIVE ALONE, SO I REALLY ONLY NEED A DESK FOR MY COMPUTER.
BUY A TABLE!
YOU'VE MOVED INTO A LARGE PLACE, SO GET A TABLE.
SHOP-PING FOR ONE IS A PAIN...
LET'S GO TOGETHER. I'LL CHOOSE FOR YOU!
Women love to buy furniture.
SIGH

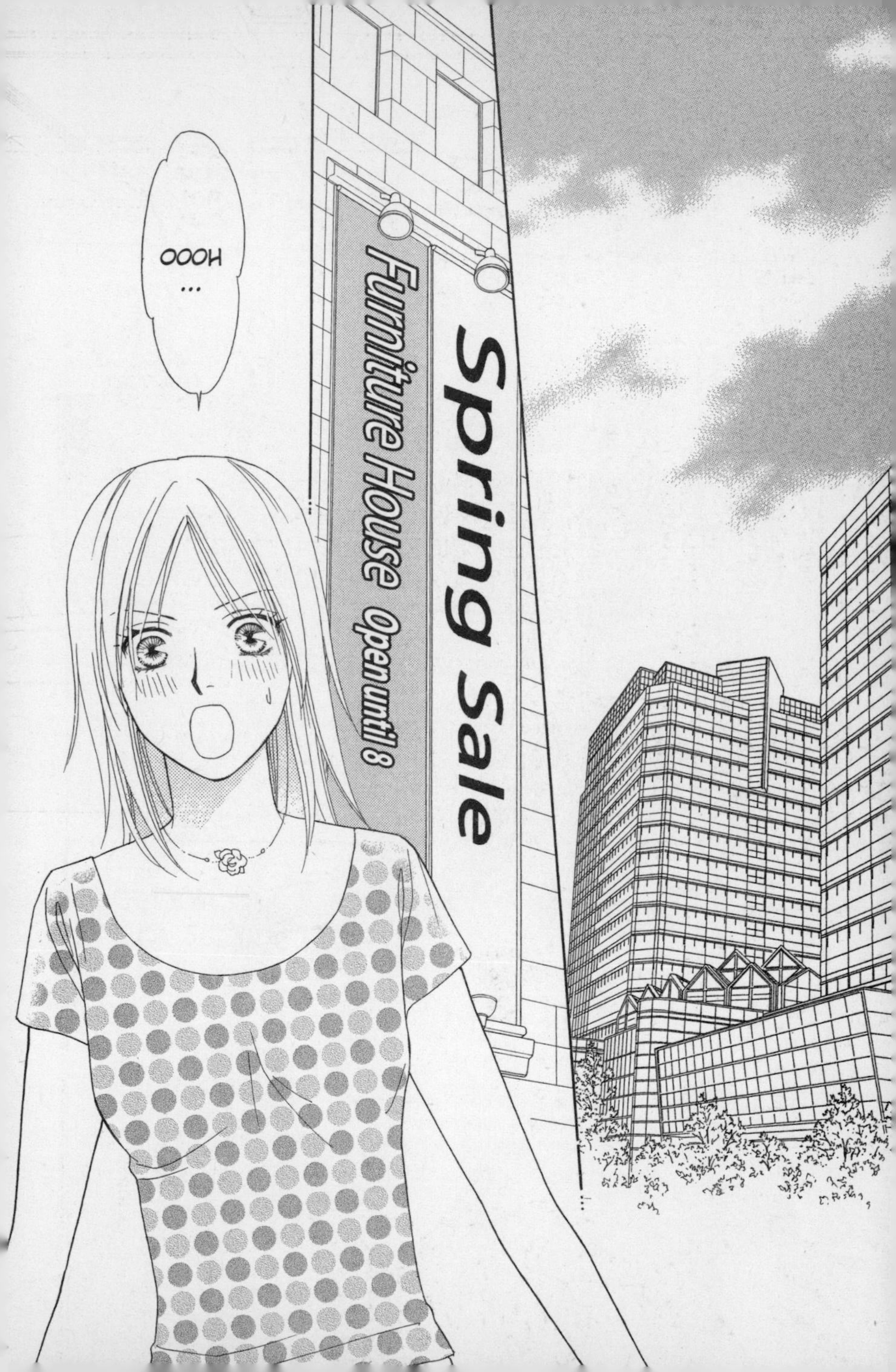
OOOH ...
Spring Sale
Furniture House open until 8

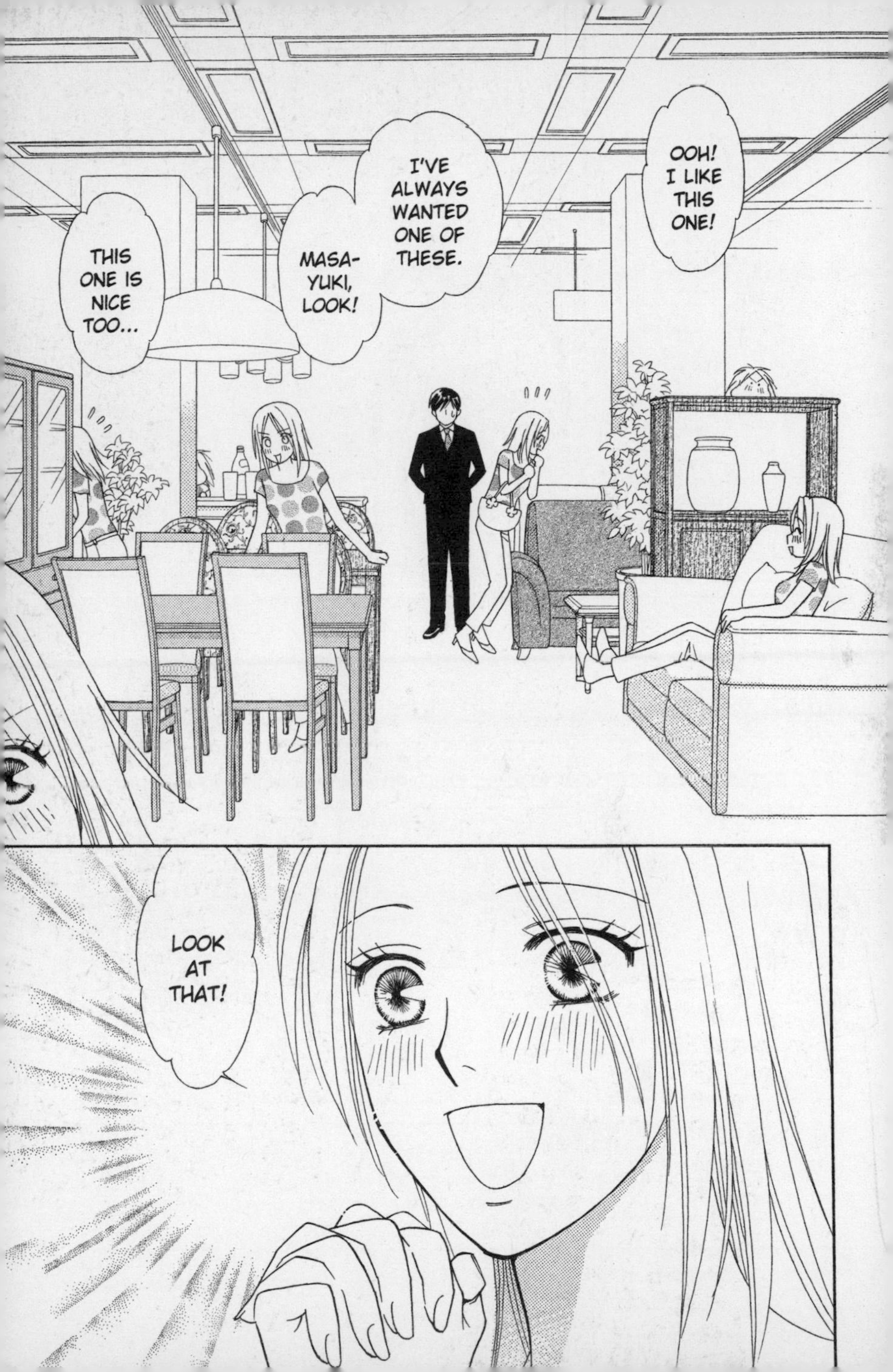
OOH! I LIKE THIS ONE!
I'VE ALWAYS WANTED ONE OF THESE.
MASA-YUKI, LOOK!
THIS ONE IS NICE TOO...
LOOK AT THAT!

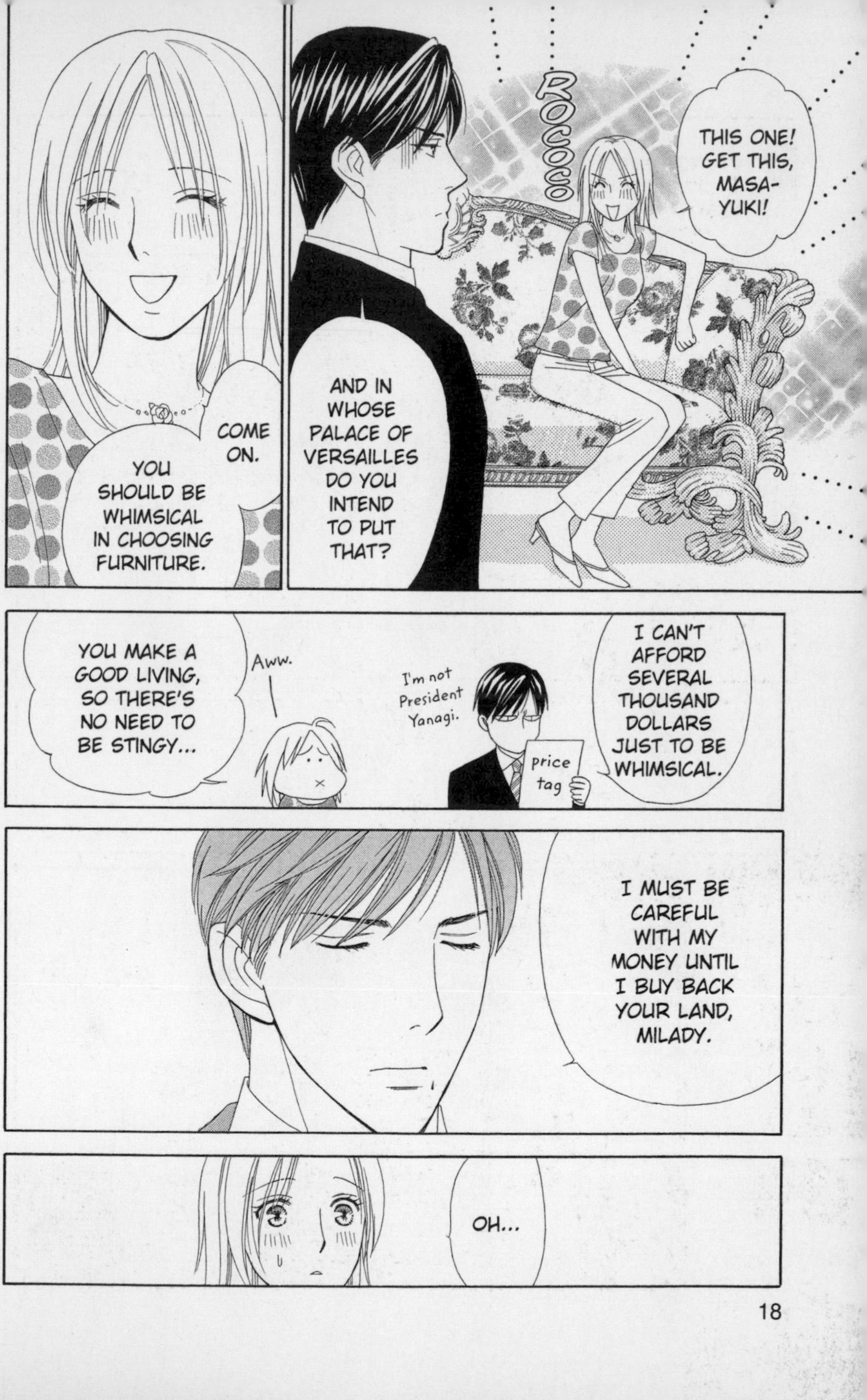

ROCOCO
THIS ONE! GET THIS, MASA-YUKI!
AND IN WHOSE PALACE OF VERSAILLES DO YOU INTEND TO PUT THAT?
COME ON.
YOU SHOULD BE WHIMSICAL IN CHOOSING FURNITURE.
I CAN'T AFFORD SEVERAL THOUSAND DOLLARS JUST TO BE WHIMSICAL.
price tag
I'm not President Yanagi.
Aww.
YOU MAKE A GOOD LIVING, SO THERE'S NO NEED TO BE STINGY...
I MUST BE CAREFUL WITH MY MONEY UNTIL I BUY BACK YOUR LAND, MILADY.
OH...

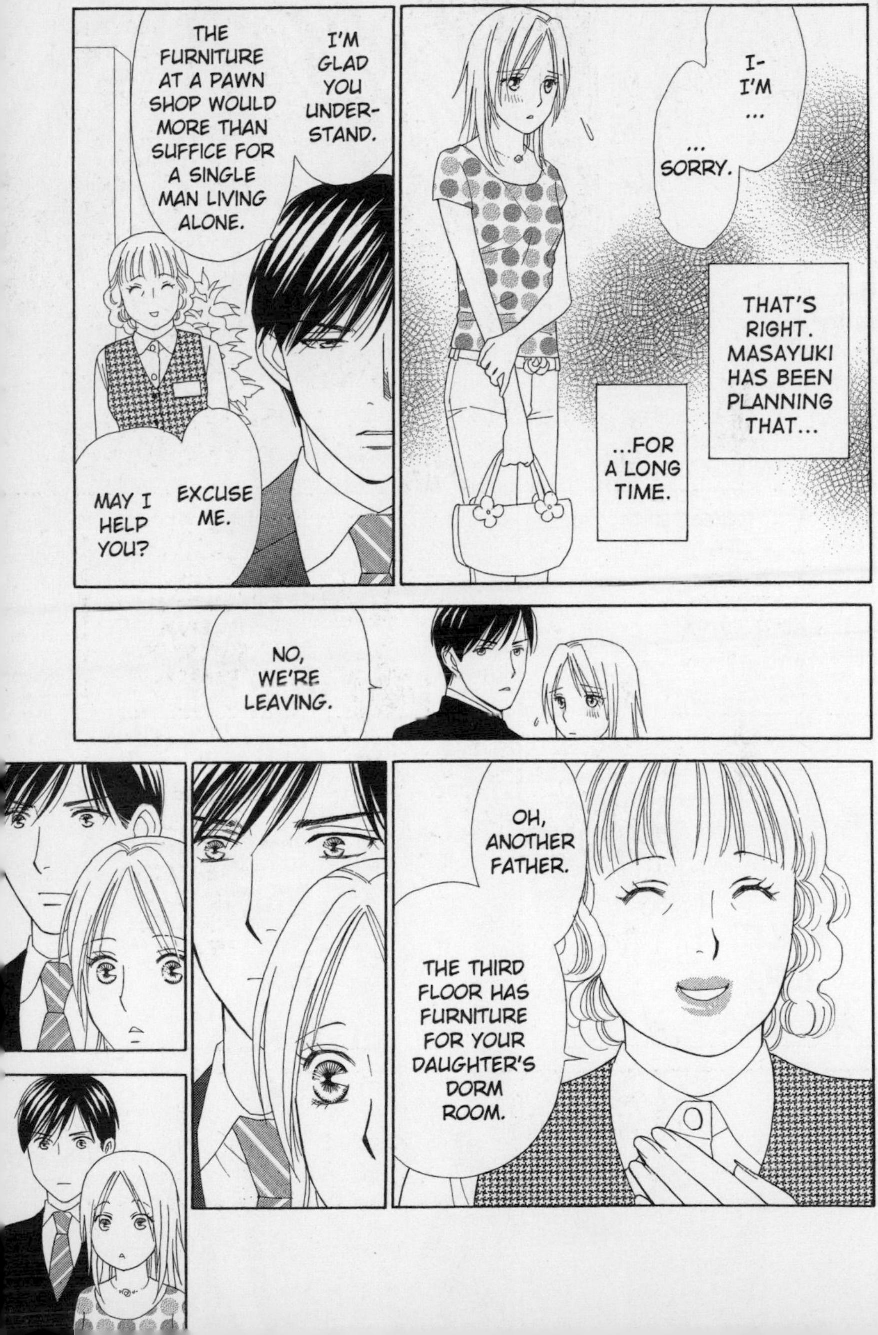
I- I'M ...
... SORRY.
THAT'S RIGHT. MASAYUKI HAS BEEN PLANNING THAT...
...FOR A LONG TIME.
I'M GLAD YOU UNDERSTAND.
THE FURNITURE AT A PAWN SHOP WOULD MORE THAN SUFFICE FOR A SINGLE MAN LIVING ALONE.
EXCUSE ME.
MAY I HELP YOU?
NO, WE'RE LEAVING.
OH, ANOTHER FATHER.
THE THIRD FLOOR HAS FURNITURE FOR YOUR DAUGHTER'S DORM ROOM.

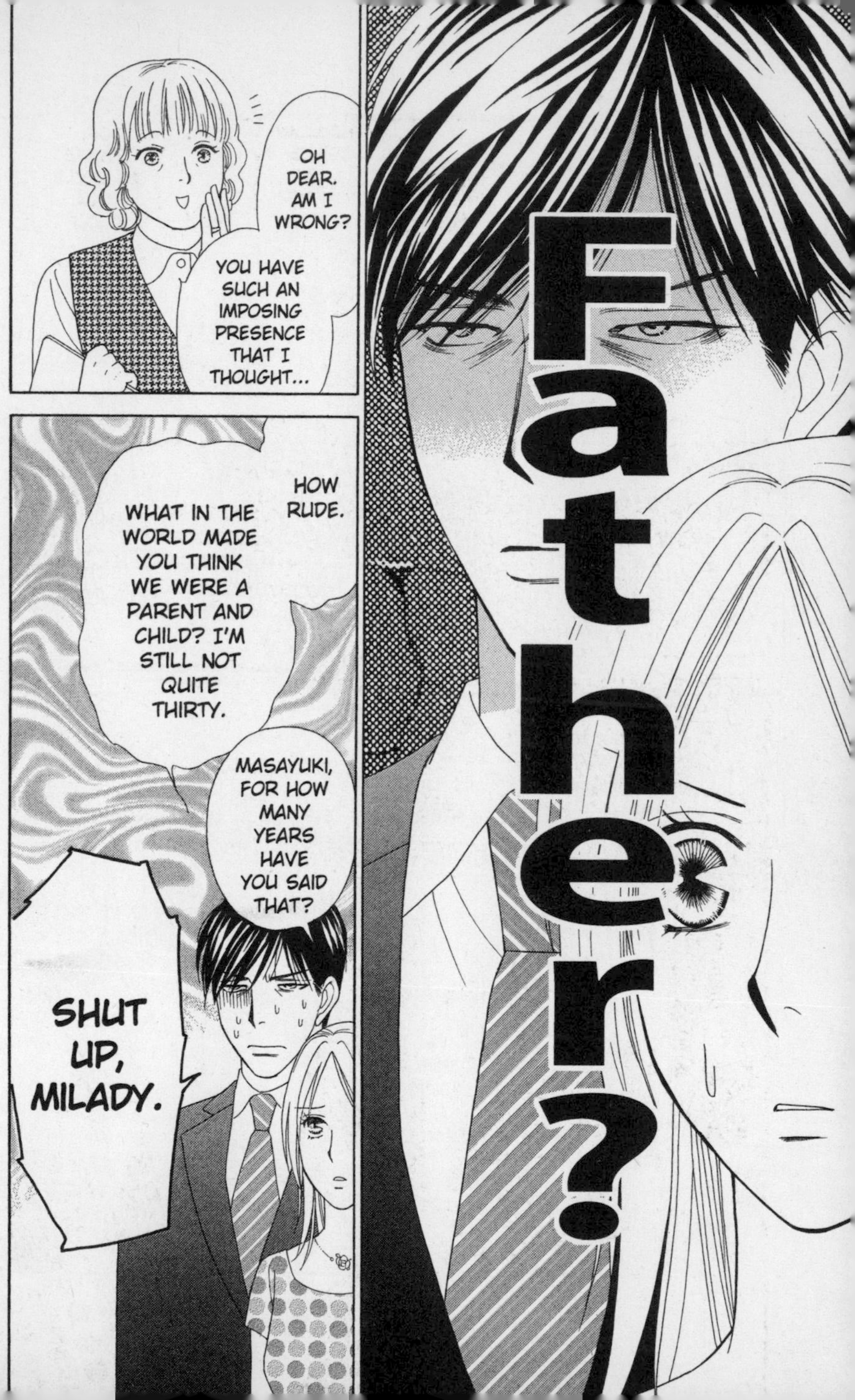
Father?
OH DEAR. AM I WRONG?
YOU HAVE SUCH AN IMPOSING PRESENCE THAT I THOUGHT...
HOW RUDE.
WHAT IN THE WORLD MADE YOU THINK WE WERE A PARENT AND CHILD? I'M STILL NOT QUITE THIRTY.
MASAYUKI, FOR HOW MANY YEARS HAVE YOU SAID THAT?
SHUT UP, MILADY.

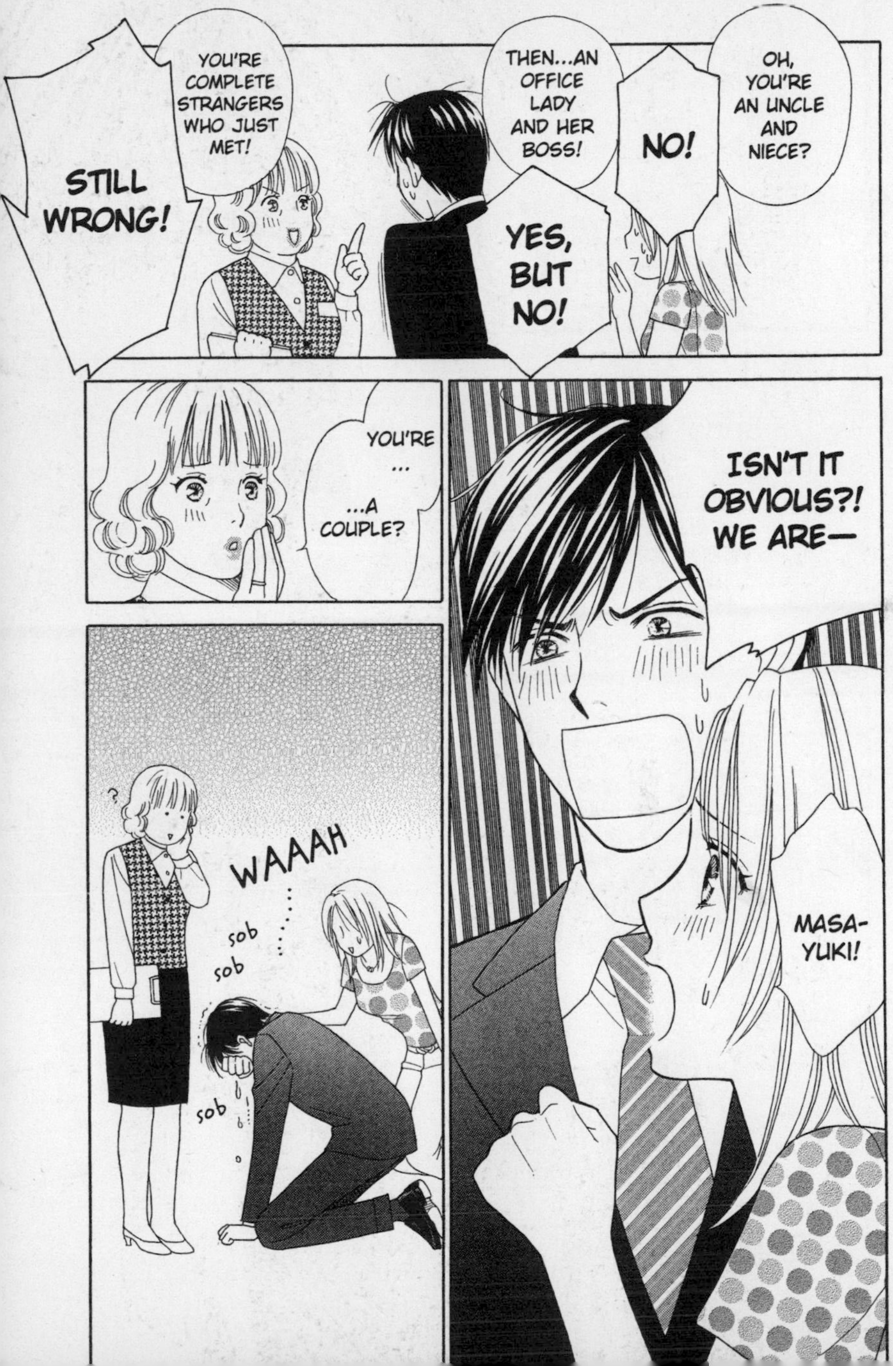
OH, YOU'RE AN UNCLE AND NIECE?
NO!
THEN...AN OFFICE LADY AND HER BOSS!
YES, BUT NO!
YOU'RE COMPLETE STRANGERS WHO JUST MET!
STILL WRONG!
ISN'T IT OBVIOUS?! WE ARE—
MASA-YUKI!
YOU'RE ... ...A COUPLE?
WAAAH
sob
sob
sob

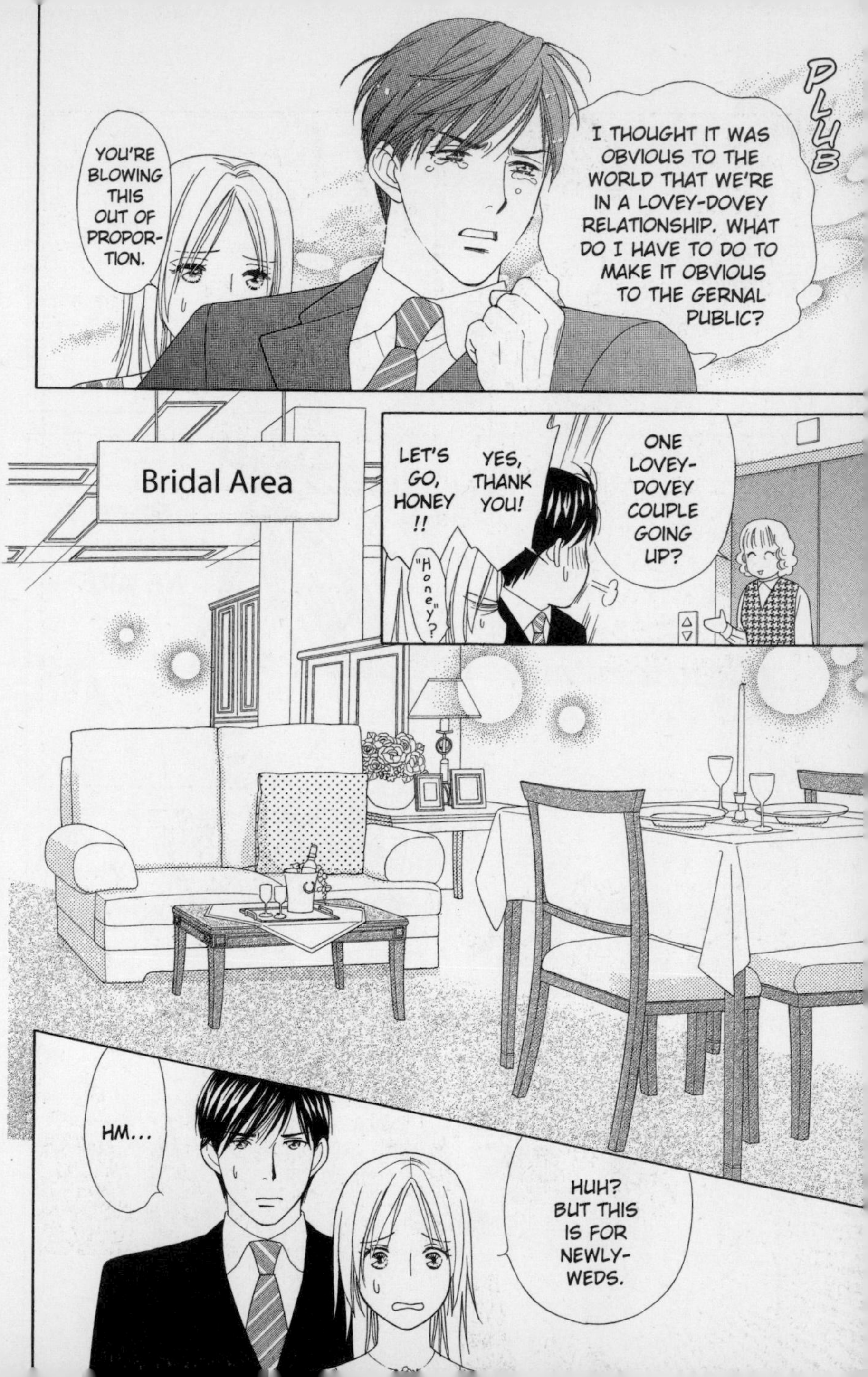
PLUB
I THOUGHT IT WAS OBVIOUS TO THE WORLD THAT WE'RE IN A LOVEY-DOVEY RELATIONSHIP. WHAT DO I HAVE TO DO TO MAKE IT OBVIOUS TO THE GERNAL PUBLIC?
YOU'RE BLOWING THIS OUT OF PROPOR-TION.
ONE LOVEY-DOVEY COUPLE GOING UP?
YES, THANK YOU!
LET'S GO, HONEY !!
"Honey"?
Bridal Area
HUH? BUT THIS IS FOR NEWLY-WEDS.
HM...

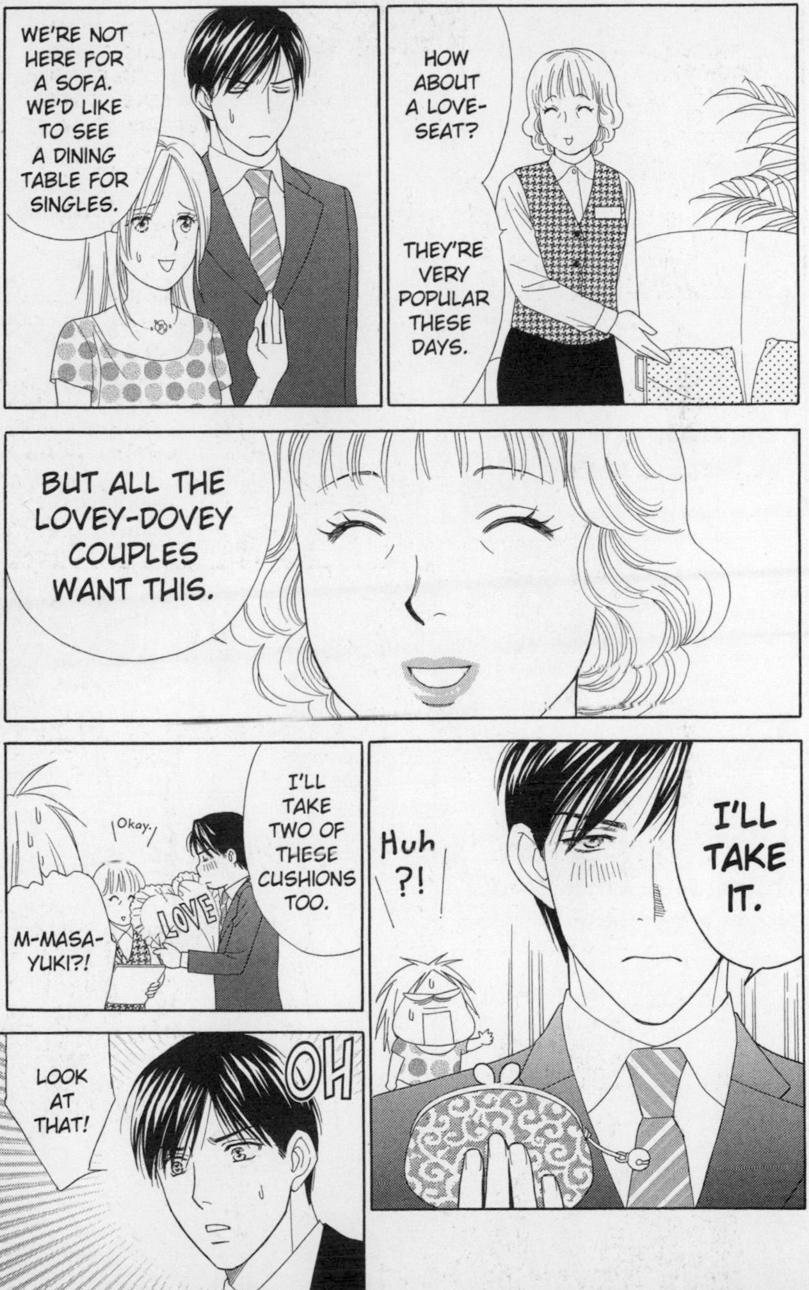
HOW ABOUT A LOVE-SEAT?
THEY'RE VERY POPULAR THESE DAYS.
WE'RE NOT HERE FOR A SOFA. WE'D LIKE TO SEE A DINING TABLE FOR SINGLES.
BUT ALL THE LOVEY-DOVEY COUPLES WANT THIS.
I'LL TAKE IT.
Huh ?!
I'LL TAKE TWO OF THESE CUSHIONS TOO.
Okay.
LOVE
M-MASA-YUKI?!
OH
LOOK AT THAT!

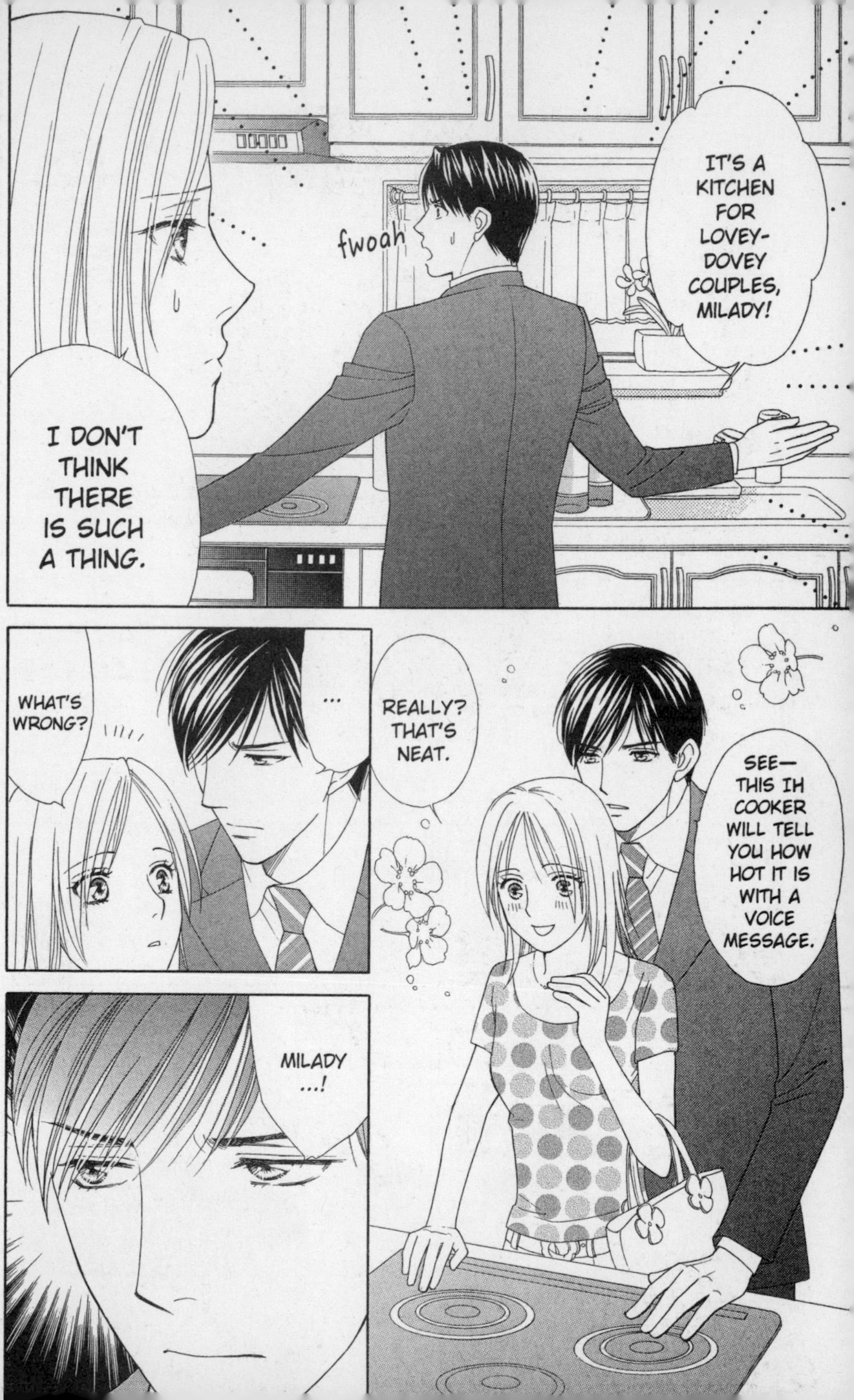
IT'S A KITCHEN FOR LOVEY-DOVEY COUPLES, MILADY!
fwoah
I DON'T THINK THERE IS SUCH A THING.
SEE— THIS IH COOKER WILL TELL YOU HOW HOT IT IS WITH A VOICE MESSAGE.
REALLY? THAT'S NEAT.
...
WHAT'S WRONG?
MILADY ...!

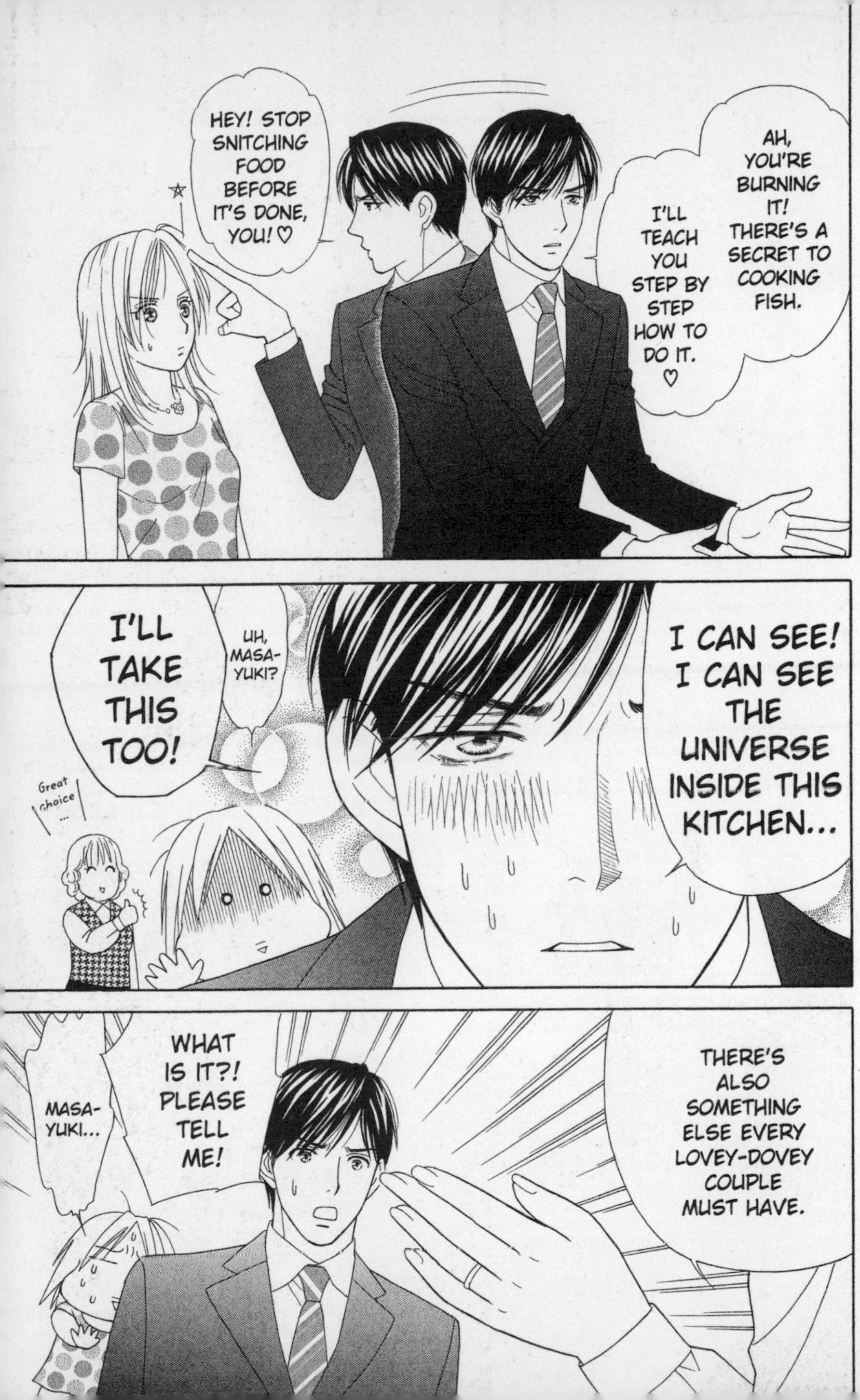
AH, YOU'RE BURNING IT! THERE'S A SECRET TO COOKING FISH.
I'LL TEACH YOU STEP BY STEP HOW TO DO IT. ♡
HEY! STOP SNITCHING FOOD BEFORE IT'S DONE, YOU! ♡
I CAN SEE! I CAN SEE THE UNIVERSE INSIDE THIS KITCHEN...
UH, MASA-YUKI?
I'LL TAKE THIS TOO!
Great choice ...
THERE'S ALSO SOMETHING ELSE EVERY LOVEY-DOVEY COUPLE MUST HAVE.
WHAT IS IT?! PLEASE TELL ME!
MASA-YUKI...

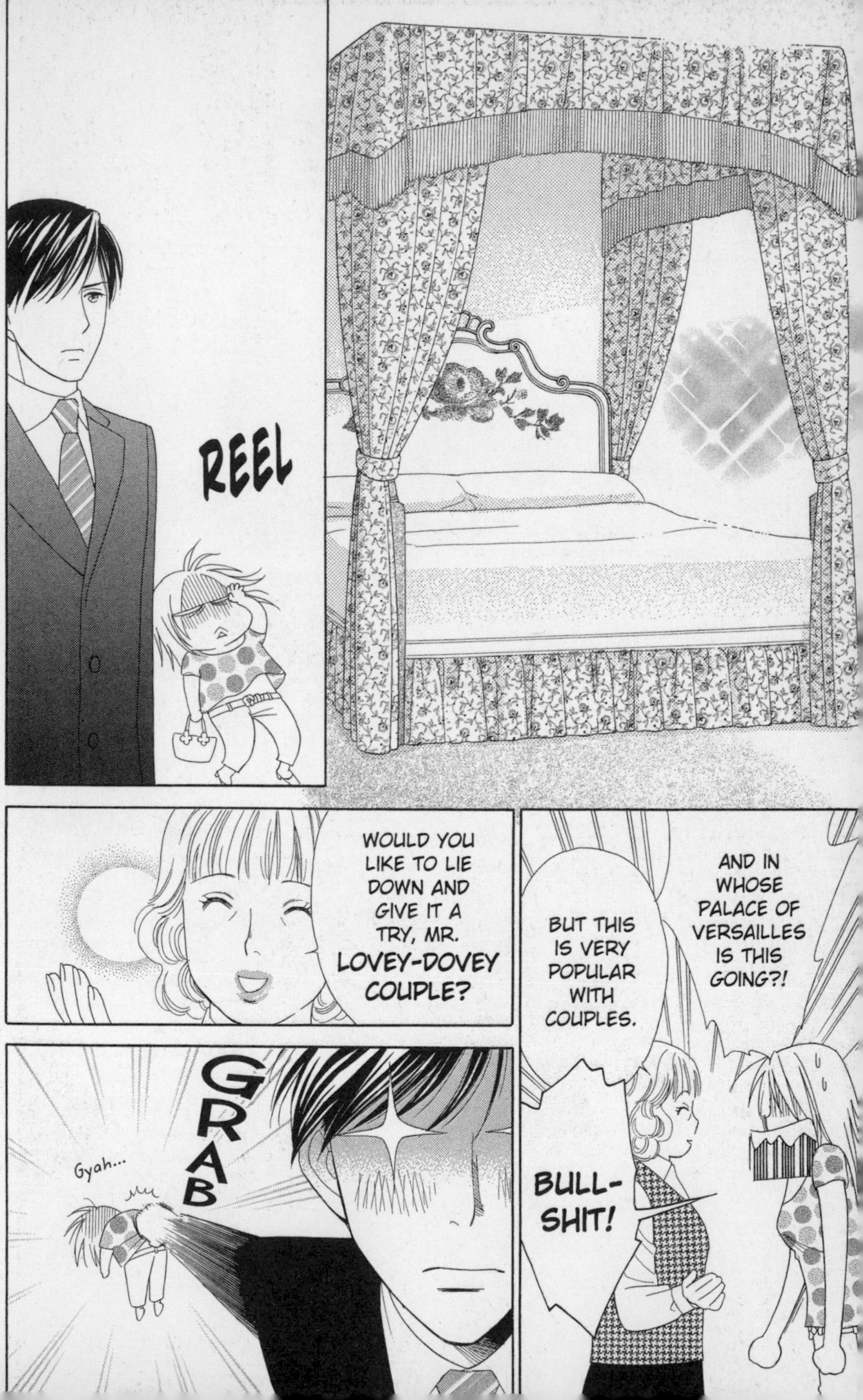

REEL
AND IN WHOSE PALACE OF VERSAILLES IS THIS GOING?!
BUT THIS IS VERY POPULAR WITH COUPLES.
BULL-SHIT!
WOULD YOU LIKE TO LIE DOWN AND GIVE IT A TRY, MR. LOVEY-DOVEY COUPLE?
GRAB
Gyah...

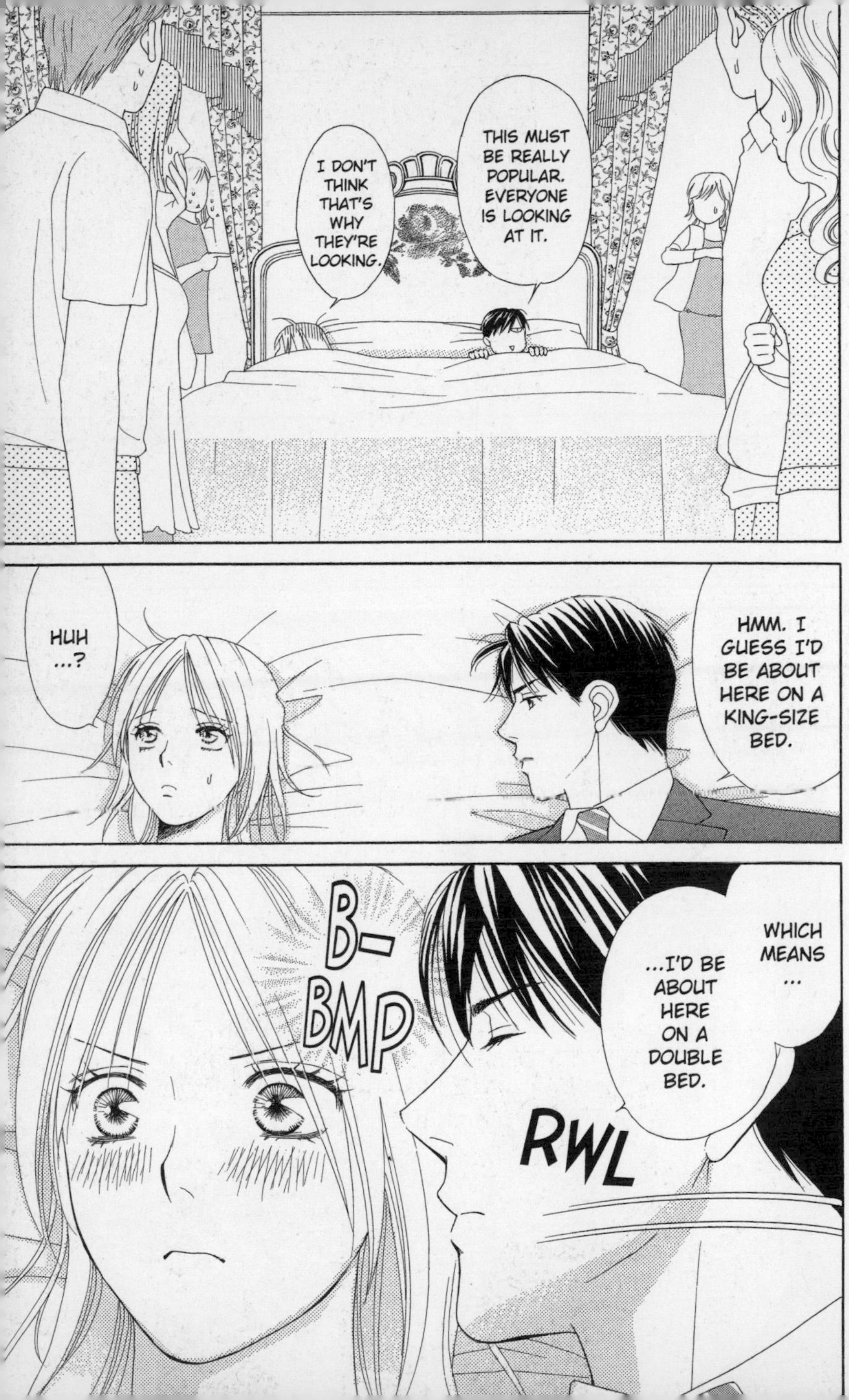
THIS MUST BE REALLY POPULAR. EVERYONE IS LOOKING AT IT.
I DON'T THINK THAT'S WHY THEY'RE LOOKING.
HMM. I GUESS I'D BE ABOUT HERE ON A KING-SIZE BED.
HUH ...?
WHICH MEANS ...
...I'D BE ABOUT HERE ON A DOUBLE BED.
B-BMP
RWL

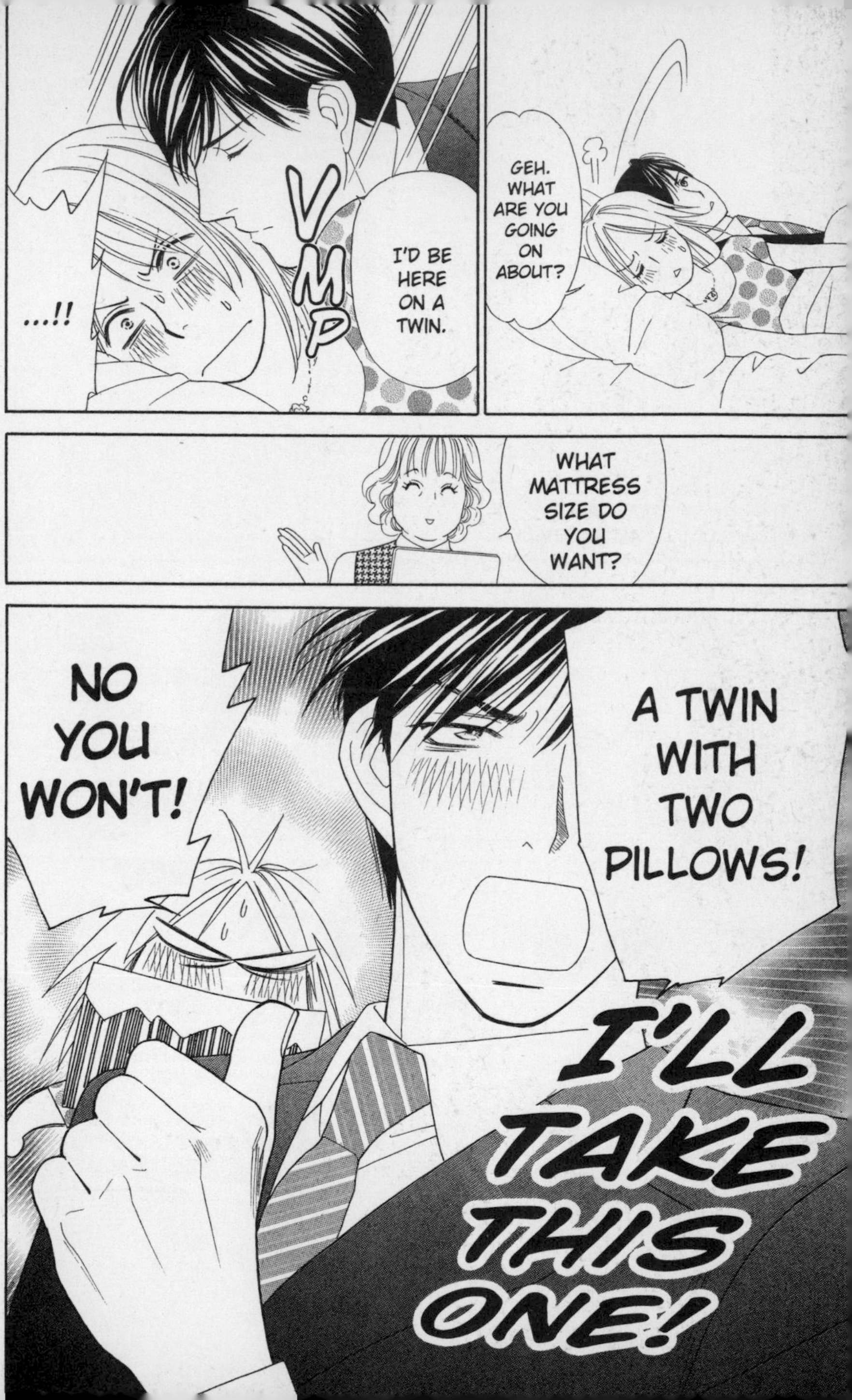
GEH. WHAT ARE YOU GOING ON ABOUT?
I'D BE HERE ON A TWIN.
VMP
...!!
WHAT MATTRESS SIZE DO YOU WANT?
A TWIN WITH TWO PILLOWS!
NO YOU WON'T!
I'LL TAKE THIS ONE!

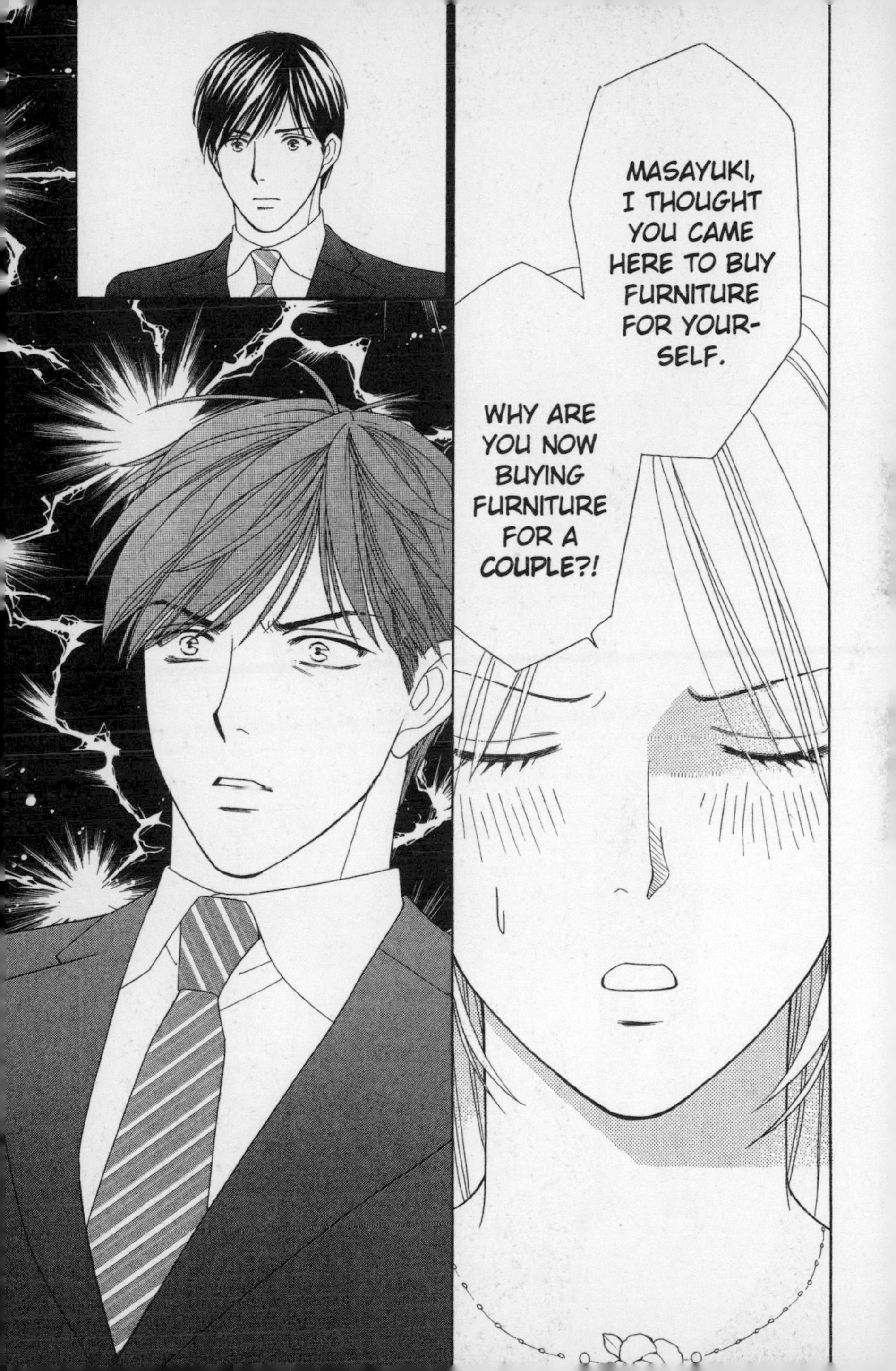
MASAYUKI, I THOUGHT YOU CAME HERE TO BUY FURNITURE FOR YOUR-SELF.
WHY ARE YOU NOW BUYING FURNITURE FOR A COUPLE?!

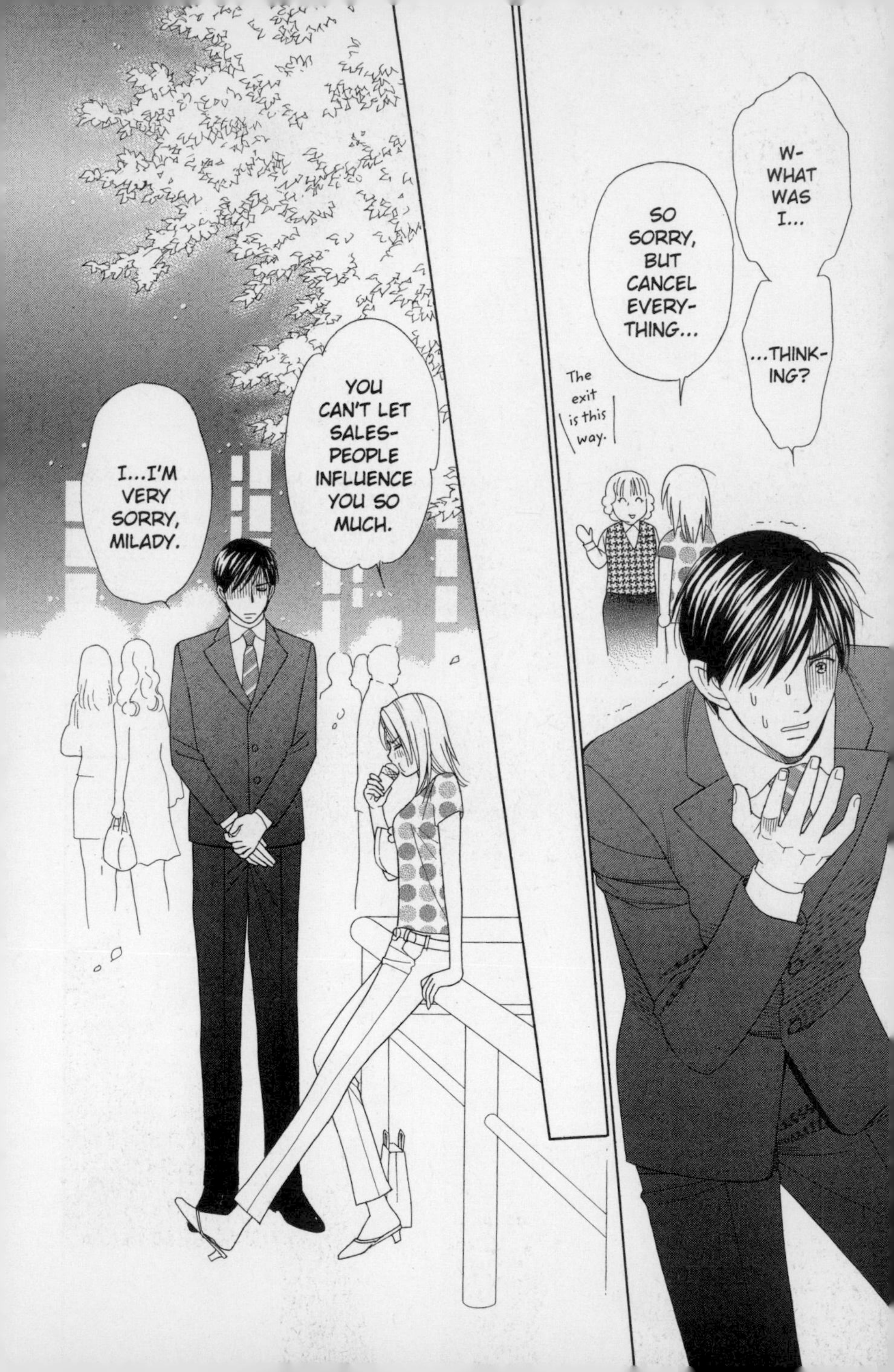

W- WHAT WAS I...
...THINKING?
SO SORRY, BUT CANCEL EVERYTHING...
The exit is this way.
YOU CAN'T LET SALES-PEOPLE INFLUENCE YOU SO MUCH.
I...I'M VERY SORRY, MILADY.

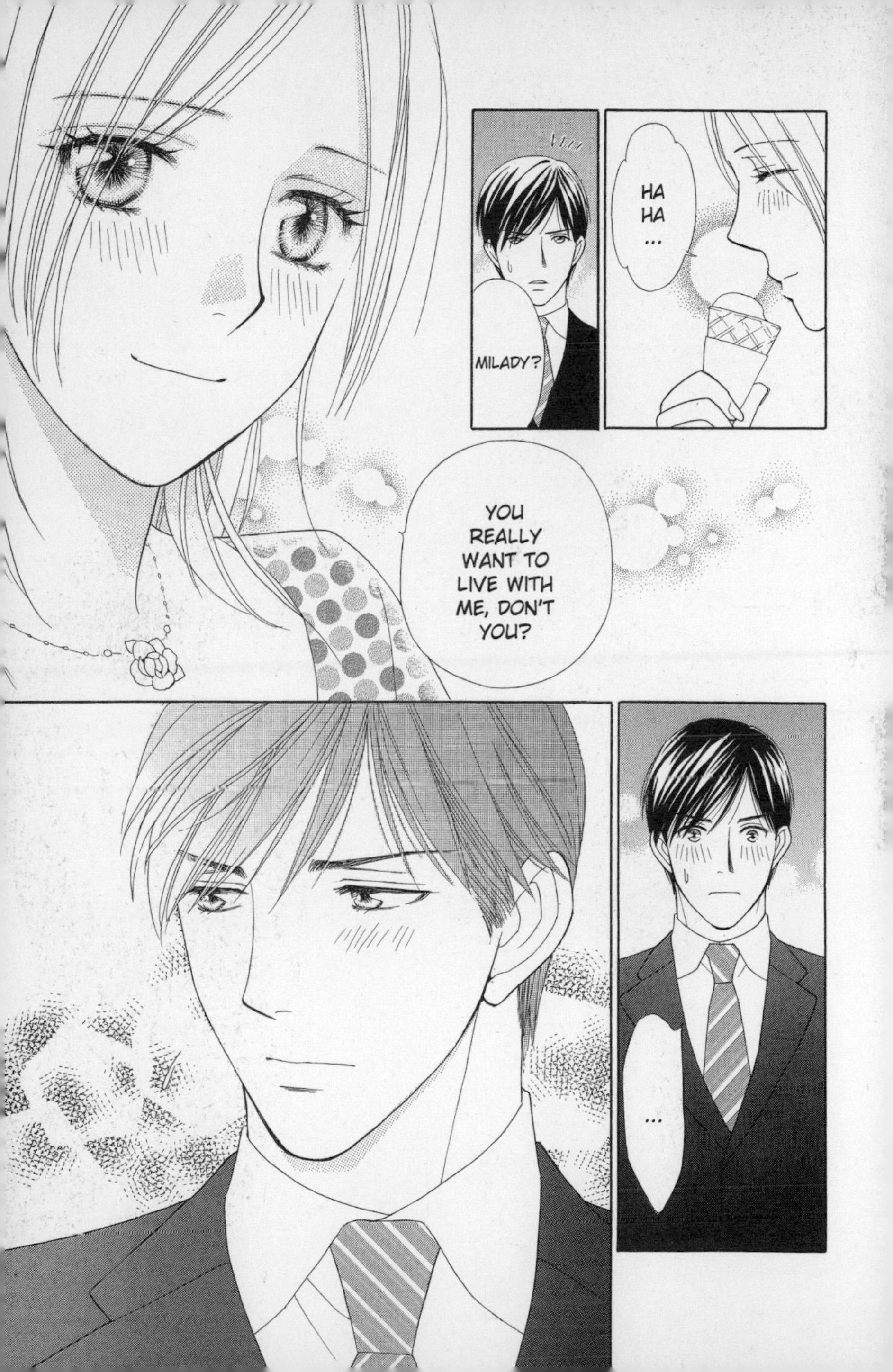
HA
HA
...
MILADY?
YOU REALLY WANT TO LIVE WITH ME, DON'T YOU?
...

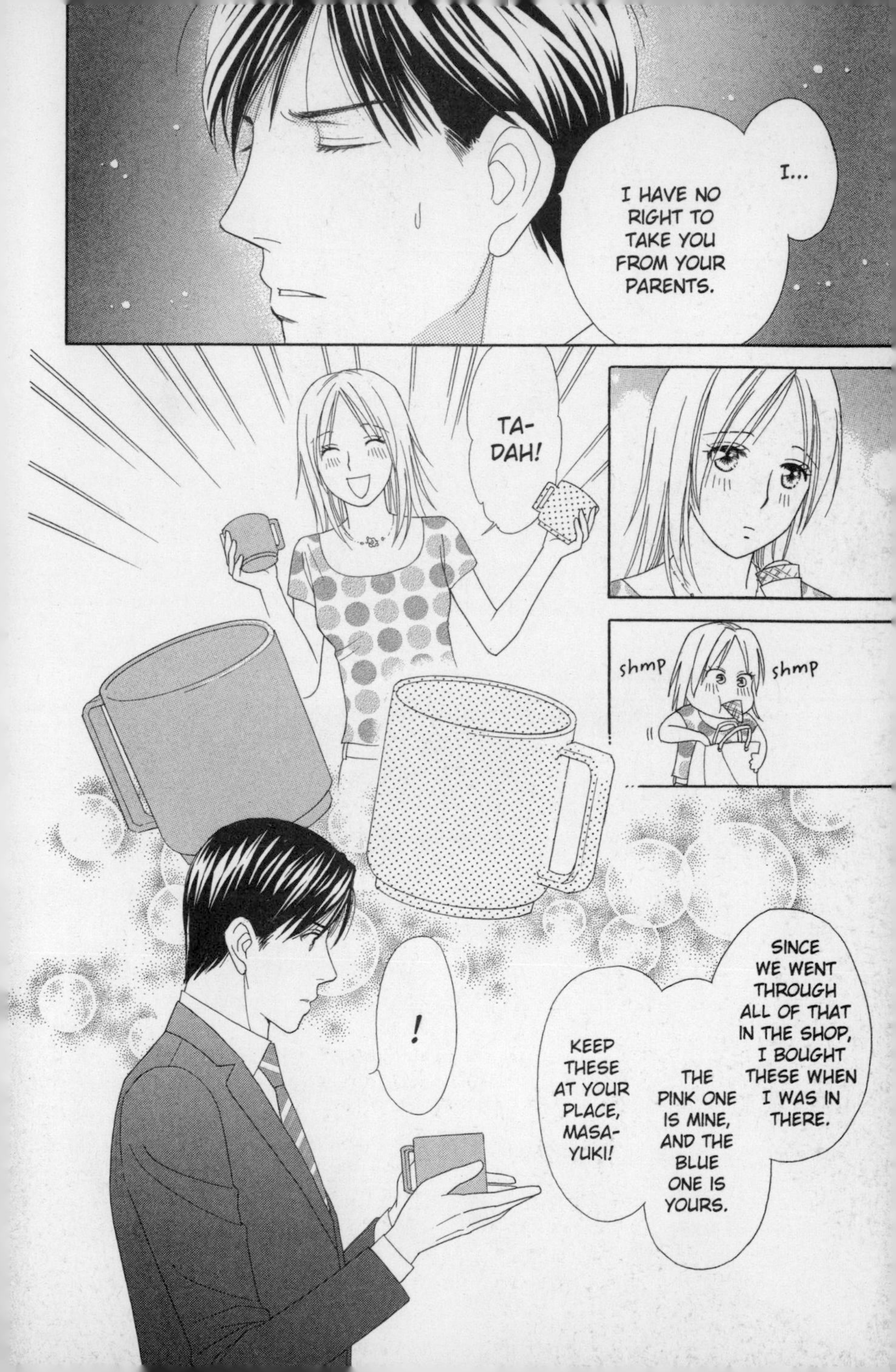
I...
I HAVE NO RIGHT TO TAKE YOU FROM YOUR PARENTS.
shmp
shmp
TA-DAH!
SINCE WE WENT THROUGH ALL OF THAT IN THE SHOP, I BOUGHT THESE WHEN I WAS IN THERE.
THE PINK ONE IS MINE, AND THE BLUE ONE IS YOURS.
KEEP THESE AT YOUR PLACE, MASA-YUKI!
!

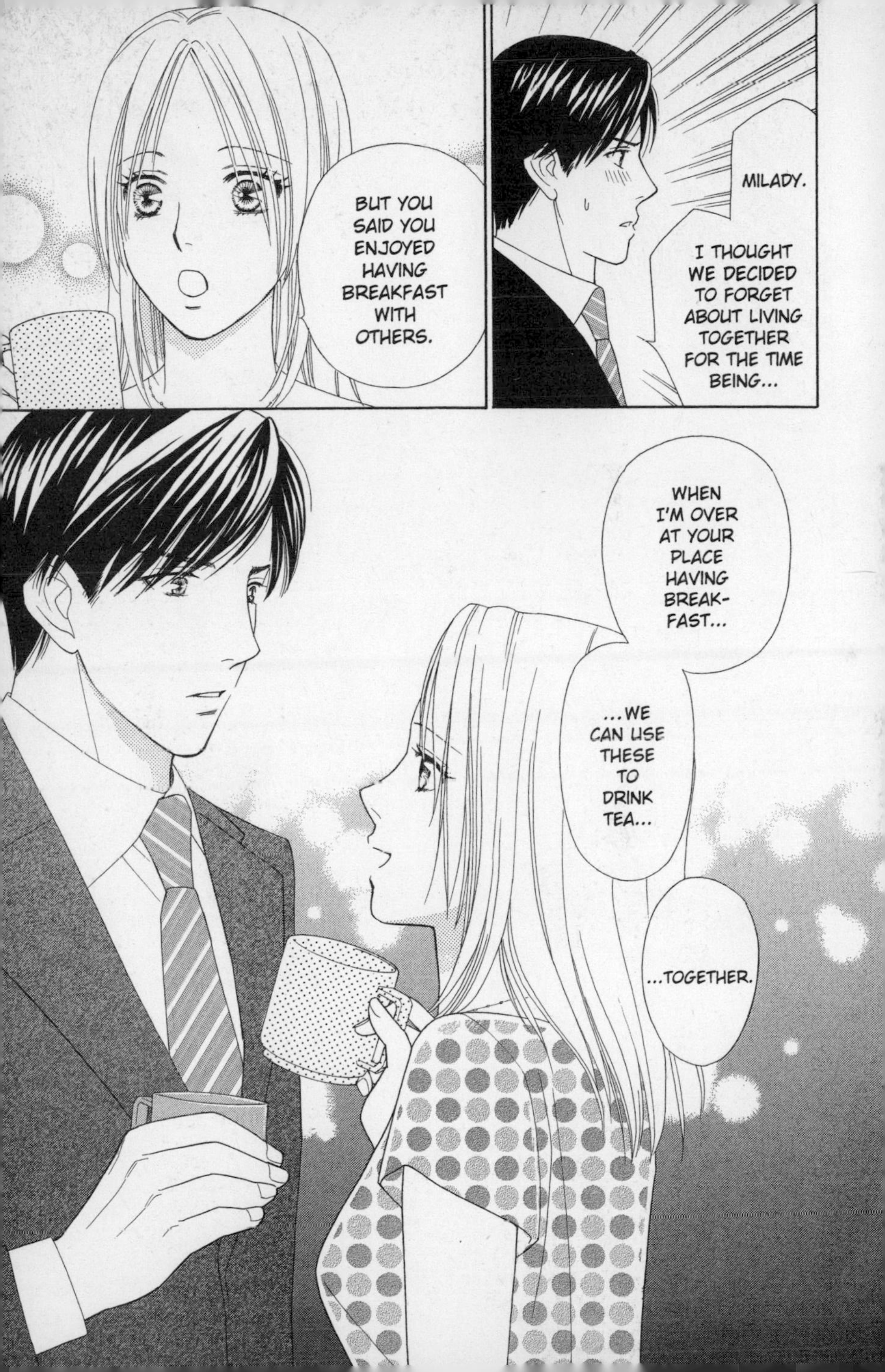
MILADY.
I THOUGHT WE DECIDED TO FORGET ABOUT LIVING TOGETHER FOR THE TIME BEING...
BUT YOU SAID YOU ENJOYED HAVING BREAKFAST WITH OTHERS.
WHEN I'M OVER AT YOUR PLACE HAVING BREAK-FAST...
...WE CAN USE THESE TO DRINK TEA...
...TOGETHER.

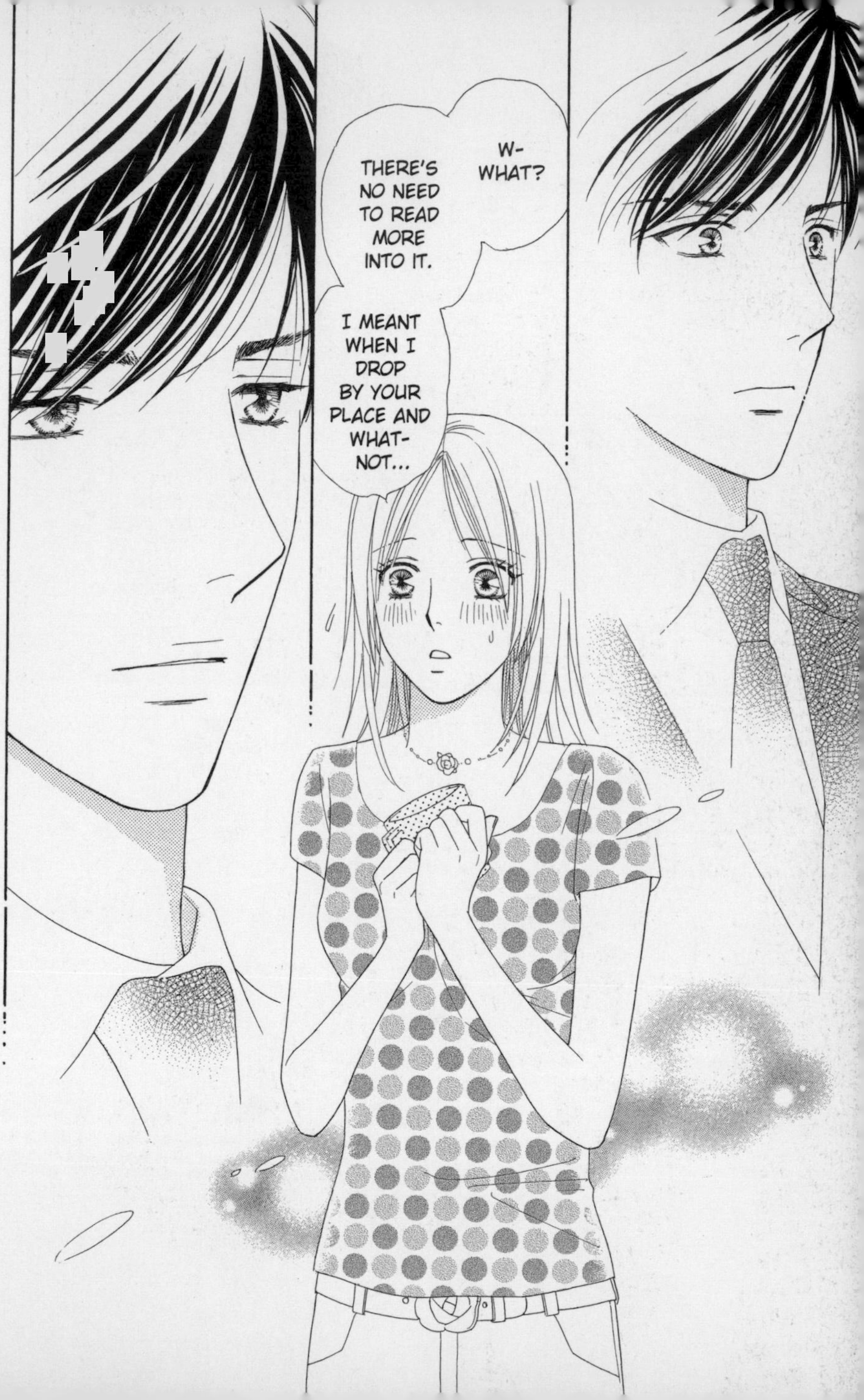
W- WHAT?
THERE'S NO NEED TO READ MORE INTO IT.
I MEANT WHEN I DROP BY YOUR PLACE AND WHAT-NOT...

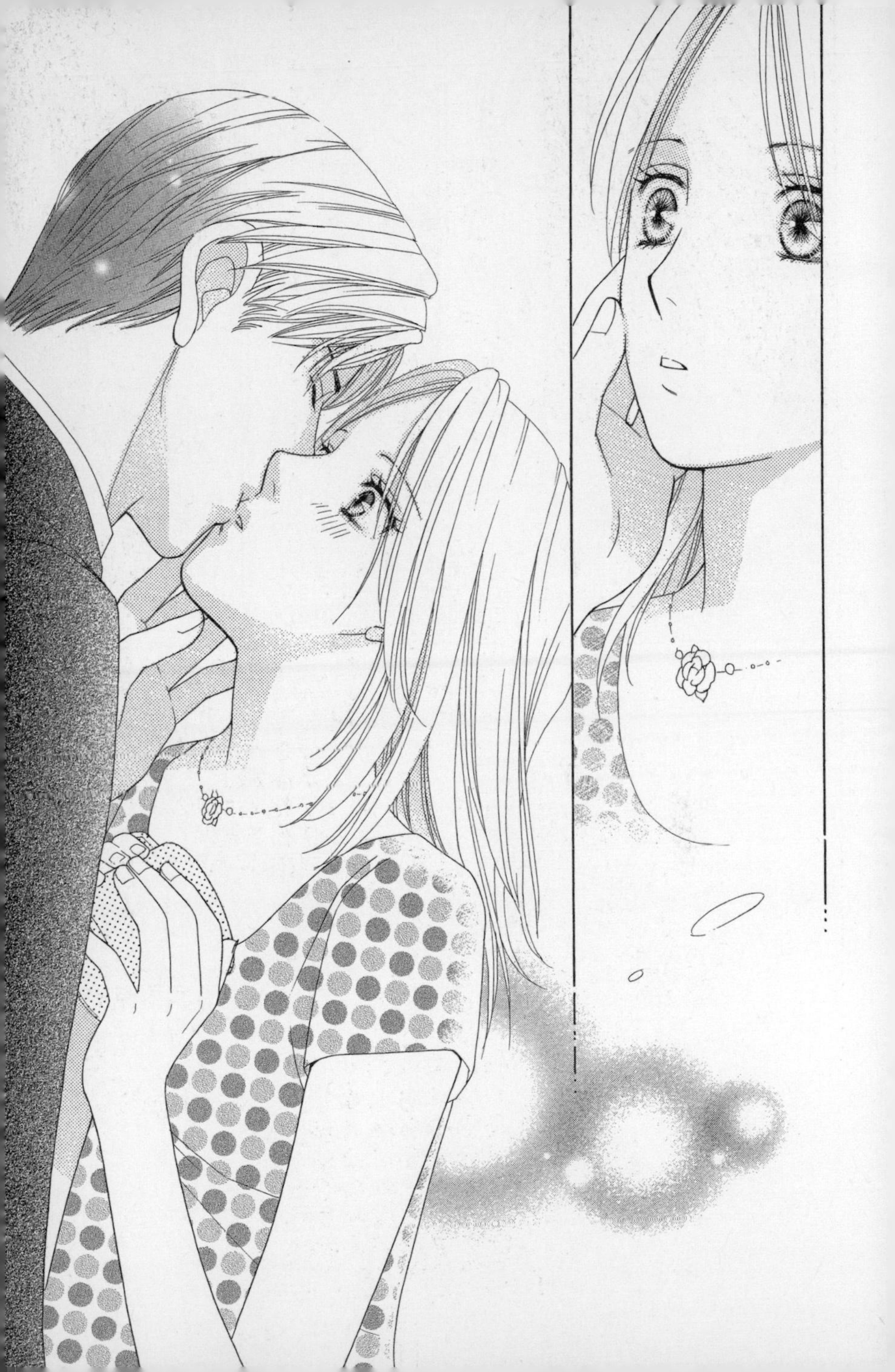

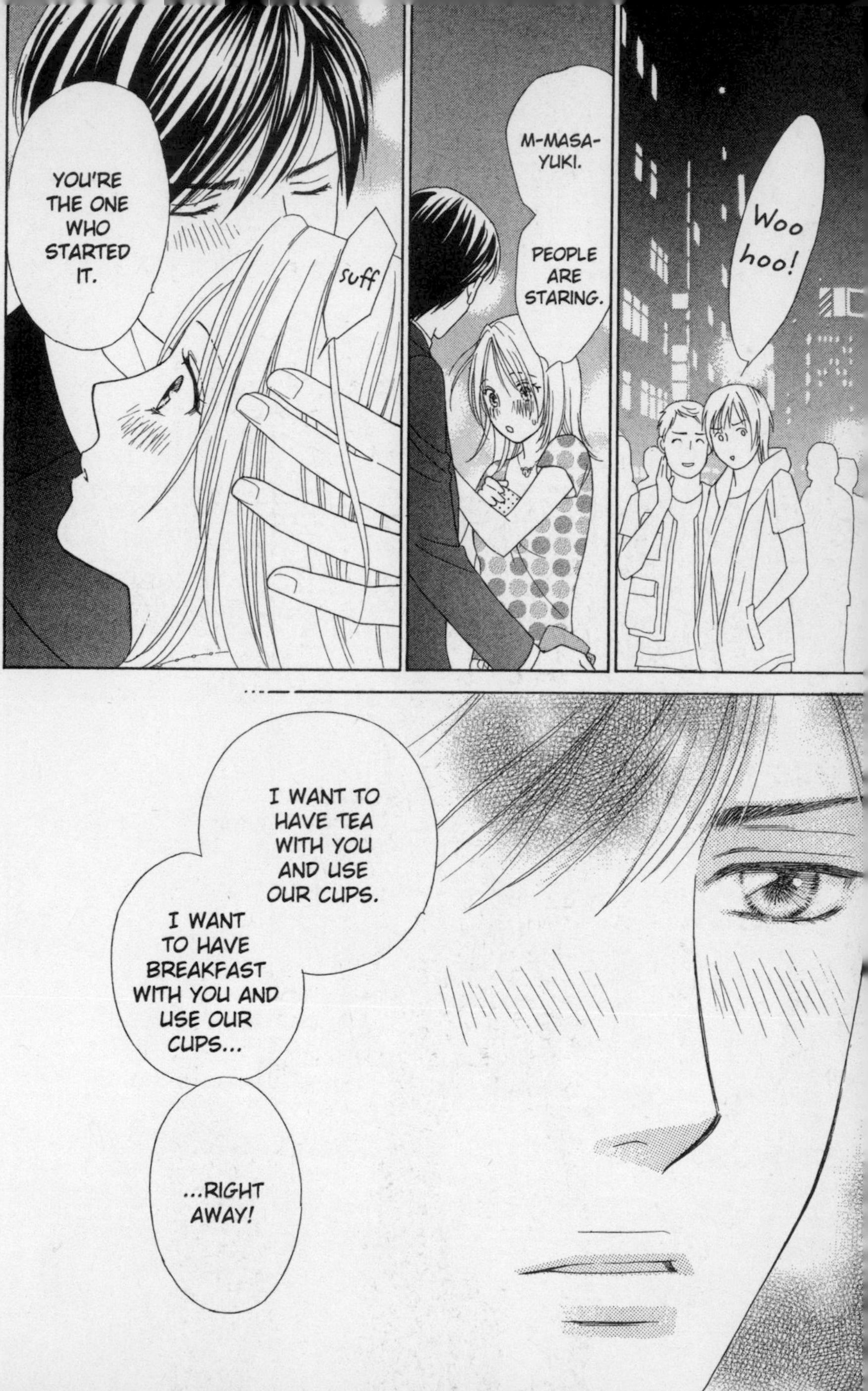
Woo hoo!
M-MASA-YUKI.
PEOPLE ARE STARING.
YOU'RE THE ONE WHO STARTED IT.
suff
I WANT TO HAVE TEA WITH YOU AND USE OUR CUPS.
I WANT TO HAVE BREAKFAST WITH YOU AND USE OUR CUPS...
...RIGHT AWAY!

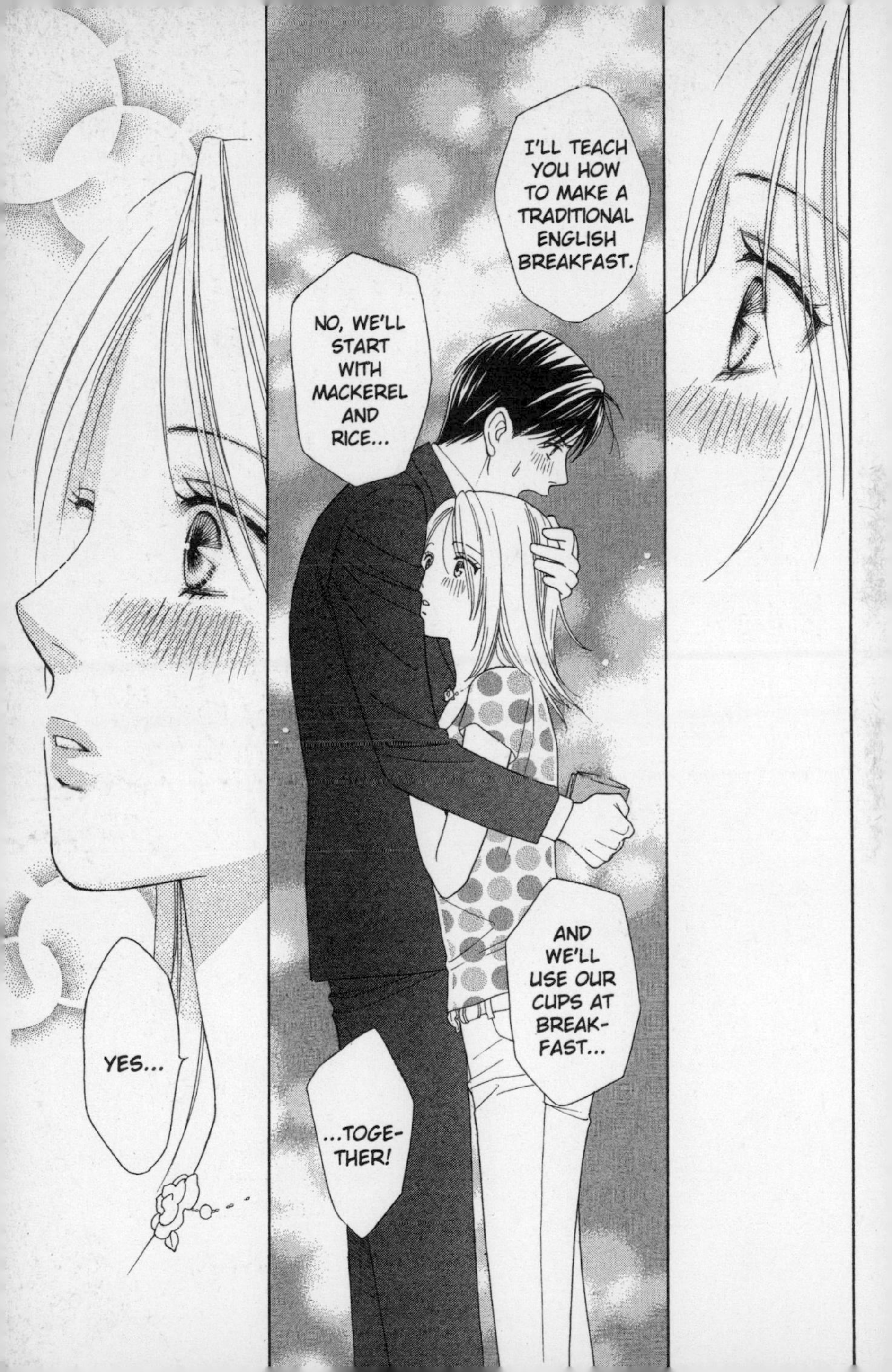
I'LL TEACH YOU HOW TO MAKE A TRADITIONAL ENGLISH BREAKFAST.
NO, WE'LL START WITH MACKEREL AND RICE...
AND WE'LL USE OUR CUPS AT BREAK-FAST...
...TOGE-THER!
YES...

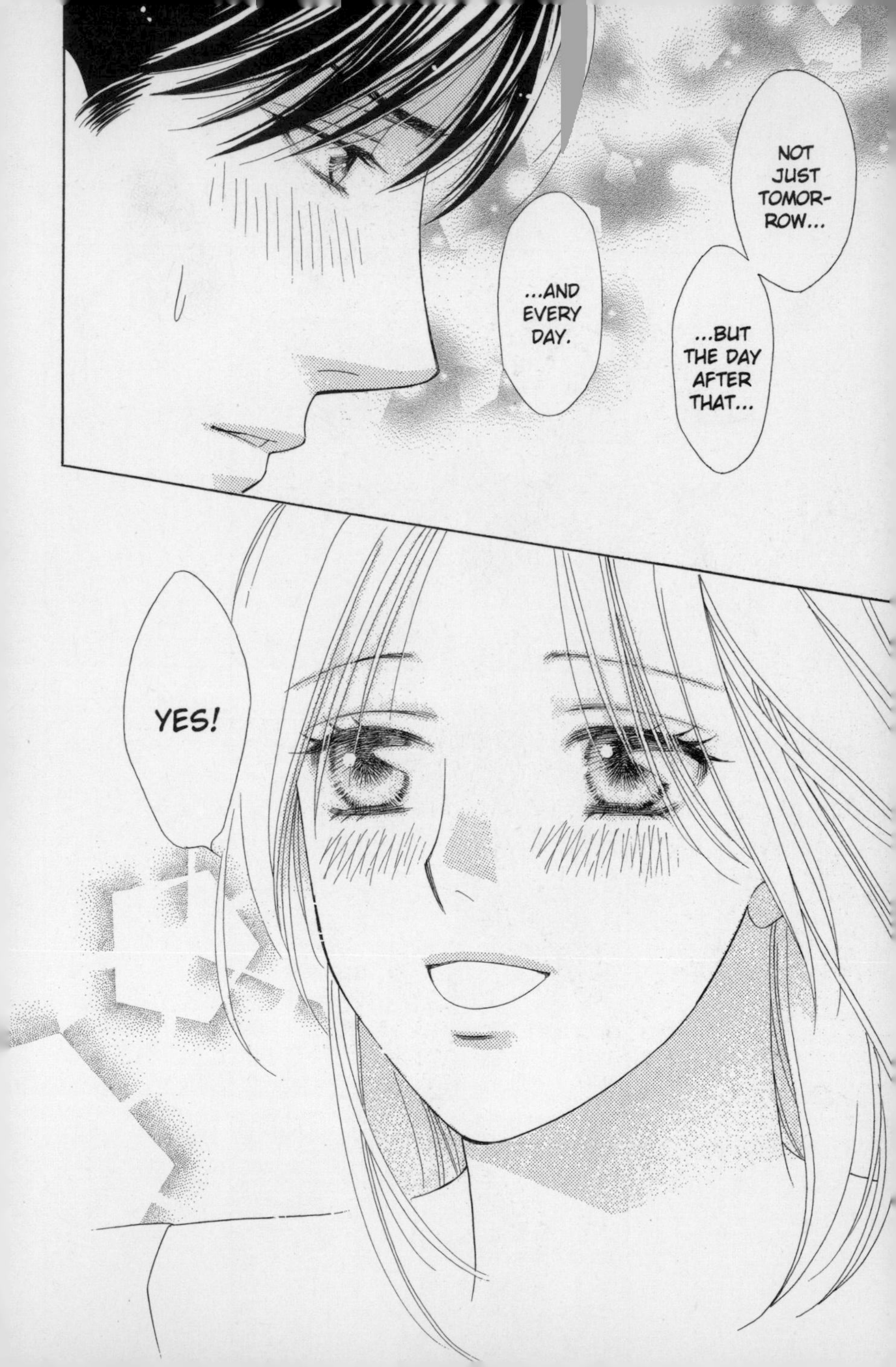
NOT JUST TOMORROW...
...BUT THE DAY AFTER THAT...
...AND EVERY DAY.
YES!

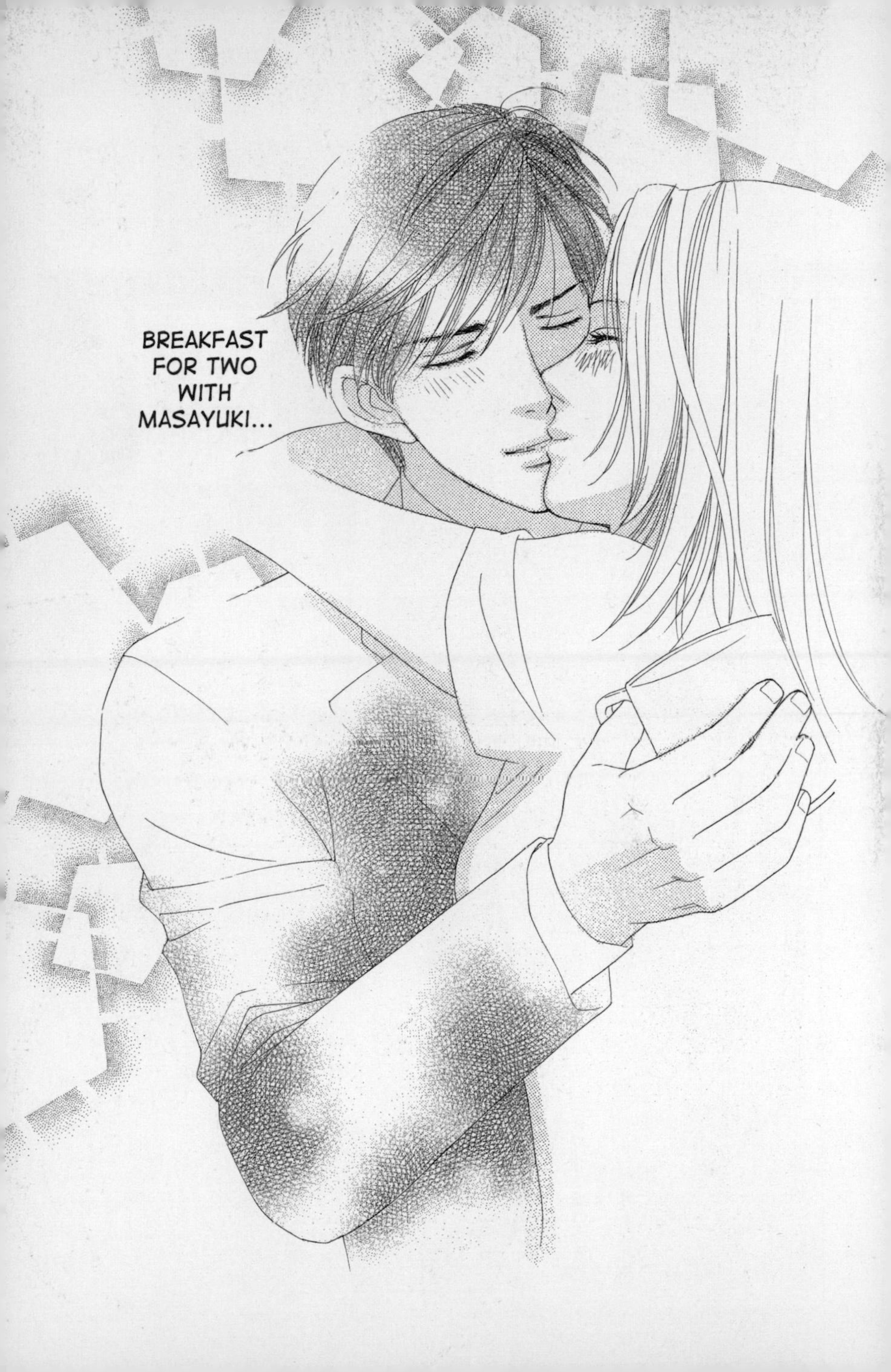
BREAKFAST FOR TWO WITH MASAYUKI...

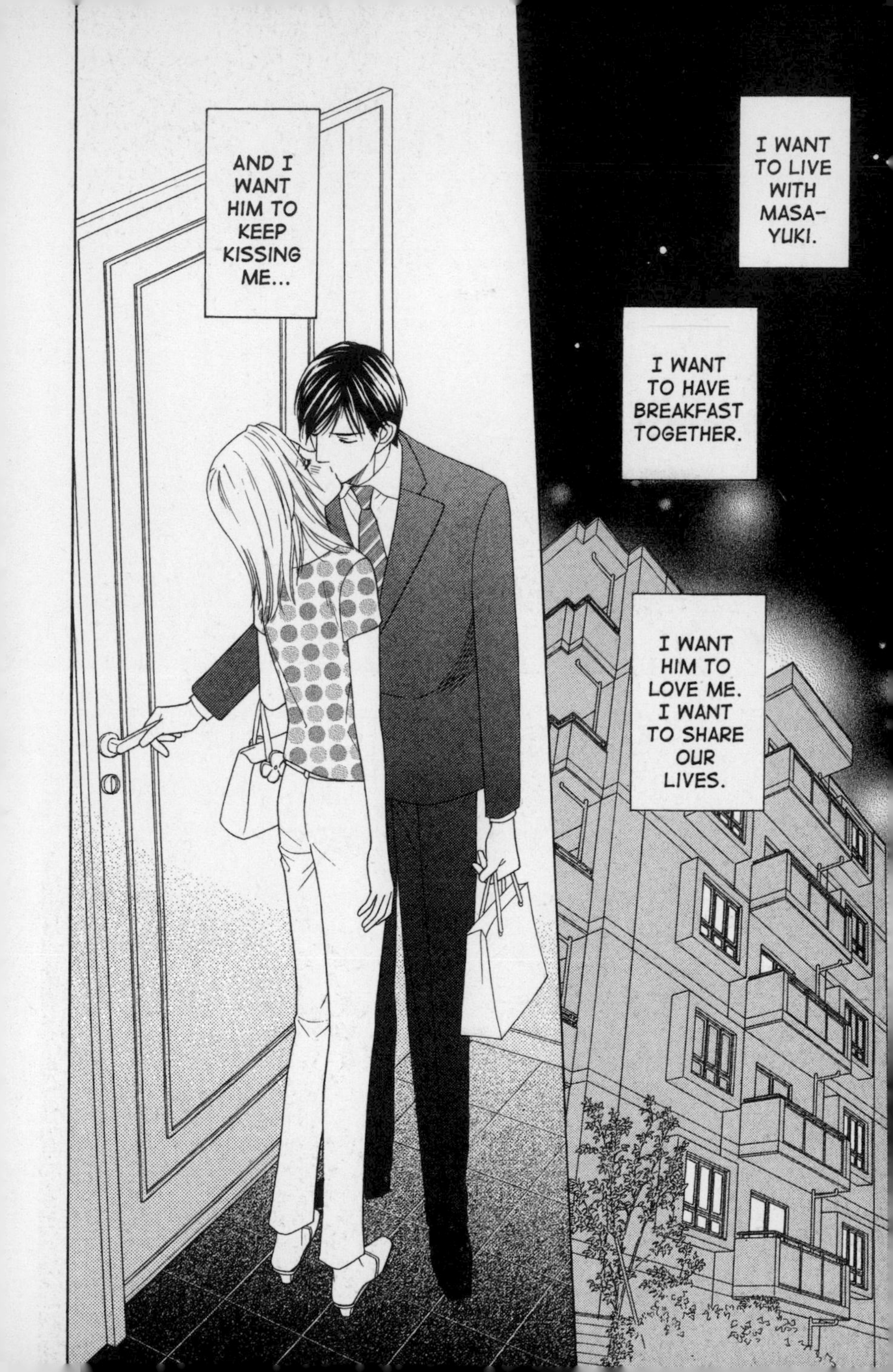
I WANT TO LIVE WITH MASA-YUKI.
I WANT TO HAVE BREAKFAST TOGETHER.
I WANT HIM TO LOVE ME.
I WANT TO SHARE OUR LIVES.
AND I WANT HIM TO KEEP KISSING ME...

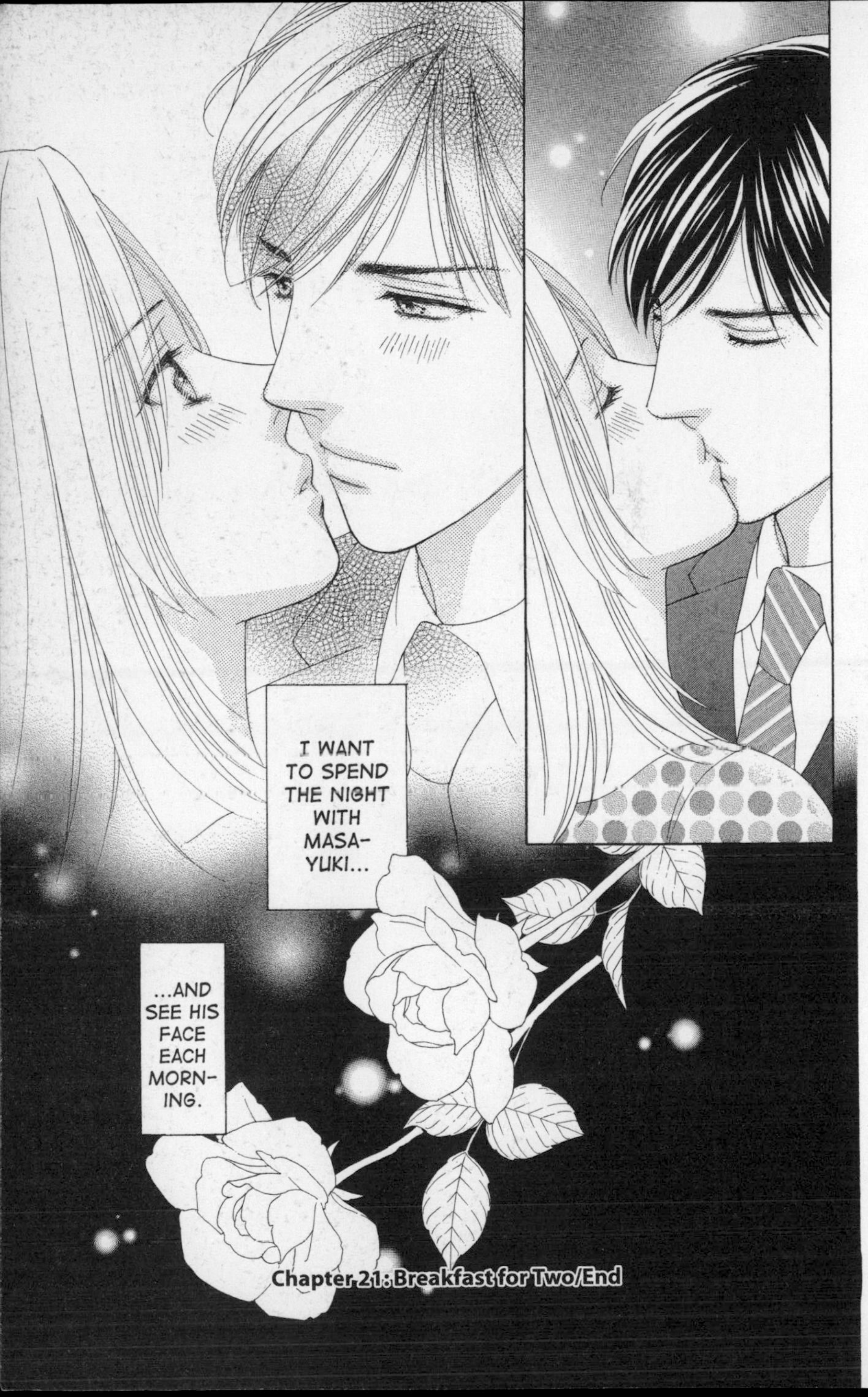
I WANT TO SPEND THE NIGHT WITH MASA-YUKI...
...AND SEE HIS FACE EACH MORN-ING.
Chapter 21: Breakfast for Two/End

SERVANT DIARY

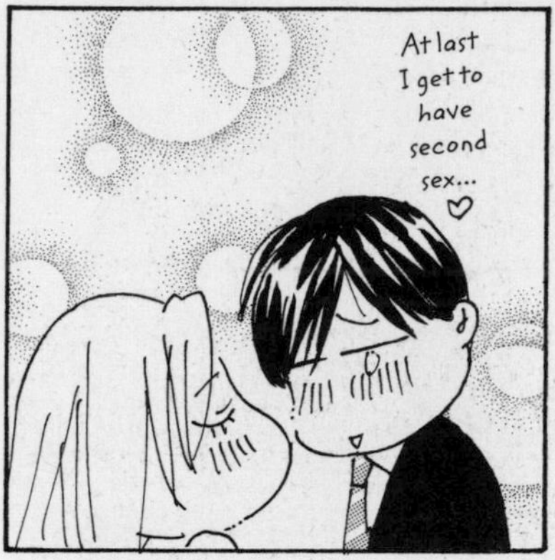
At last I get to have second sex...

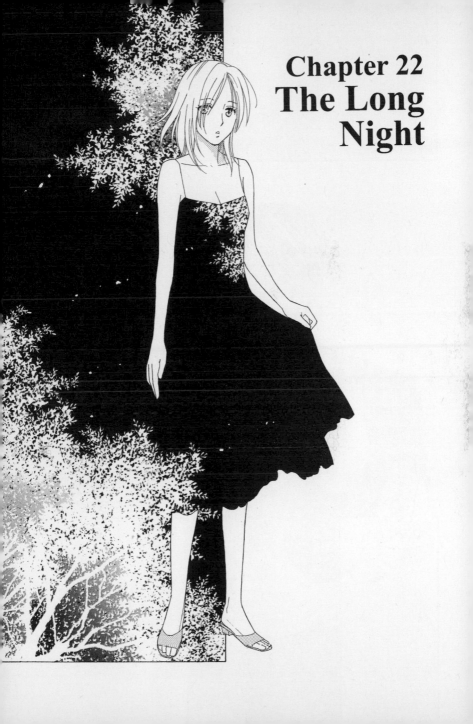

Chapter 22
The Long Night

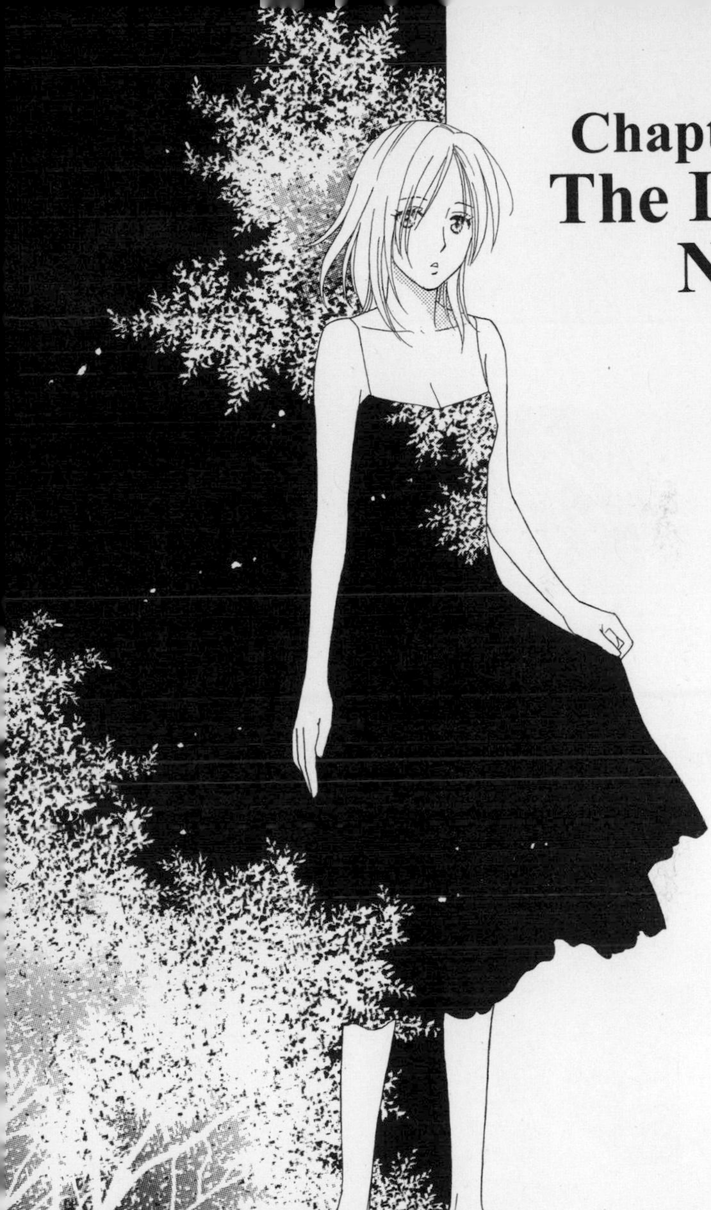

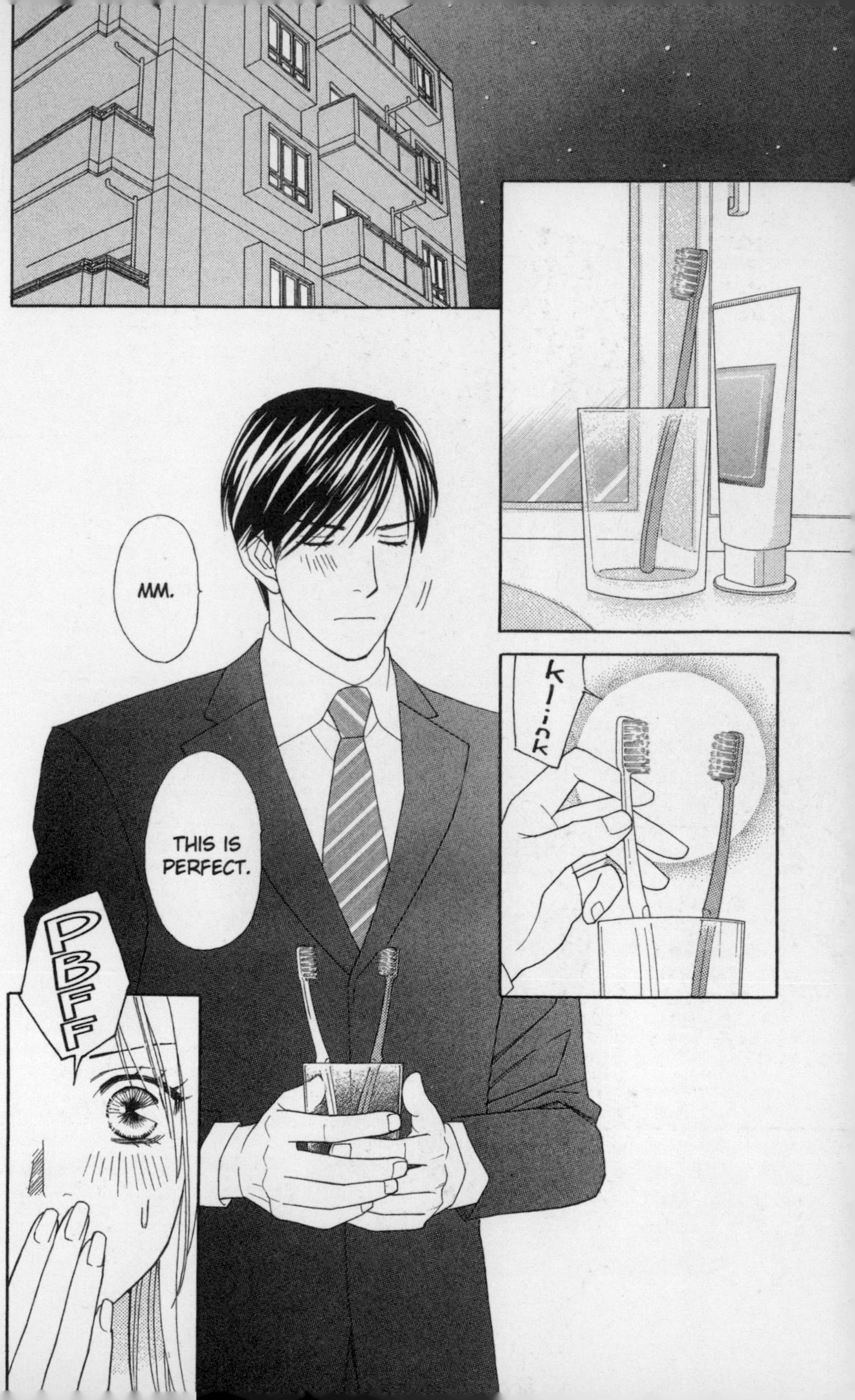

klink
MM.
THIS IS PERFECT.
PBFF

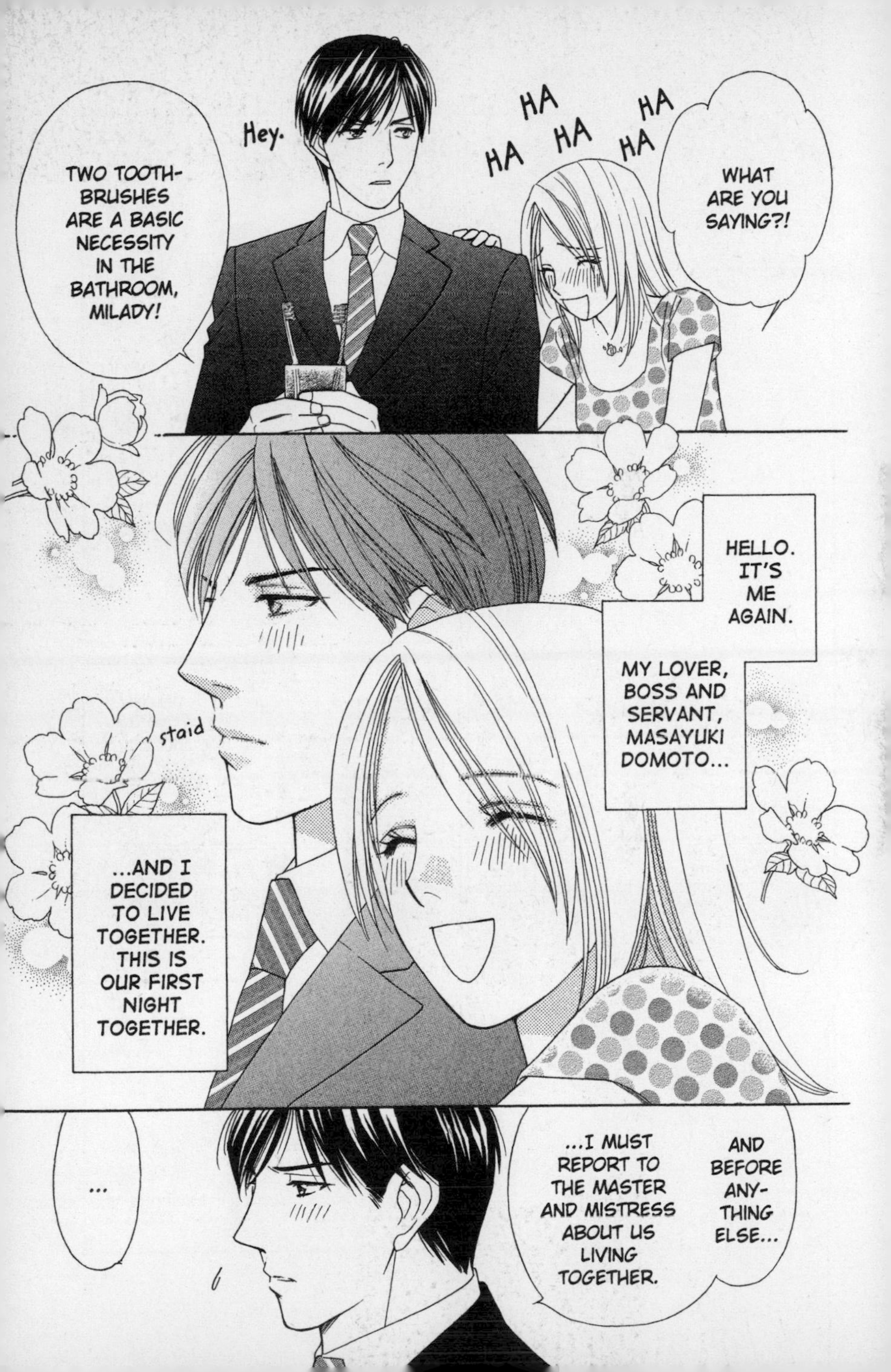
HA HA HA HA HA
WHAT ARE YOU SAYING?!
Hey.
TWO TOOTH-BRUSHES ARE A BASIC NECESSITY IN THE BATHROOM, MILADY!
HELLO. IT'S ME AGAIN.
MY LOVER, BOSS AND SERVANT, MASAYUKI DOMOTO...
staid
...AND I DECIDED TO LIVE TOGETHER. THIS IS OUR FIRST NIGHT TOGETHER.
AND BEFORE ANY-THING ELSE...
...I MUST REPORT TO THE MASTER AND MISTRESS ABOUT US LIVING TOGETHER.
...

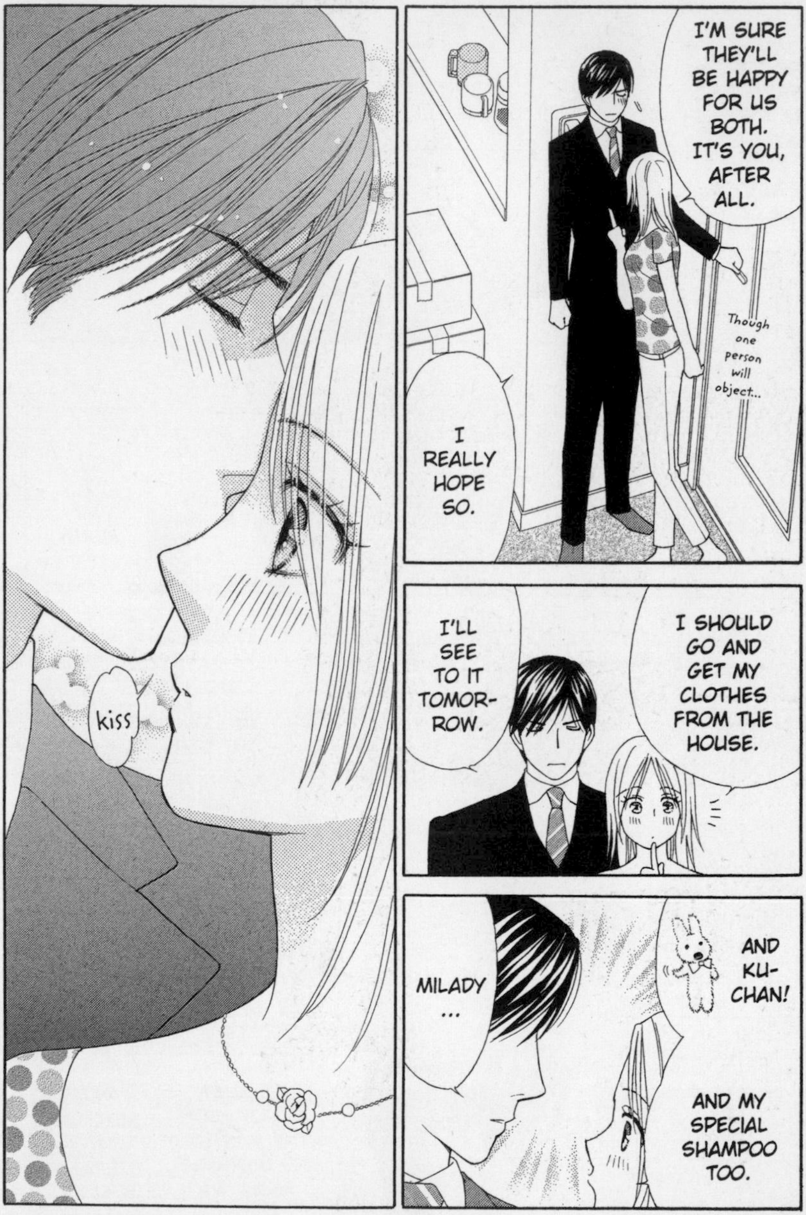
I'M SURE THEY'LL BE HAPPY FOR US BOTH. IT'S YOU, AFTER ALL.
Though one person will object...
I REALLY HOPE SO.
I SHOULD GO AND GET MY CLOTHES FROM THE HOUSE.
I'LL SEE TO IT TOMORROW.
AND KU-CHAN!
AND MY SPECIAL SHAMPOO TOO.
MILADY ...
kiss

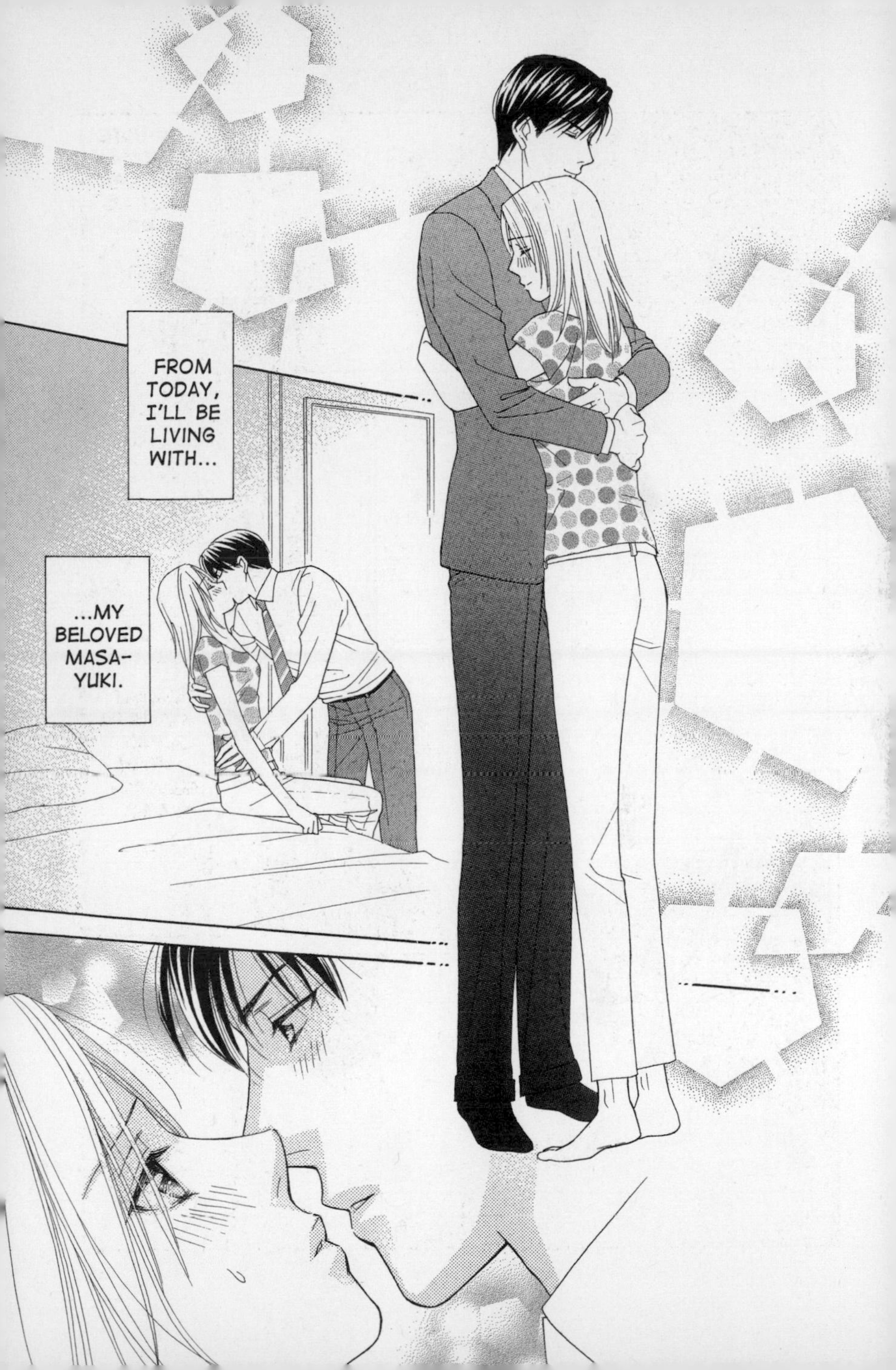
FROM TODAY, I'LL BE LIVING WITH...
...MY BELOVED MASA-YUKI.

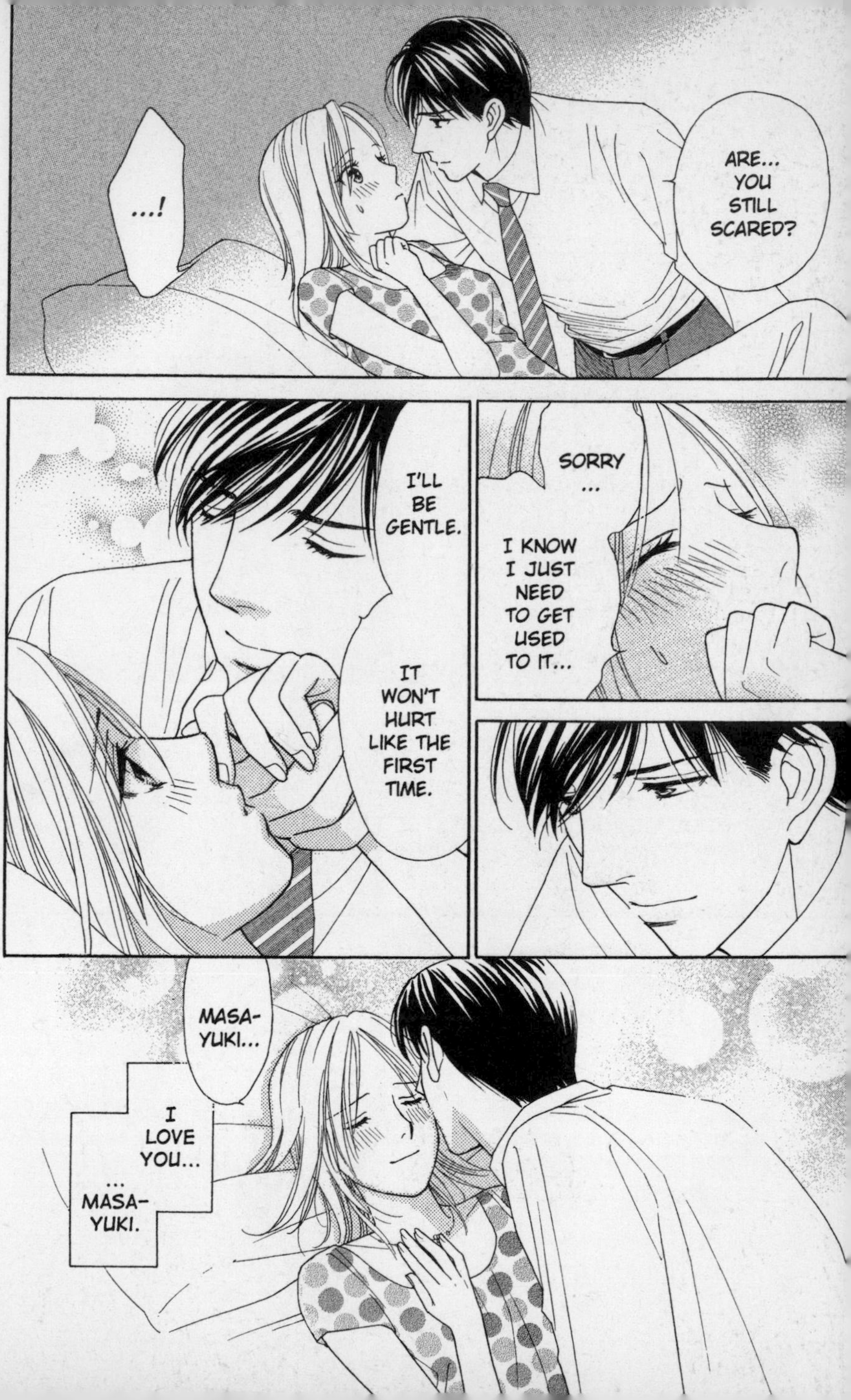
ARE... YOU STILL SCARED?
...!
SORRY ...
I KNOW I JUST NEED TO GET USED TO IT...
I'LL BE GENTLE.
IT WON'T HURT LIKE THE FIRST TIME.
MASA-YUKI...
I LOVE YOU... ... MASA-YUKI.

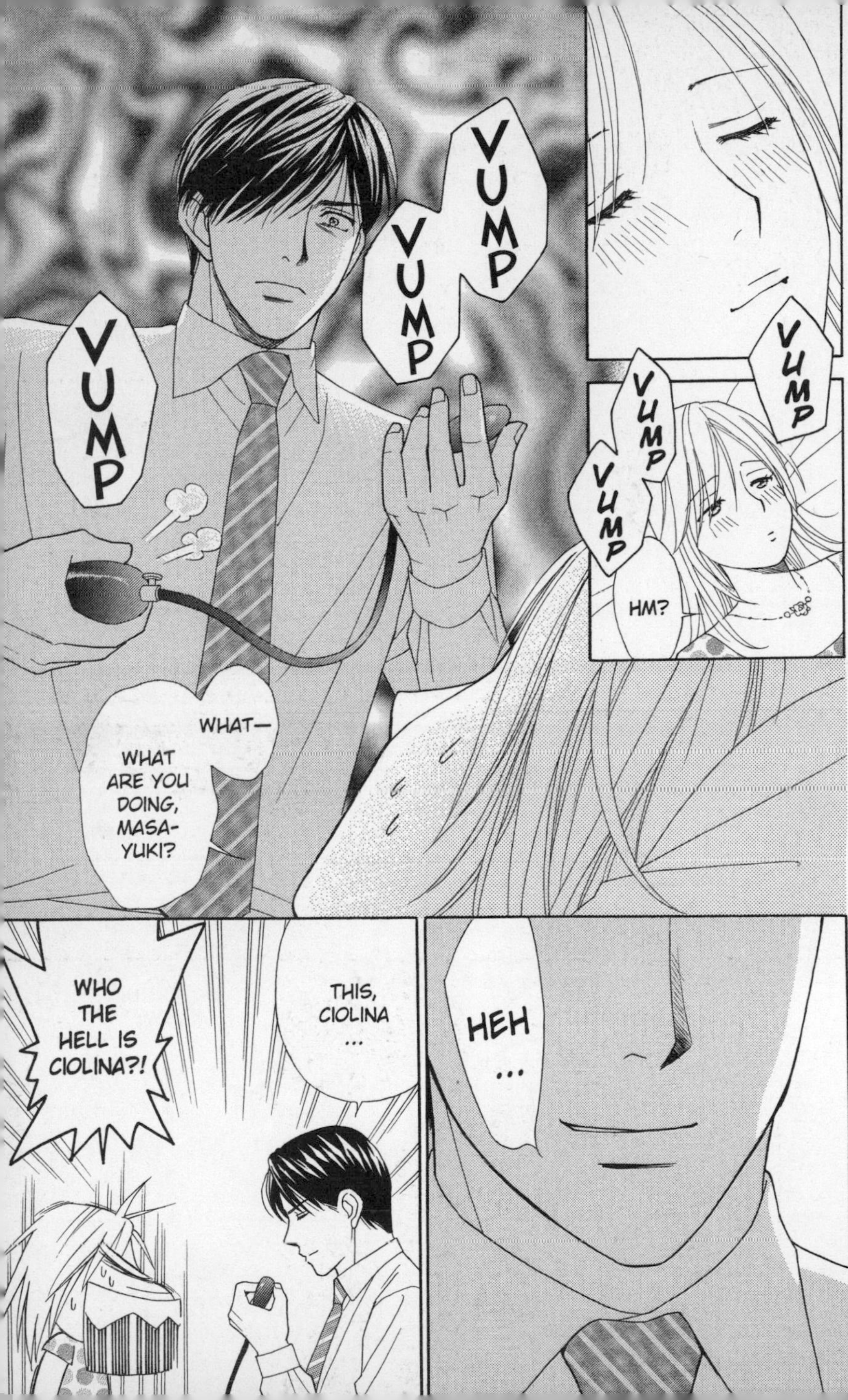
VUMP
VUMP
VUMP
HM?
VUMP
VUMP
VUMP
VUMP
WHAT—
WHAT ARE YOU DOING, MASA-YUKI?
HEH ...
THIS, CIOLINA ...
WHO THE HELL IS CIOLINA?!

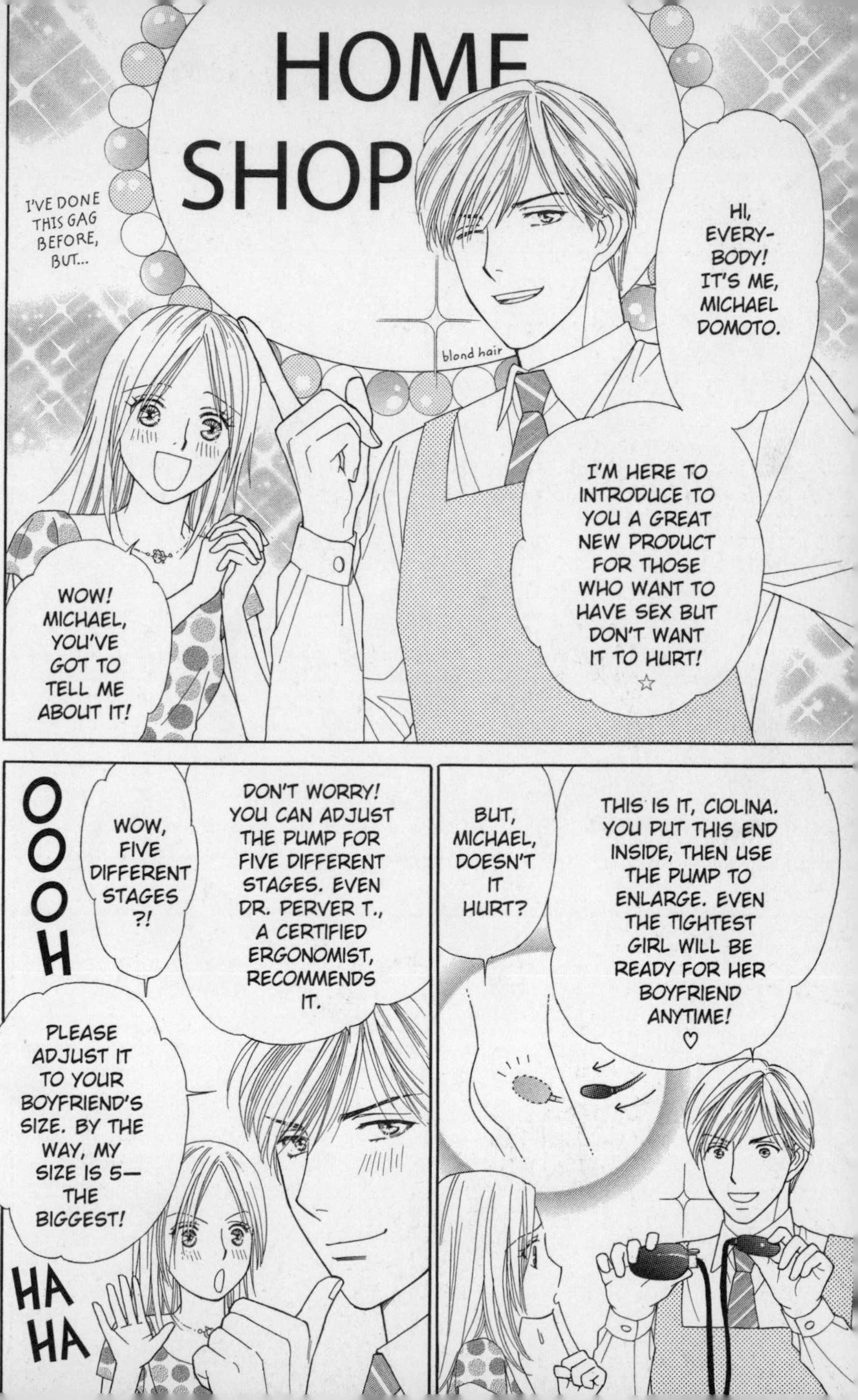
HOME SHOP
HI, EVERYBODY! IT'S ME, MICHAEL DOMOTO.
blond hair
I'VE DONE THIS GAG BEFORE, BUT...
I'M HERE TO INTRODUCE TO YOU A GREAT NEW PRODUCT FOR THOSE WHO WANT TO HAVE SEX BUT DON'T WANT IT TO HURT! ☆
WOW! MICHAEL, YOU'VE GOT TO TELL ME ABOUT IT!
THIS IS IT, CIOLINA. YOU PUT THIS END INSIDE, THEN USE THE PUMP TO ENLARGE. EVEN THE TIGHTEST GIRL WILL BE READY FOR HER BOYFRIEND ANYTIME! ♡
BUT, MICHAEL, DOESN'T IT HURT?
DON'T WORRY! YOU CAN ADJUST THE PUMP FOR FIVE DIFFERENT STAGES. EVEN DR. PERVER T., A CERTIFIED ERGONOMIST, RECOMMENDS IT.
WOW, FIVE DIFFERENT STAGES ?!
OOOH
PLEASE ADJUST IT TO YOUR BOYFRIEND'S SIZE. BY THE WAY, MY SIZE IS 5— THE BIGGEST!
HA HA

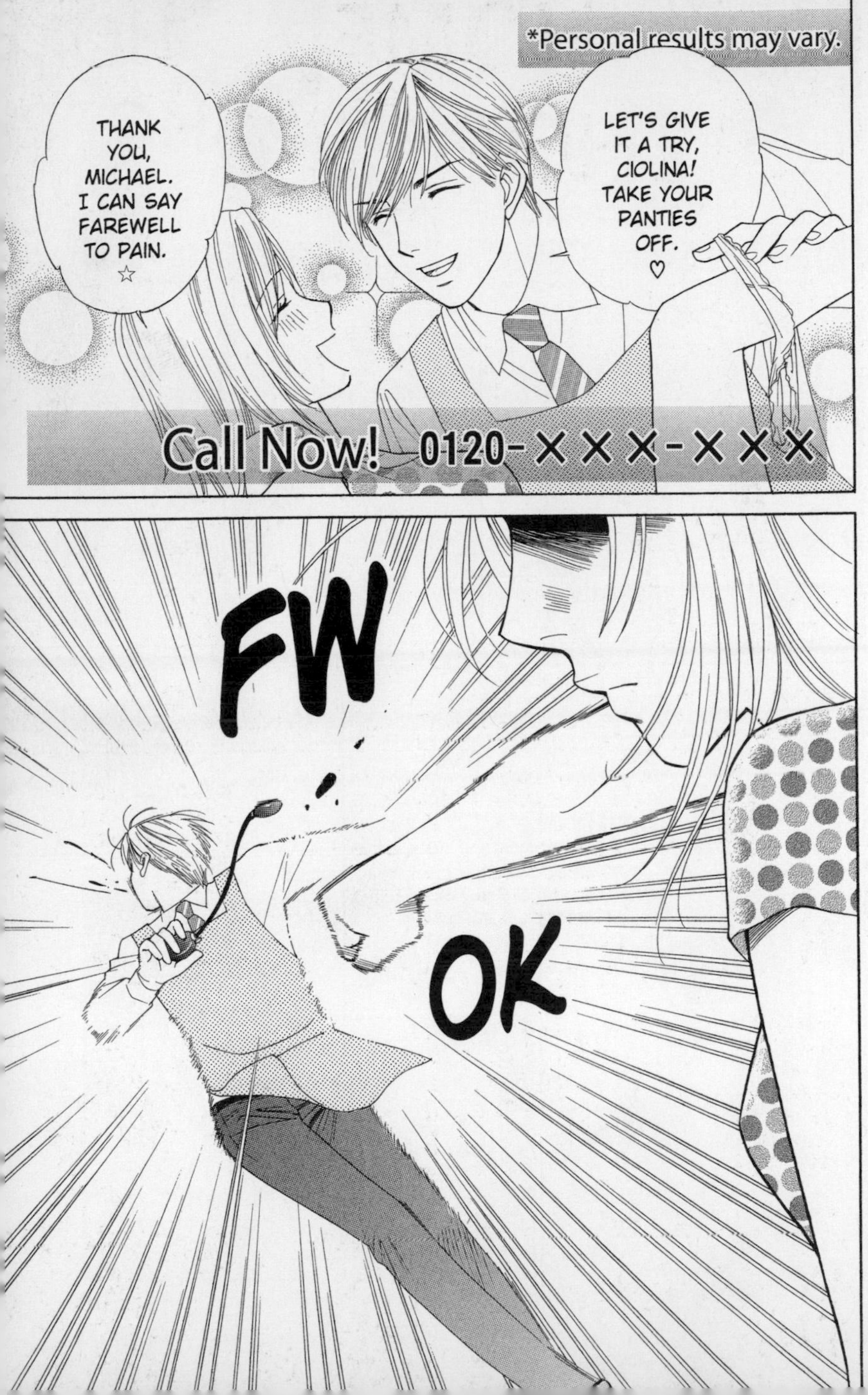
*Personal results may vary.
LET'S GIVE IT A TRY, CIOLINA! TAKE YOUR PANTIES OFF. ♡
THANK YOU, MICHAEL. I CAN SAY FAREWELL TO PAIN. ☆
Call Now! 0120-×××-×××
FW
OK

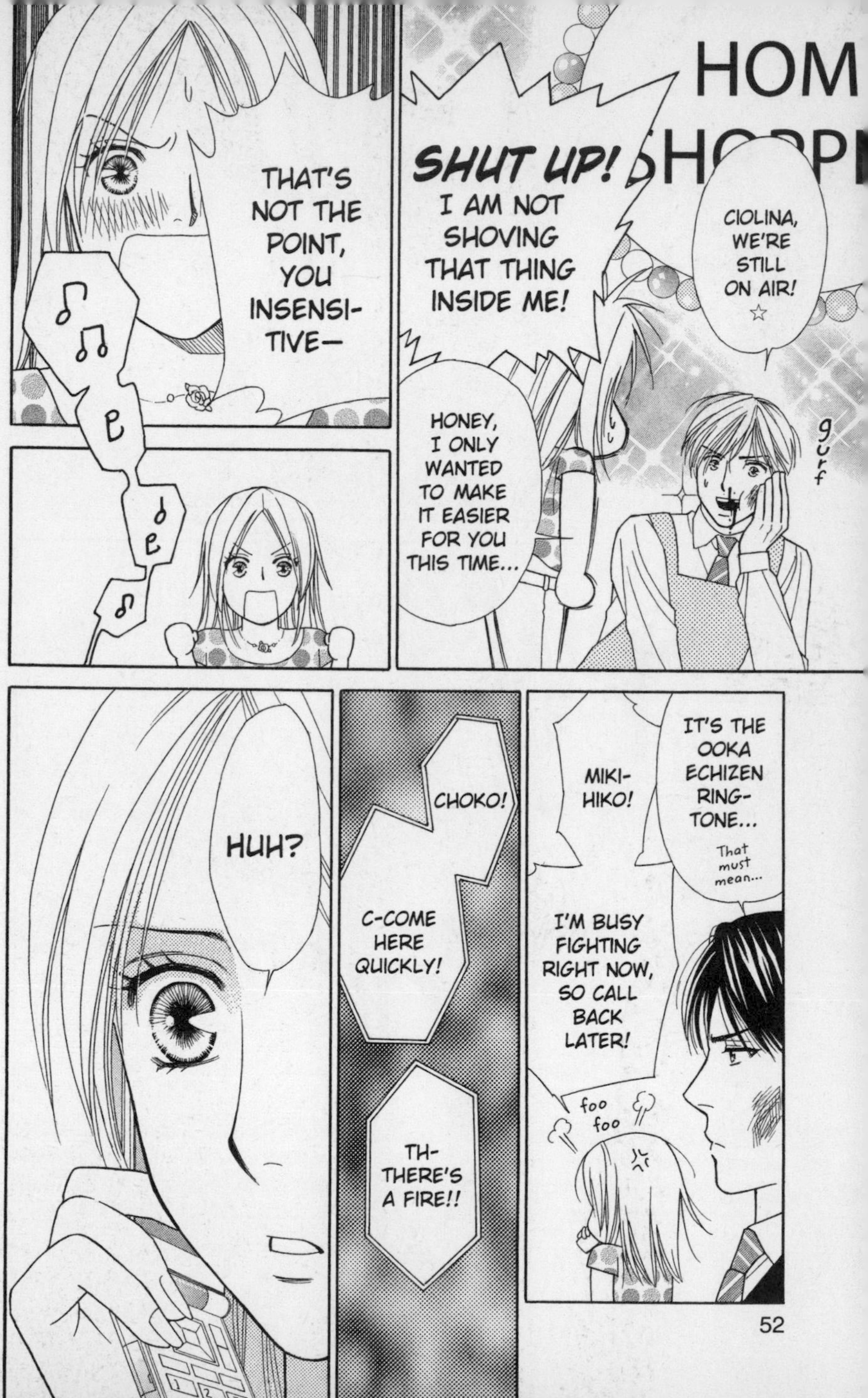
HOM
CIOLINA, WE'RE STILL ON AIR! ☆
gurf
SHUT UP!
I AM NOT SHOVING THAT THING INSIDE ME!
HONEY, I ONLY WANTED TO MAKE IT EASIER FOR YOU THIS TIME...
THAT'S NOT THE POINT, YOU INSENSITIVE—
IT'S THE OOKA ECHIZEN RING-TONE...
That must mean...
MIKI-HIKO!
I'M BUSY FIGHTING RIGHT NOW, SO CALL BACK LATER!
foo foo
CHOKO!
C-COME HERE QUICKLY!
TH-THERE'S A FIRE!!
HUH?

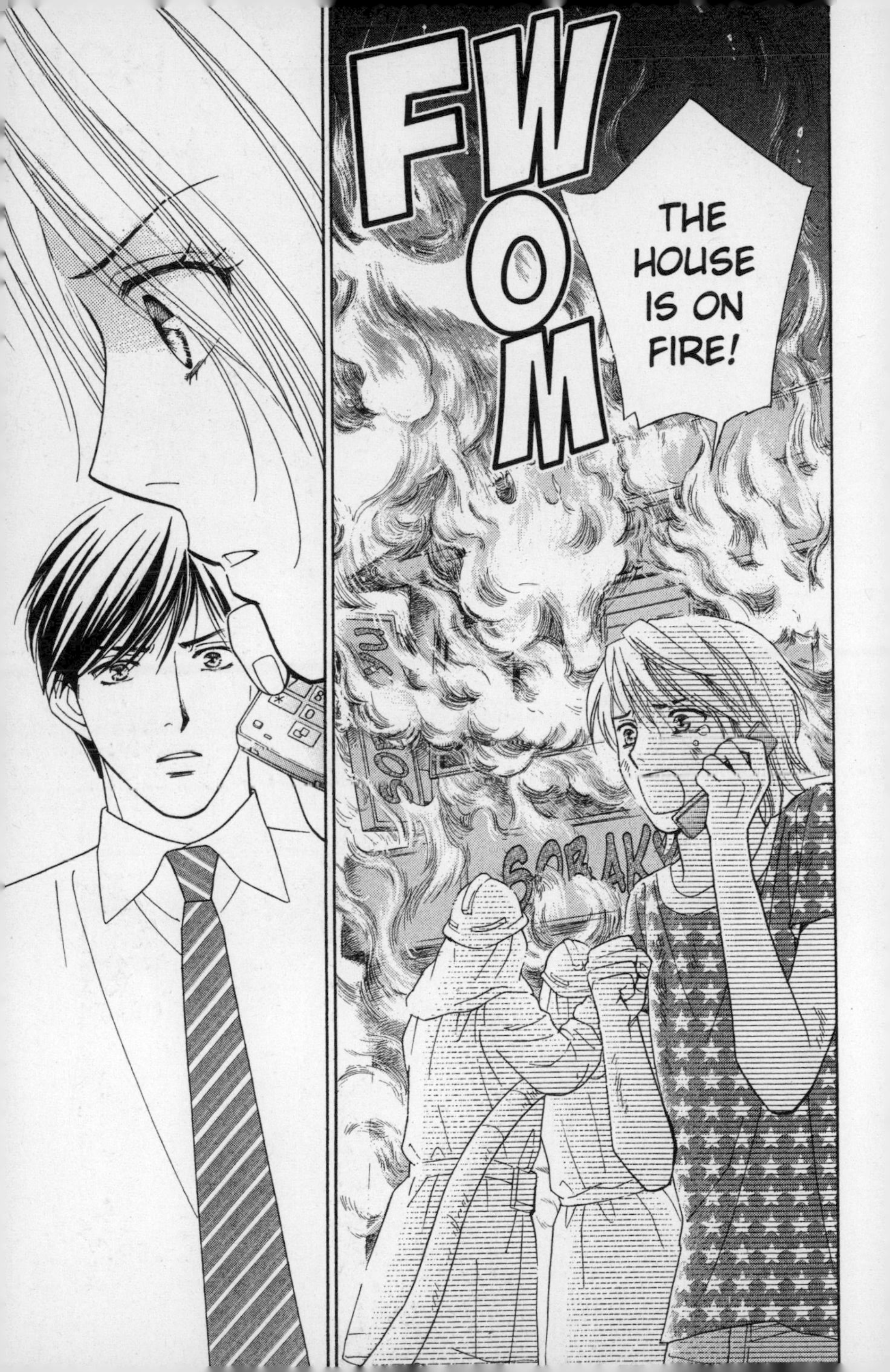
FWOM
THE HOUSE IS ON FIRE!

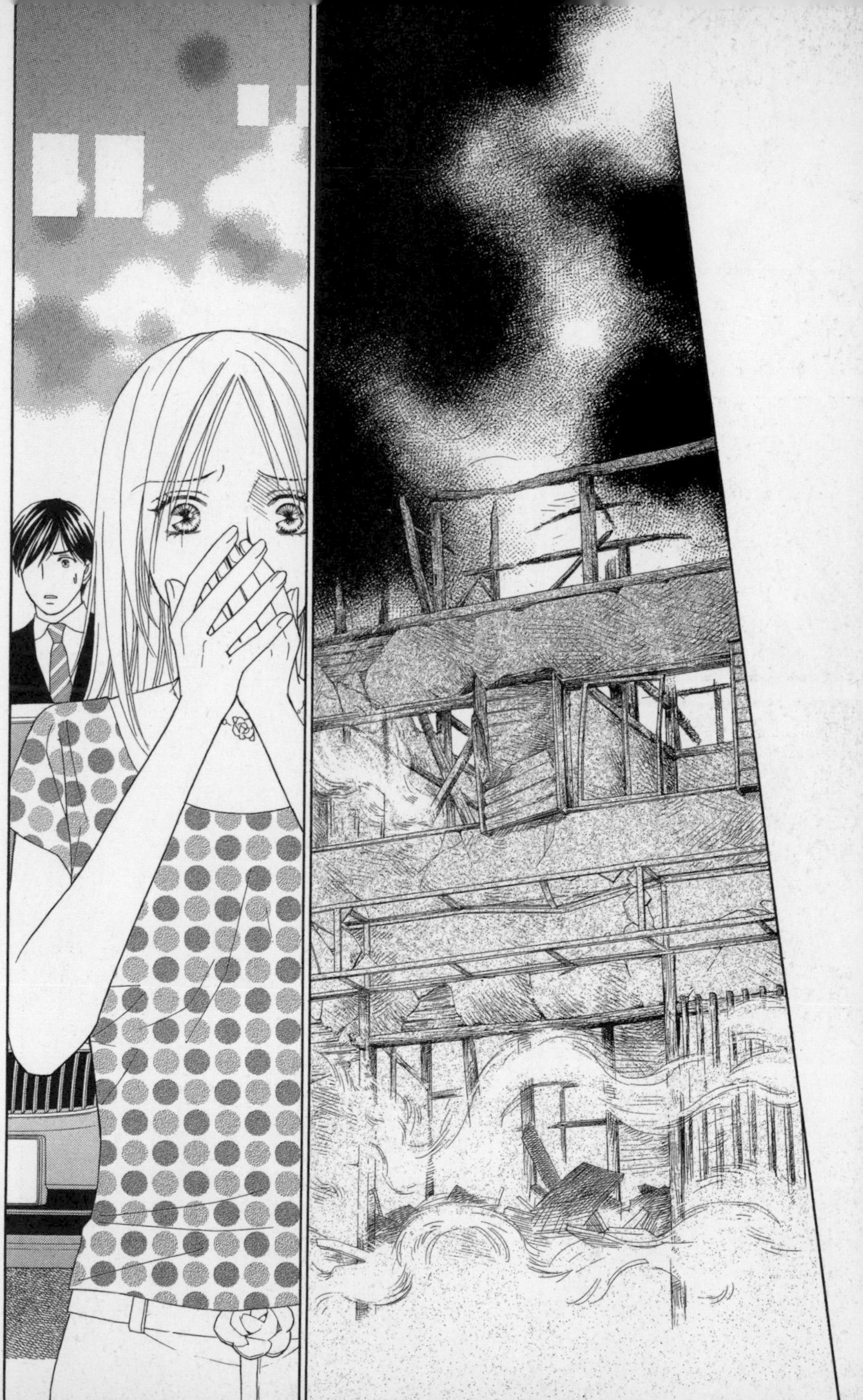

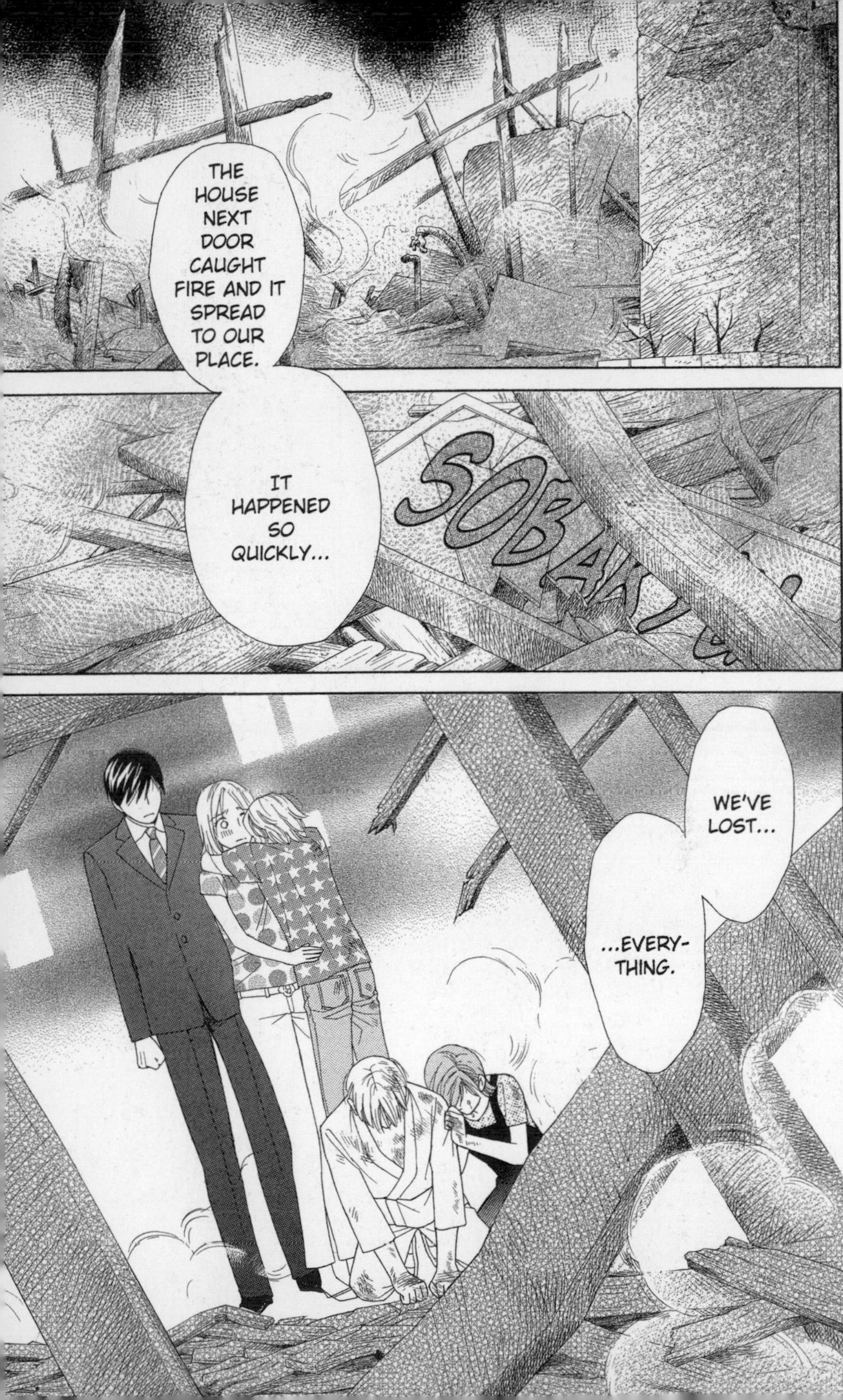
THE HOUSE NEXT DOOR CAUGHT FIRE AND IT SPREAD TO OUR PLACE.
IT HAPPENED SO QUICKLY...
WE'VE LOST...
...EVERY-THING.

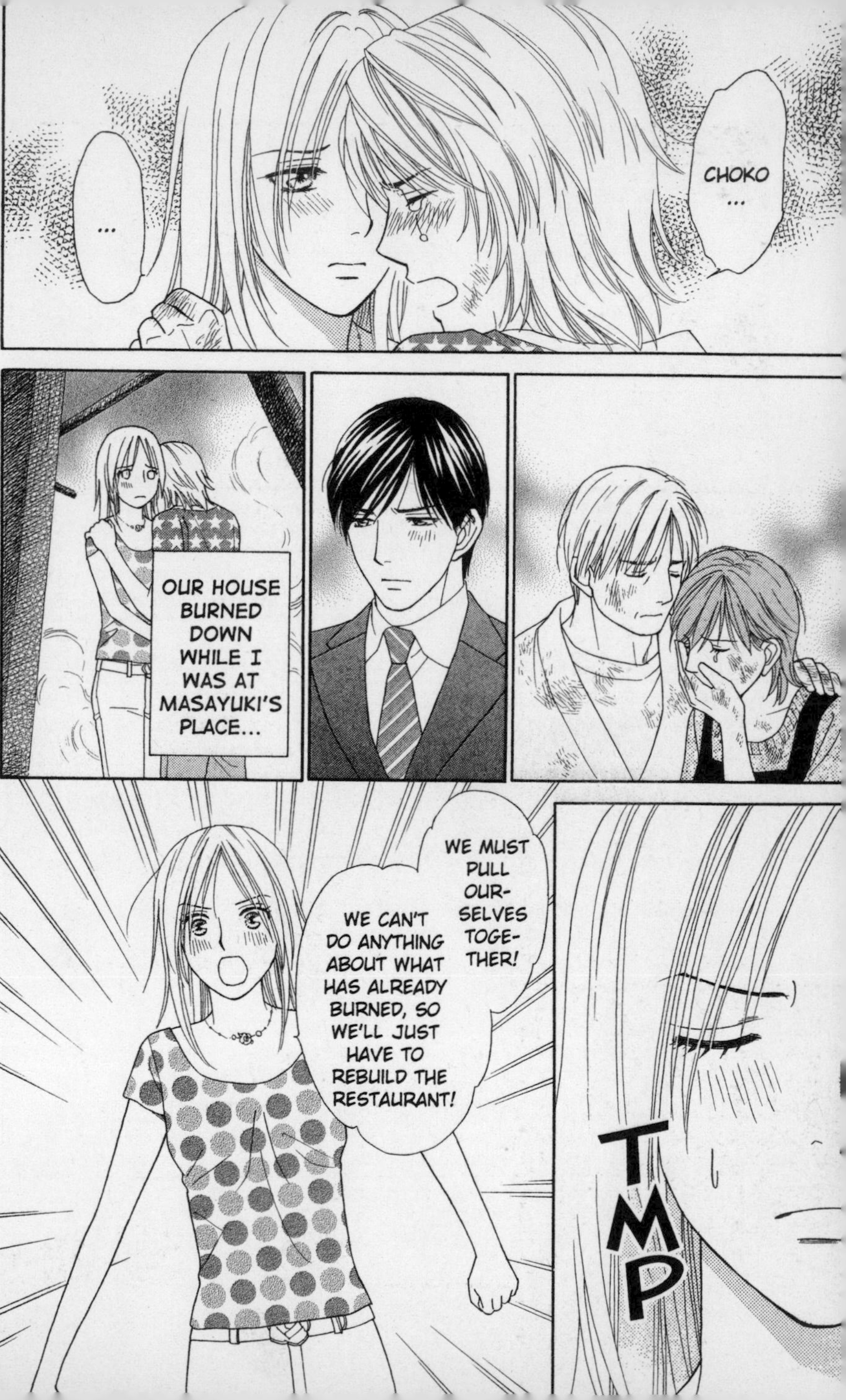
CHOKO ...
...
OUR HOUSE BURNED DOWN WHILE I WAS AT MASAYUKI'S PLACE...
TMP
WE MUST PULL OURSELVES TOGETHER!
WE CAN'T DO ANYTHING ABOUT WHAT HAS ALREADY BURNED, SO WE'LL JUST HAVE TO REBUILD THE RESTAURANT!

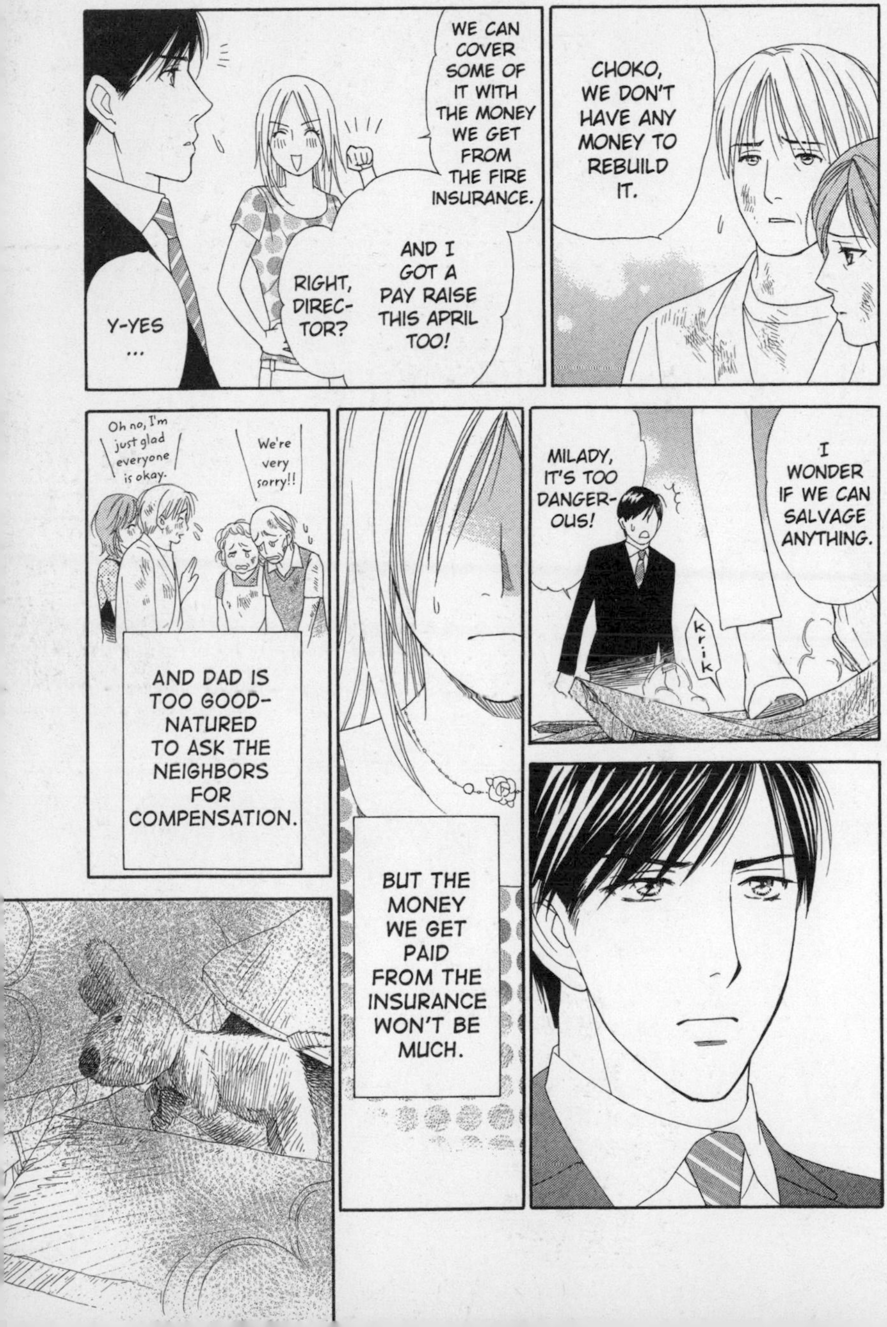
CHOKO, WE DON'T HAVE ANY MONEY TO REBUILD IT.
WE CAN COVER SOME OF IT WITH THE MONEY WE GET FROM THE FIRE INSURANCE.
AND I GOT A PAY RAISE THIS APRIL TOO!
RIGHT, DIRECTOR?
Y-YES ...
I WONDER IF WE CAN SALVAGE ANYTHING.
MILADY, IT'S TOO DANGEROUS!
kr-i-k
BUT THE MONEY WE GET PAID FROM THE INSURANCE WON'T BE MUCH.
We're very sorry!!
Oh no, I'm just glad everyone is okay.
AND DAD IS TOO GOOD-NATURED TO ASK THE NEIGHBORS FOR COMPENSATION.

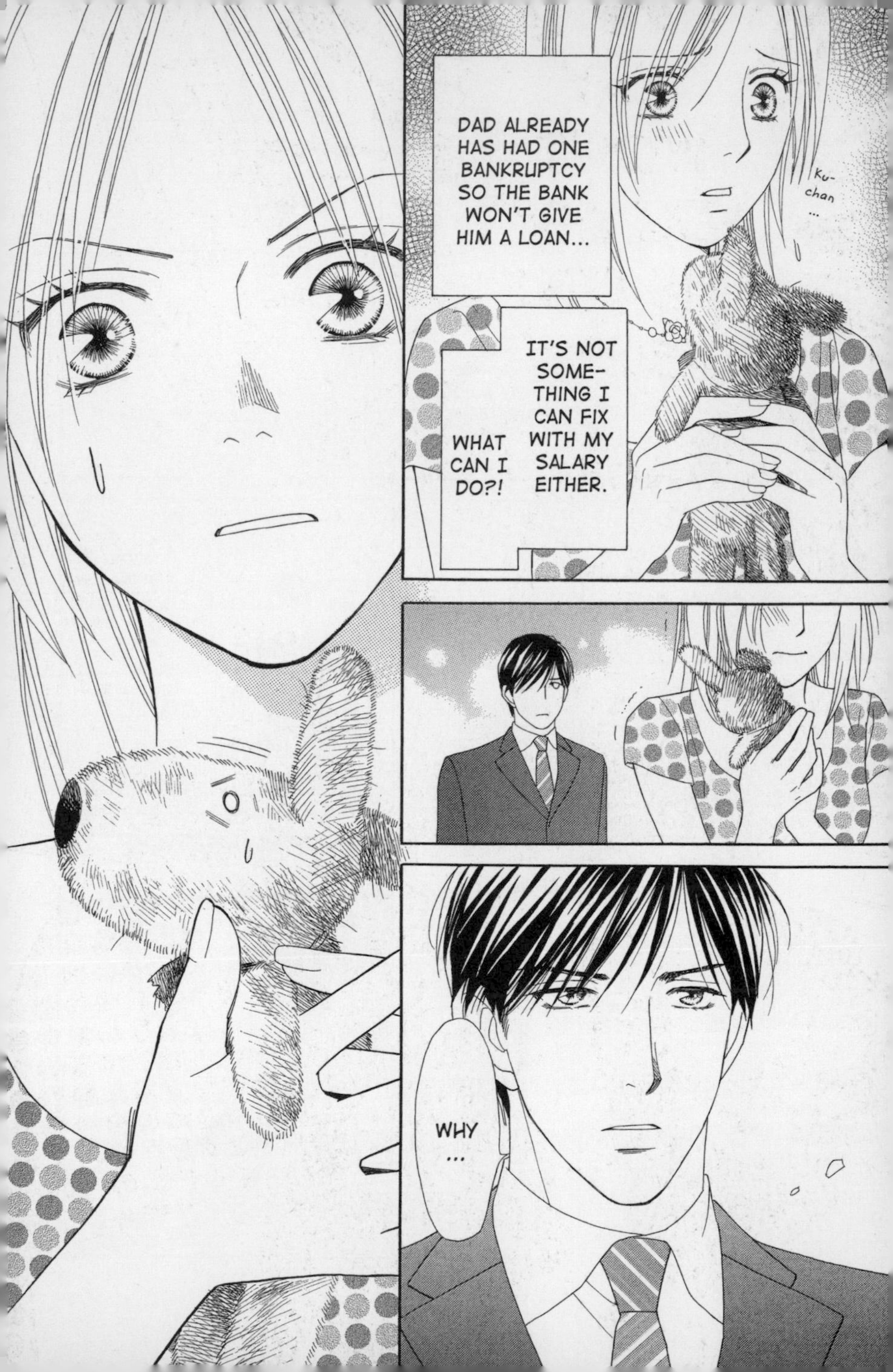

Ku-chan...
DAD ALREADY HAS HAD ONE BANKRUPTCY SO THE BANK WON'T GIVE HIM A LOAN...
IT'S NOT SOMETHING I CAN FIX WITH MY SALARY EITHER.
WHAT CAN I DO?!
WHY...

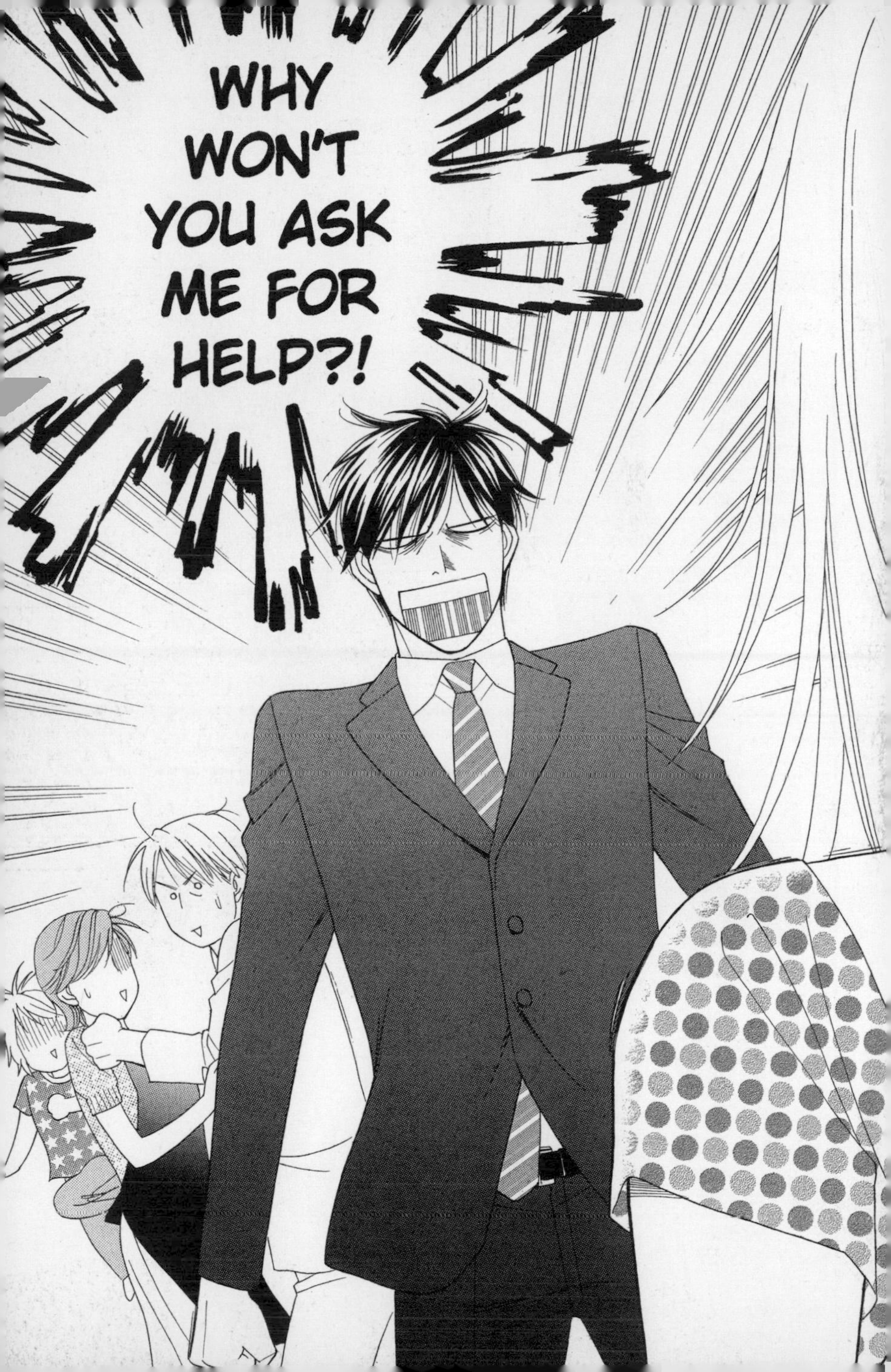
WHY WON'T YOU ASK ME FOR HELP?!

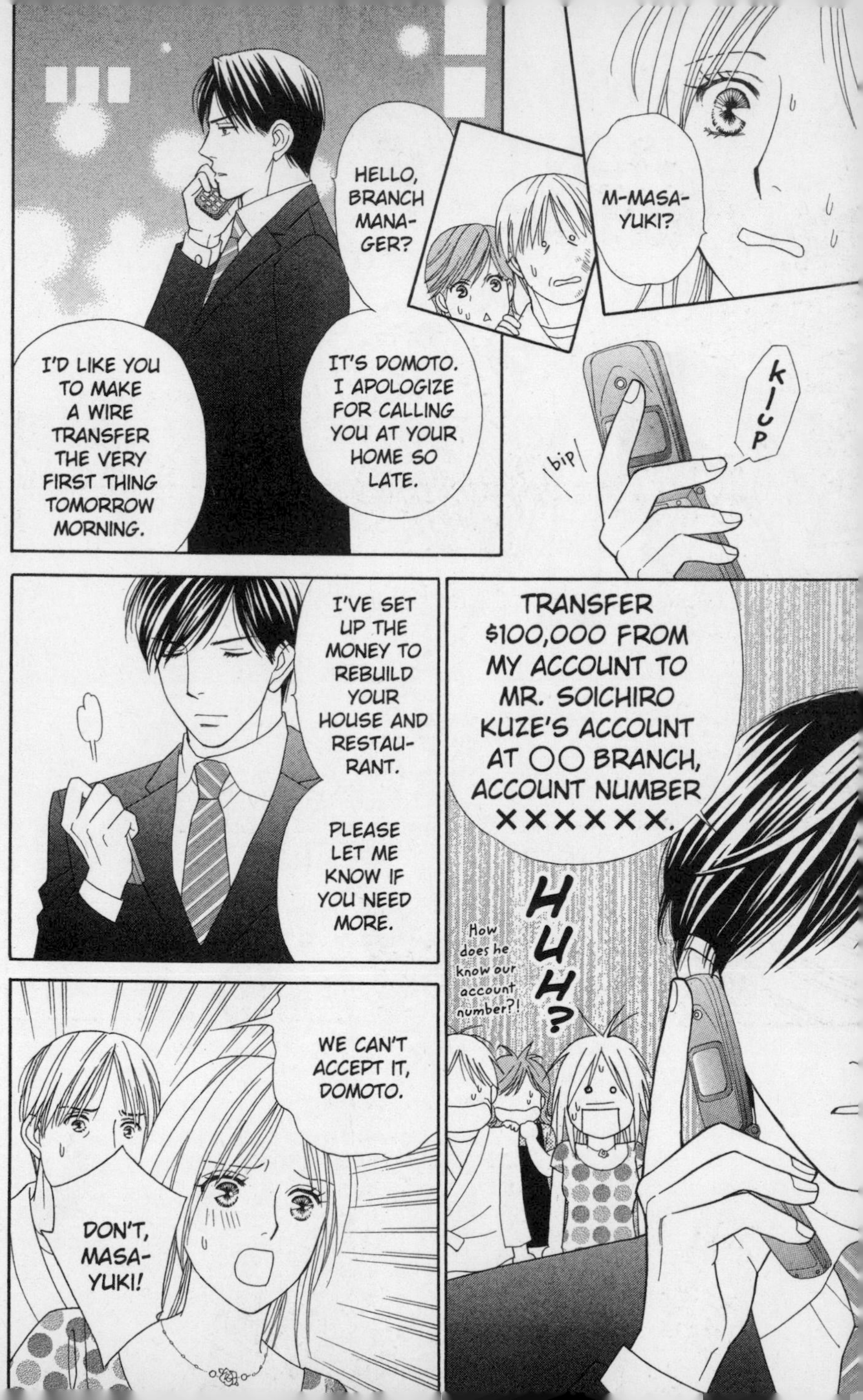
M-MASA-YUKI?
KLUP
bip
HELLO, BRANCH MANA-GER?
IT'S DOMOTO. I APOLOGIZE FOR CALLING YOU AT YOUR HOME SO LATE.
I'D LIKE YOU TO MAKE A WIRE TRANSFER THE VERY FIRST THING TOMORROW MORNING.
TRANSFER $100,000 FROM MY ACCOUNT TO MR. SOICHIRO KUZE'S ACCOUNT AT ○○ BRANCH, ACCOUNT NUMBER ××××××.
HUH?
How does he know our account number?!
I'VE SET UP THE MONEY TO REBUILD YOUR HOUSE AND RESTAU-RANT.
PLEASE LET ME KNOW IF YOU NEED MORE.
WE CAN'T ACCEPT IT, DOMOTO.
DON'T, MASA-YUKI!

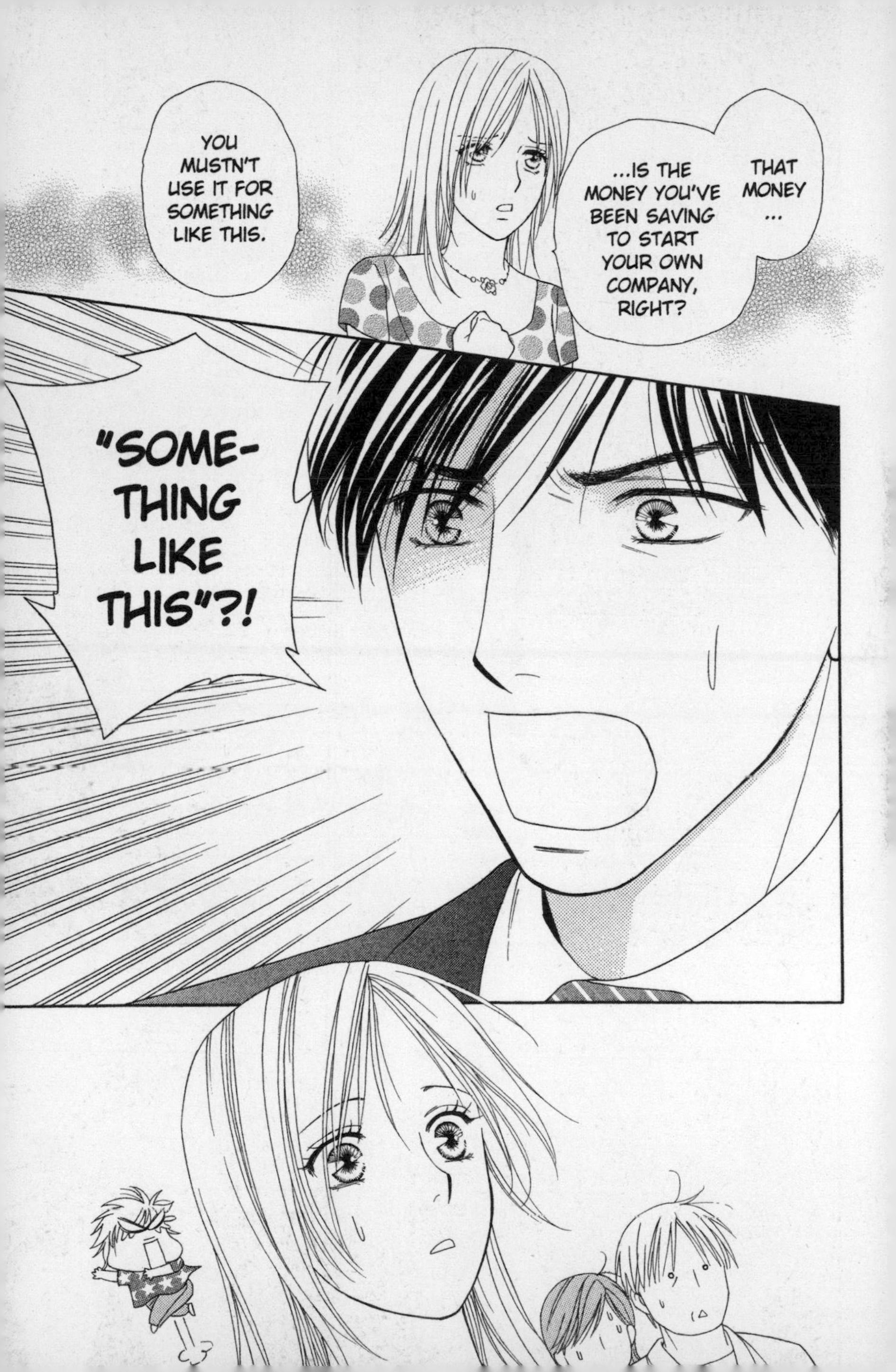
THAT MONEY ...
...IS THE MONEY YOU'VE BEEN SAVING TO START YOUR OWN COMPANY, RIGHT?
YOU MUSTN'T USE IT FOR SOMETHING LIKE THIS.
"SOME-THING LIKE THIS"?!

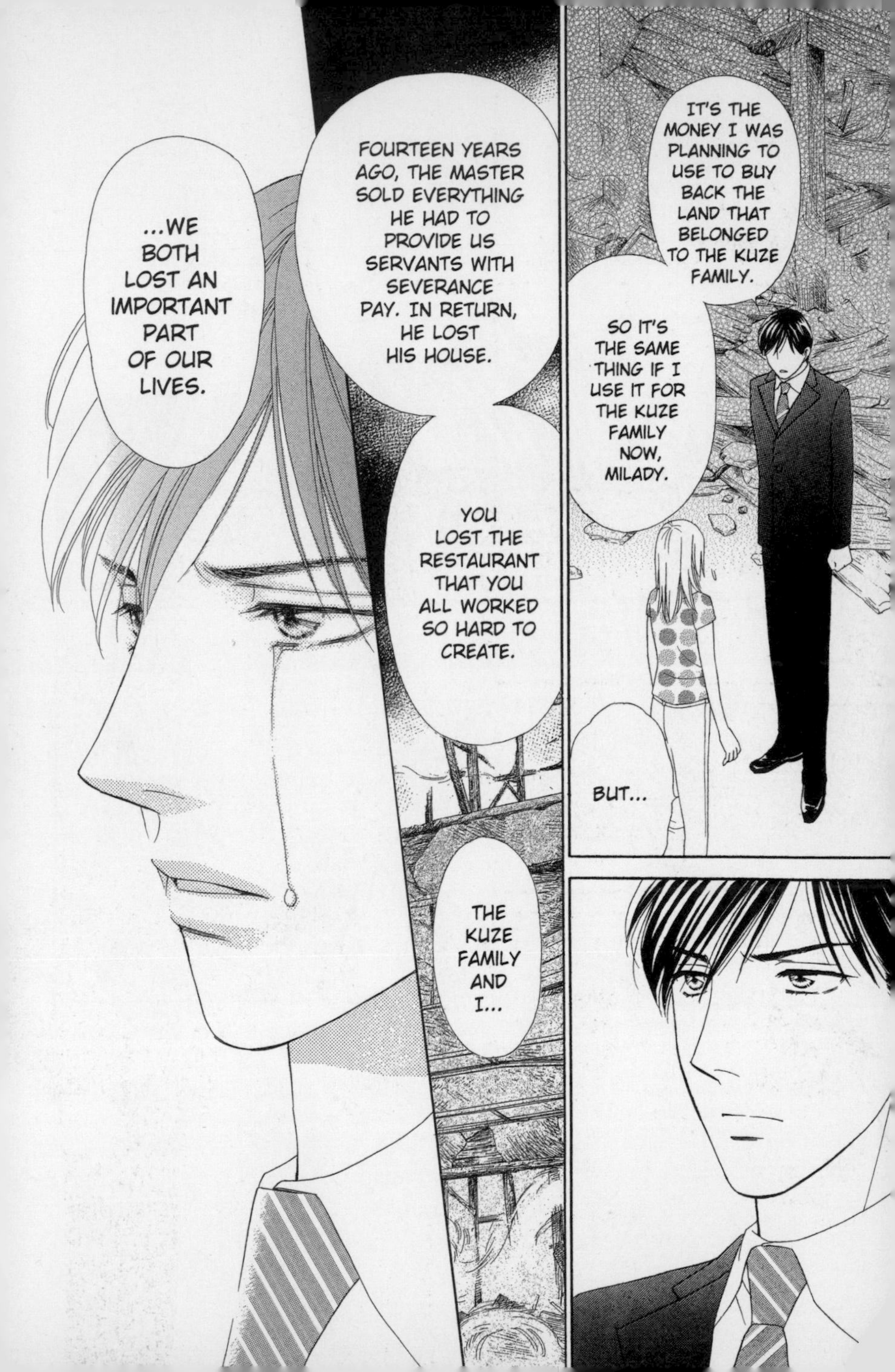
IT'S THE MONEY I WAS PLANNING TO USE TO BUY BACK THE LAND THAT BELONGED TO THE KUZE FAMILY.
SO IT'S THE SAME THING IF I USE IT FOR THE KUZE FAMILY NOW, MILADY.
BUT...
FOURTEEN YEARS AGO, THE MASTER SOLD EVERYTHING HE HAD TO PROVIDE US SERVANTS WITH SEVERANCE PAY. IN RETURN, HE LOST HIS HOUSE.
YOU LOST THE RESTAURANT THAT YOU ALL WORKED SO HARD TO CREATE.
THE KUZE FAMILY AND I...
...WE BOTH LOST AN IMPORTANT PART OF OUR LIVES.

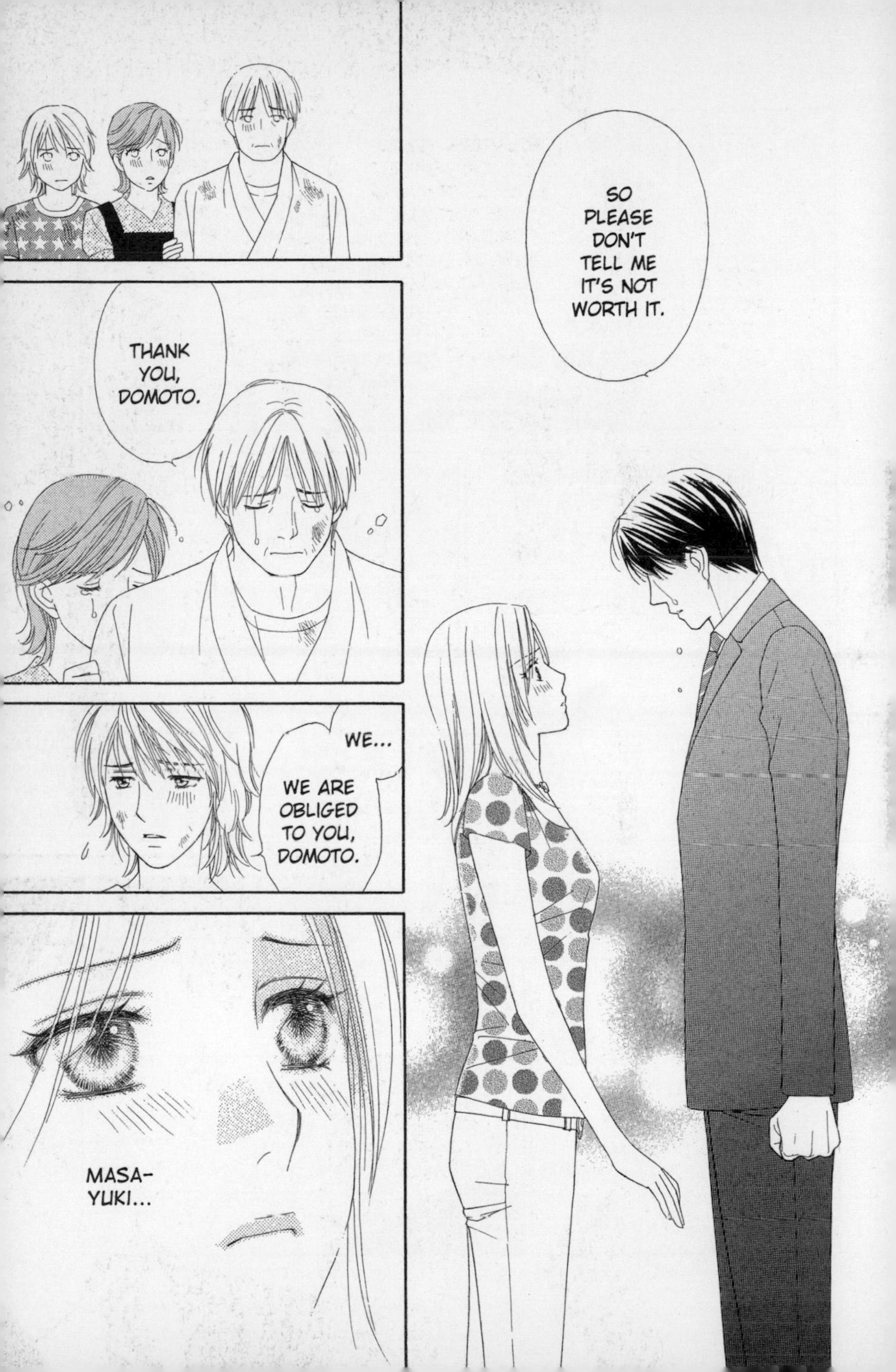
SO PLEASE DON'T TELL ME IT'S NOT WORTH IT.
THANK YOU, DOMOTO.
WE...
WE ARE OBLIGED TO YOU, DOMOTO.
MASA-YUKI...

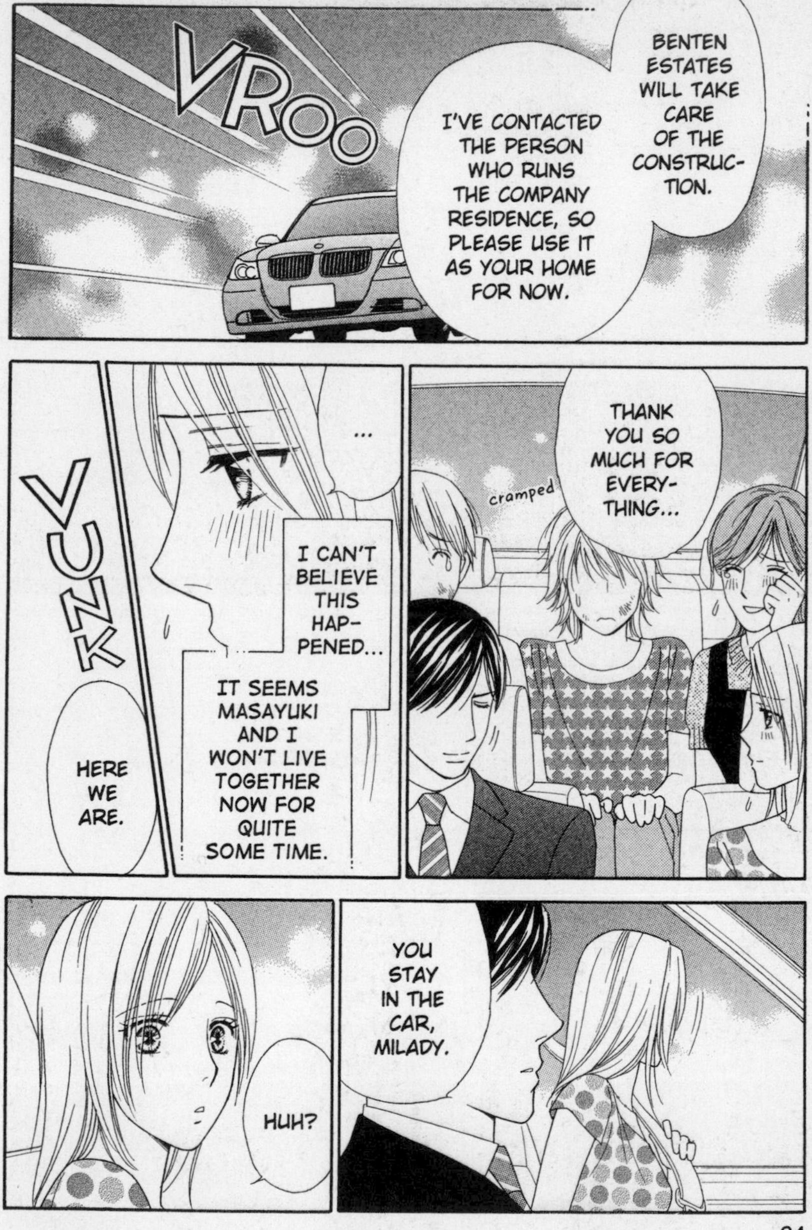
BENTEN ESTATES WILL TAKE CARE OF THE CONSTRUCTION.
I'VE CONTACTED THE PERSON WHO RUNS THE COMPANY RESIDENCE, SO PLEASE USE IT AS YOUR HOME FOR NOW.
VROOO
THANK YOU SO MUCH FOR EVERYTHING...
cramped
...
I CAN'T BELIEVE THIS HAPPENED...
IT SEEMS MASAYUKI AND I WON'T LIVE TOGETHER NOW FOR QUITE SOME TIME.
VUNK
HERE WE ARE.
YOU STAY IN THE CAR, MILADY.
HUH?

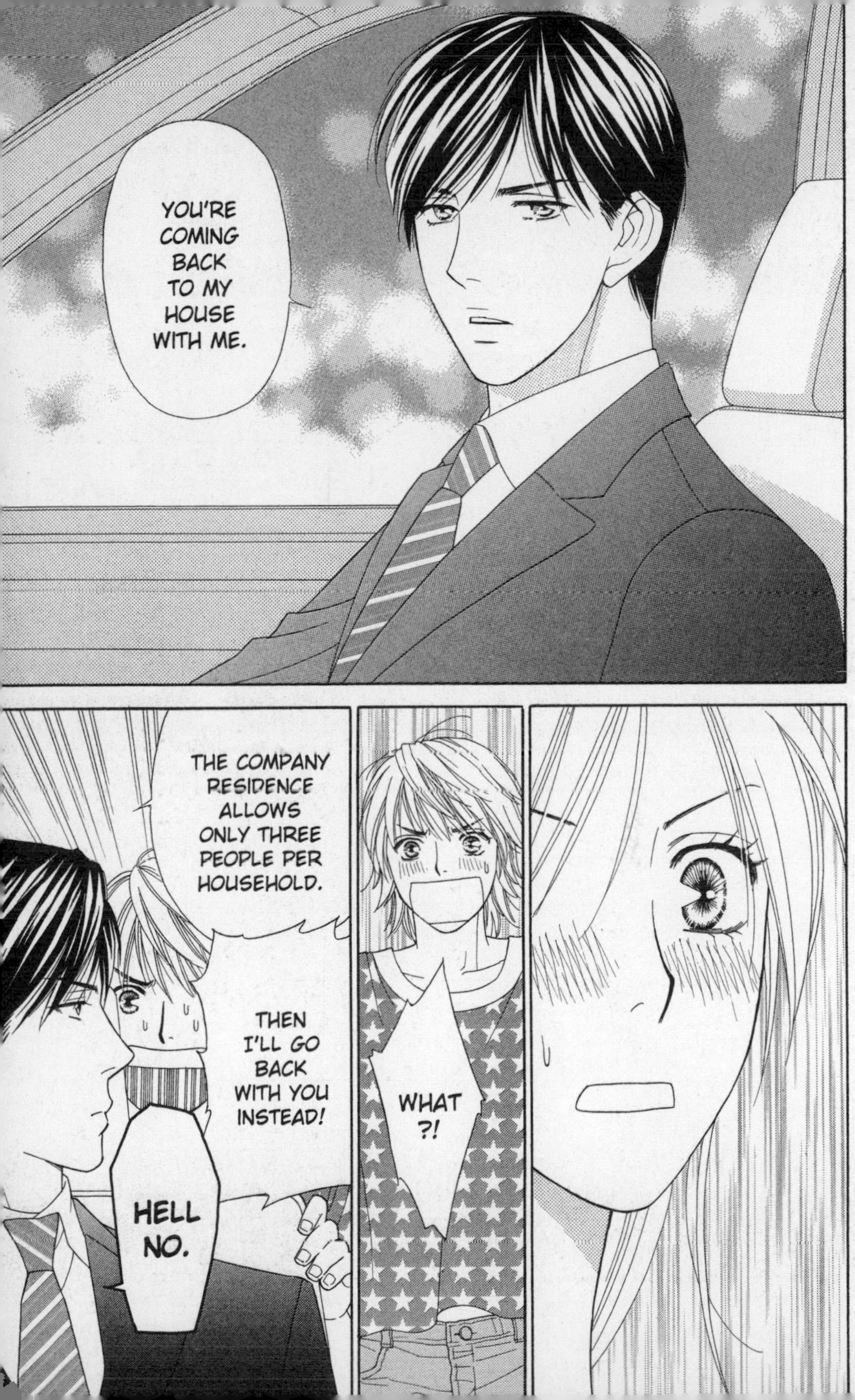

YOU'RE COMING BACK TO MY HOUSE WITH ME.
THE COMPANY RESIDENCE ALLOWS ONLY THREE PEOPLE PER HOUSEHOLD.
THEN I'LL GO BACK WITH YOU INSTEAD!
WHAT ?!
HELL NO.

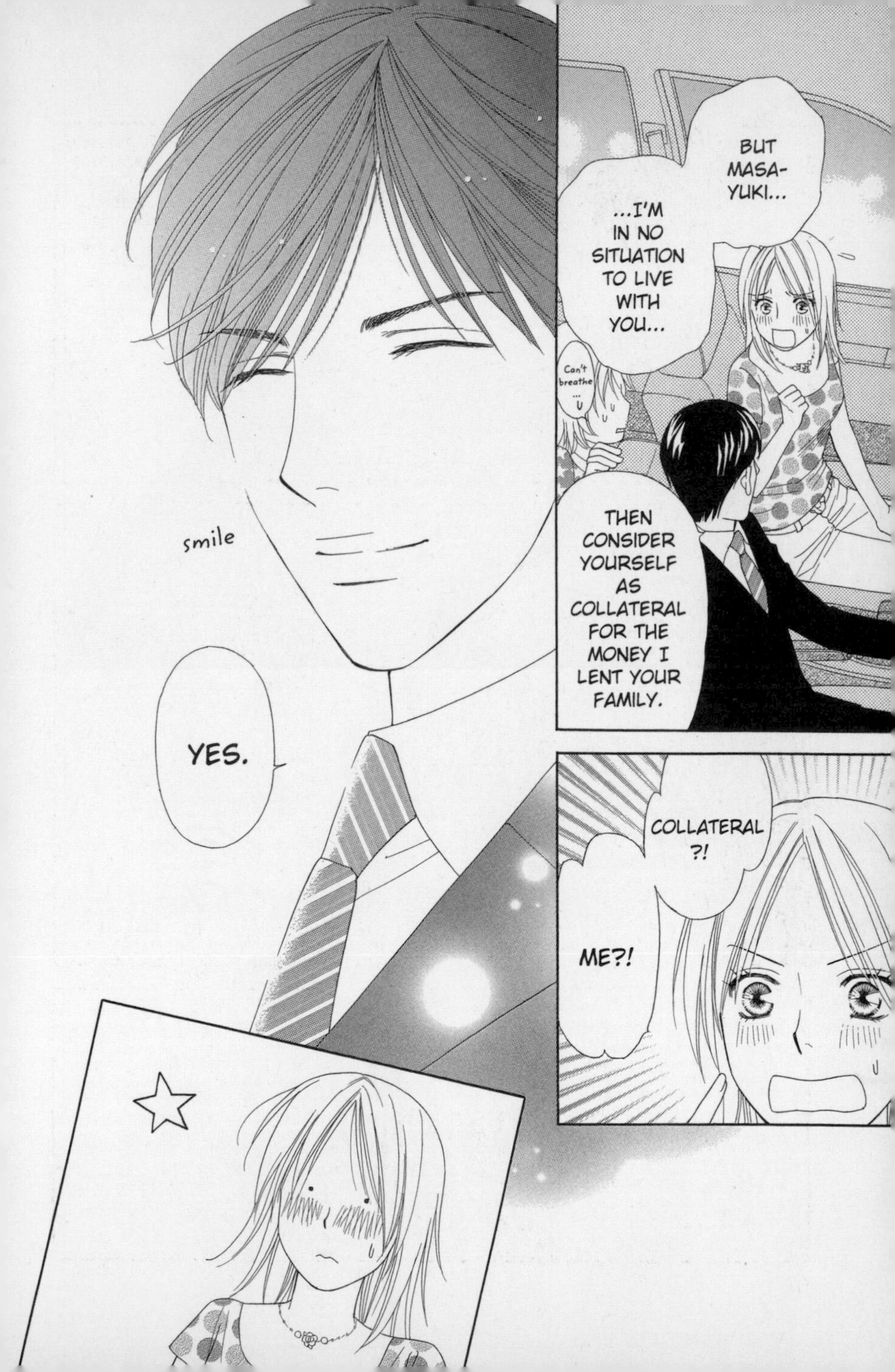
BUT MASA-YUKI...
...I'M IN NO SITUATION TO LIVE WITH YOU...
Can't breathe...
THEN CONSIDER YOURSELF AS COLLATERAL FOR THE MONEY I LENT YOUR FAMILY.
COLLATERAL?!
ME?!
smile
YES.

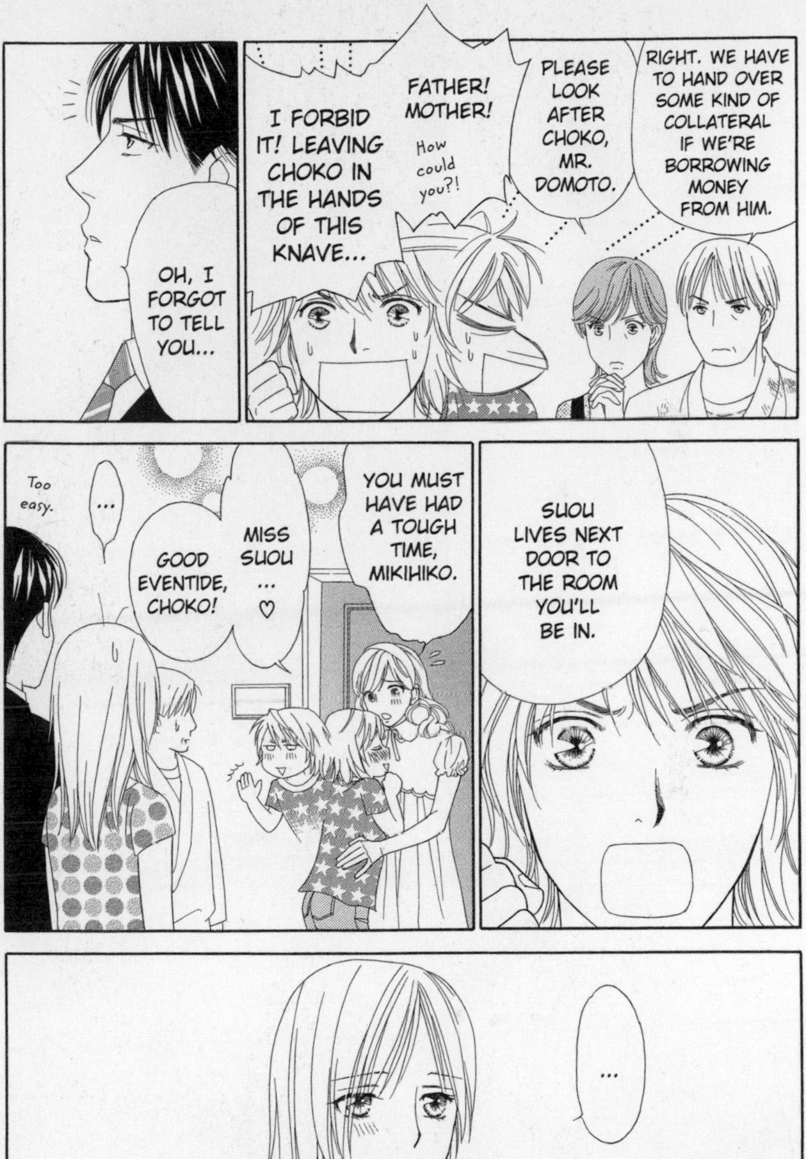
RIGHT. WE HAVE TO HAND OVER SOME KIND OF COLLATERAL IF WE'RE BORROWING MONEY FROM HIM.
PLEASE LOOK AFTER CHOKO, MR. DOMOTO.
FATHER! MOTHER!
How could you?!
I FORBID IT! LEAVING CHOKO IN THE HANDS OF THIS KNAVE...
OH, I FORGOT TO TELL YOU...
SUOU LIVES NEXT DOOR TO THE ROOM YOU'LL BE IN.
YOU MUST HAVE HAD A TOUGH TIME, MIKIHIKO.
MISS SUOU ... ♡
GOOD EVENTIDE, CHOKO!
...
Too easy.
...

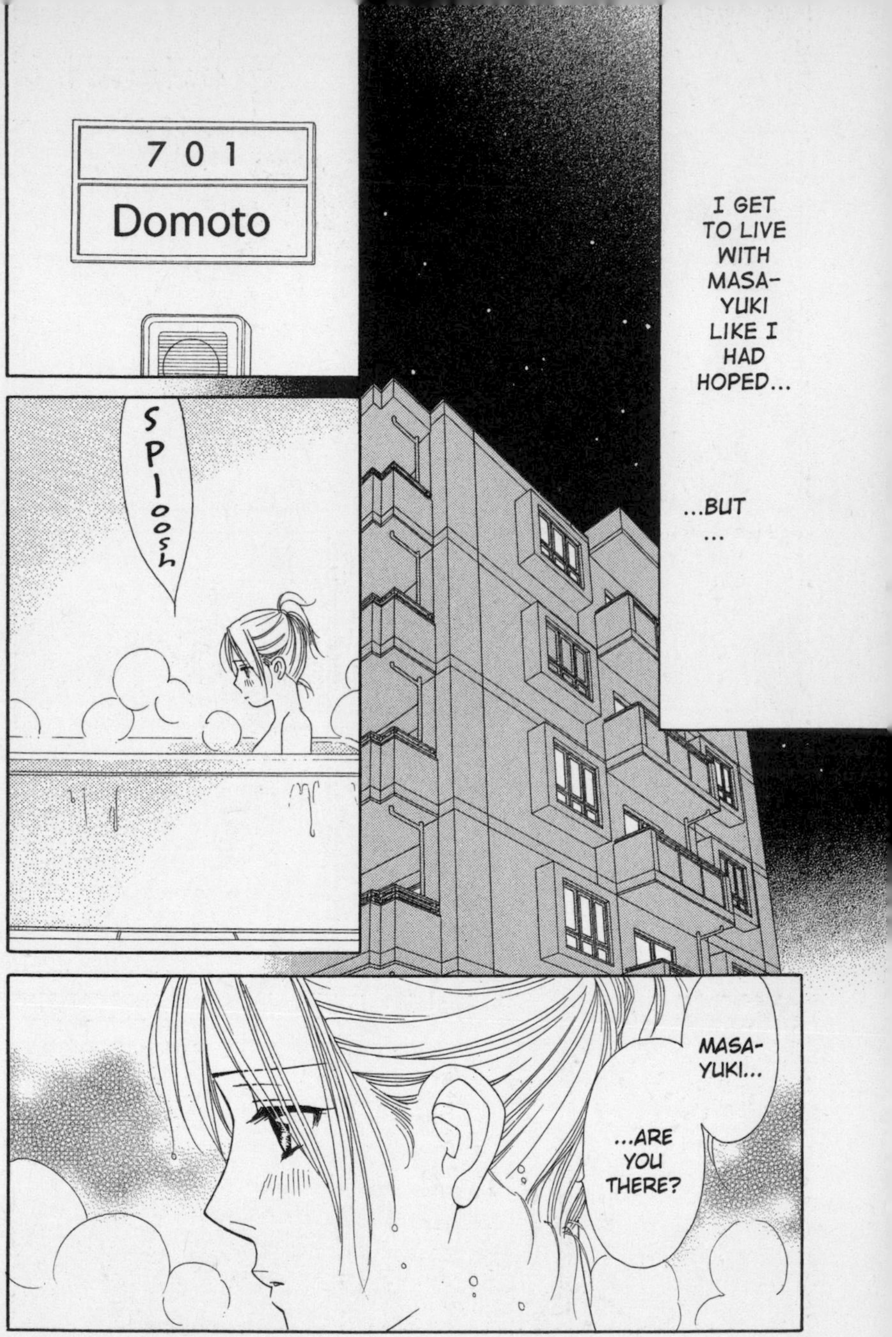

I GET TO LIVE WITH MASA-YUKI LIKE I HAD HOPED...
...BUT ...
701
Domoto
SPlOOSH
MASA-YUKI...
...ARE YOU THERE?

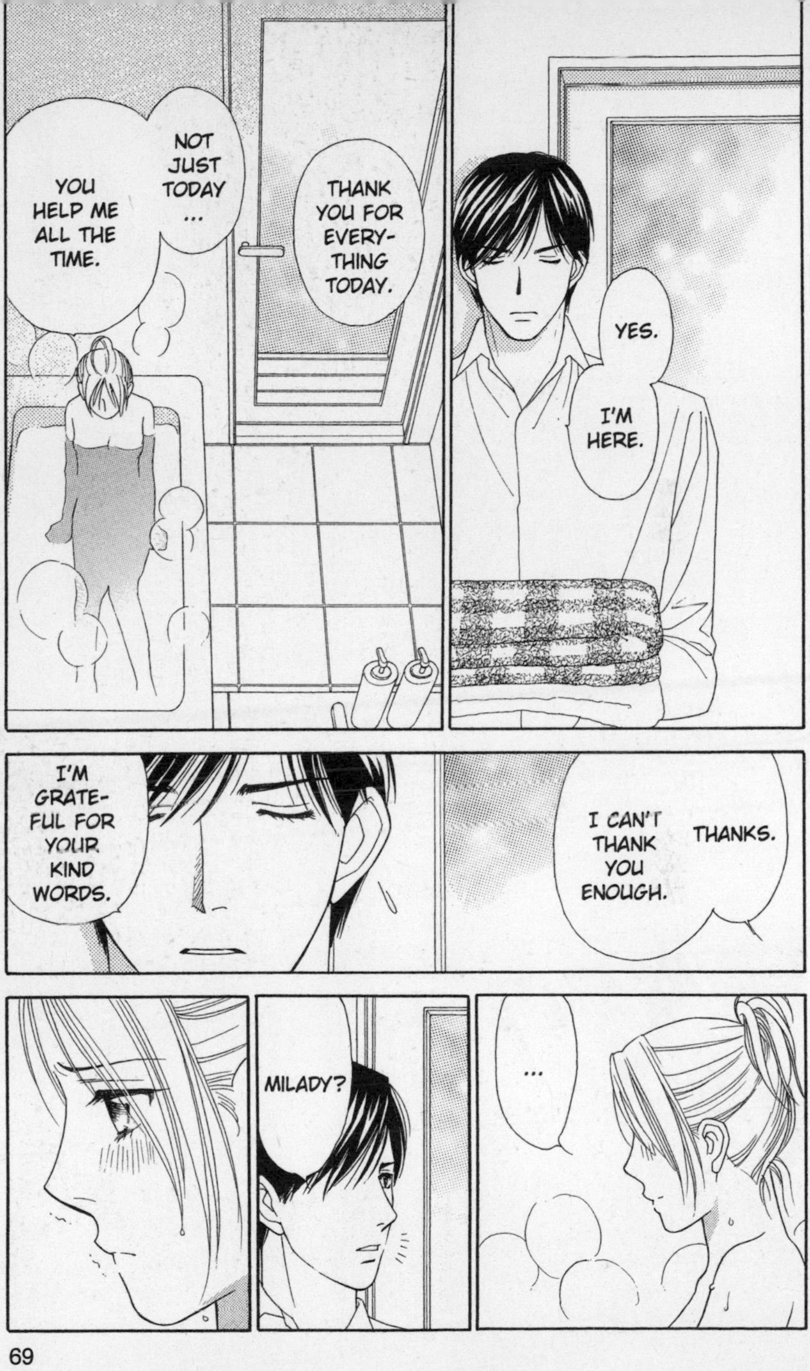
YES.
I'M HERE.
THANK YOU FOR EVERYTHING TODAY.
NOT JUST TODAY ...
YOU HELP ME ALL THE TIME.
THANKS.
I CAN'T THANK YOU ENOUGH.
I'M GRATEFUL FOR YOUR KIND WORDS.
...
MILADY?

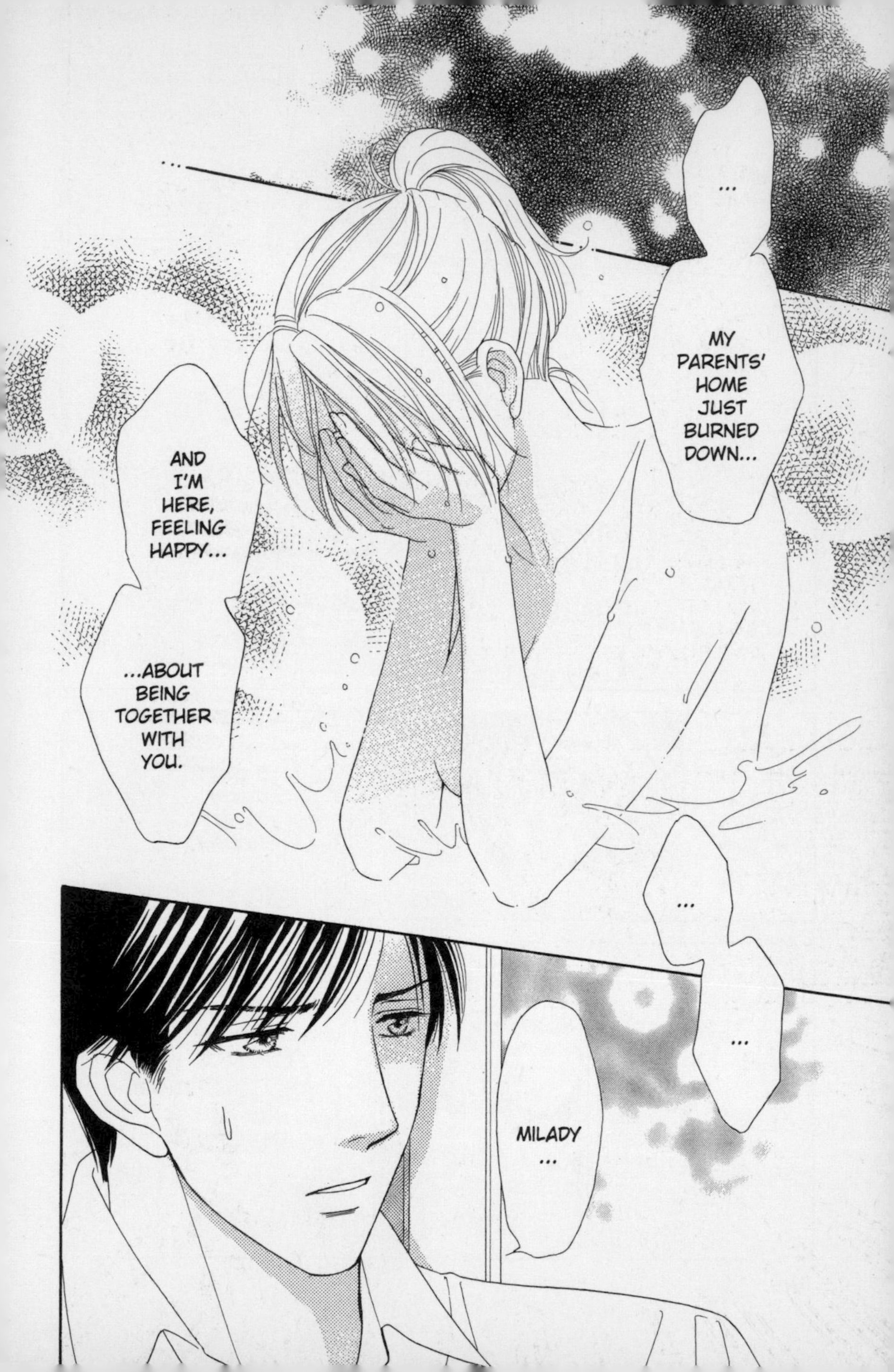
...
MY PARENTS' HOME JUST BURNED DOWN...
...
AND I'M HERE, FEELING HAPPY...
...ABOUT BEING TOGETHER WITH YOU.
...
...
MILADY ...

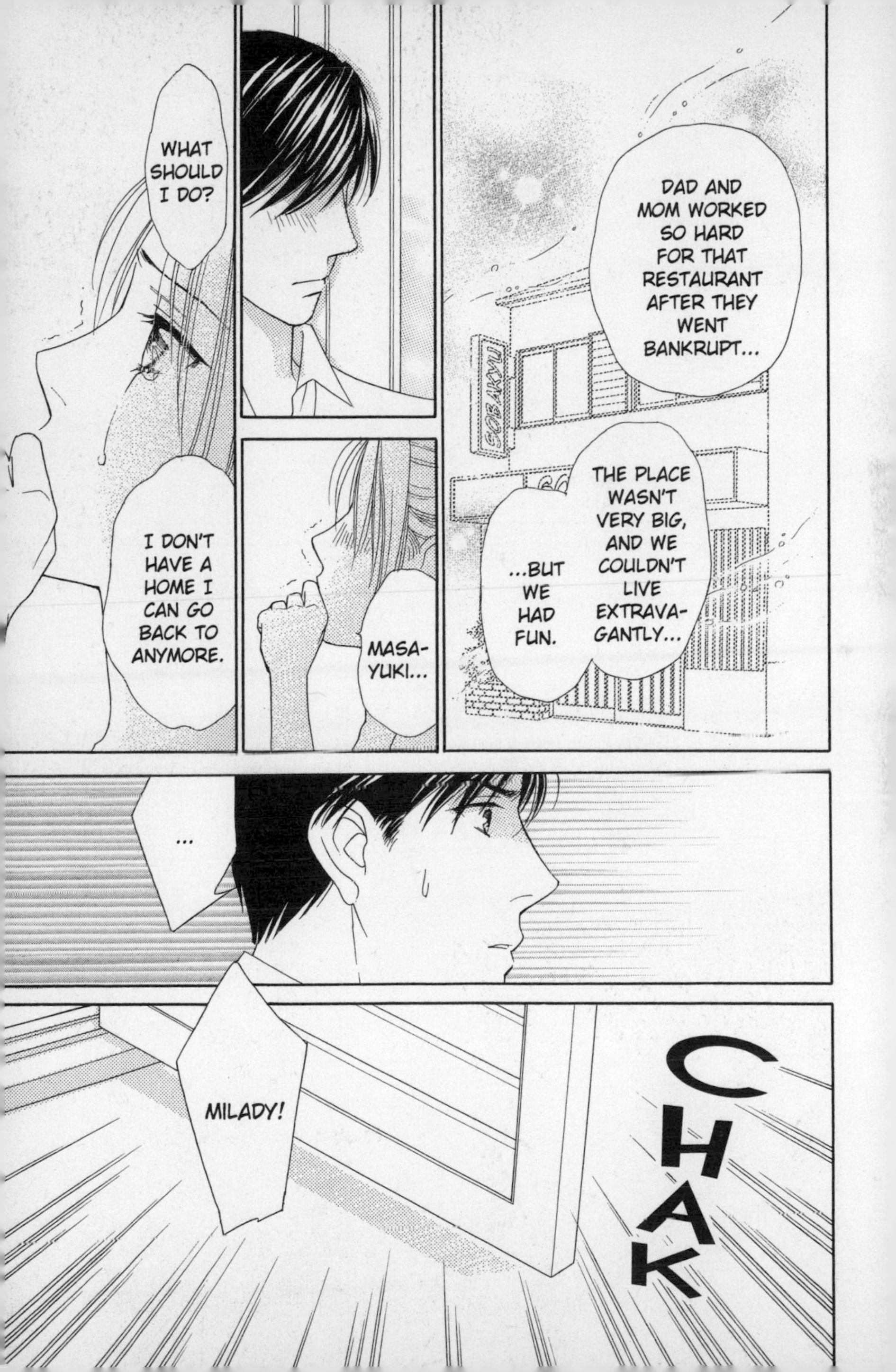
DAD AND MOM WORKED SO HARD FOR THAT RESTAURANT AFTER THEY WENT BANKRUPT...
SOBAKYU
THE PLACE WASN'T VERY BIG, AND WE COULDN'T LIVE EXTRAVA-GANTLY...
...BUT WE HAD FUN.
MASA-YUKI...
WHAT SHOULD I DO?
I DON'T HAVE A HOME I CAN GO BACK TO ANYMORE.
...
CHAK
MILADY!

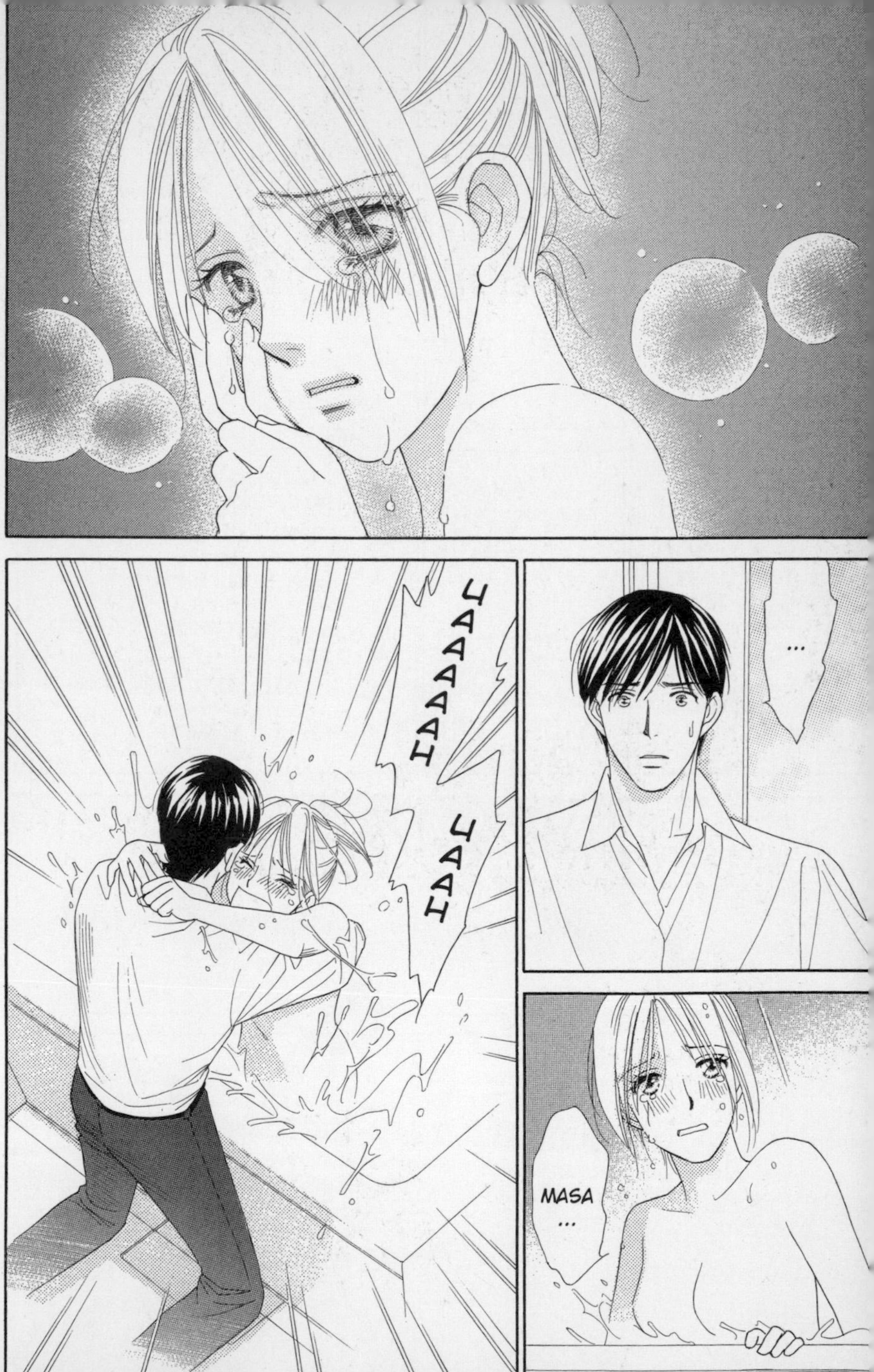
...
MASA ...
UAAAAAAH
UAAAH

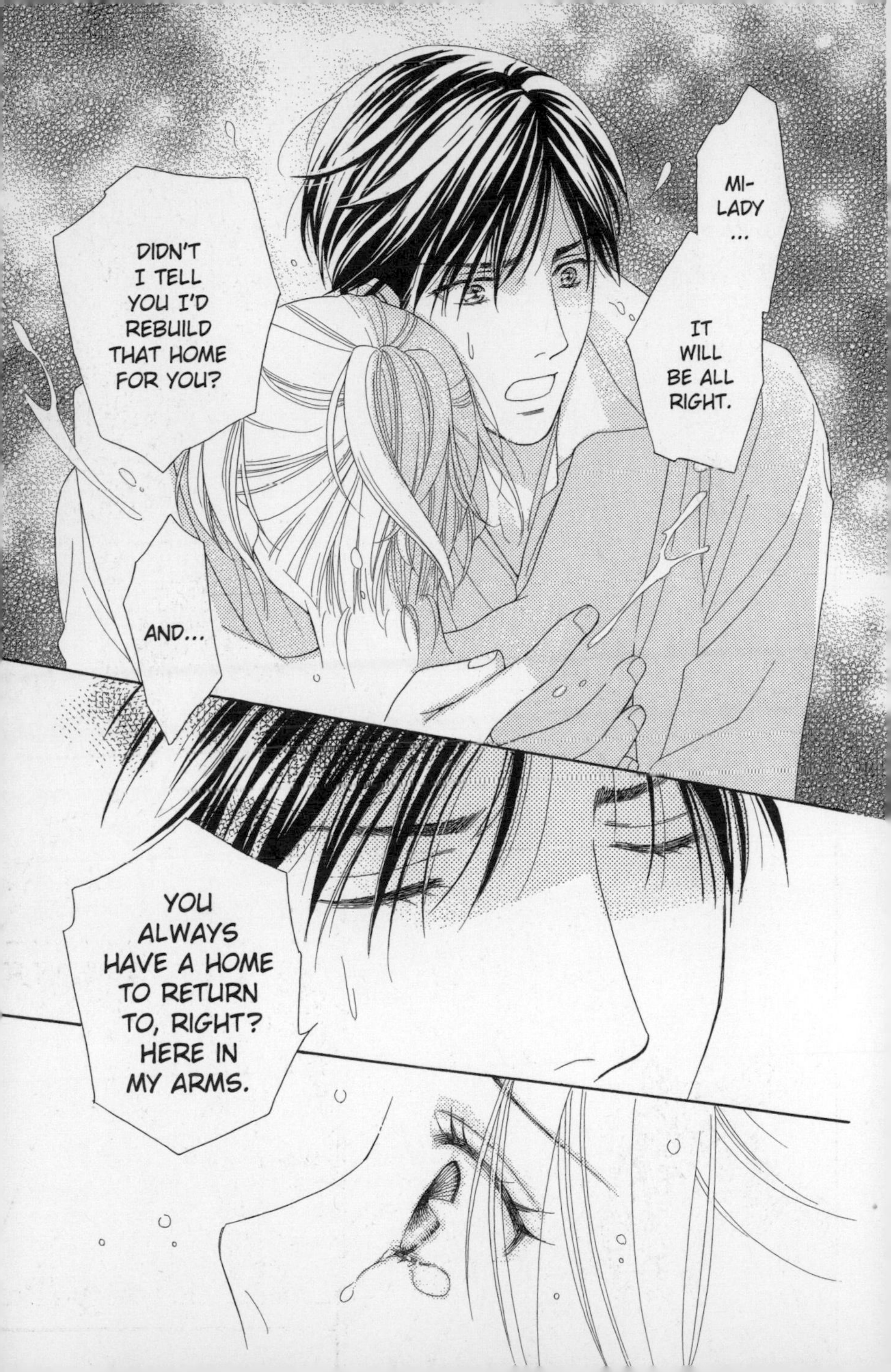
MI-LADY...
IT WILL BE ALL RIGHT.
DIDN'T I TELL YOU I'D REBUILD THAT HOME FOR YOU?
AND...
YOU ALWAYS HAVE A HOME TO RETURN TO, RIGHT? HERE IN MY ARMS.

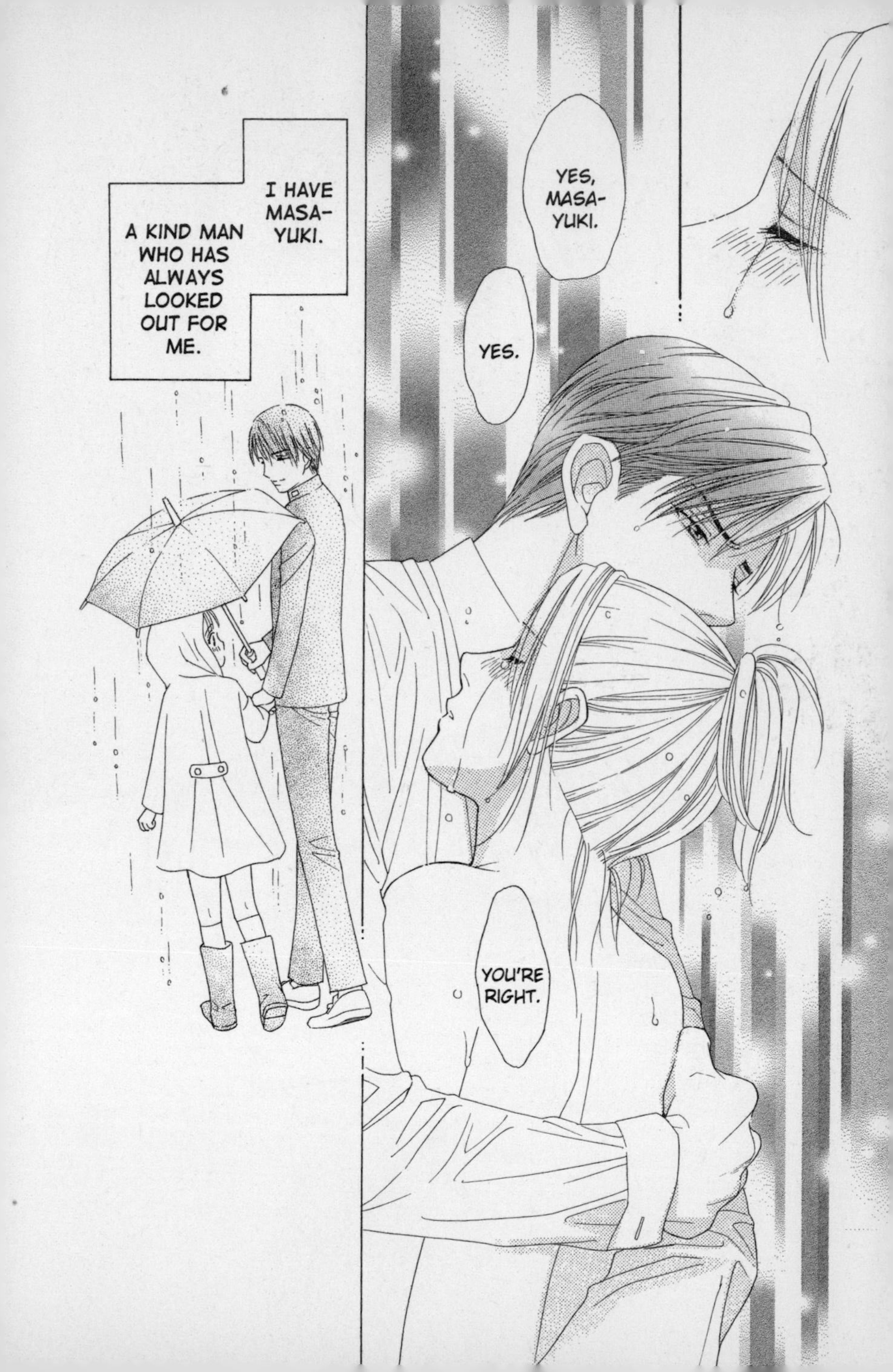
YES, MASA-YUKI.
YES.
YOU'RE RIGHT.
I HAVE MASA-YUKI.
A KIND MAN WHO HAS ALWAYS LOOKED OUT FOR ME.

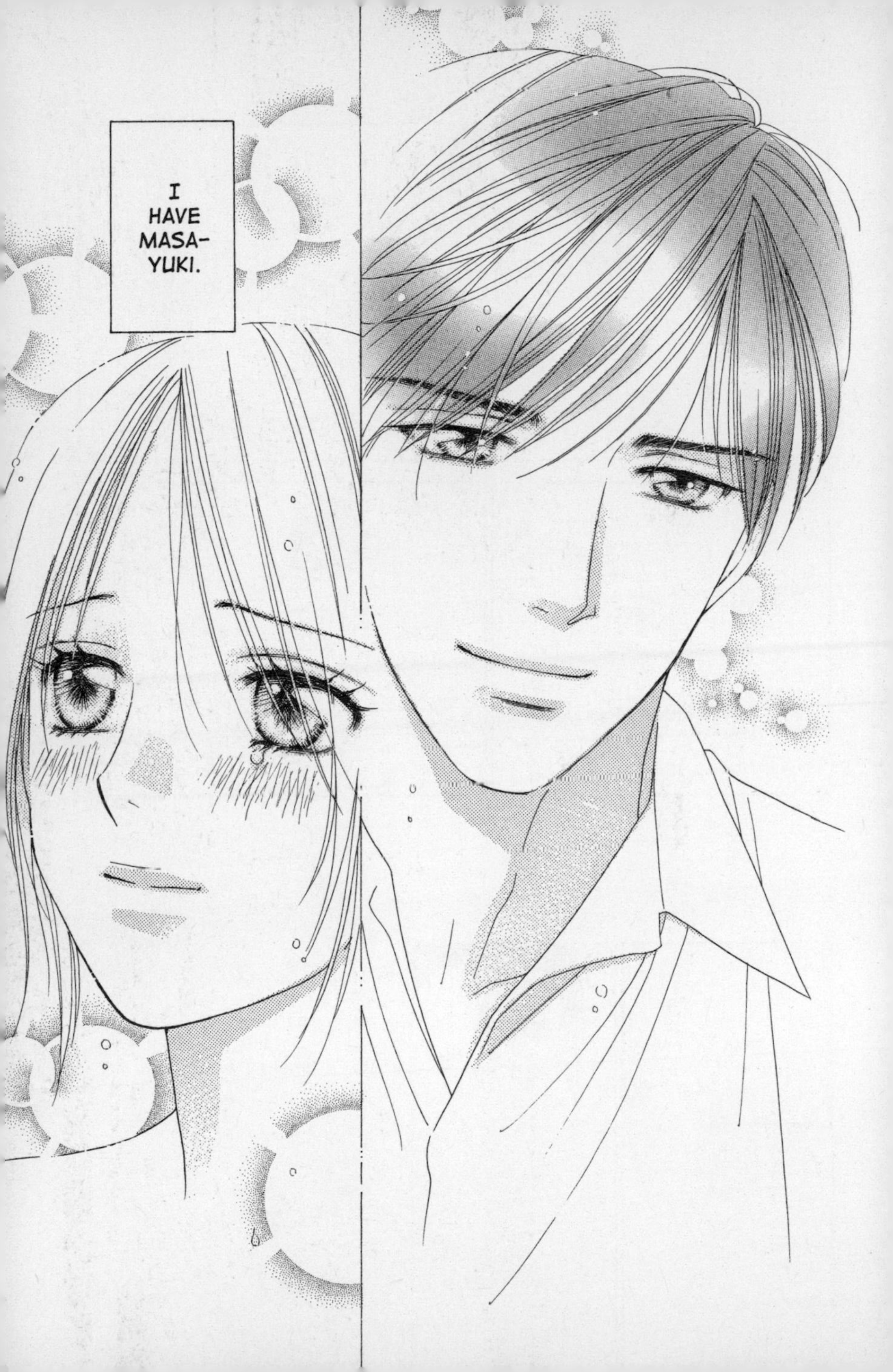
I HAVE MASA-YUKI.

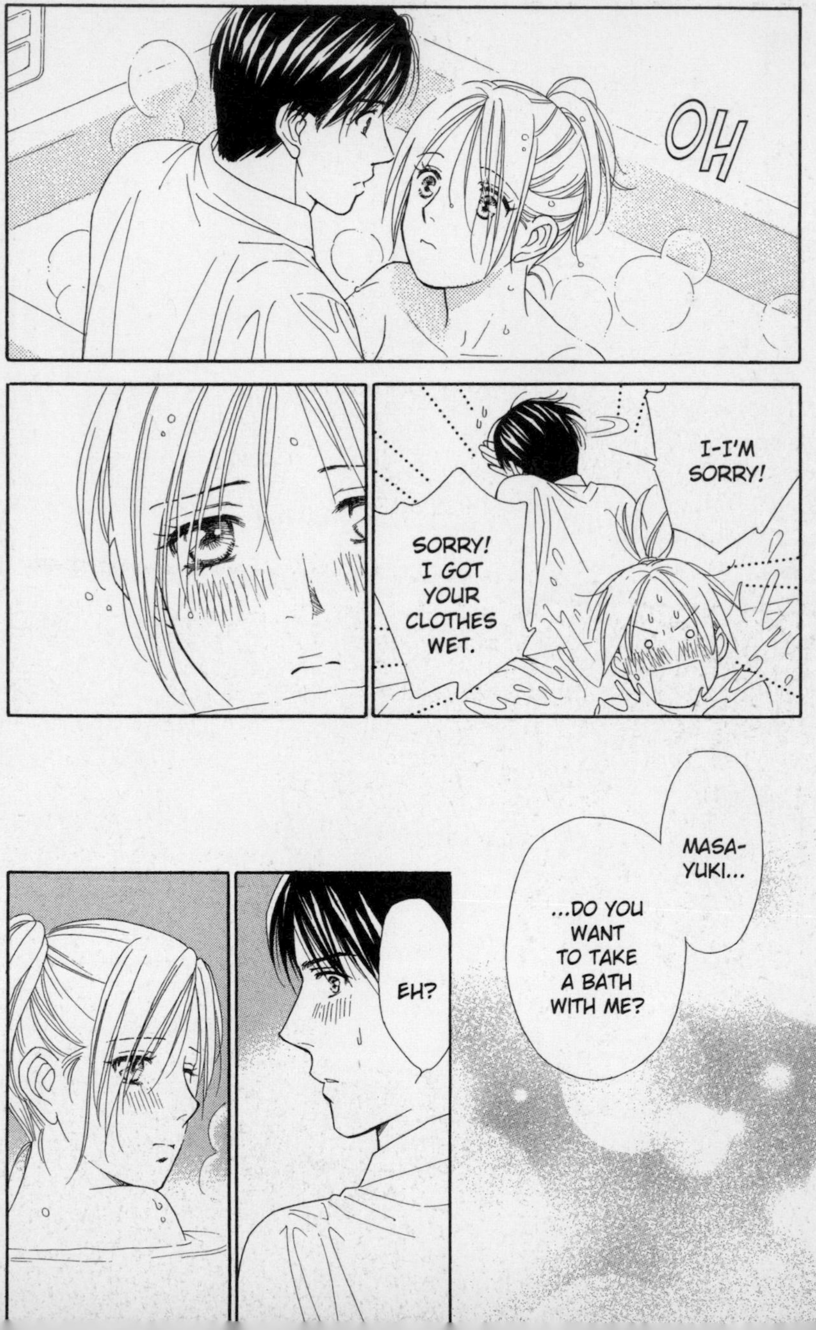
OH
I-I'M SORRY!
SORRY! I GOT YOUR CLOTHES WET.
MASA-YUKI...
...DO YOU WANT TO TAKE A BATH WITH ME?
EH?

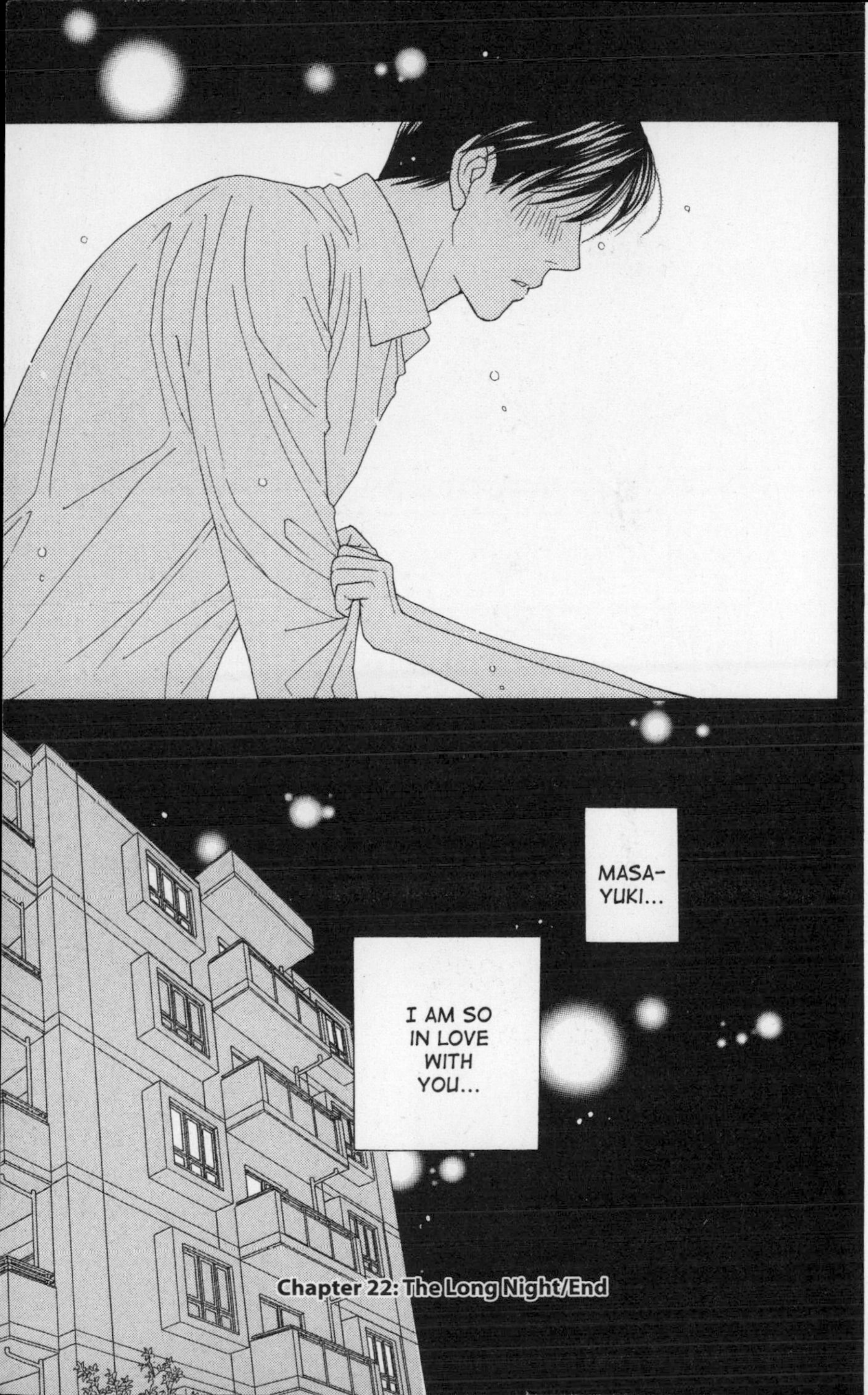
MASA-YUKI...
I AM SO IN LOVE WITH YOU...
Chapter 22: The Long Night/End

SERVANT DIARY

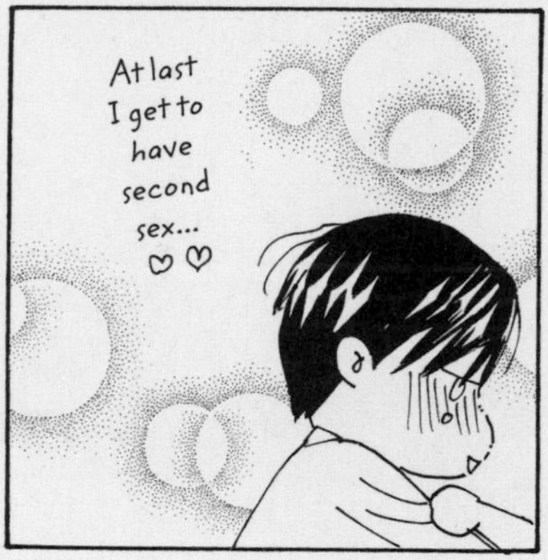
At last I get to have second sex... ♡ ♡

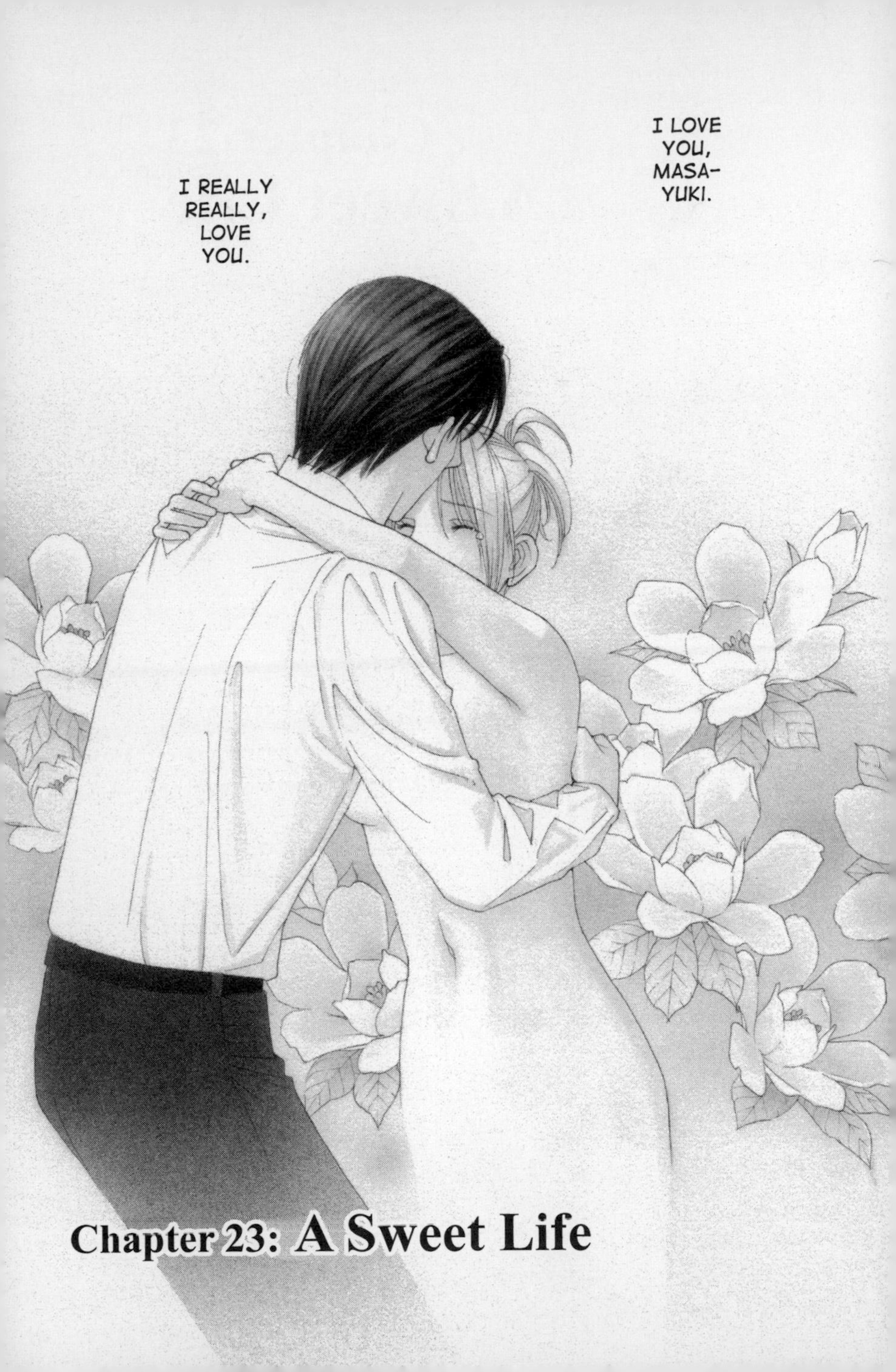
I LOVE YOU, MASA-YUKI.
I REALLY REALLY, LOVE YOU.

Chapter 23: A Sweet Life

Chapter 23
A Sweet Life

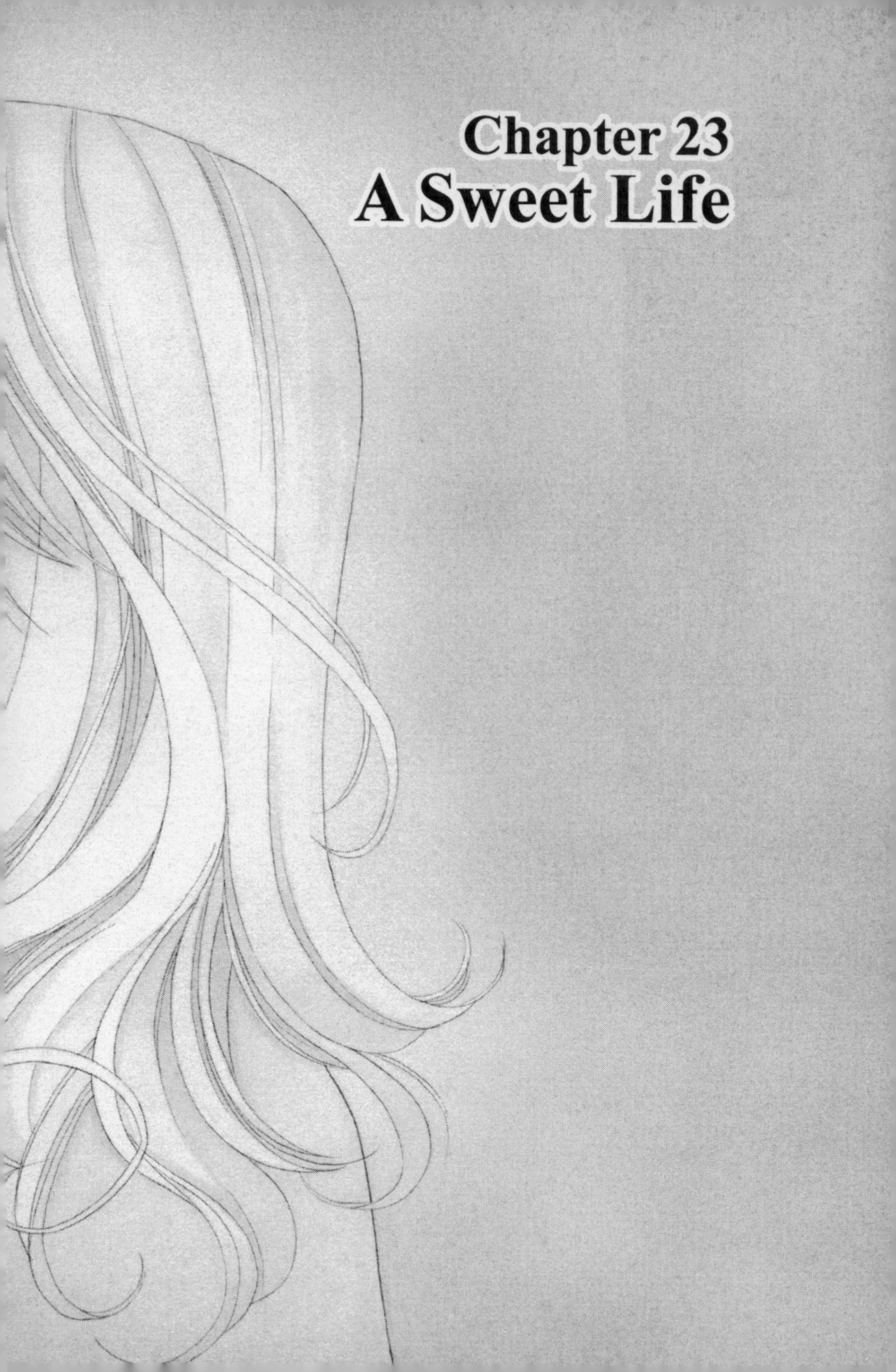

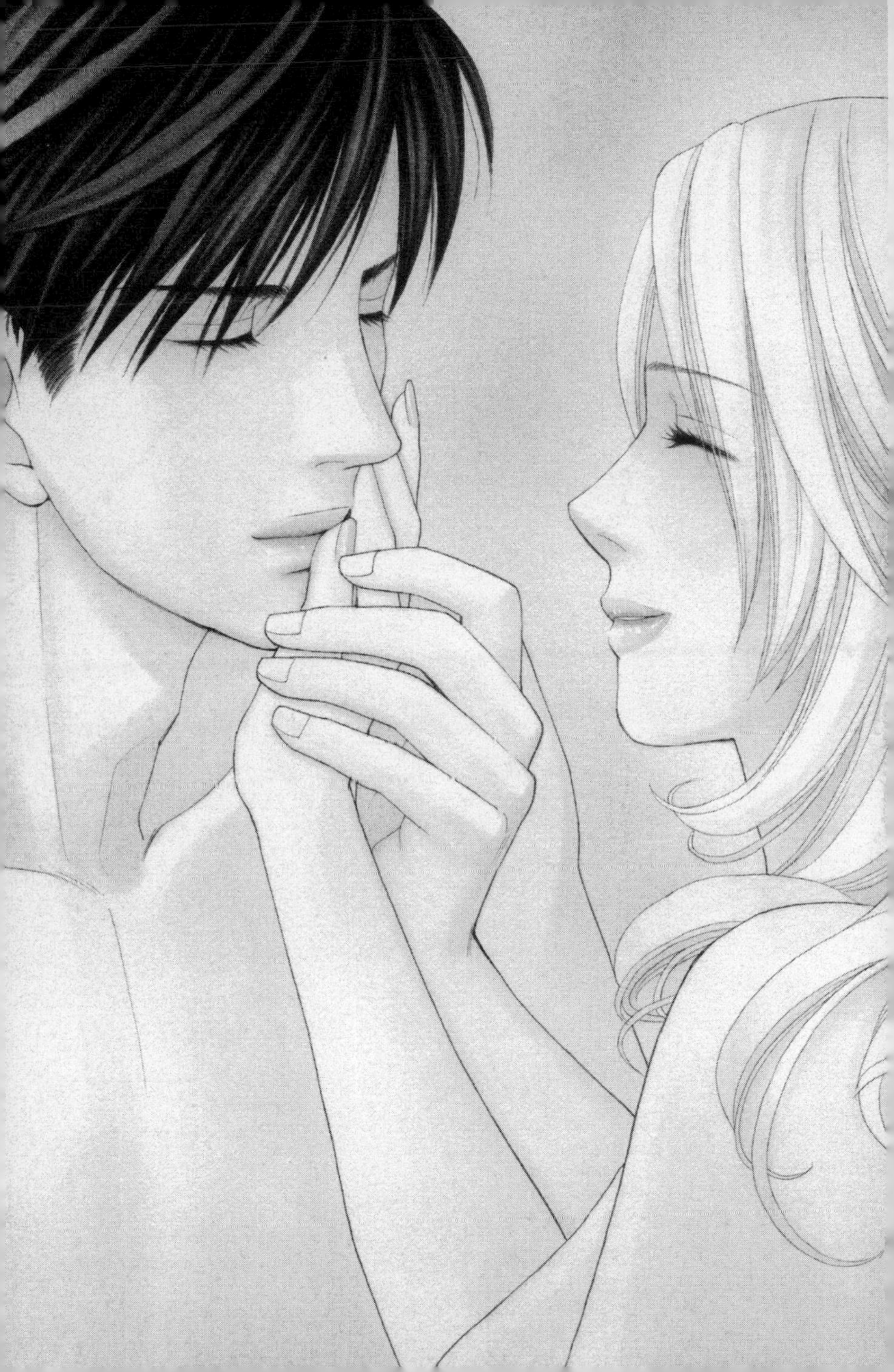

SERVANT DIARY

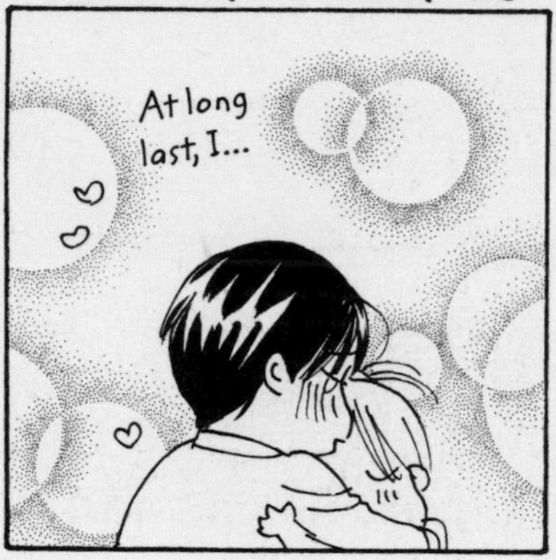
At long last, I...

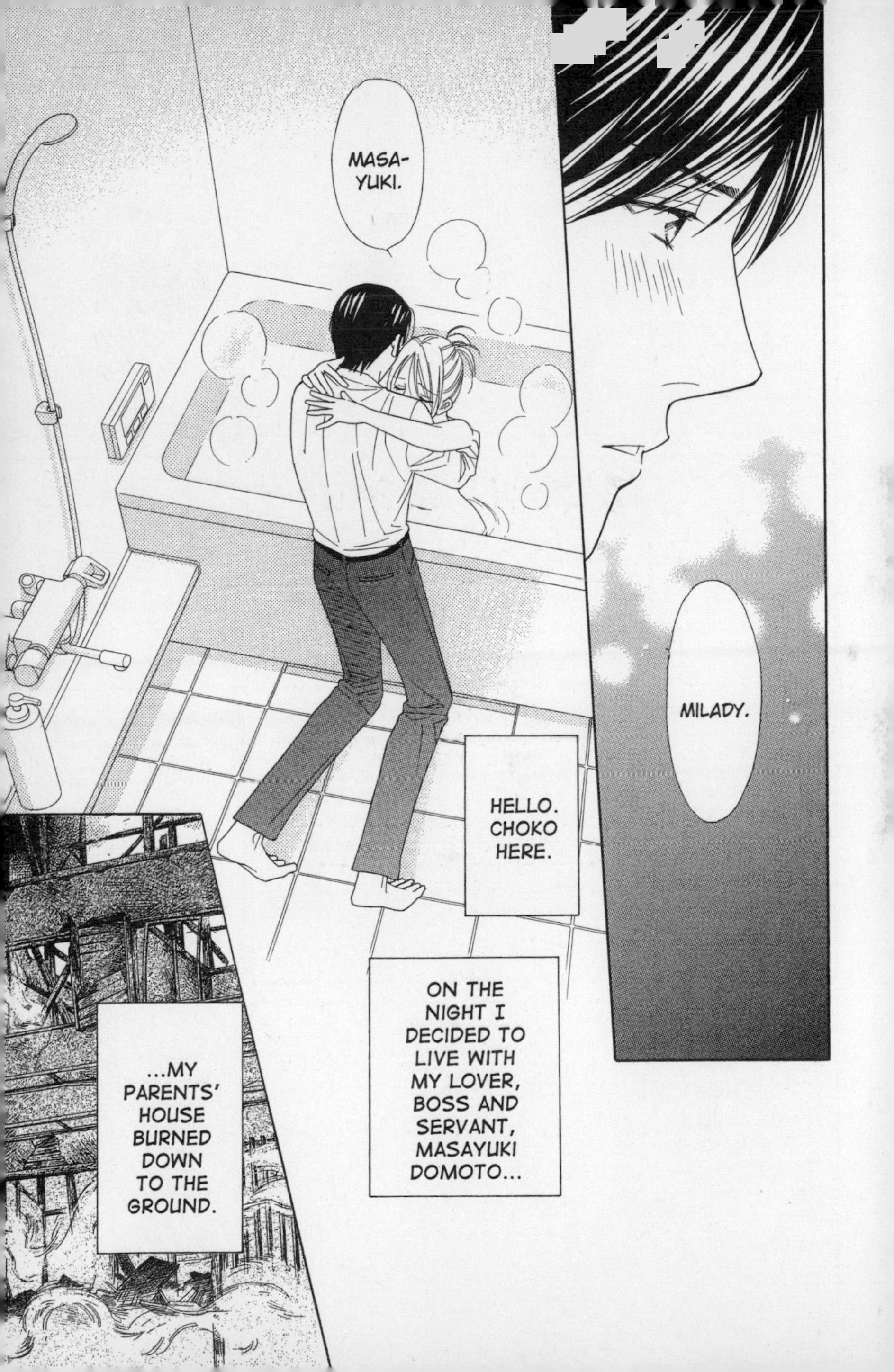
MILADY.
MASA-YUKI.
HELLO. CHOKO HERE.
ON THE NIGHT I DECIDED TO LIVE WITH MY LOVER, BOSS AND SERVANT, MASAYUKI DOMOTO...
...MY PARENTS' HOUSE BURNED DOWN TO THE GROUND.

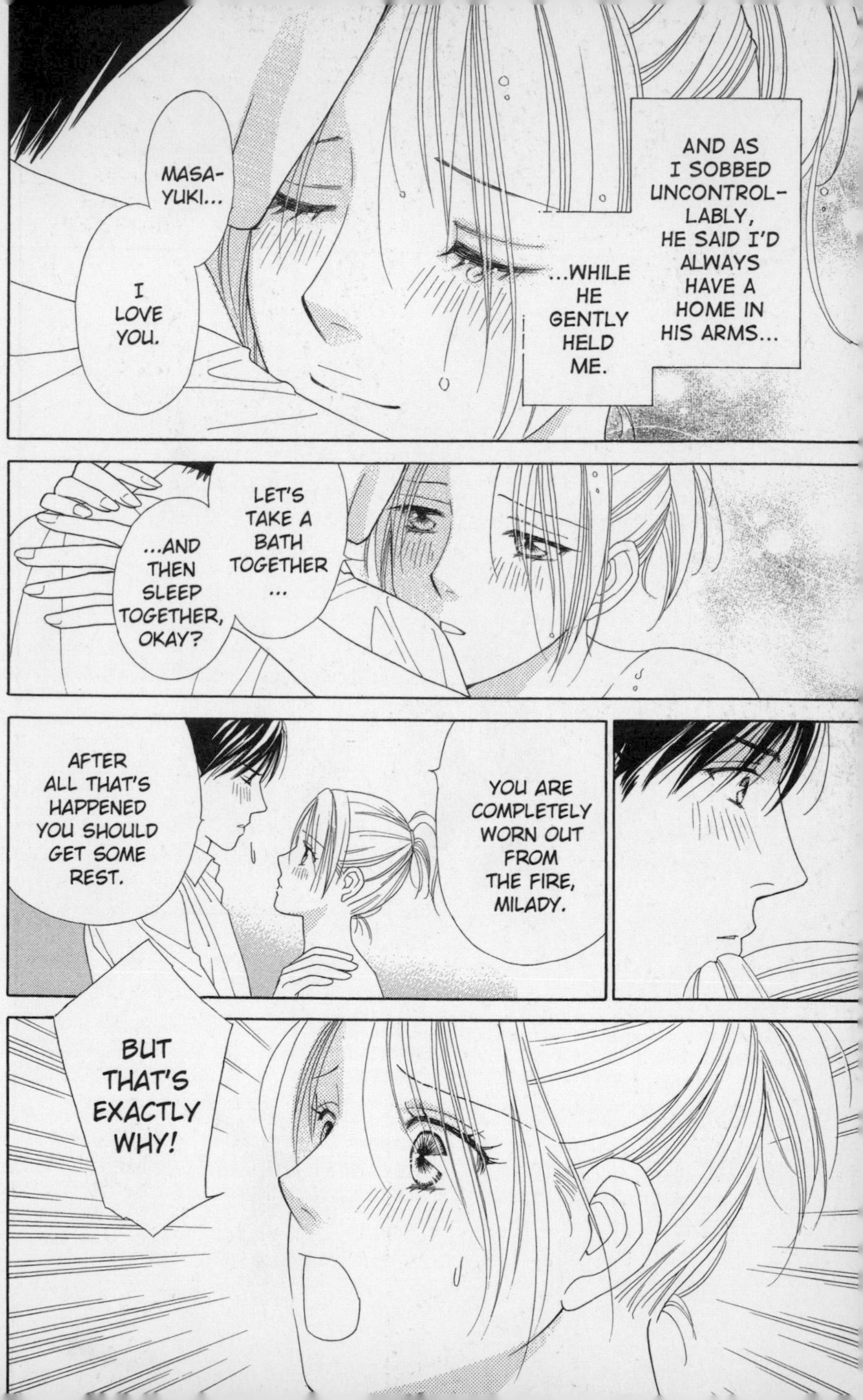
AND AS I SOBBED UNCONTROL-LABLY, HE SAID I'D ALWAYS HAVE A HOME IN HIS ARMS...
...WHILE HE GENTLY HELD ME.
MASA-YUKI...
I LOVE YOU.
LET'S TAKE A BATH TOGETHER...
...AND THEN SLEEP TOGETHER, OKAY?
YOU ARE COMPLETELY WORN OUT FROM THE FIRE, MILADY.
AFTER ALL THAT'S HAPPENED YOU SHOULD GET SOME REST.
BUT THAT'S EXACTLY WHY!

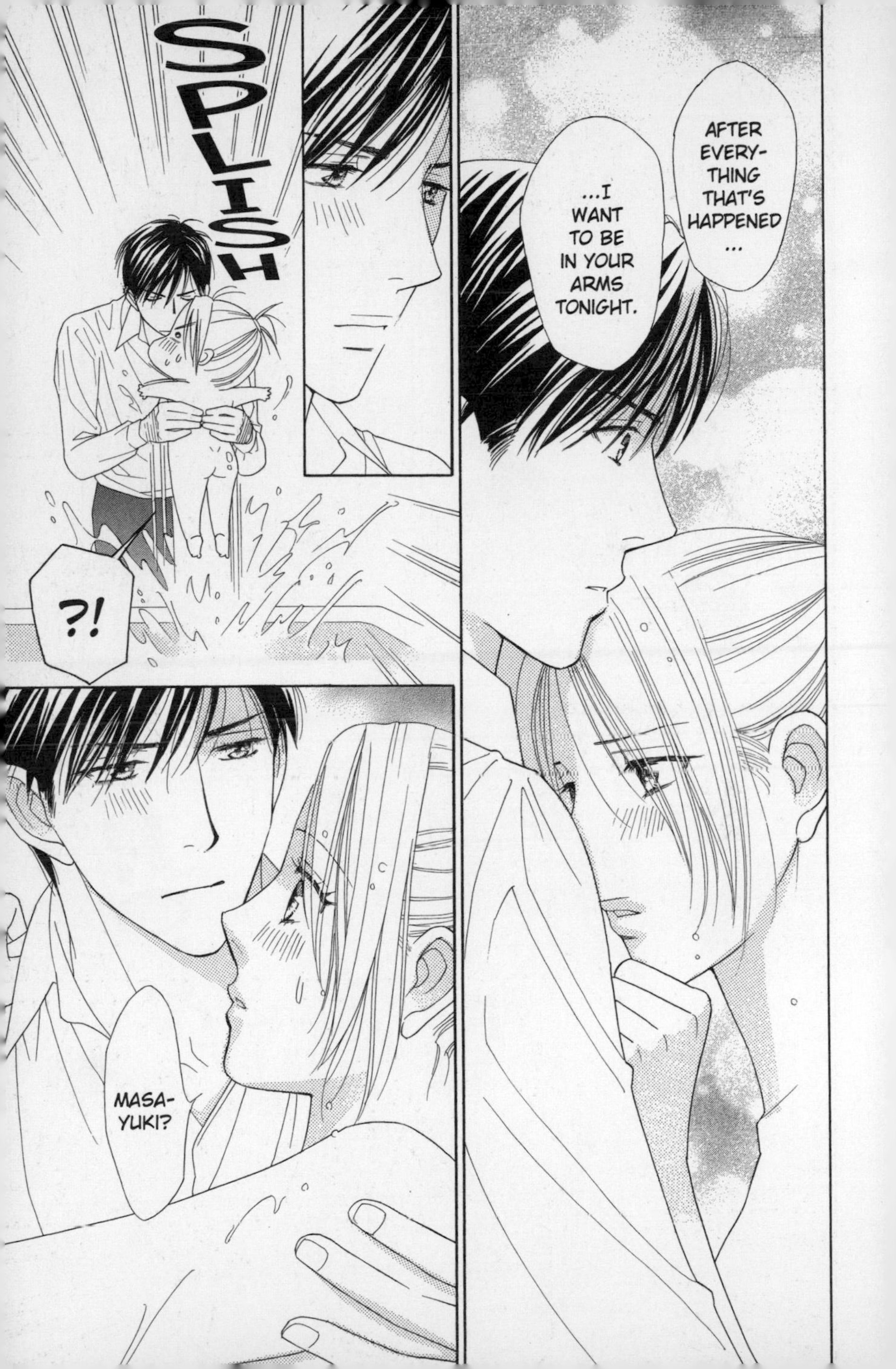
AFTER EVERY-THING THAT'S HAPPENED ...
...I WANT TO BE IN YOUR ARMS TONIGHT.
SPLISH
?!
MASA-YUKI?

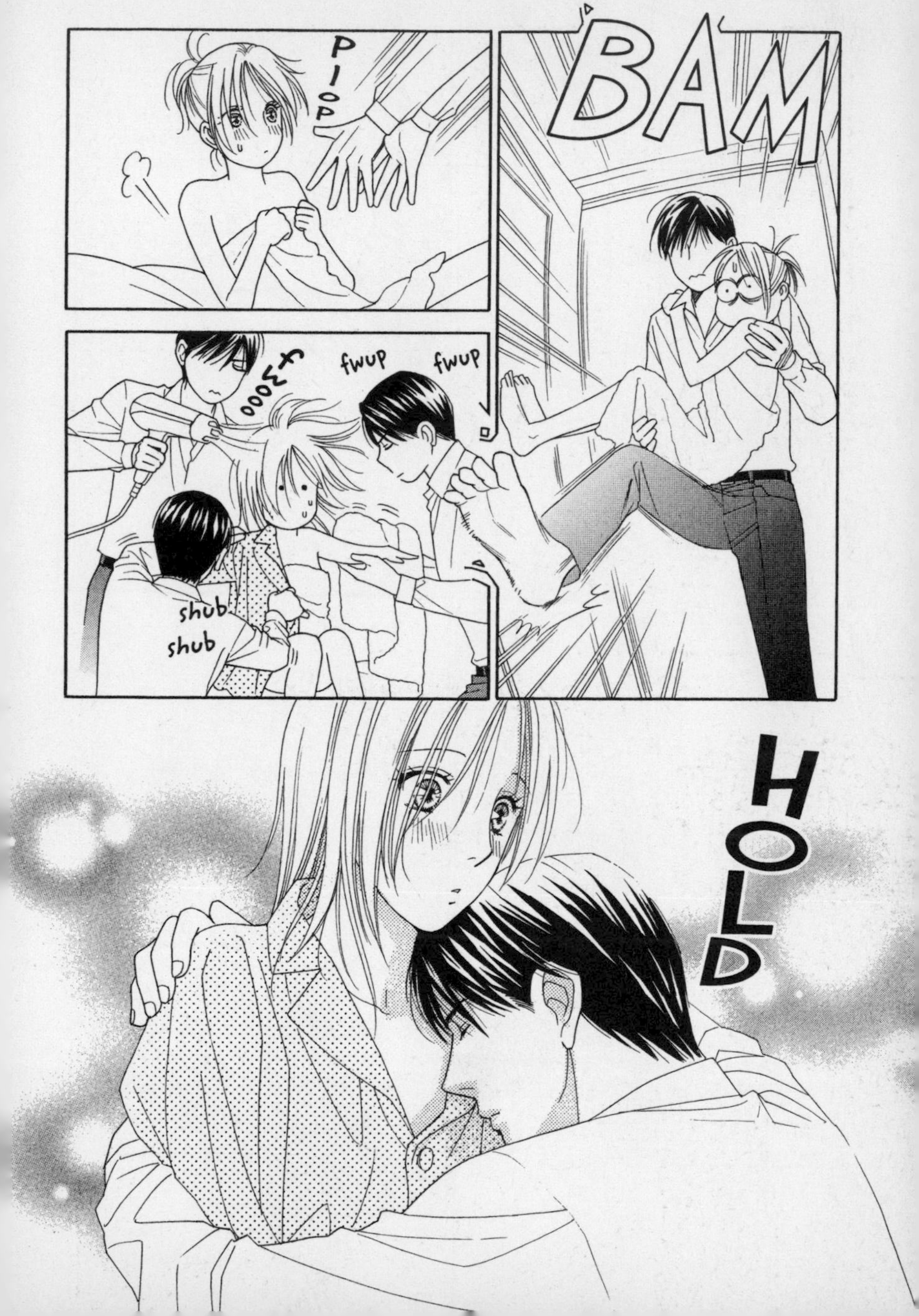
BAM
PLOP
fwup
fwup
fwoooo
shub
shub
HOLD

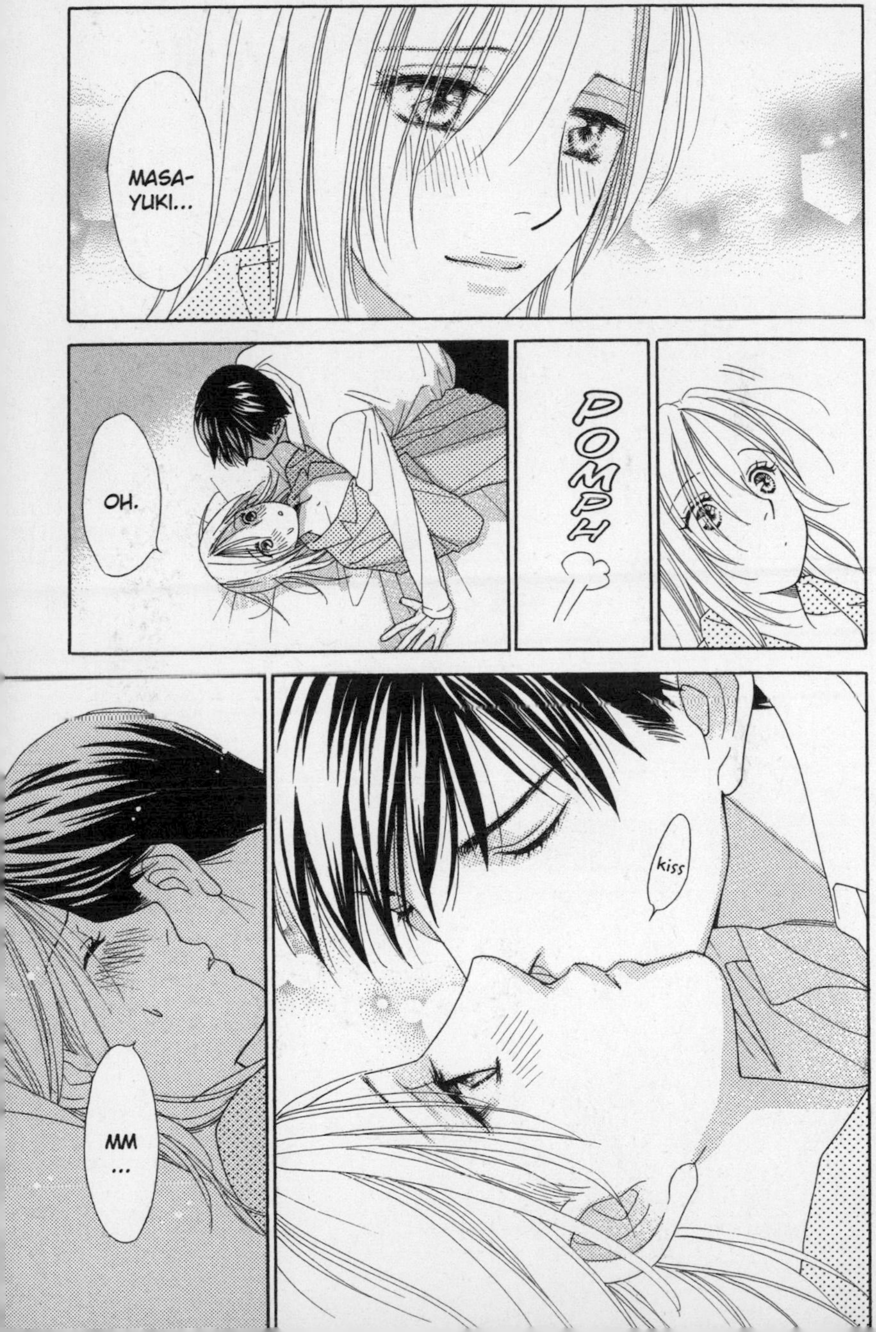
MASA-YUKI...
POMPH
OH.
kiss
MM ...

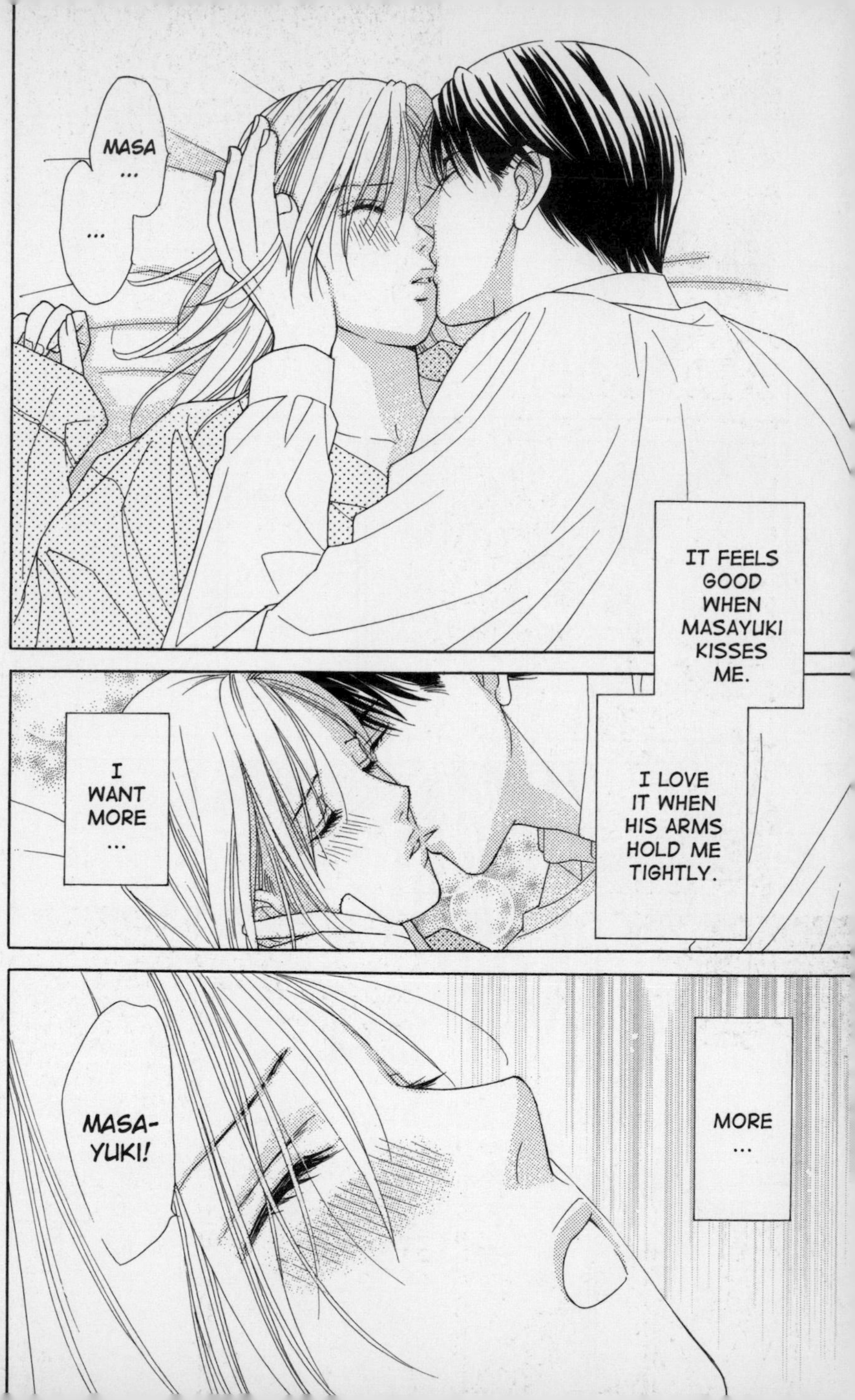
MASA ...
...
IT FEELS GOOD WHEN MASAYUKI KISSES ME.
I LOVE IT WHEN HIS ARMS HOLD ME TIGHTLY.
I WANT MORE ...
MORE ...
MASA-YUKI!

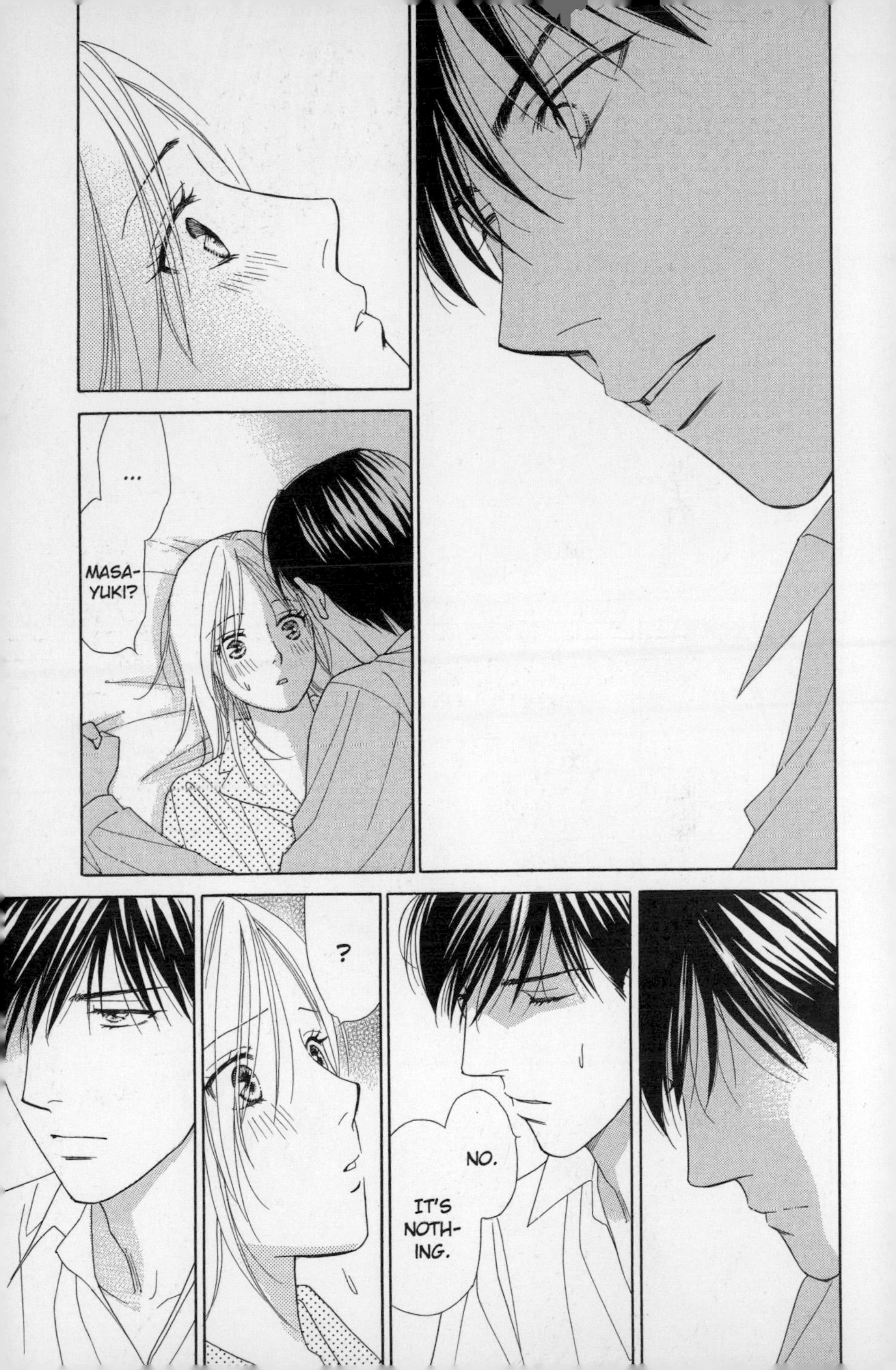
...
MASA-YUKI?
NO.
IT'S NOTH-ING.
?

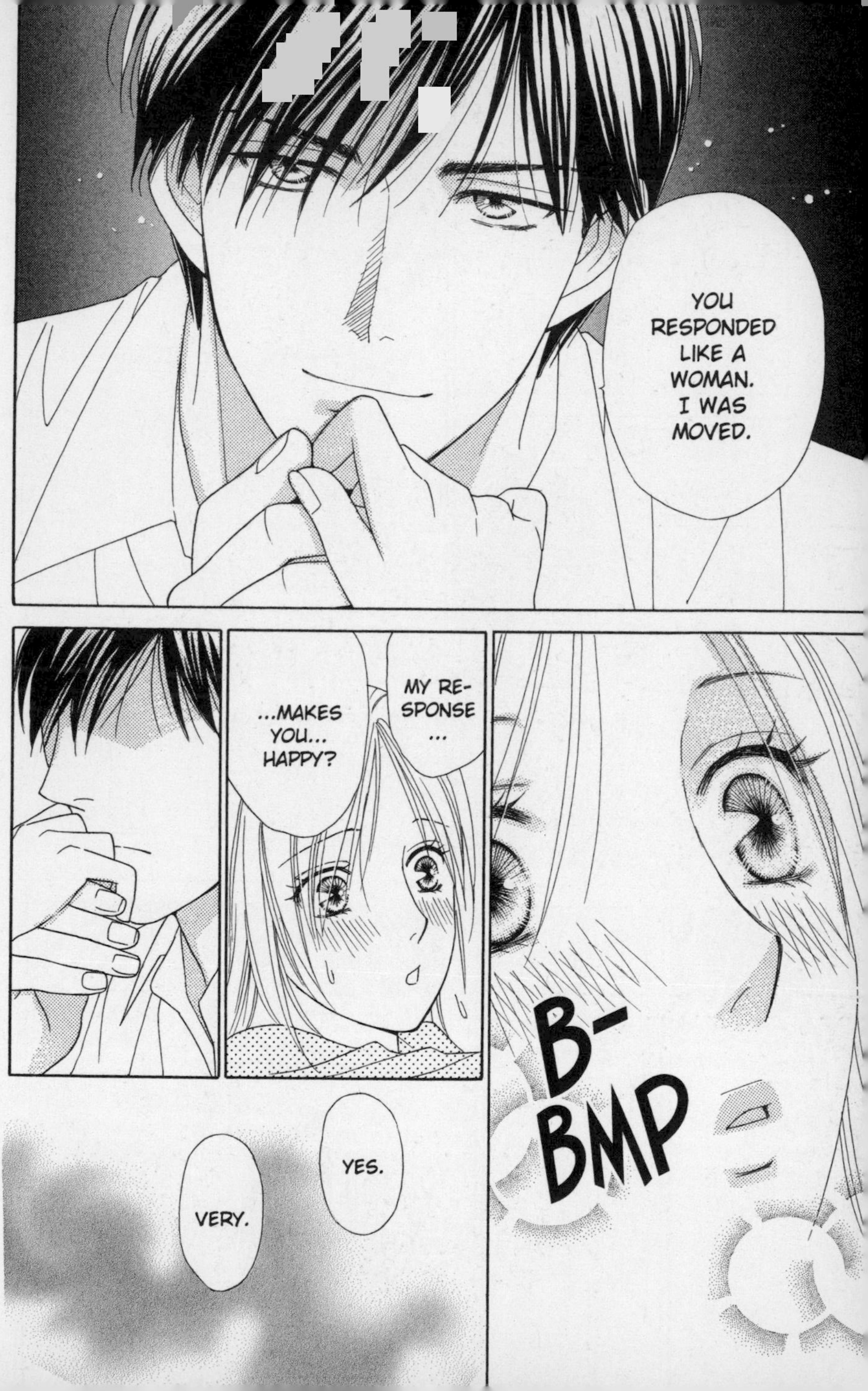
YOU RESPONDED LIKE A WOMAN. I WAS MOVED.
B-BMP
MY RE-SPONSE...
...MAKES YOU... HAPPY?
YES.
VERY.

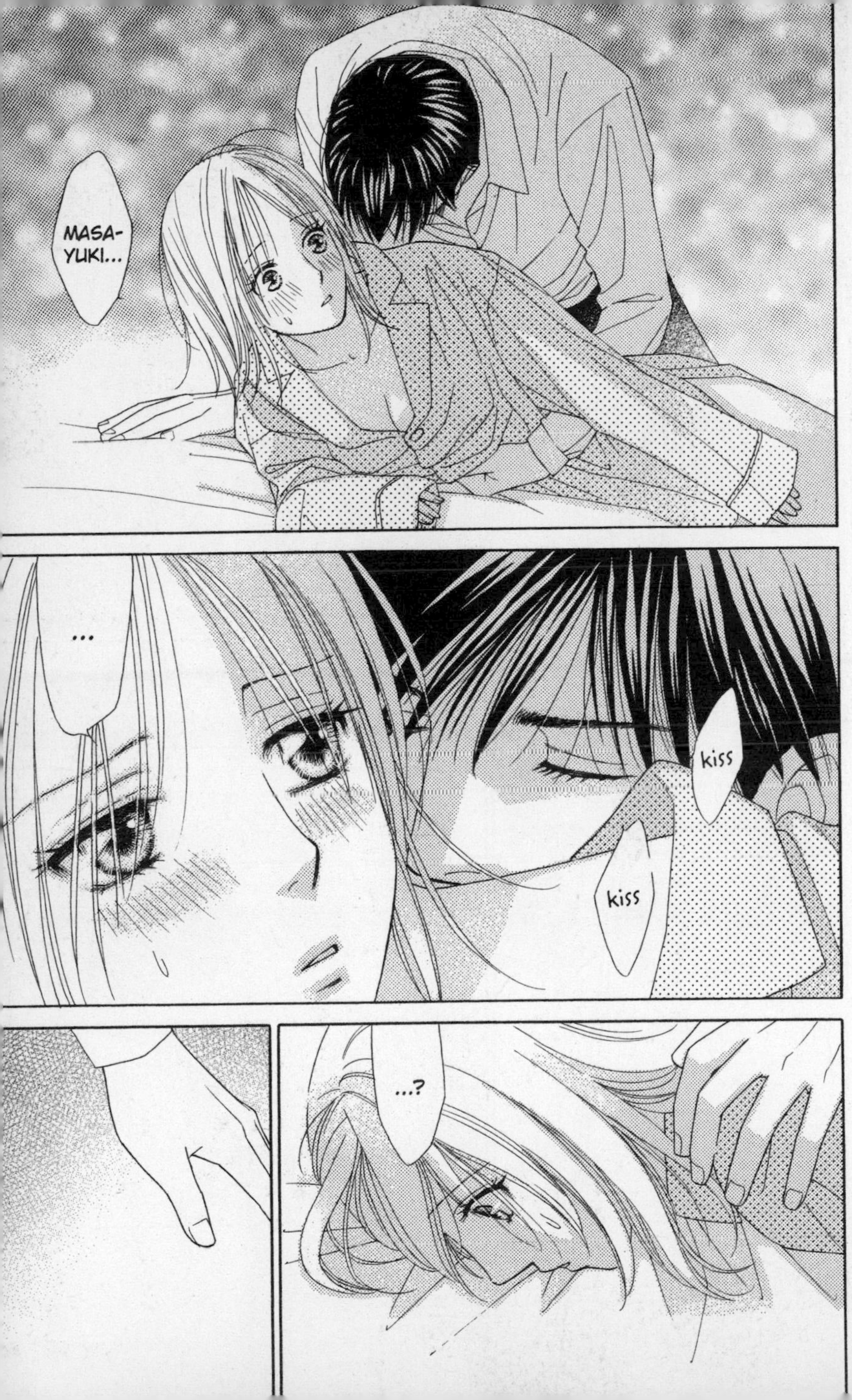
MASA-YUKI...
kiss
kiss
...
...?

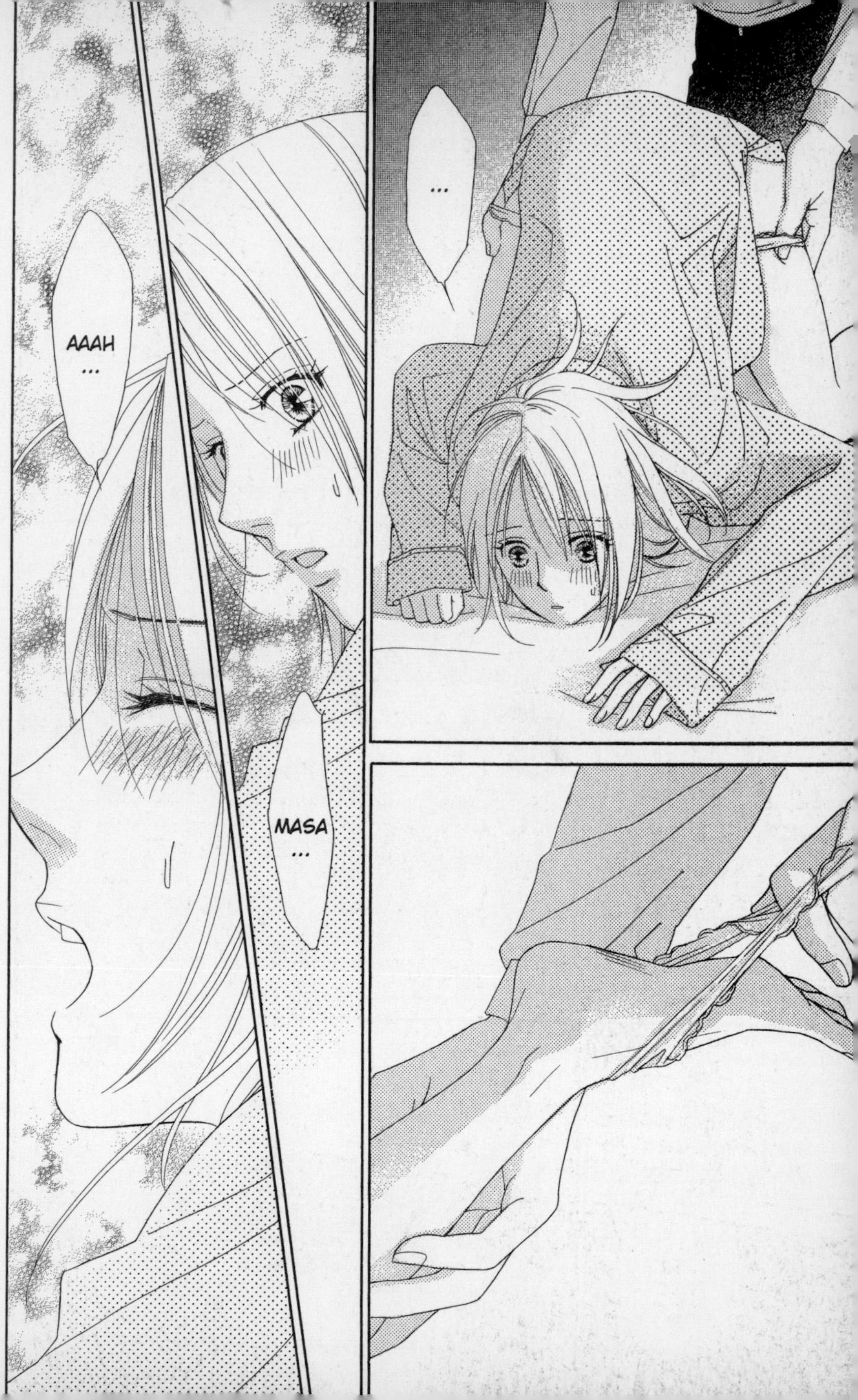
...
AAAH ...
MASA ...

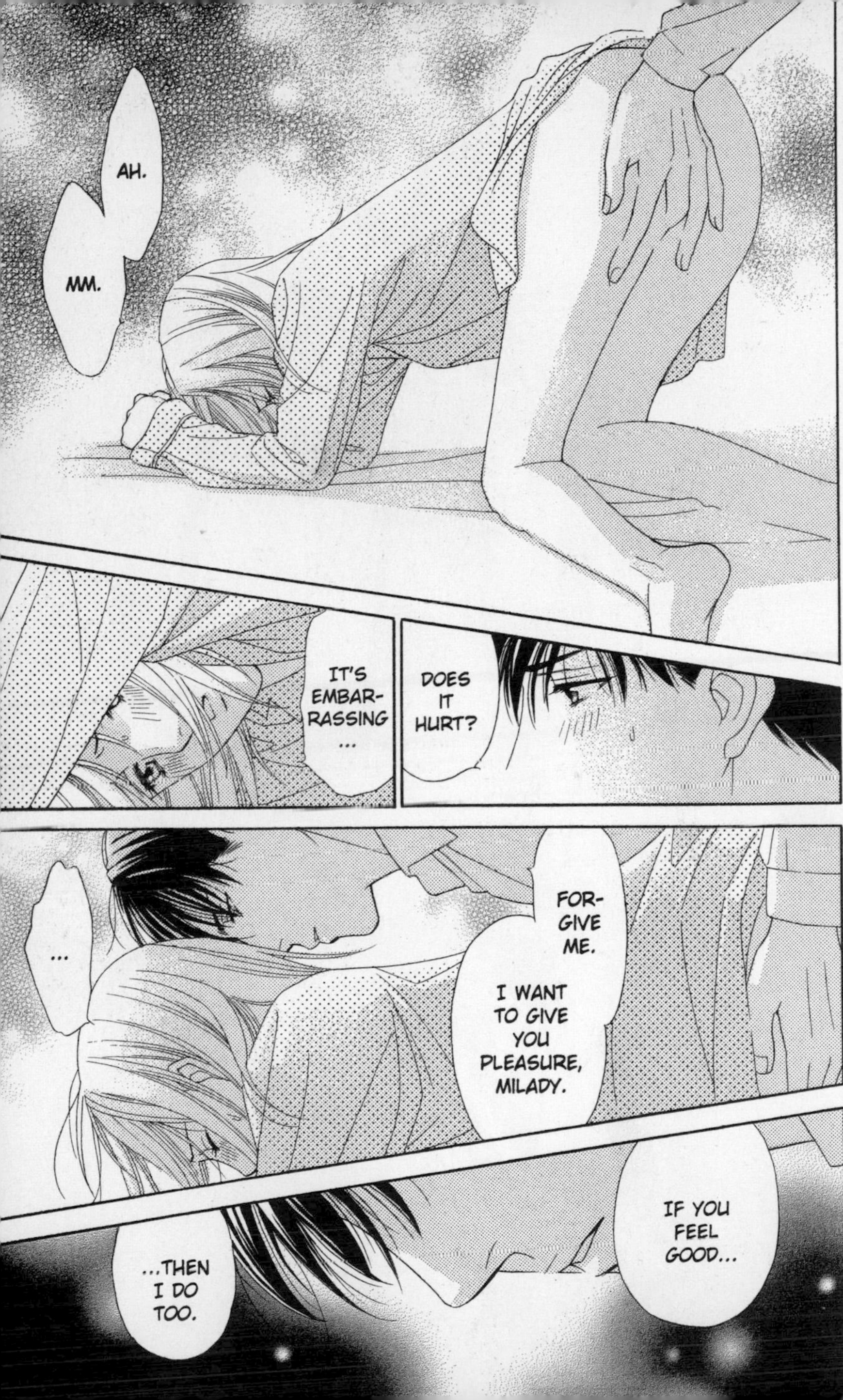
AH.
MM.
DOES IT HURT?
IT'S EMBAR-RASSING...
FOR-GIVE ME.
I WANT TO GIVE YOU PLEASURE, MILADY.
...
IF YOU FEEL GOOD...
...THEN I DO TOO.

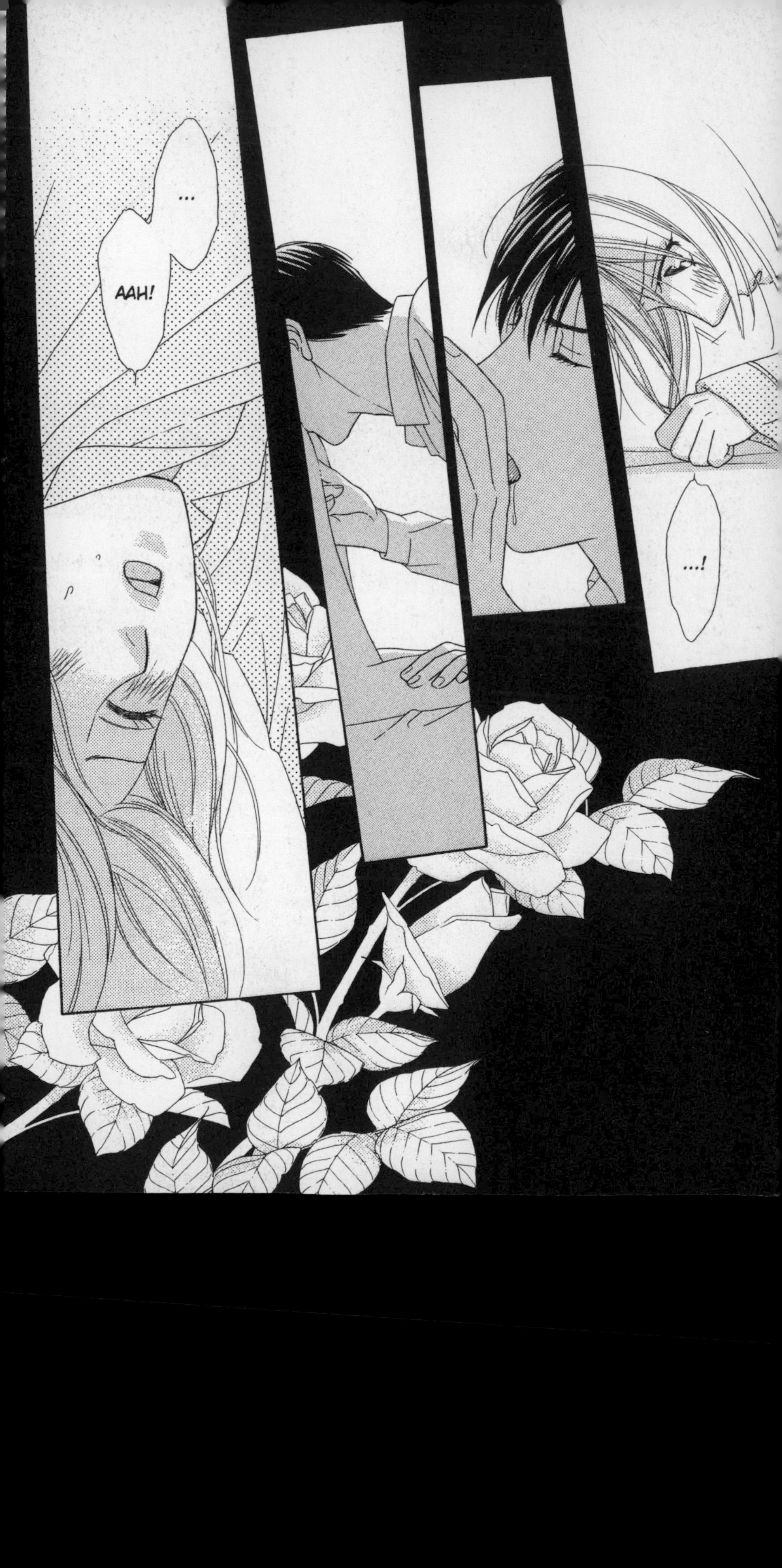
...!
...
AAH!

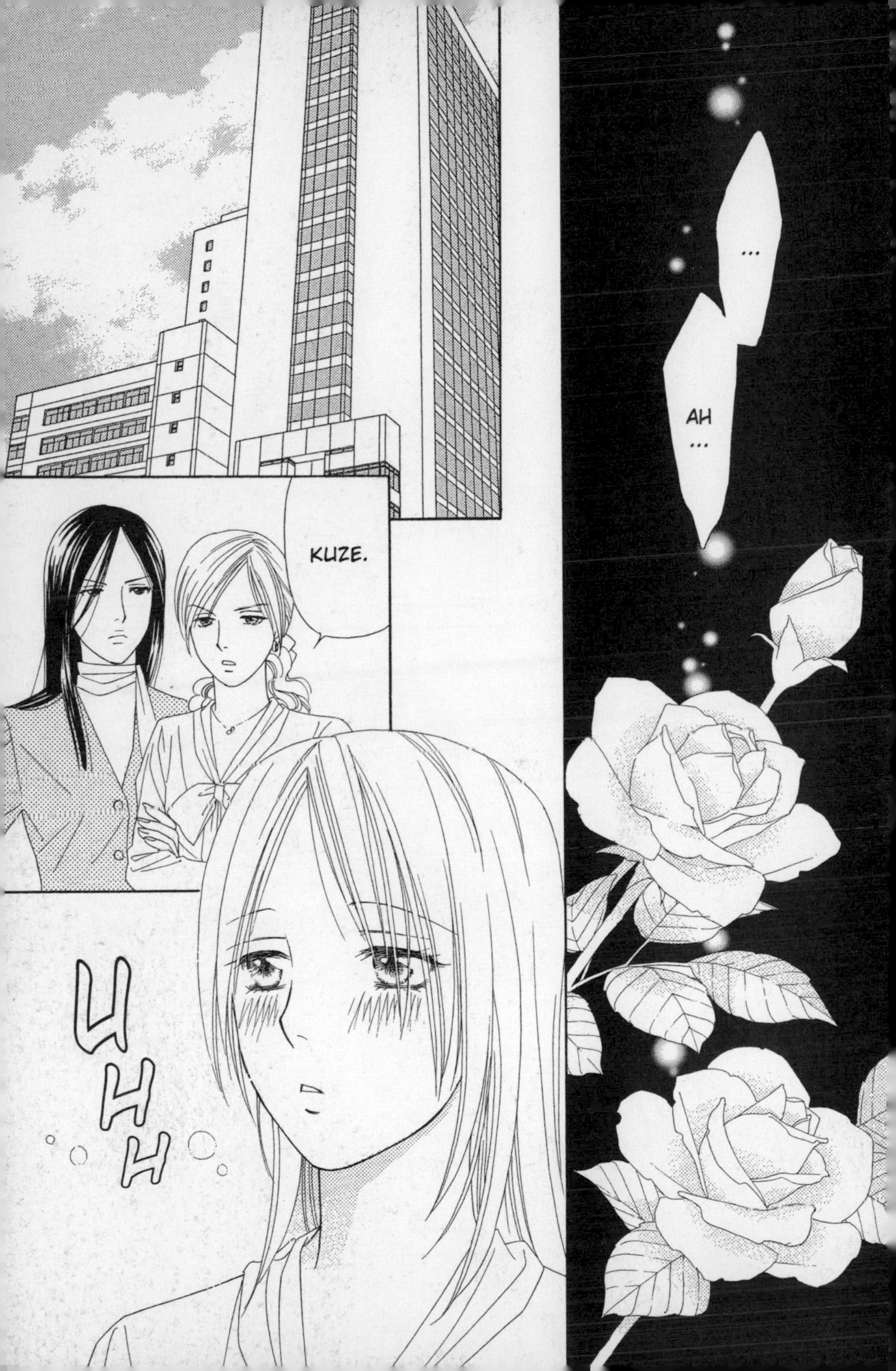
...
AH ...
KUZE.
UHHH

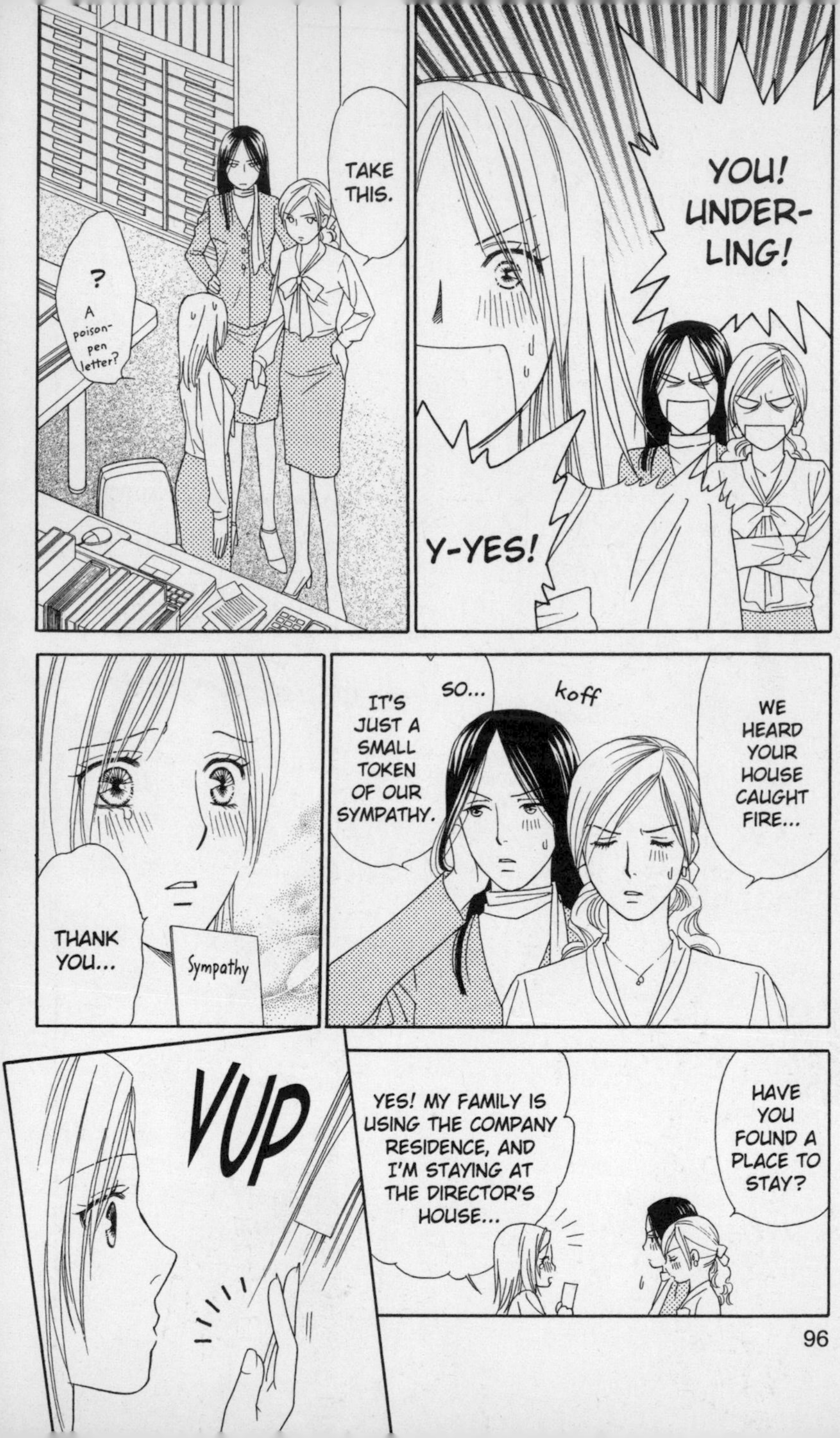
YOU! UNDER-LING!
Y-YES!
TAKE THIS.
?
A poison-pen letter?
WE HEARD YOUR HOUSE CAUGHT FIRE...
koff
SO...
IT'S JUST A SMALL TOKEN OF OUR SYMPATHY.
THANK YOU...
Sympathy
HAVE YOU FOUND A PLACE TO STAY?
YES! MY FAMILY IS USING THE COMPANY RESIDENCE, AND I'M STAYING AT THE DIRECTOR'S HOUSE...
VUP

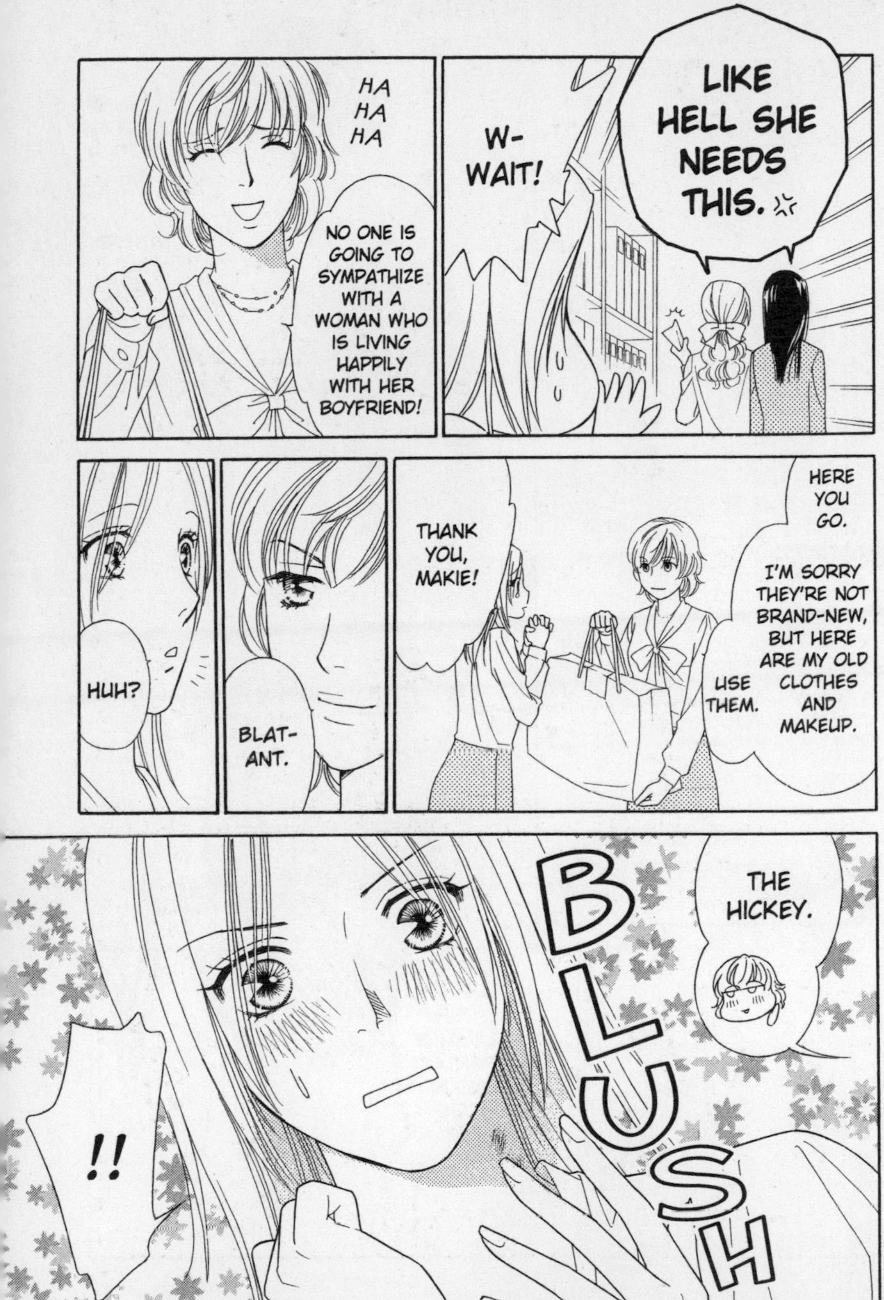
LIKE HELL SHE NEEDS THIS.
W-WAIT!
HA HA HA
NO ONE IS GOING TO SYMPATHIZE WITH A WOMAN WHO IS LIVING HAPPILY WITH HER BOYFRIEND!
HERE YOU GO.
I'M SORRY THEY'RE NOT BRAND-NEW, BUT HERE ARE MY OLD CLOTHES AND MAKEUP.
USE THEM.
THANK YOU, MAKIE!
BLAT-ANT.
HUH?
THE HICKEY.
BLUSH
!!

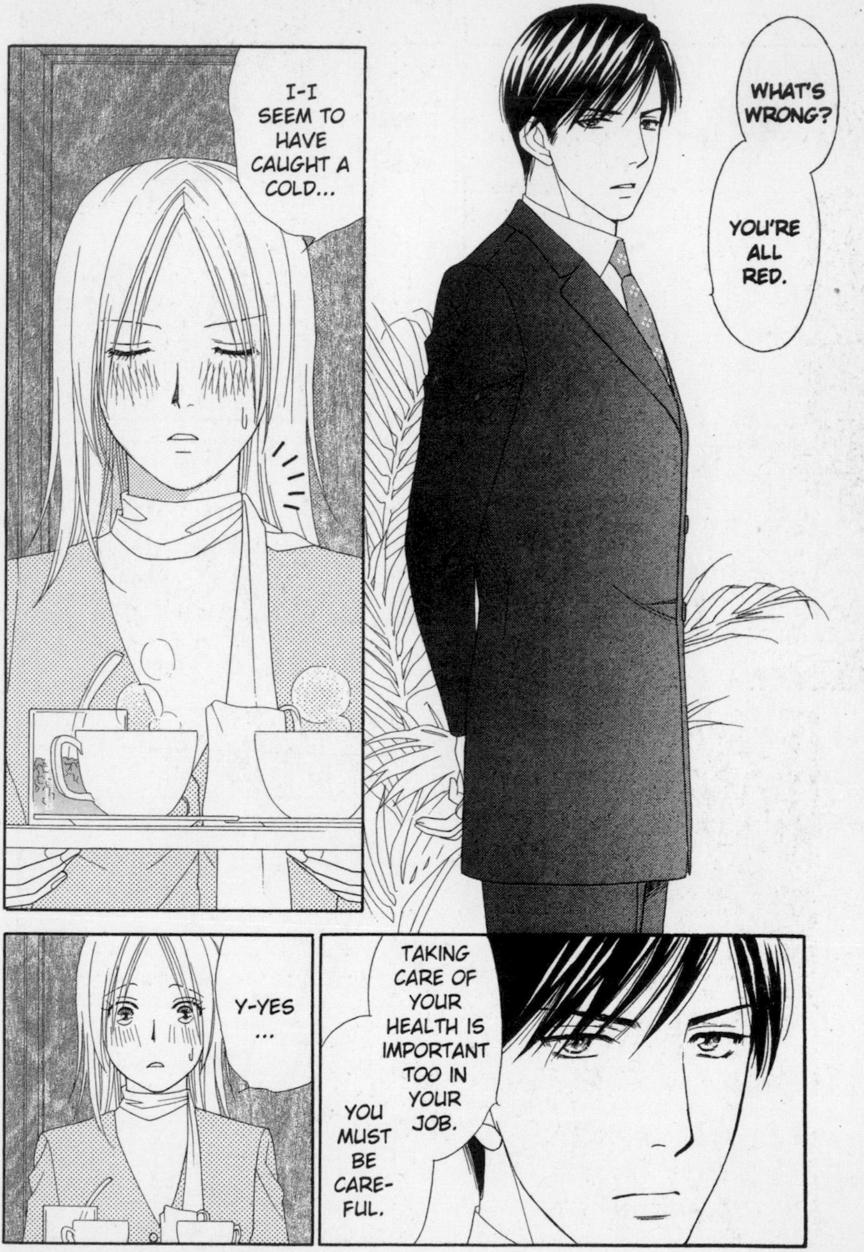
WHAT'S WRONG?
YOU'RE ALL RED.
I-I SEEM TO HAVE CAUGHT A COLD...
TAKING CARE OF YOUR HEALTH IS IMPORTANT TOO IN YOUR JOB.
YOU MUST BE CARE-FUL.
Y-YES ...

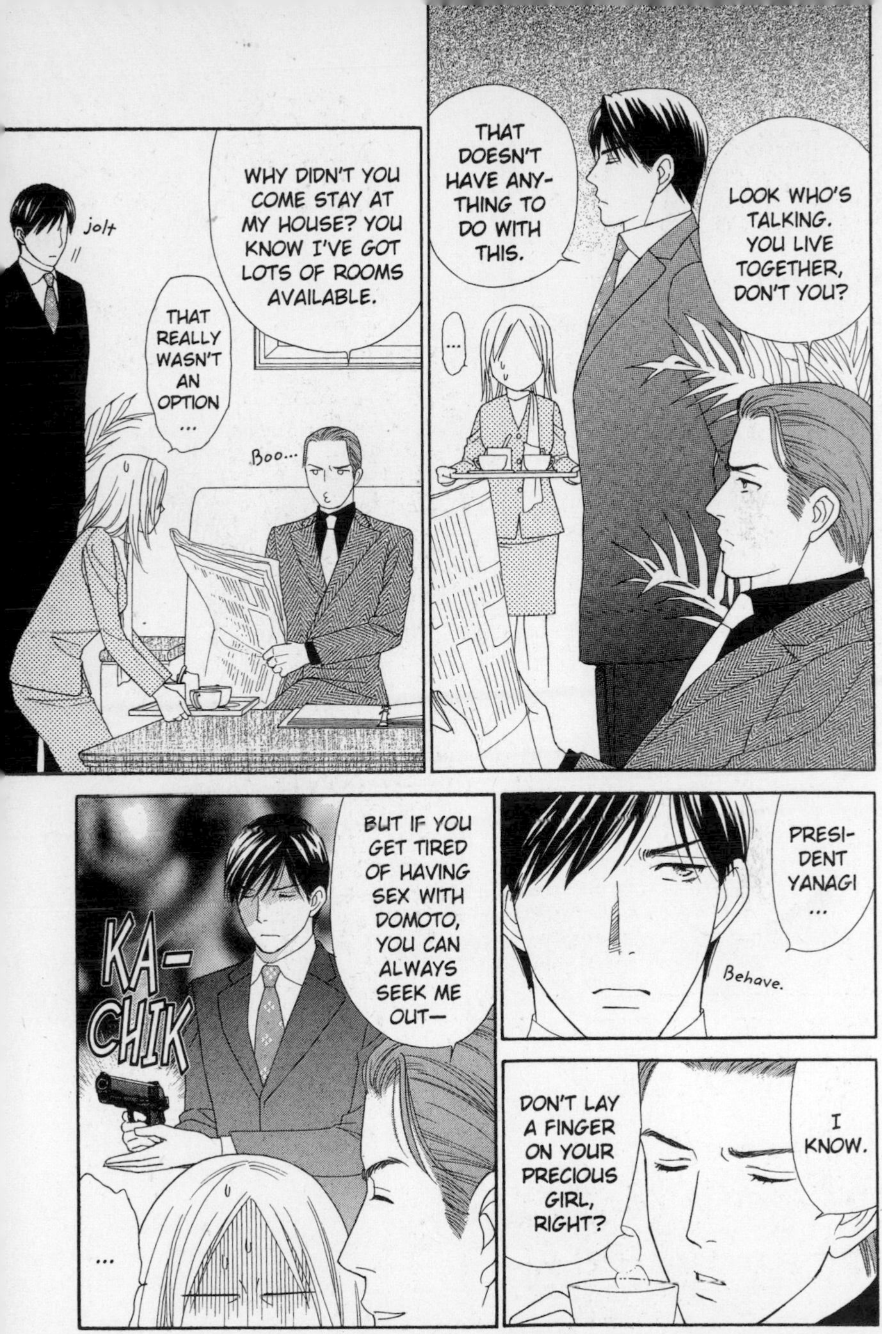
LOOK WHO'S TALKING. YOU LIVE TOGETHER, DON'T YOU?
THAT DOESN'T HAVE ANY-THING TO DO WITH THIS.
...
WHY DIDN'T YOU COME STAY AT MY HOUSE? YOU KNOW I'VE GOT LOTS OF ROOMS AVAILABLE.
jolt
THAT REALLY WASN'T AN OPTION ...
Boo...
PRESI-DENT YANAGI ...
Behave.
I KNOW.
DON'T LAY A FINGER ON YOUR PRECIOUS GIRL, RIGHT?
BUT IF YOU GET TIRED OF HAVING SEX WITH DOMOTO, YOU CAN ALWAYS SEEK ME OUT—
KA-CHIK
...

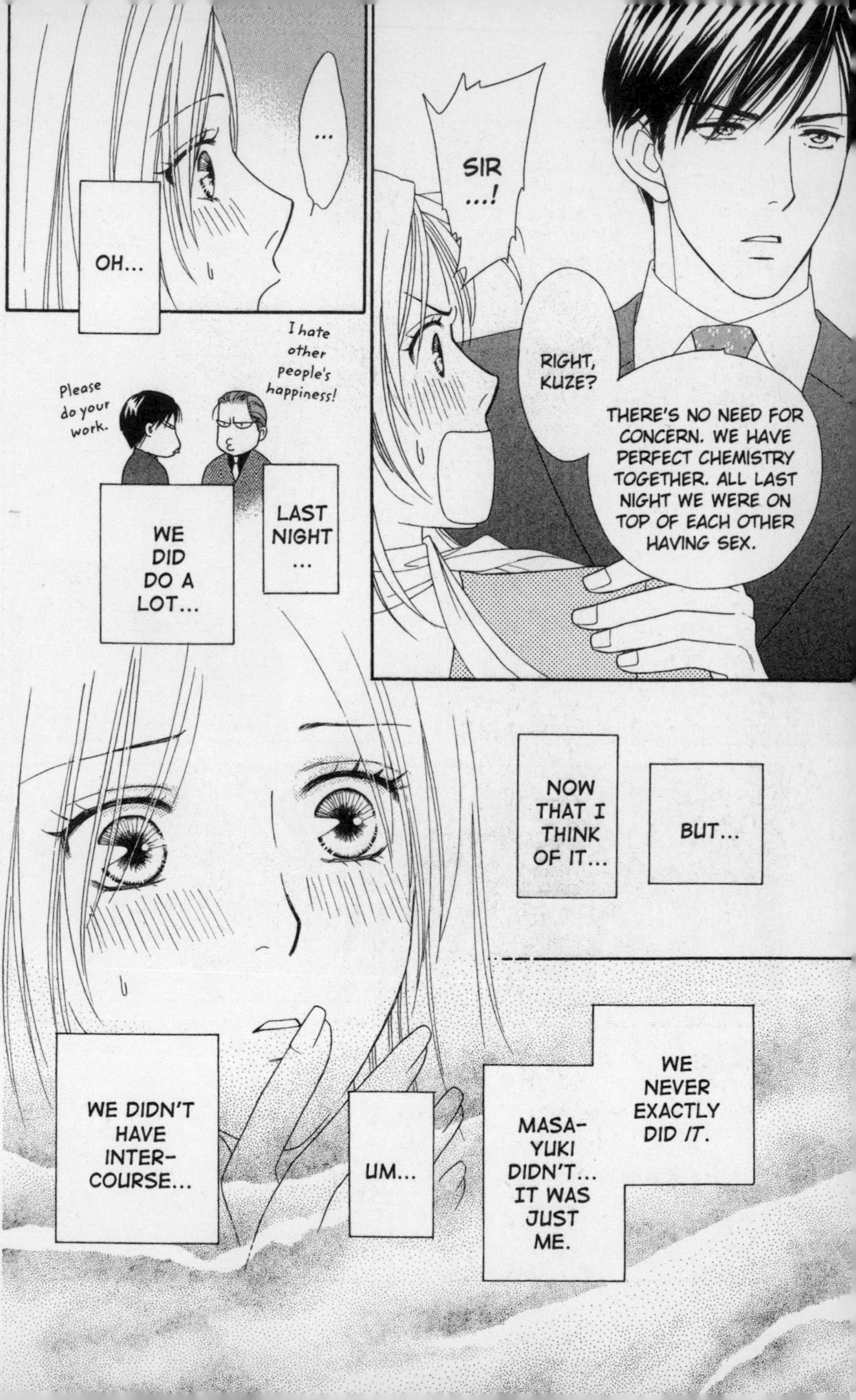
SIR ...!
THERE'S NO NEED FOR CONCERN. WE HAVE PERFECT CHEMISTRY TOGETHER. ALL LAST NIGHT WE WERE ON TOP OF EACH OTHER HAVING SEX.
RIGHT, KUZE?
...
OH...
LAST NIGHT ...
WE DID DO A LOT...
I hate other people's happiness!
Please do your work.
BUT...
NOW THAT I THINK OF IT...
WE NEVER EXACTLY DID *IT*.
MASA-YUKI DIDN'T... IT WAS JUST ME.
UM...
WE DIDN'T HAVE INTER-COURSE...

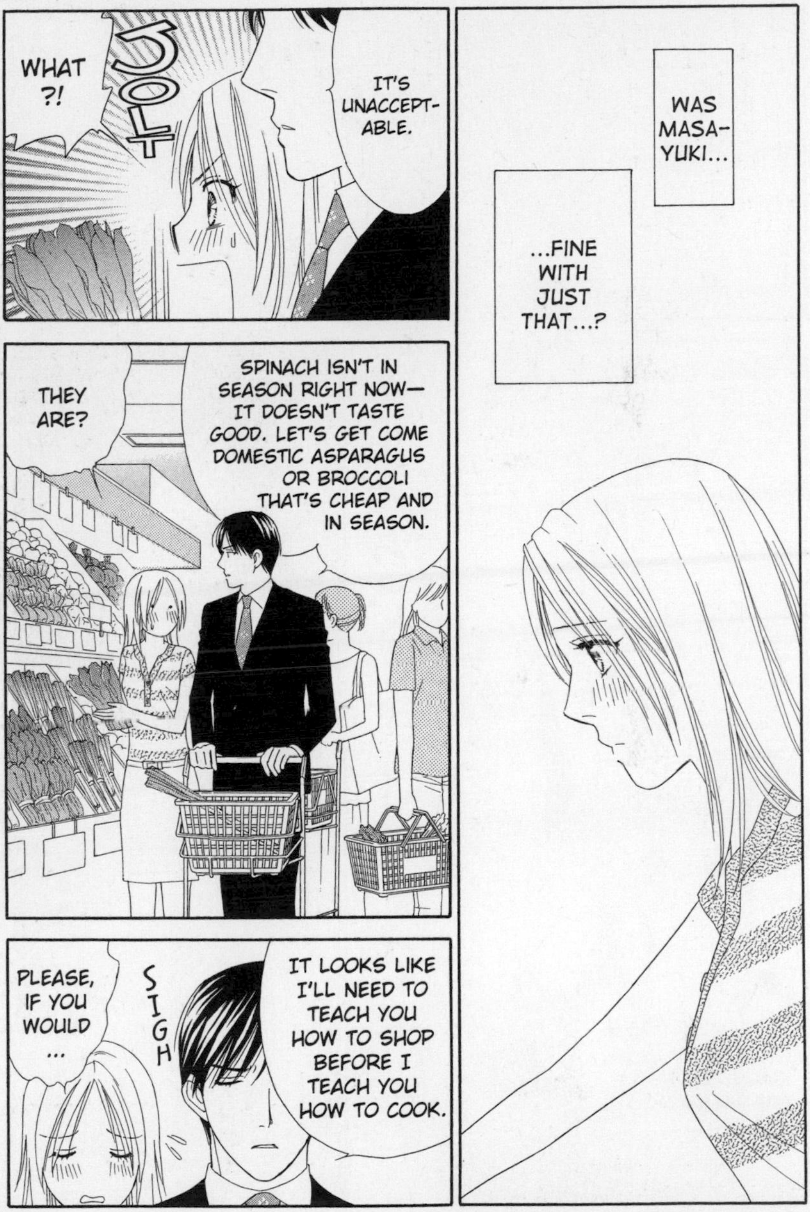
WAS MASA-YUKI...
...FINE WITH JUST THAT...?
IT'S UNACCEPT-ABLE.
JOLT
WHAT ?!
SPINACH ISN'T IN SEASON RIGHT NOW—IT DOESN'T TASTE GOOD. LET'S GET COME DOMESTIC ASPARAGUS OR BROCCOLI THAT'S CHEAP AND IN SEASON.
THEY ARE?
IT LOOKS LIKE I'LL NEED TO TEACH YOU HOW TO SHOP BEFORE I TEACH YOU HOW TO COOK.
SIGH
PLEASE, IF YOU WOULD ...

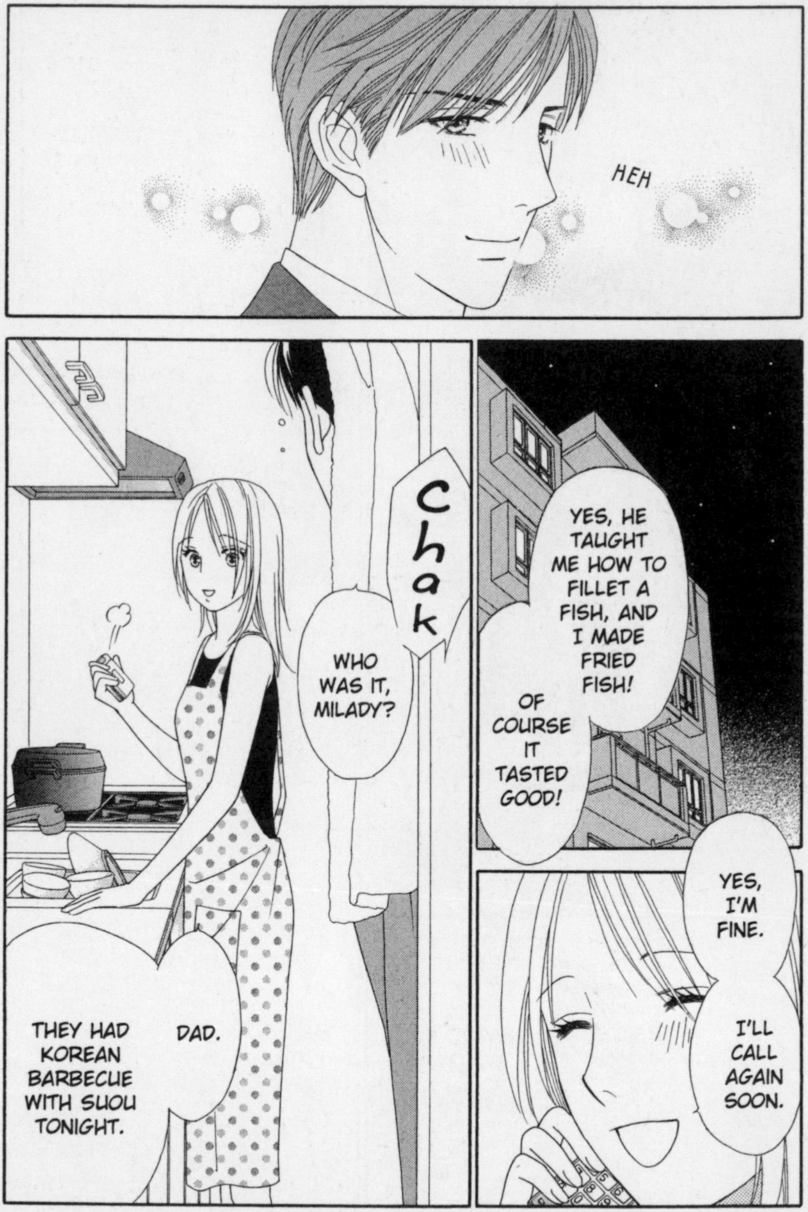
HEH
YES, HE TAUGHT ME HOW TO FILLET A FISH, AND I MADE FRIED FISH!
OF COURSE IT TASTED GOOD!
YES, I'M FINE.
I'LL CALL AGAIN SOON.
Chak
WHO WAS IT, MILADY?
DAD.
THEY HAD KOREAN BARBECUE WITH SUOU TONIGHT.

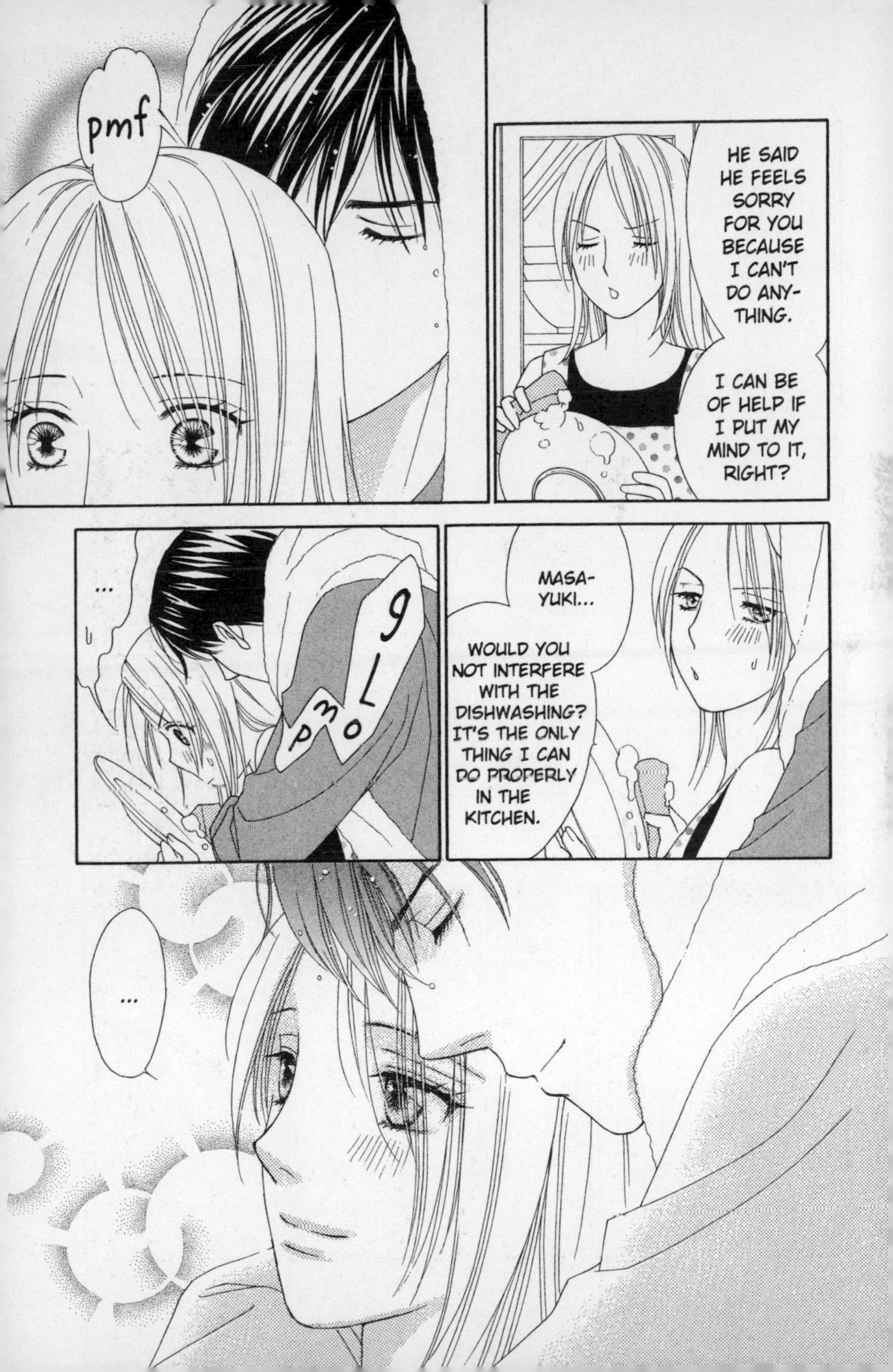
HE SAID HE FEELS SORRY FOR YOU BECAUSE I CAN'T DO ANY-THING.
I CAN BE OF HELP IF I PUT MY MIND TO IT, RIGHT?
pmf
MASA-YUKI...
WOULD YOU NOT INTERFERE WITH THE DISHWASHING? IT'S THE ONLY THING I CAN DO PROPERLY IN THE KITCHEN.
...
glomp
...

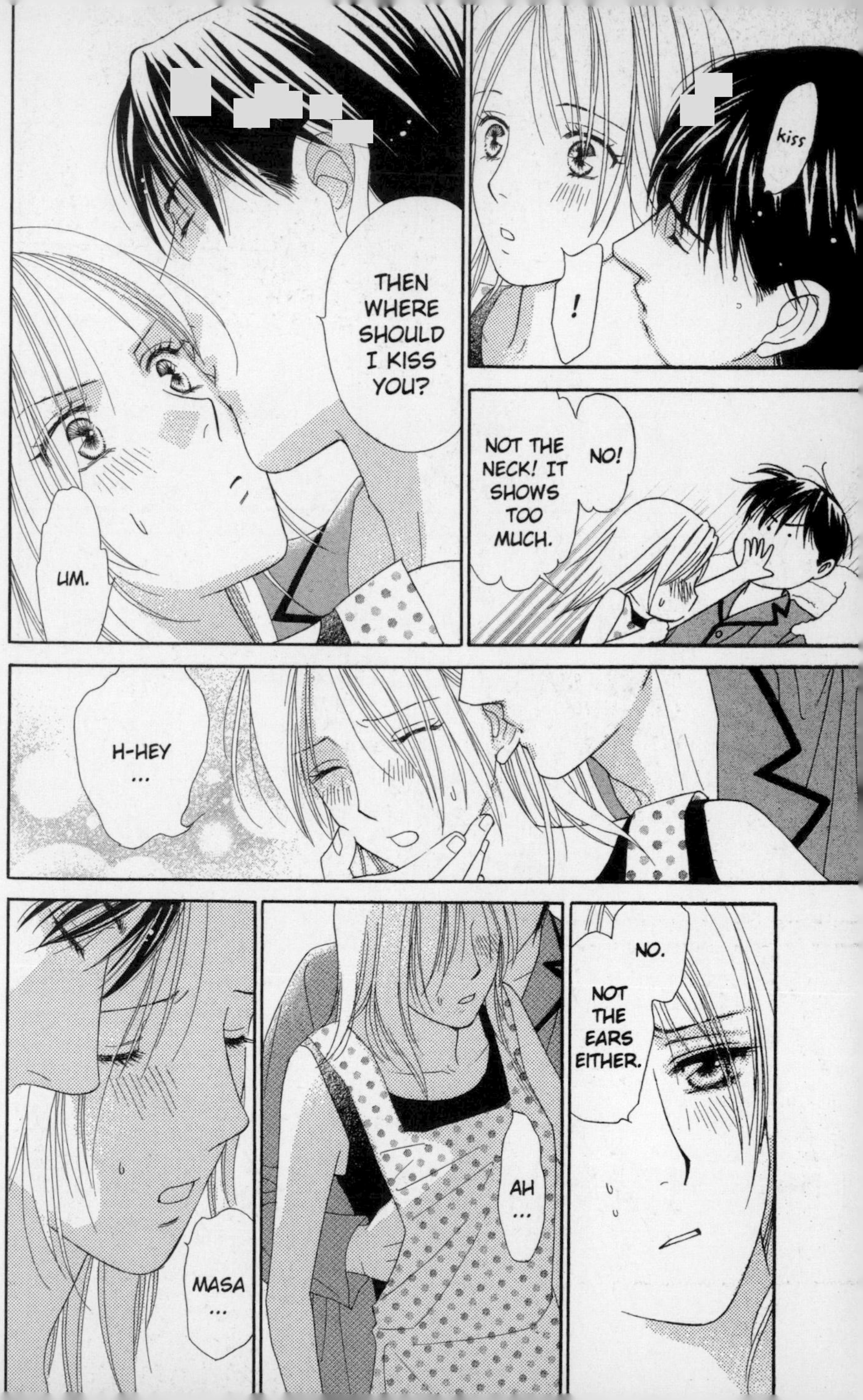
kiss
!
NO!
NOT THE NECK! IT SHOWS TOO MUCH.
THEN WHERE SHOULD I KISS YOU?
UM.
H-HEY ...
NO.
NOT THE EARS EITHER.
AH ...
MASA ...

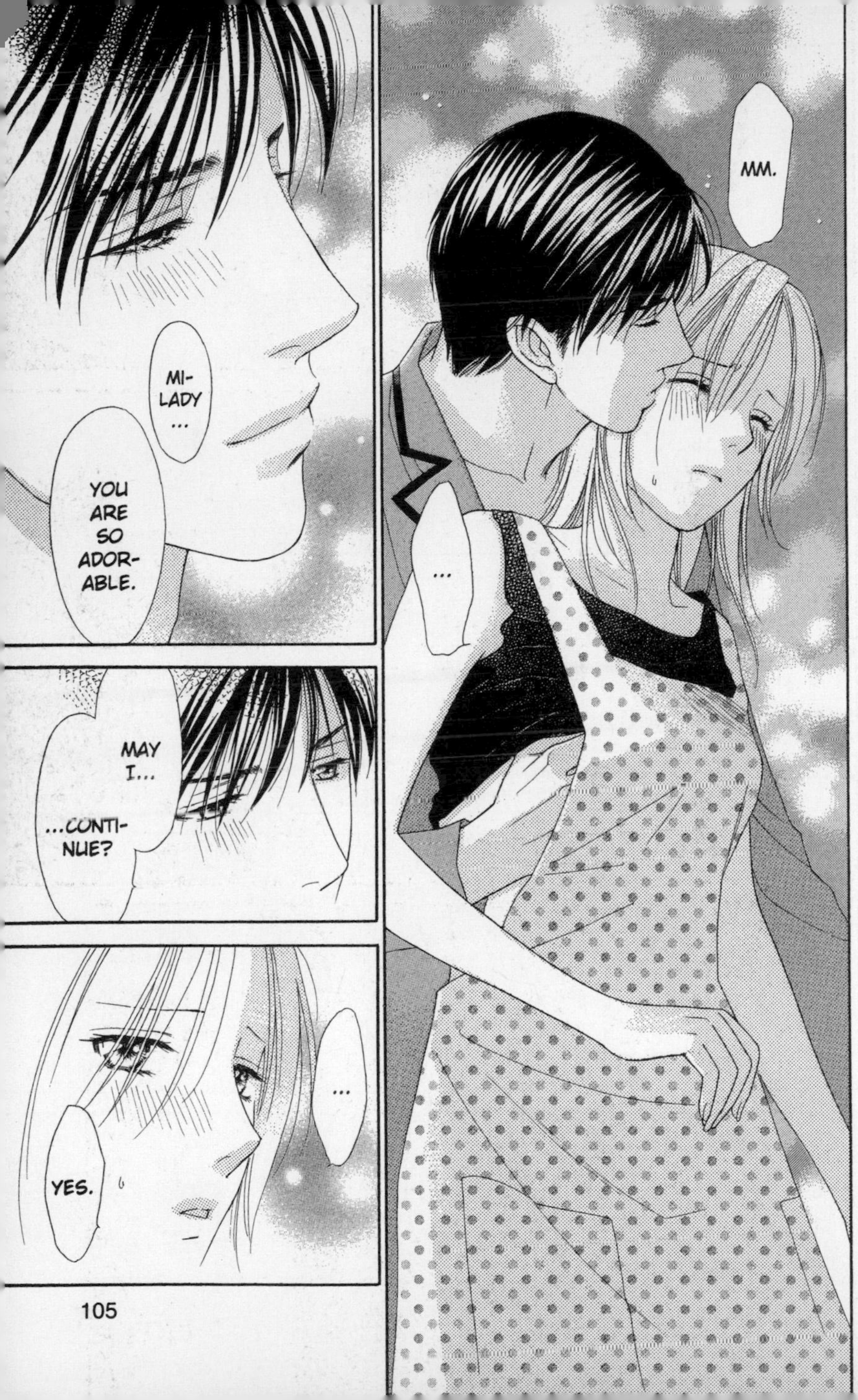
MM.
...
MI-LADY ...
YOU ARE SO ADOR-ABLE.
MAY I...
...CONTI-NUE?
...
YES.

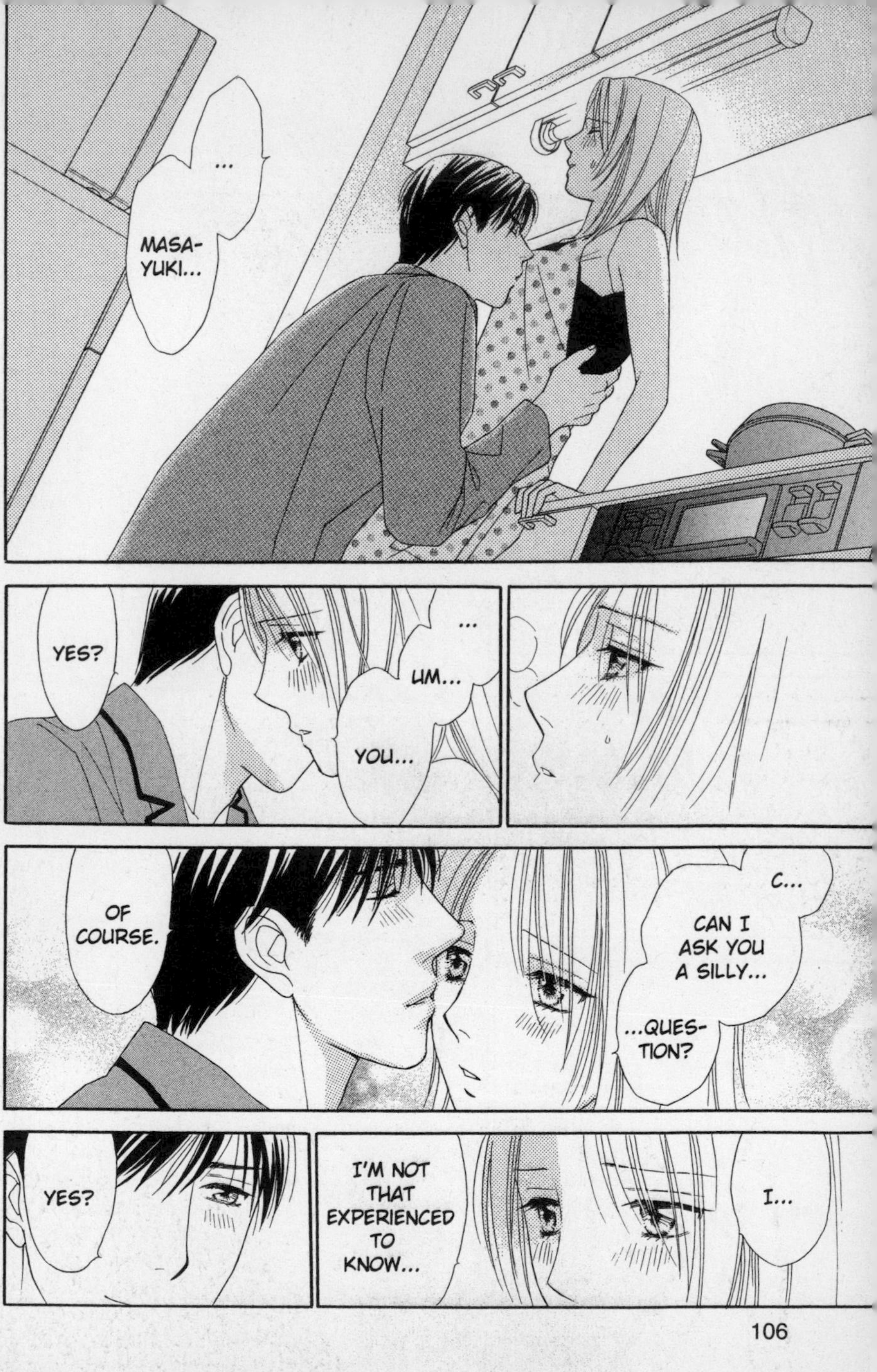
...
MASA-YUKI...
...
UM...
YOU...
YES?
C...
CAN I ASK YOU A SILLY...
...QUES-TION?
OF COURSE.
I...
I'M NOT THAT EXPERIENCED TO KNOW...
YES?

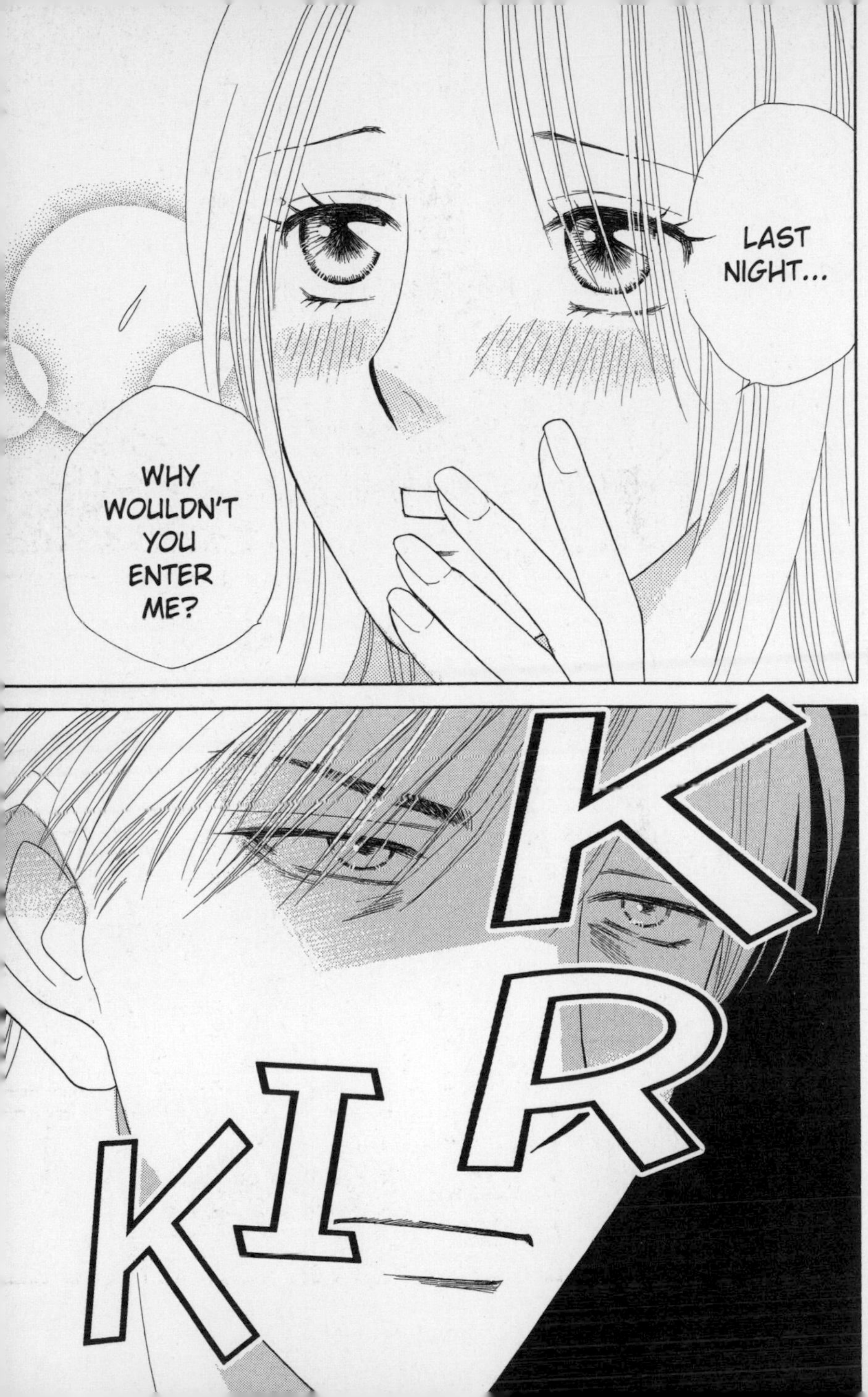
LAST NIGHT...
WHY WOULDN'T YOU ENTER ME?
KIRK

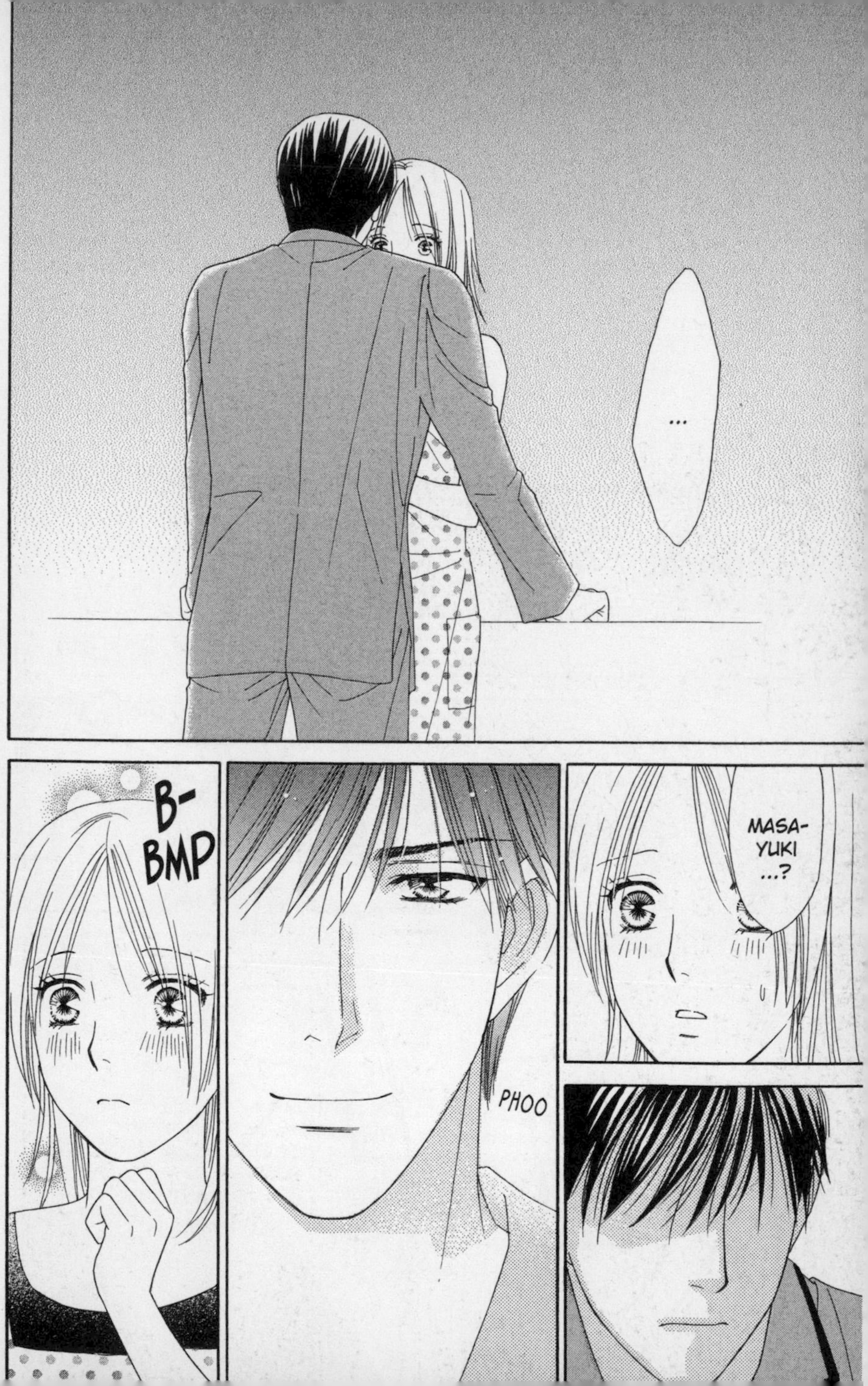
...
MASA-YUKI ...?
PHOO
B-BMP

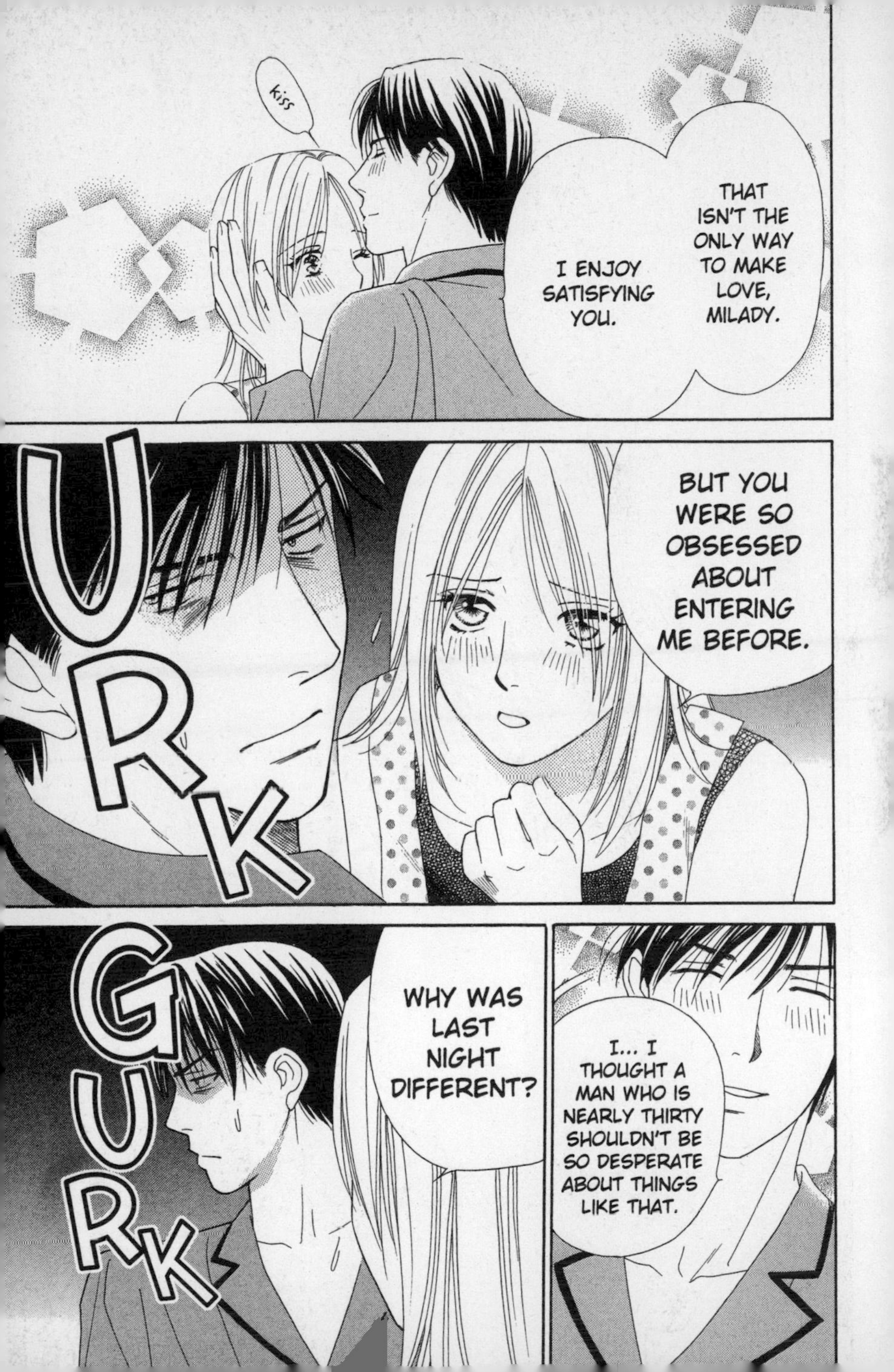
THAT ISN'T THE ONLY WAY TO MAKE LOVE, MILADY.
I ENJOY SATISFYING YOU.
kiss
BUT YOU WERE SO OBSESSED ABOUT ENTERING ME BEFORE.
URK
I... I THOUGHT A MAN WHO IS NEARLY THIRTY SHOULDN'T BE SO DESPERATE ABOUT THINGS LIKE THAT.
WHY WAS LAST NIGHT DIFFERENT?
GURK

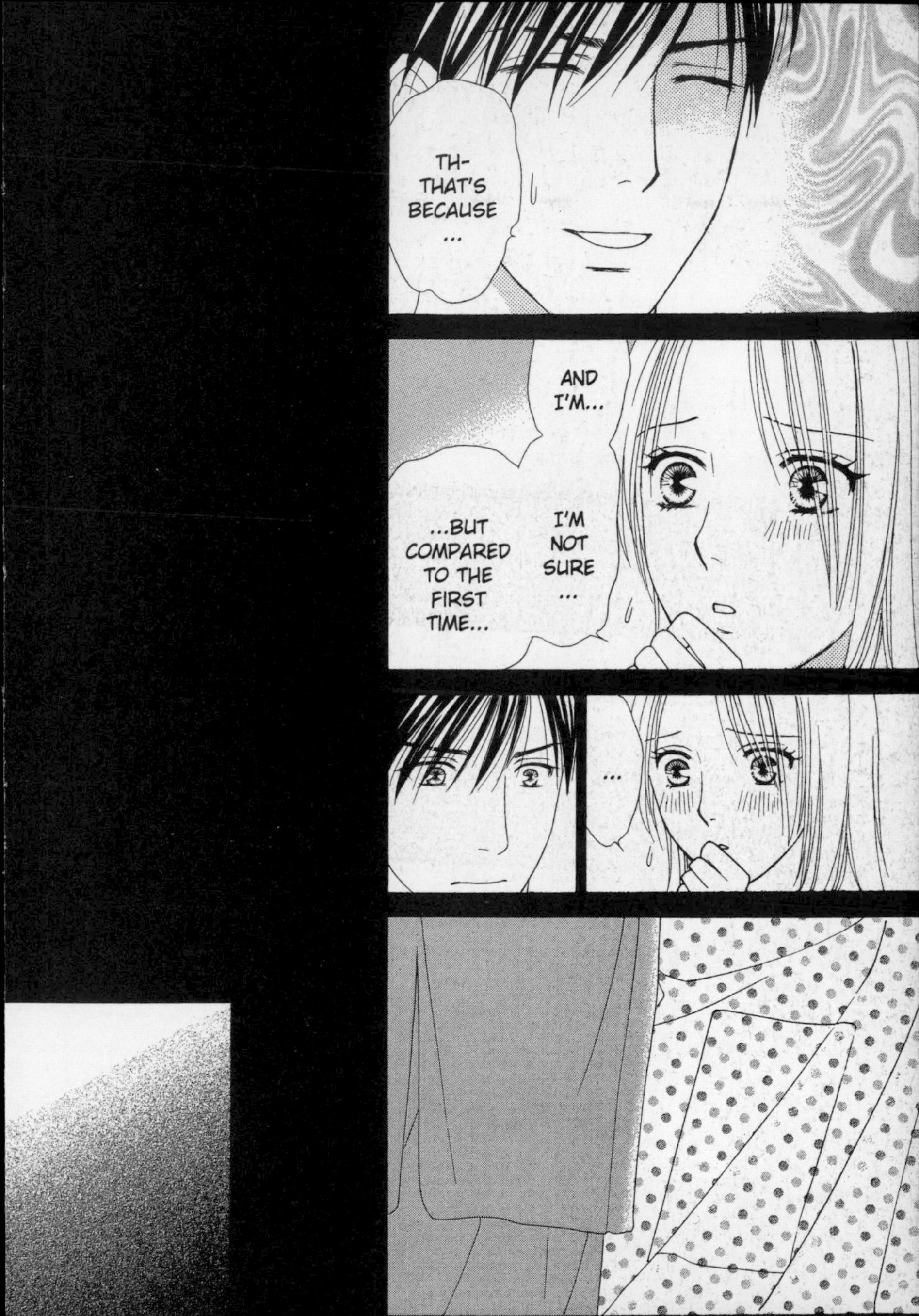
TH- THAT'S BECAUSE ...
AND I'M...
I'M NOT SURE ...
...BUT COMPARED TO THE FIRST TIME...
...

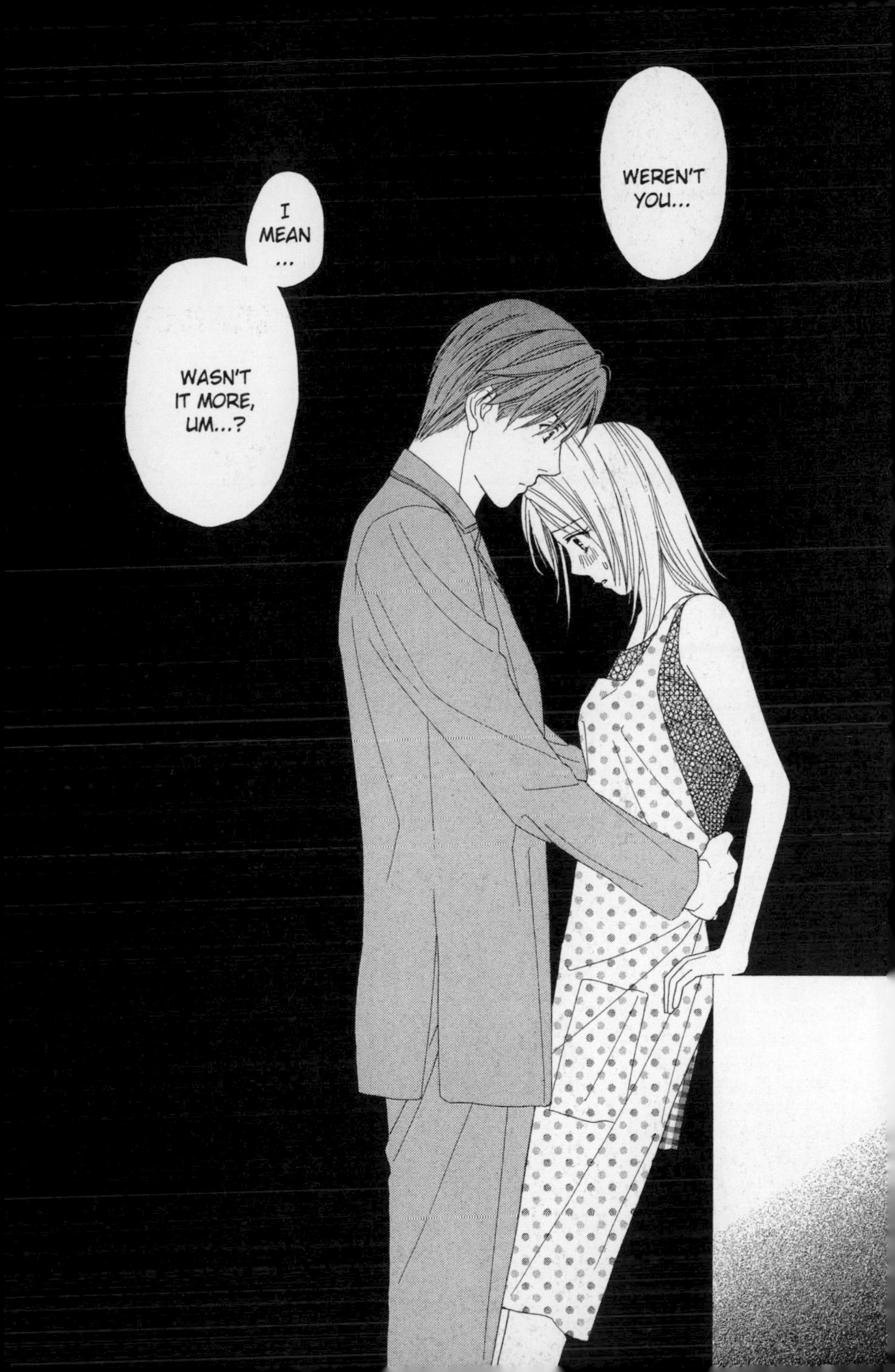
WEREN'T YOU...
I MEAN ...
WASN'T IT MORE, UM...?

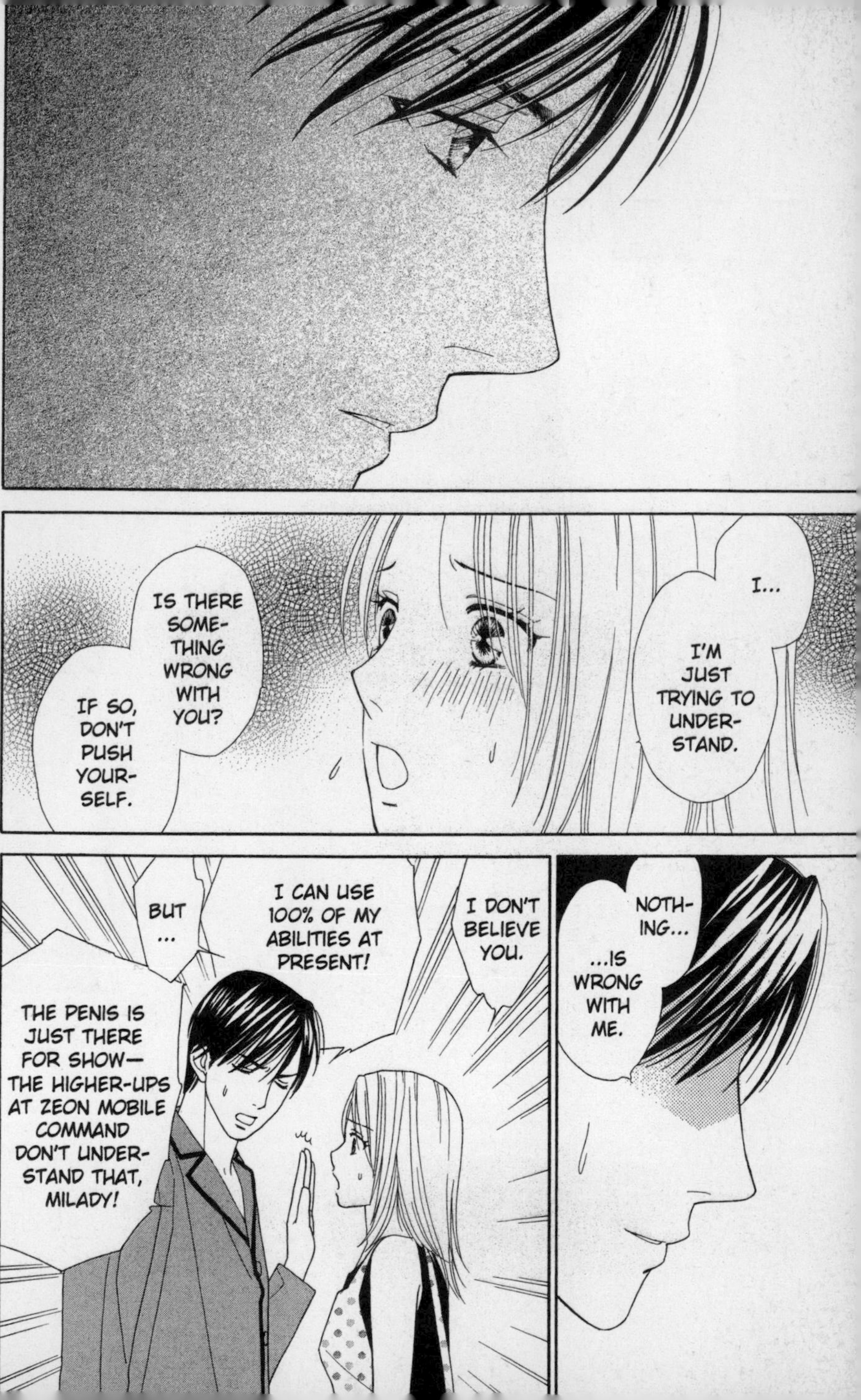
I...
I'M JUST TRYING TO UNDER-STAND.
IS THERE SOME-THING WRONG WITH YOU?
IF SO, DON'T PUSH YOUR-SELF.
NOTH-ING...
...IS WRONG WITH ME.
I DON'T BELIEVE YOU.
I CAN USE 100% OF MY ABILITIES AT PRESENT!
BUT ...
THE PENIS IS JUST THERE FOR SHOW—THE HIGHER-UPS AT ZEON MOBILE COMMAND DON'T UNDER-STAND THAT, MILADY!

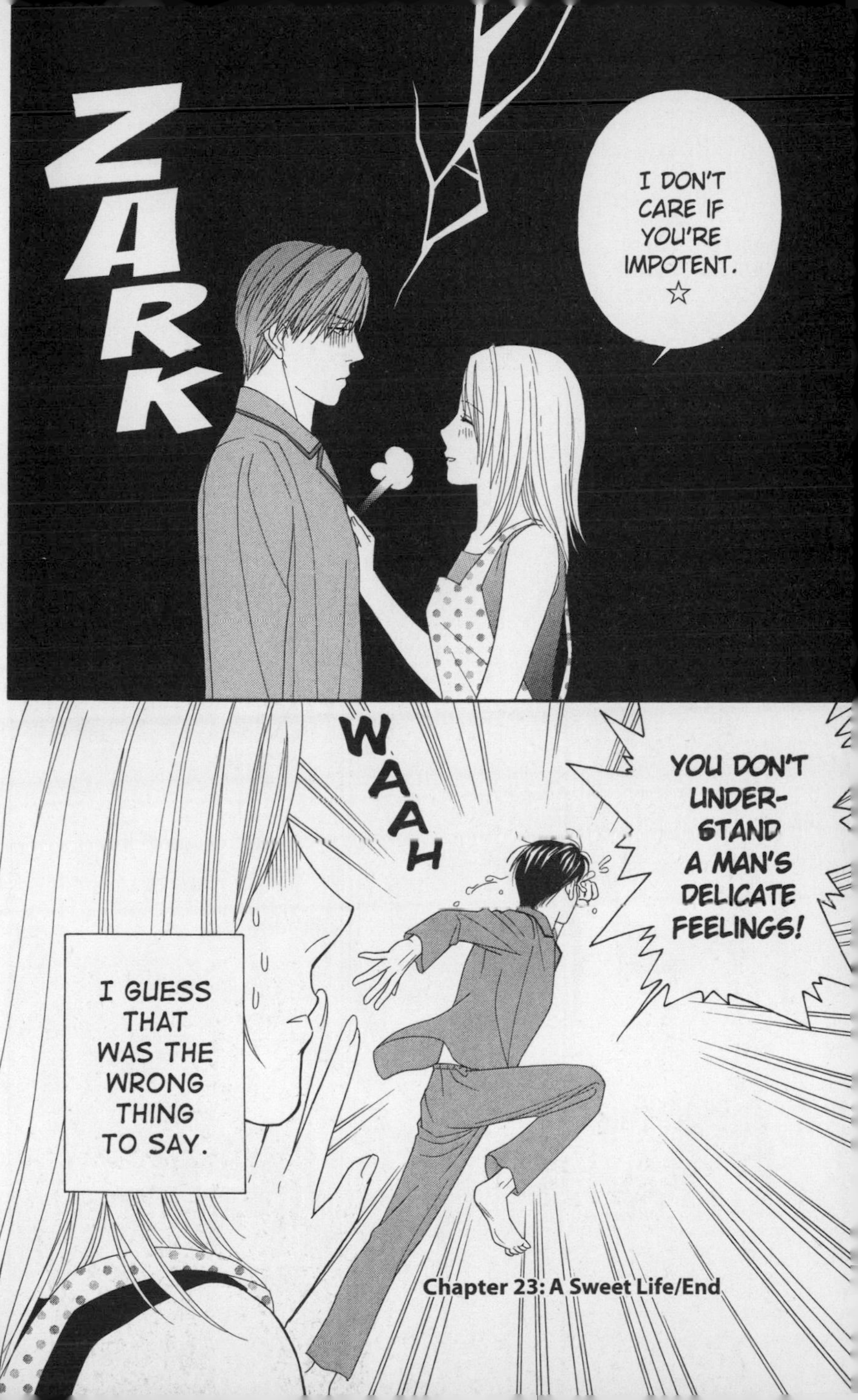
ZARK
I DON'T CARE IF YOU'RE IMPOTENT. ☆
YOU DON'T UNDER-STAND A MAN'S DELICATE FEELINGS!
WAAH
I GUESS THAT WAS THE WRONG THING TO SAY.

Chapter 23: A Sweet Life/End

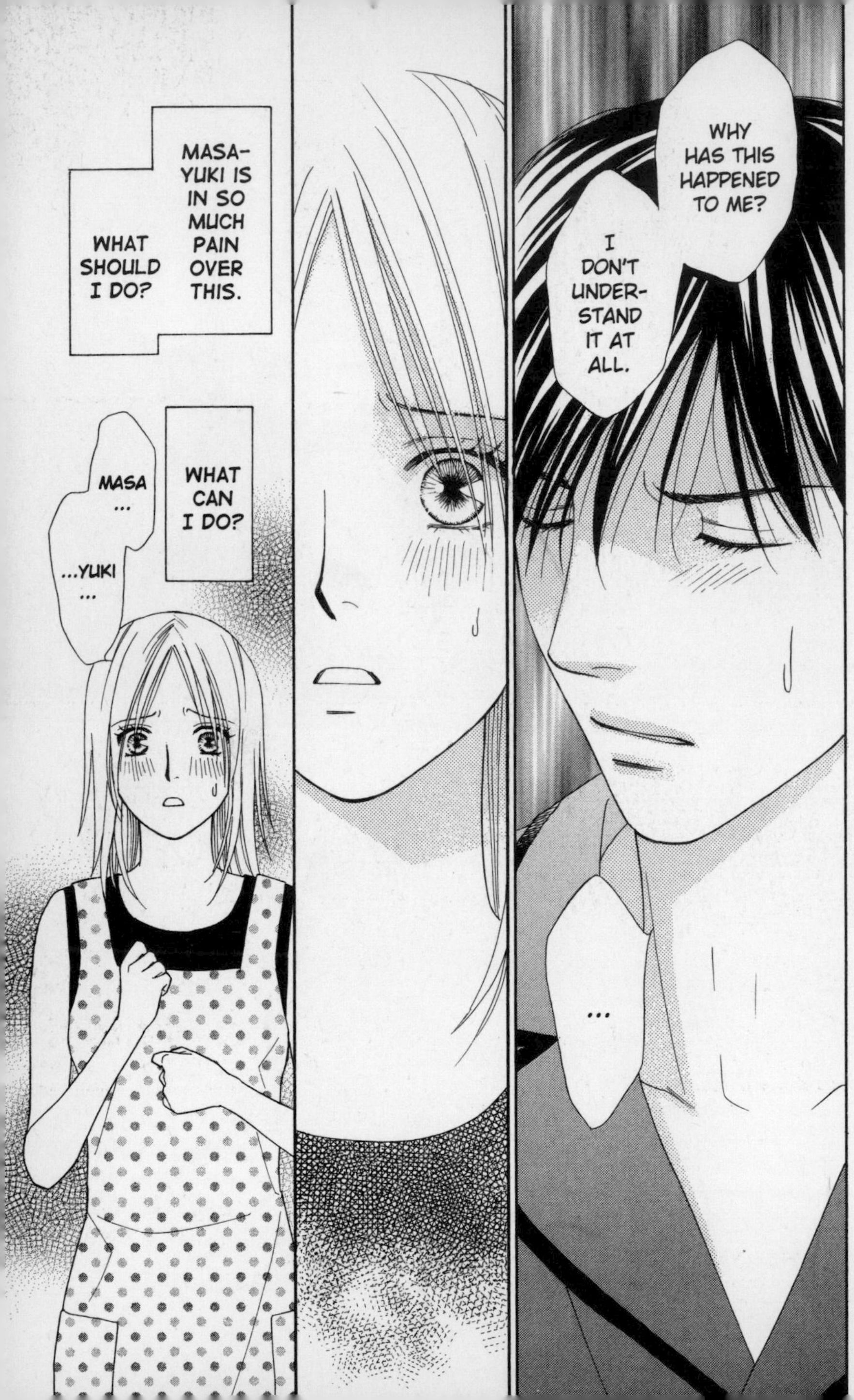
WHY HAS THIS HAPPENED TO ME?
I DON'T UNDER-STAND IT AT ALL.
...
MASA-YUKI IS IN SO MUCH PAIN OVER THIS.
WHAT SHOULD I DO?
WHAT CAN I DO?
MASA ...
...YUKI ...

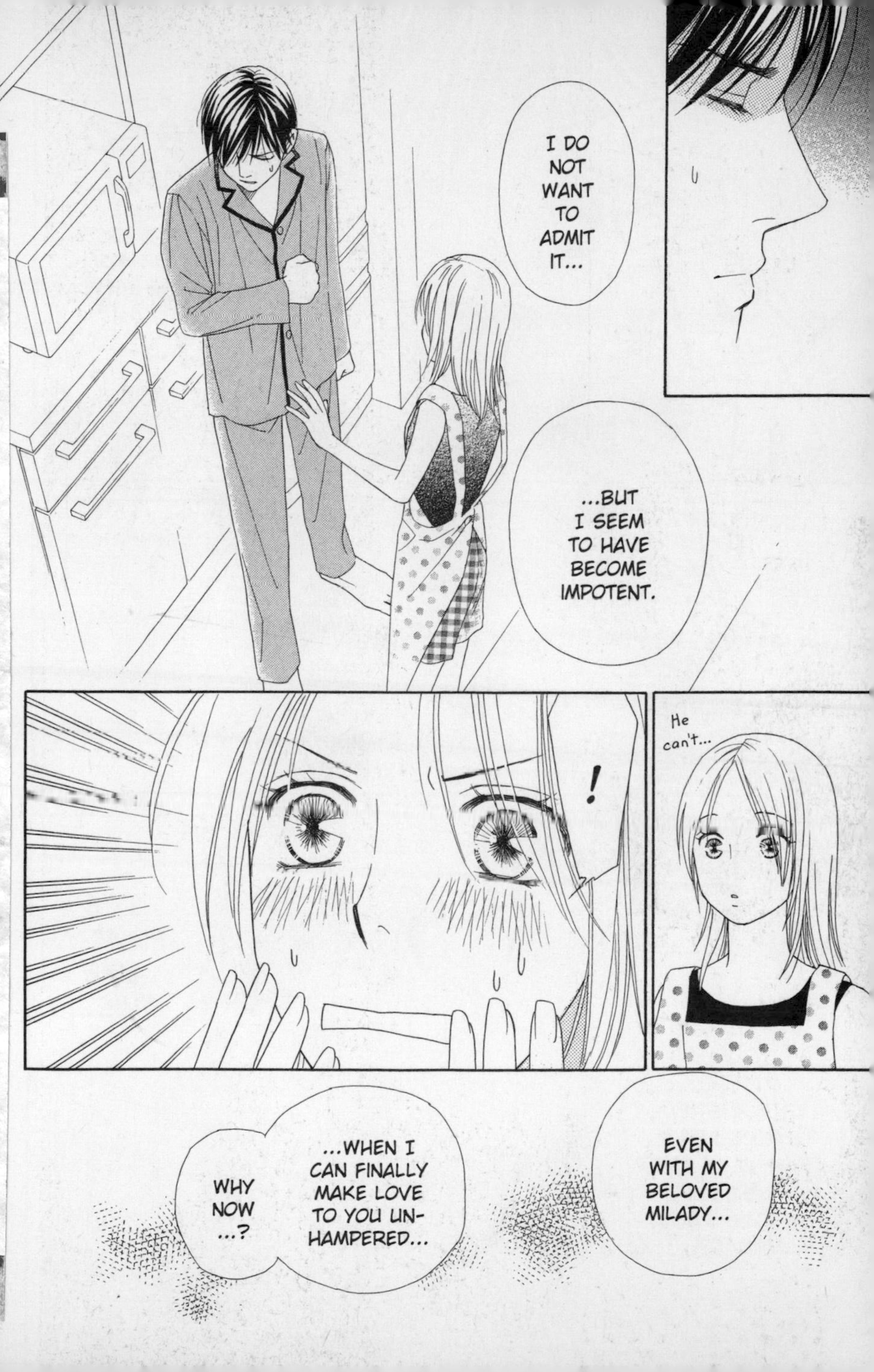
I DO NOT WANT TO ADMIT IT...
...BUT I SEEM TO HAVE BECOME IMPOTENT.
He can't...
!
EVEN WITH MY BELOVED MILADY...
...WHEN I CAN FINALLY MAKE LOVE TO YOU UN-HAMPERED...
WHY NOW ...?

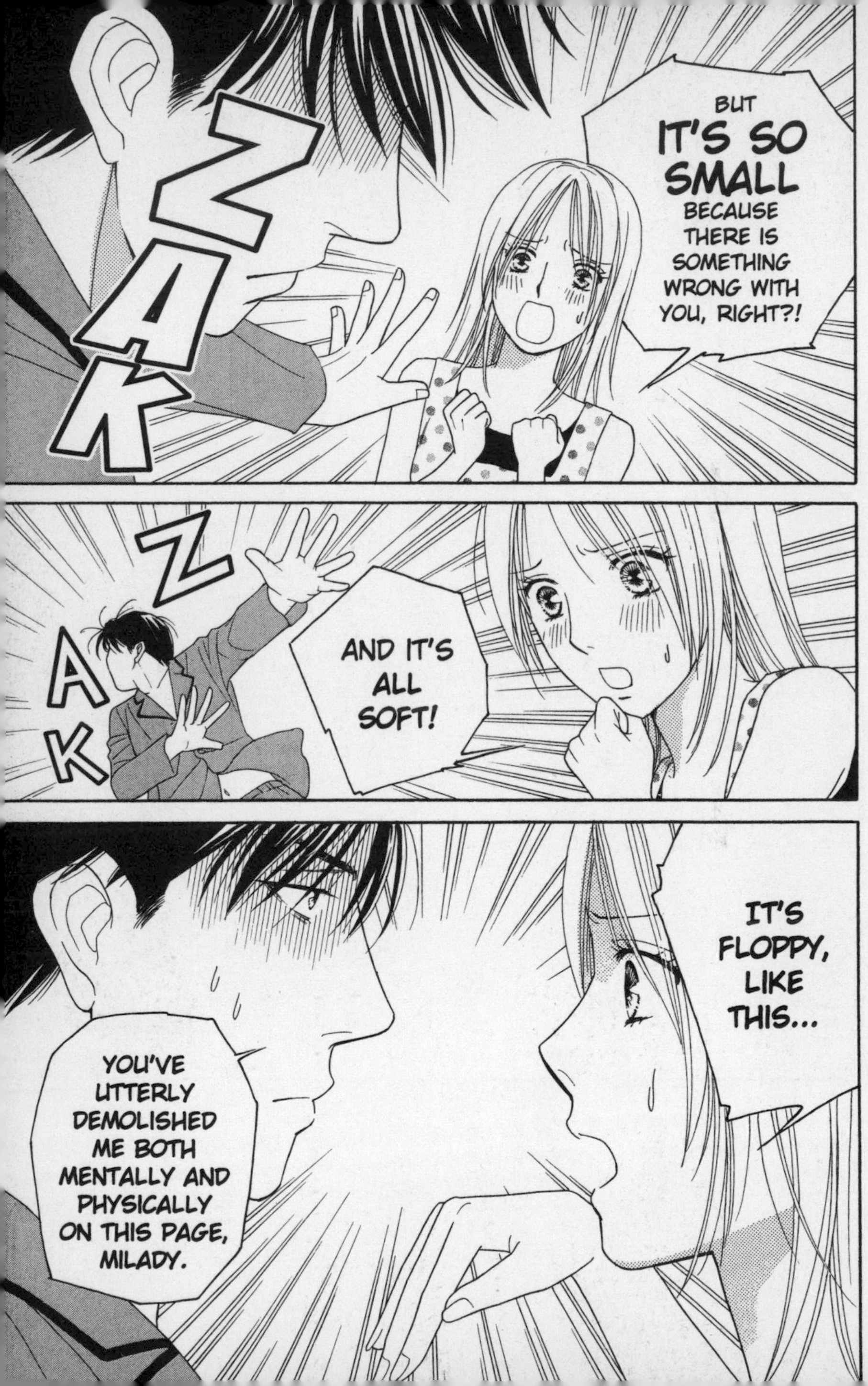
BUT IT'S SO SMALL BECAUSE THERE IS SOMETHING WRONG WITH YOU, RIGHT?!
ZAK
AND IT'S ALL SOFT!
ZAK
IT'S FLOPPY, LIKE THIS...
YOU'VE UTTERLY DEMOLISHED ME BOTH MENTALLY AND PHYSICALLY ON THIS PAGE, MILADY.

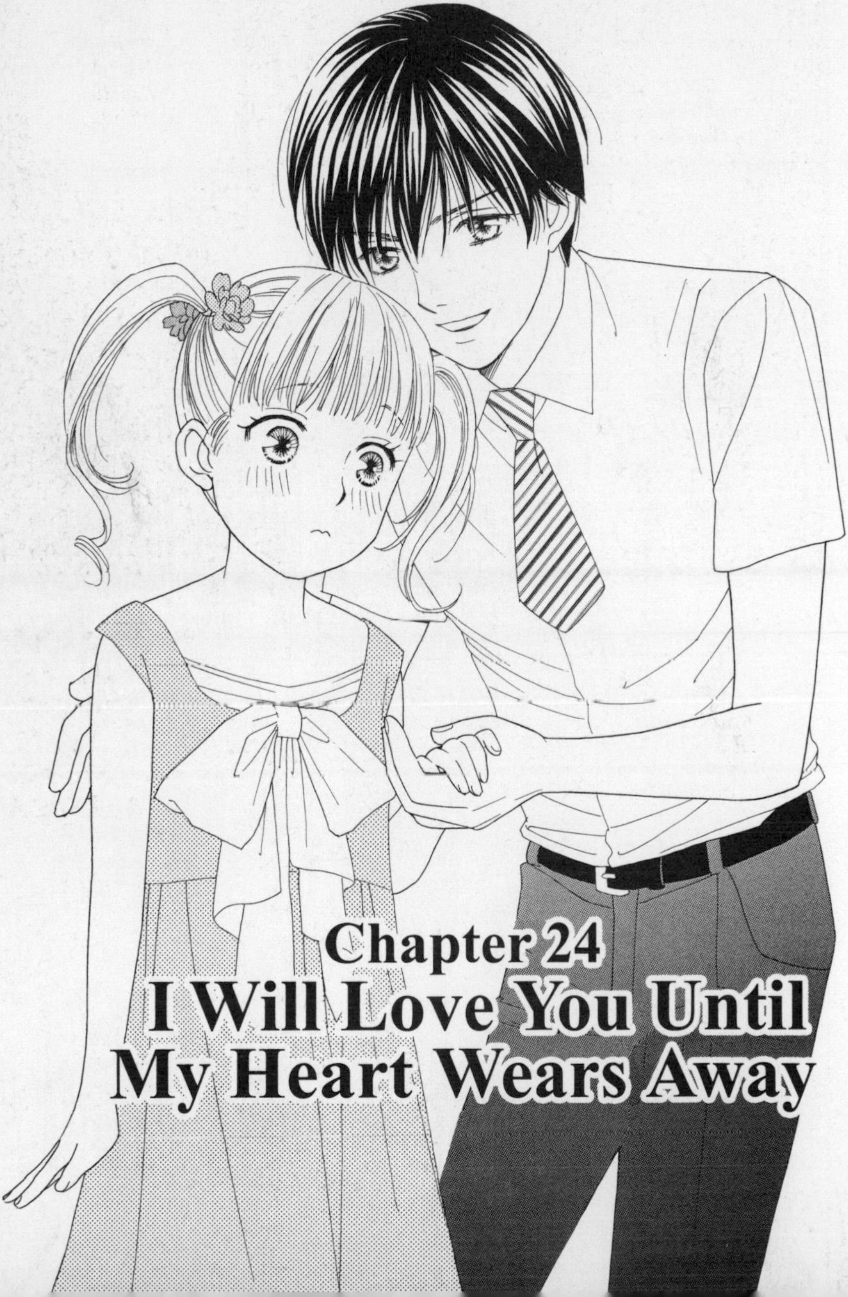
Chapter 24
I Will Love You Until
My Heart Wears Away

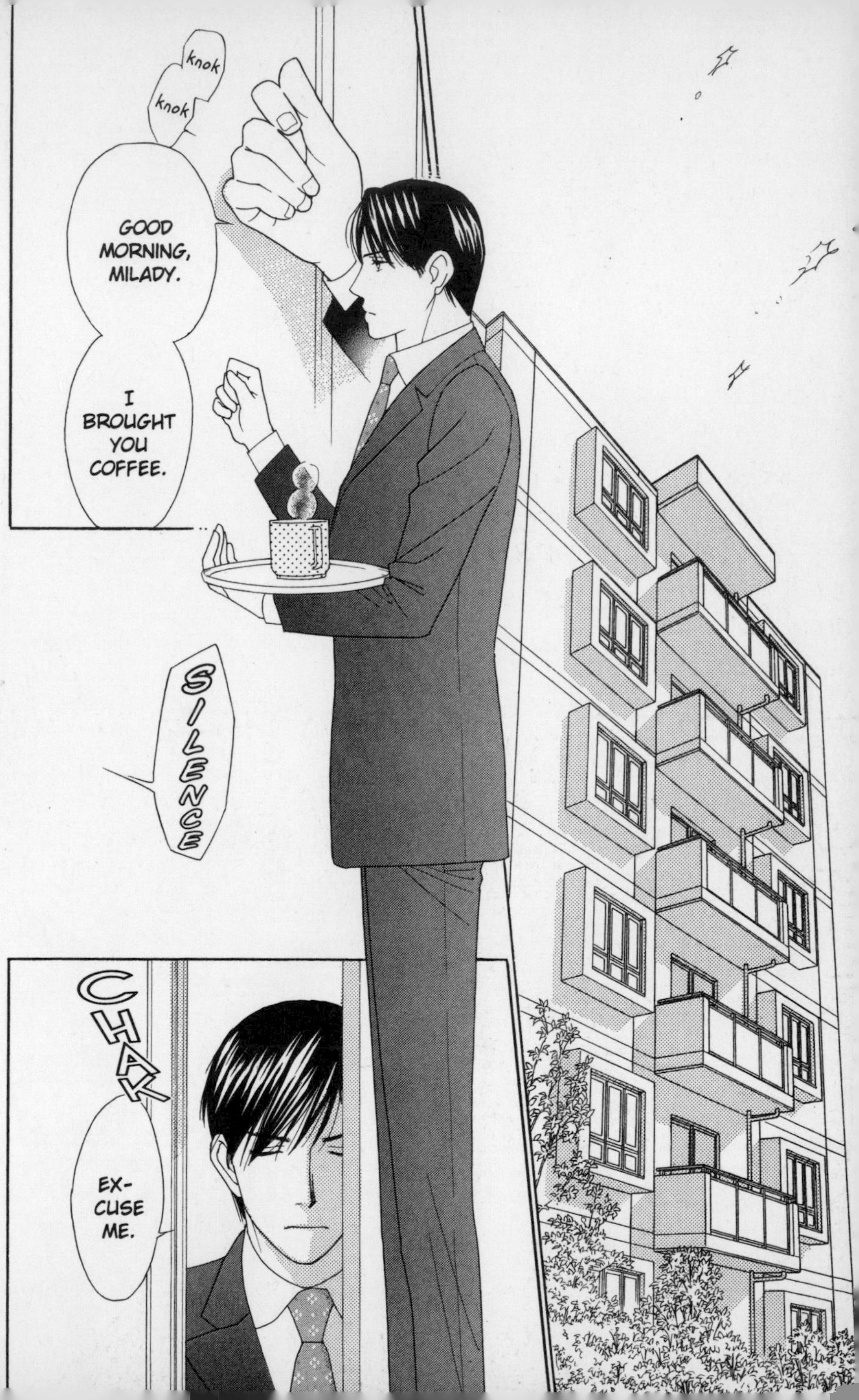
knok
knok
GOOD MORNING, MILADY.
I BROUGHT YOU COFFEE.
SILENCE
CHAK
EX-CUSE ME.

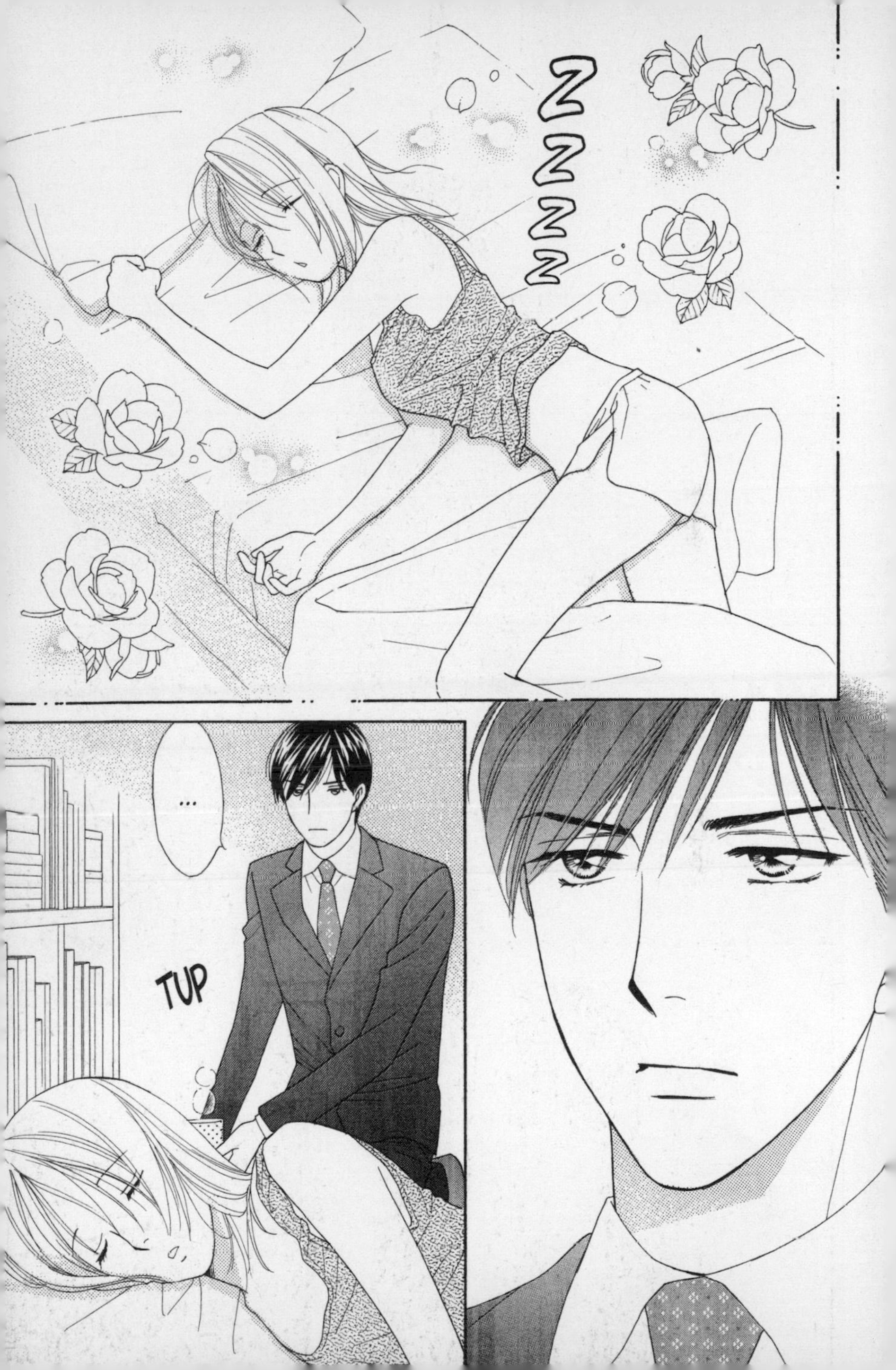
ZZZZ
...
TUP

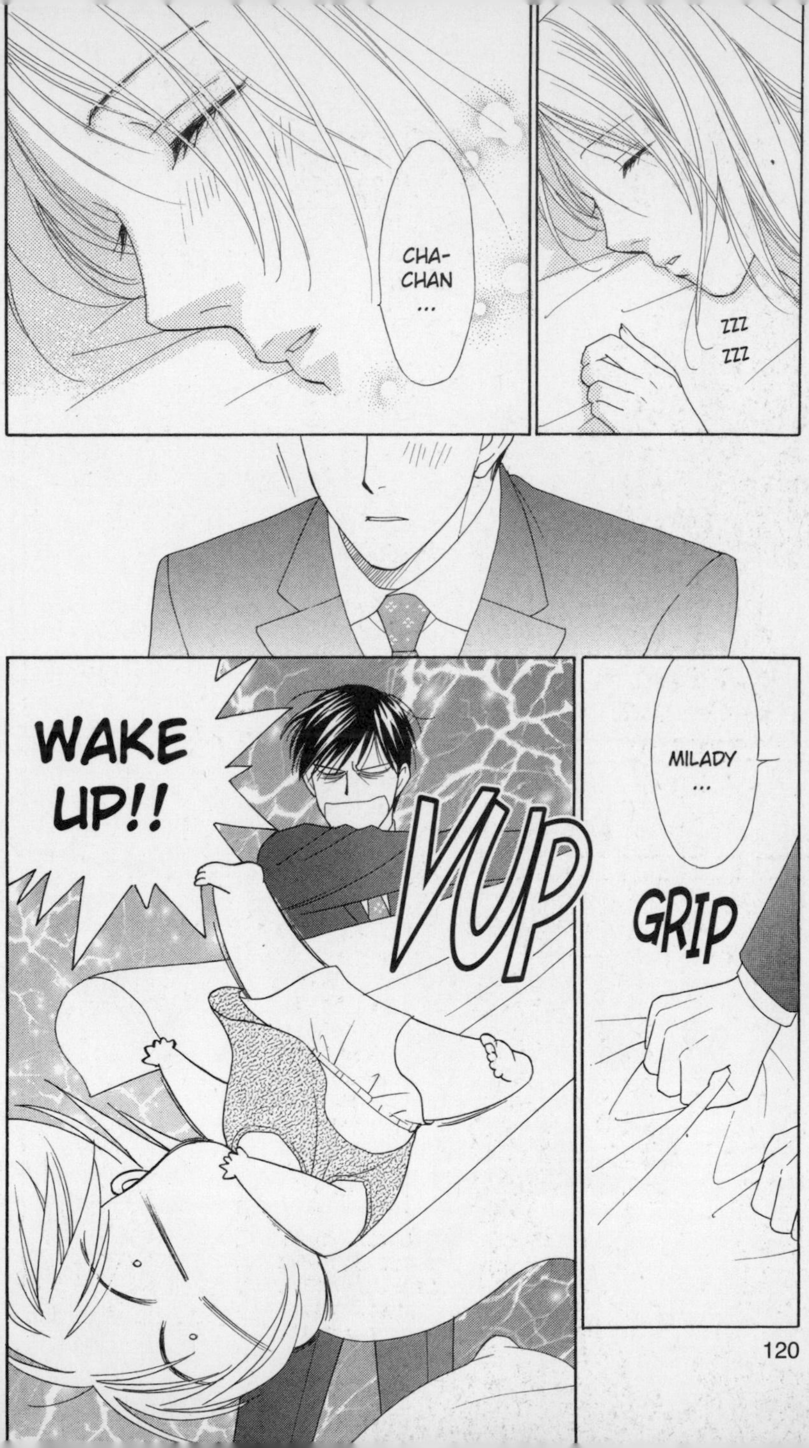
ZZZ
ZZZ
CHA-CHAN ...
MILADY ...
GRIP
WAKE UP!!
YUP

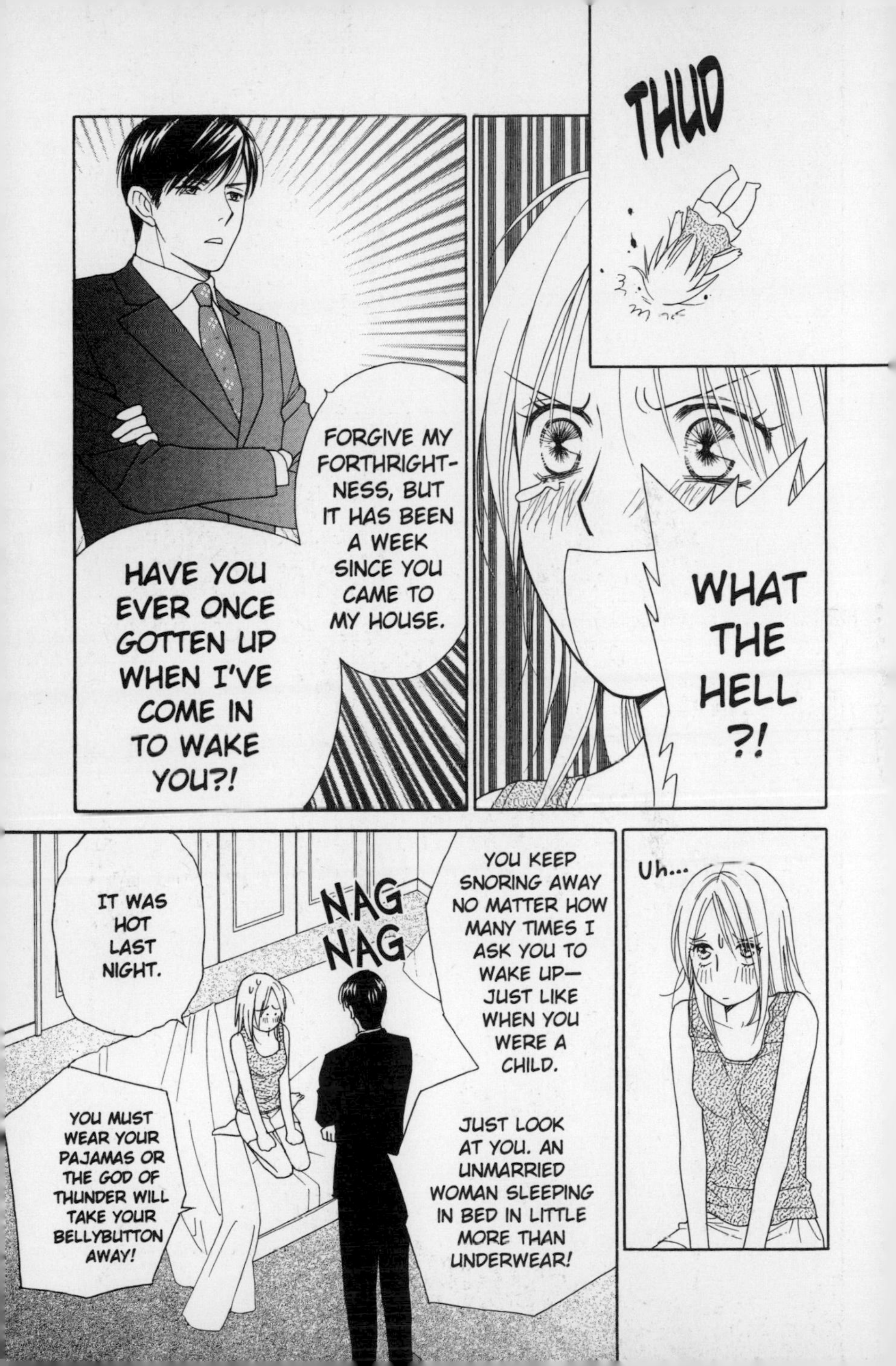
THUD
WHAT THE HELL?!
FORGIVE MY FORTHRIGHTNESS, BUT IT HAS BEEN A WEEK SINCE YOU CAME TO MY HOUSE.
HAVE YOU EVER ONCE GOTTEN UP WHEN I'VE COME IN TO WAKE YOU?!
Uh...
YOU KEEP SNORING AWAY NO MATTER HOW MANY TIMES I ASK YOU TO WAKE UP—JUST LIKE WHEN YOU WERE A CHILD.
NAG NAG
IT WAS HOT LAST NIGHT.
JUST LOOK AT YOU. AN UNMARRIED WOMAN SLEEPING IN BED IN LITTLE MORE THAN UNDERWEAR!
YOU MUST WEAR YOUR PAJAMAS OR THE GOD OF THUNDER WILL TAKE YOUR BELLYBUTTON AWAY!

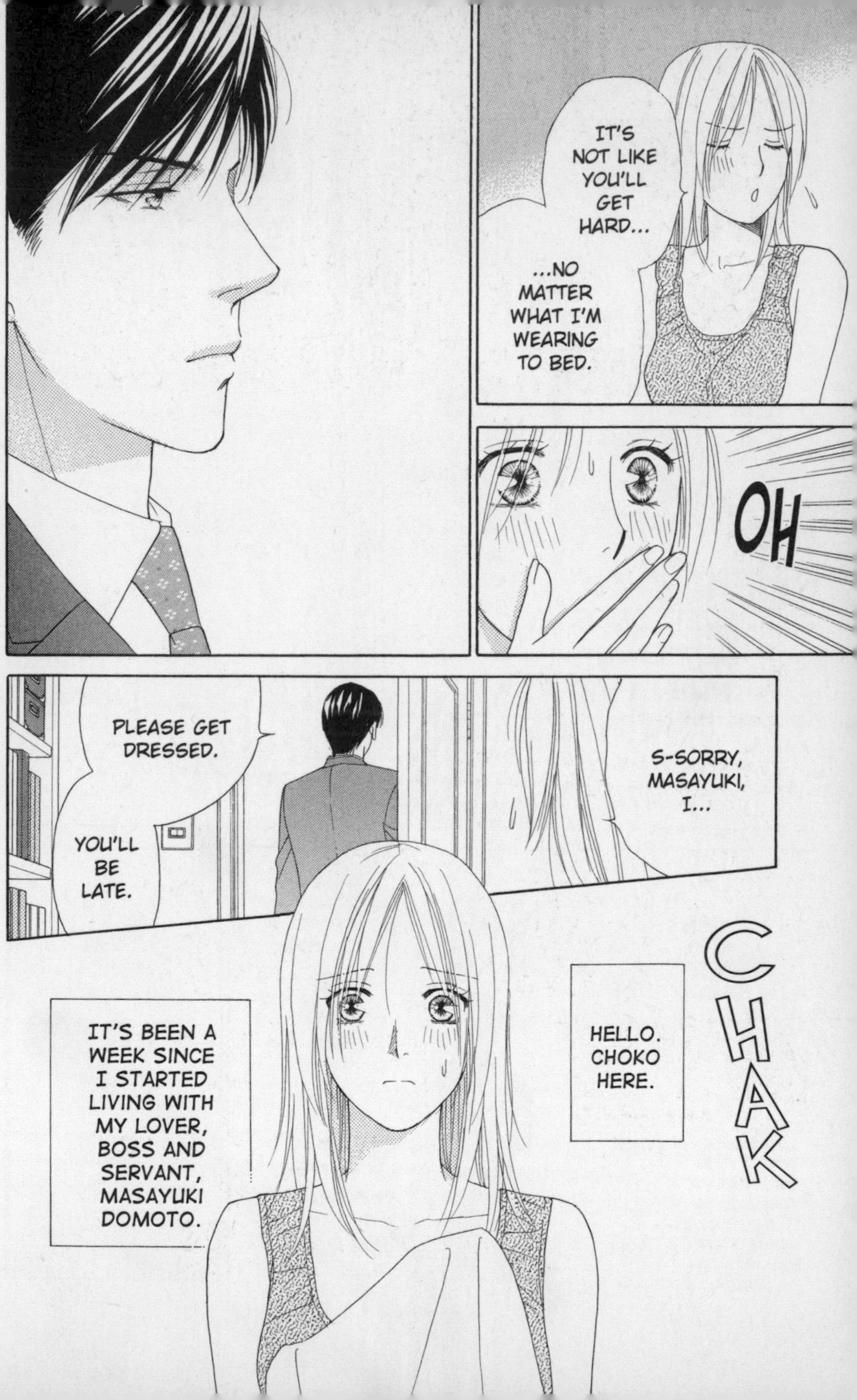
IT'S NOT LIKE YOU'LL GET HARD...
...NO MATTER WHAT I'M WEARING TO BED.
OH
S-SORRY, MASAYUKI, I...
PLEASE GET DRESSED.
YOU'LL BE LATE.
CHAK
HELLO. CHOKO HERE.
IT'S BEEN A WEEK SINCE I STARTED LIVING WITH MY LOVER, BOSS AND SERVANT, MASAYUKI DOMOTO.

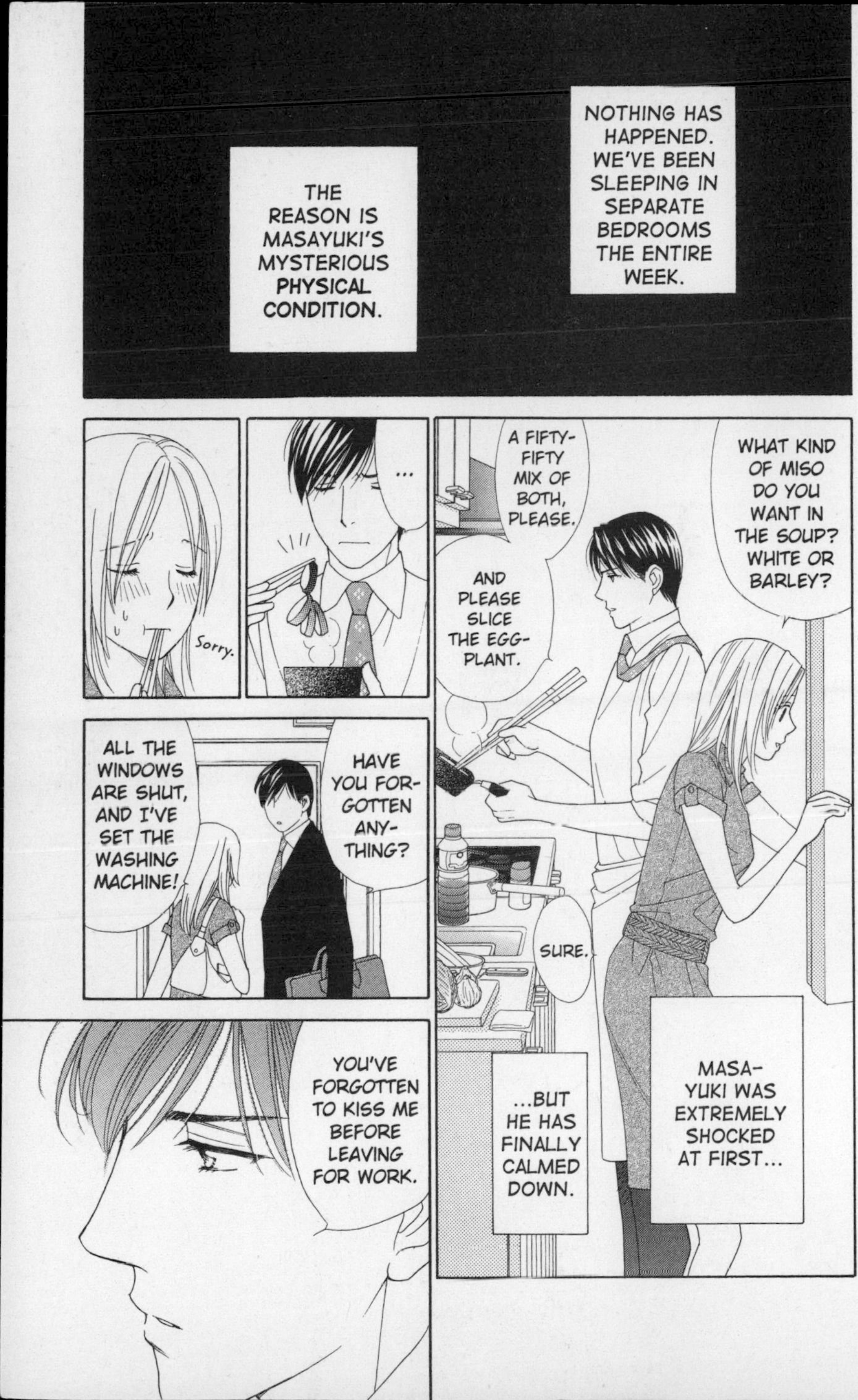
NOTHING HAS HAPPENED. WE'VE BEEN SLEEPING IN SEPARATE BEDROOMS THE ENTIRE WEEK.
THE REASON IS MASAYUKI'S MYSTERIOUS PHYSICAL CONDITION.
WHAT KIND OF MISO DO YOU WANT IN THE SOUP? WHITE OR BARLEY?
A FIFTY-FIFTY MIX OF BOTH, PLEASE.
AND PLEASE SLICE THE EGG-PLANT.
SURE.
MASA-YUKI WAS EXTREMELY SHOCKED AT FIRST...
...BUT HE HAS FINALLY CALMED DOWN.
...
Sorry.
HAVE YOU FOR-GOTTEN ANY-THING?
ALL THE WINDOWS ARE SHUT, AND I'VE SET THE WASHING MACHINE!
YOU'VE FORGOTTEN TO KISS ME BEFORE LEAVING FOR WORK.

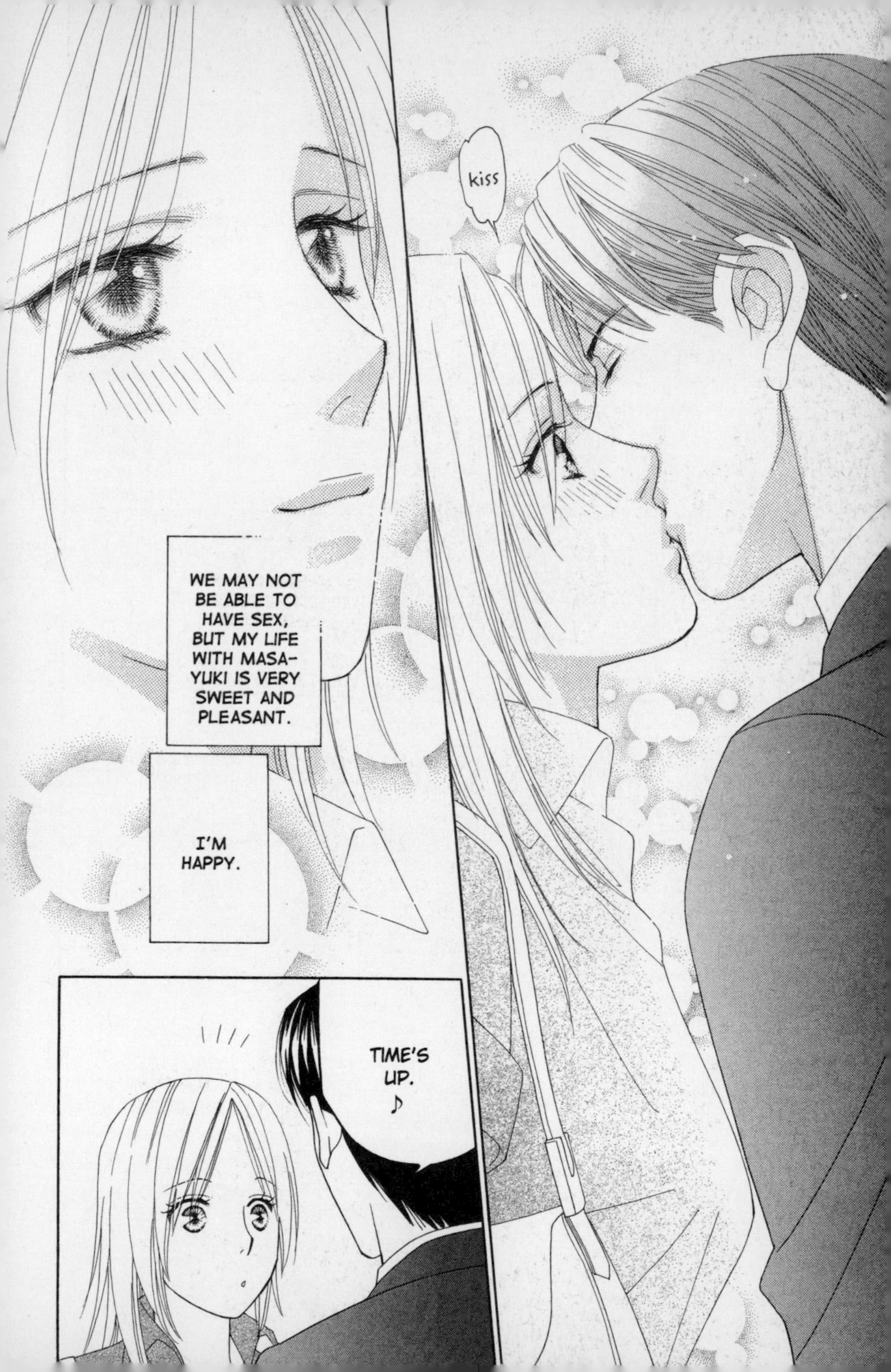
kiss
WE MAY NOT BE ABLE TO HAVE SEX, BUT MY LIFE WITH MASA-YUKI IS VERY SWEET AND PLEASANT.
I'M HAPPY.
TIME'S UP. ♪

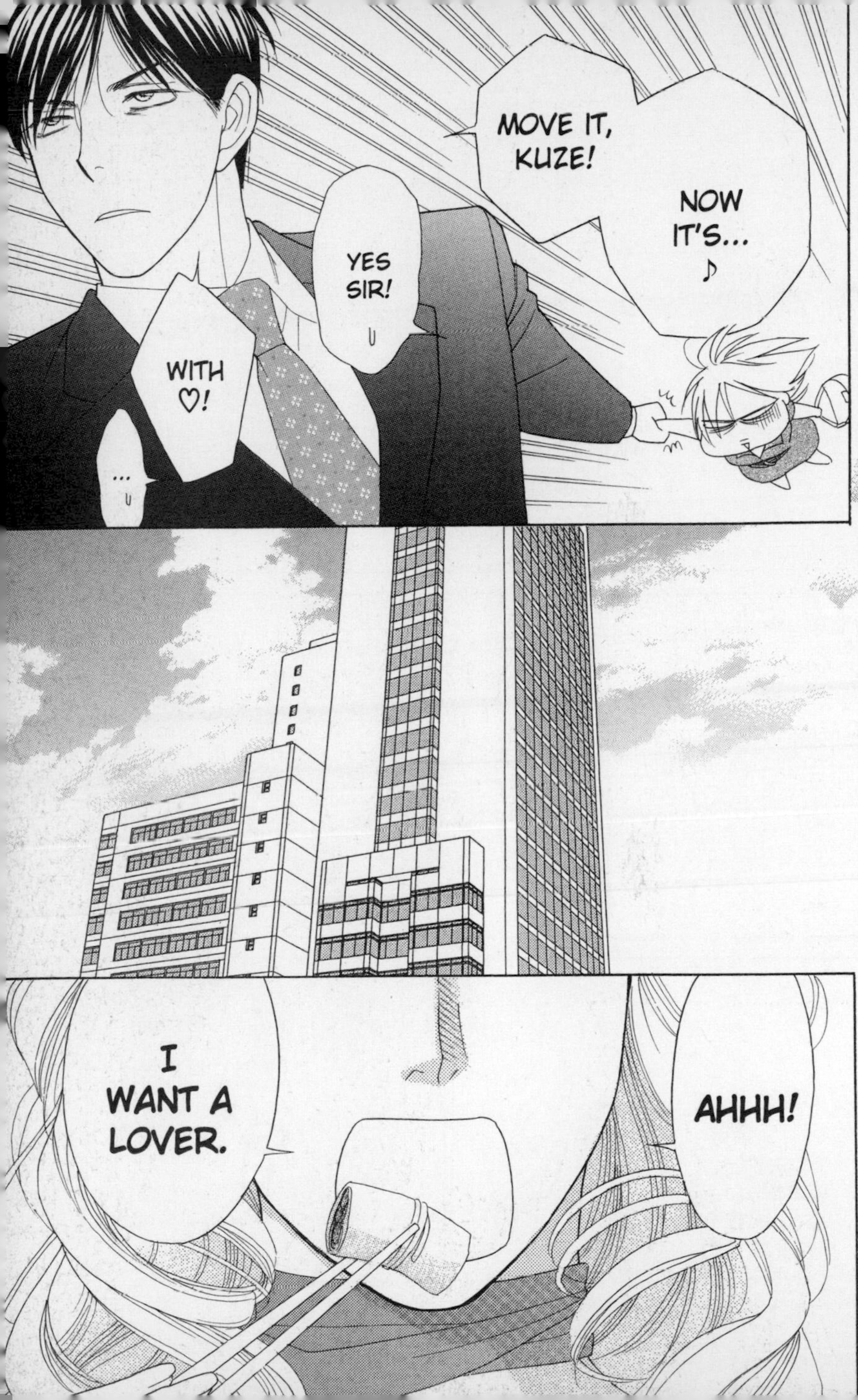
MOVE IT, KUZE!
NOW IT'S... ♪
YES SIR!
WITH ♡!
...
AHHH!
I WANT A LOVER.

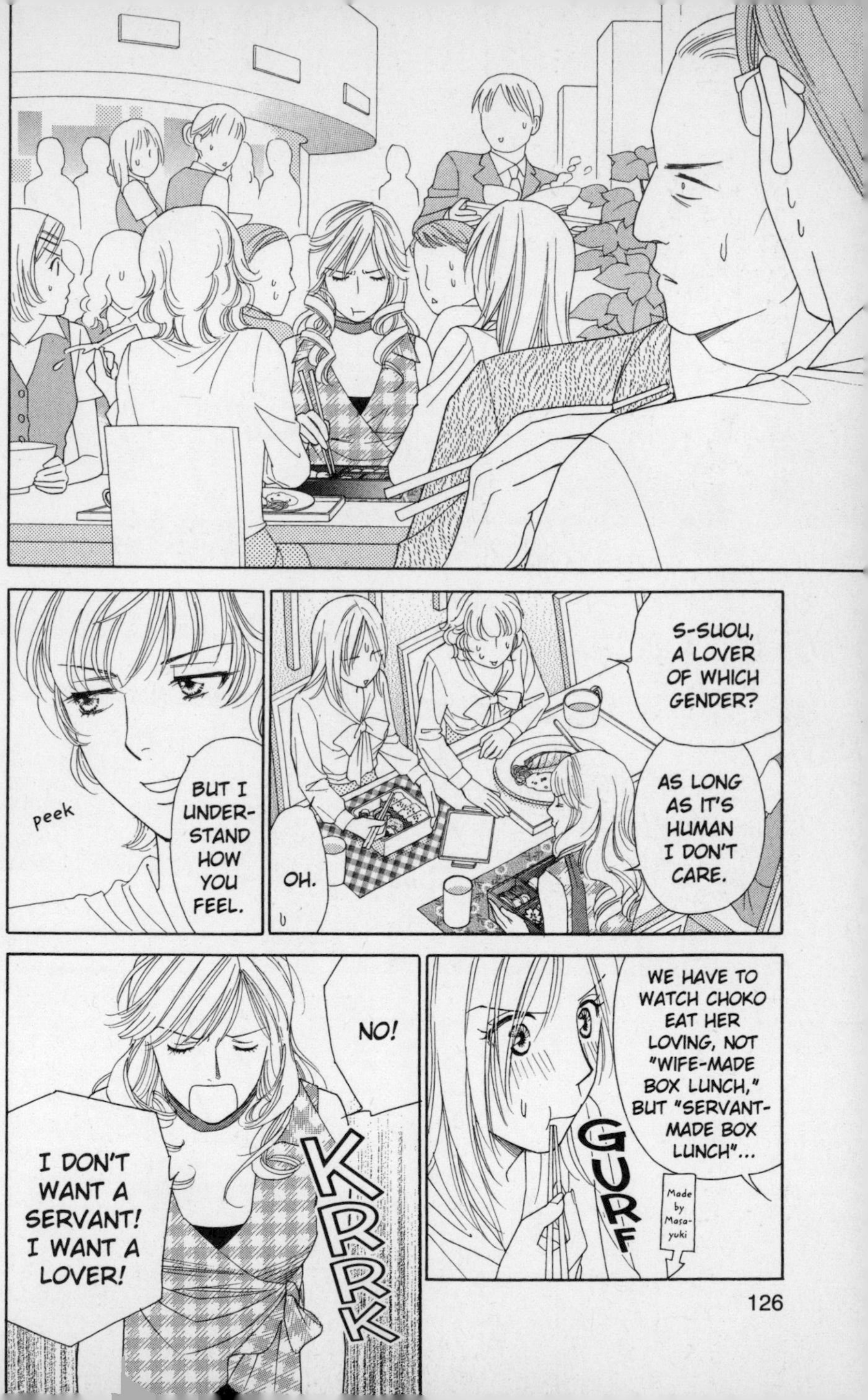
S-SUOU, A LOVER OF WHICH GENDER?
AS LONG AS IT'S HUMAN I DON'T CARE.
OH.
BUT I UNDER-STAND HOW YOU FEEL.
peek
WE HAVE TO WATCH CHOKO EAT HER LOVING, NOT "WIFE-MADE BOX LUNCH," BUT "SERVANT-MADE BOX LUNCH"...
GURF
Made by Masa-yuki
NO!
KRRK
I DON'T WANT A SERVANT! I WANT A LOVER!

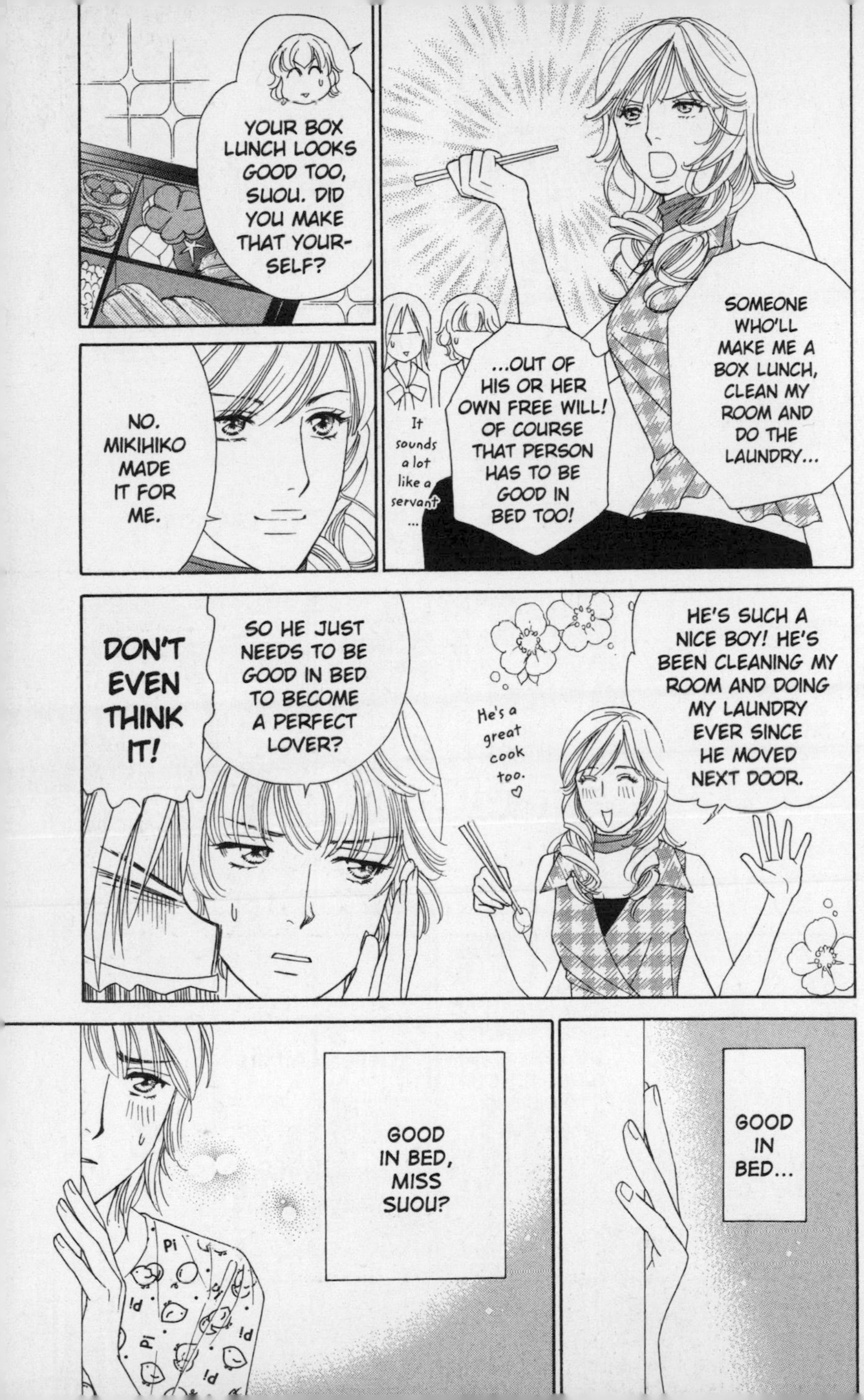
SOMEONE WHO'LL MAKE ME A BOX LUNCH, CLEAN MY ROOM AND DO THE LAUNDRY...
...OUT OF HIS OR HER OWN FREE WILL! OF COURSE THAT PERSON HAS TO BE GOOD IN BED TOO!
It sounds a lot like a servant...
YOUR BOX LUNCH LOOKS GOOD TOO, SUOU. DID YOU MAKE THAT YOUR-SELF?
NO. MIKIHIKO MADE IT FOR ME.
HE'S SUCH A NICE BOY! HE'S BEEN CLEANING MY ROOM AND DOING MY LAUNDRY EVER SINCE HE MOVED NEXT DOOR.
He's a great cook too.
SO HE JUST NEEDS TO BE GOOD IN BED TO BECOME A PERFECT LOVER?
DON'T EVEN THINK IT!
GOOD IN BED...
GOOD IN BED, MISS SUOU?

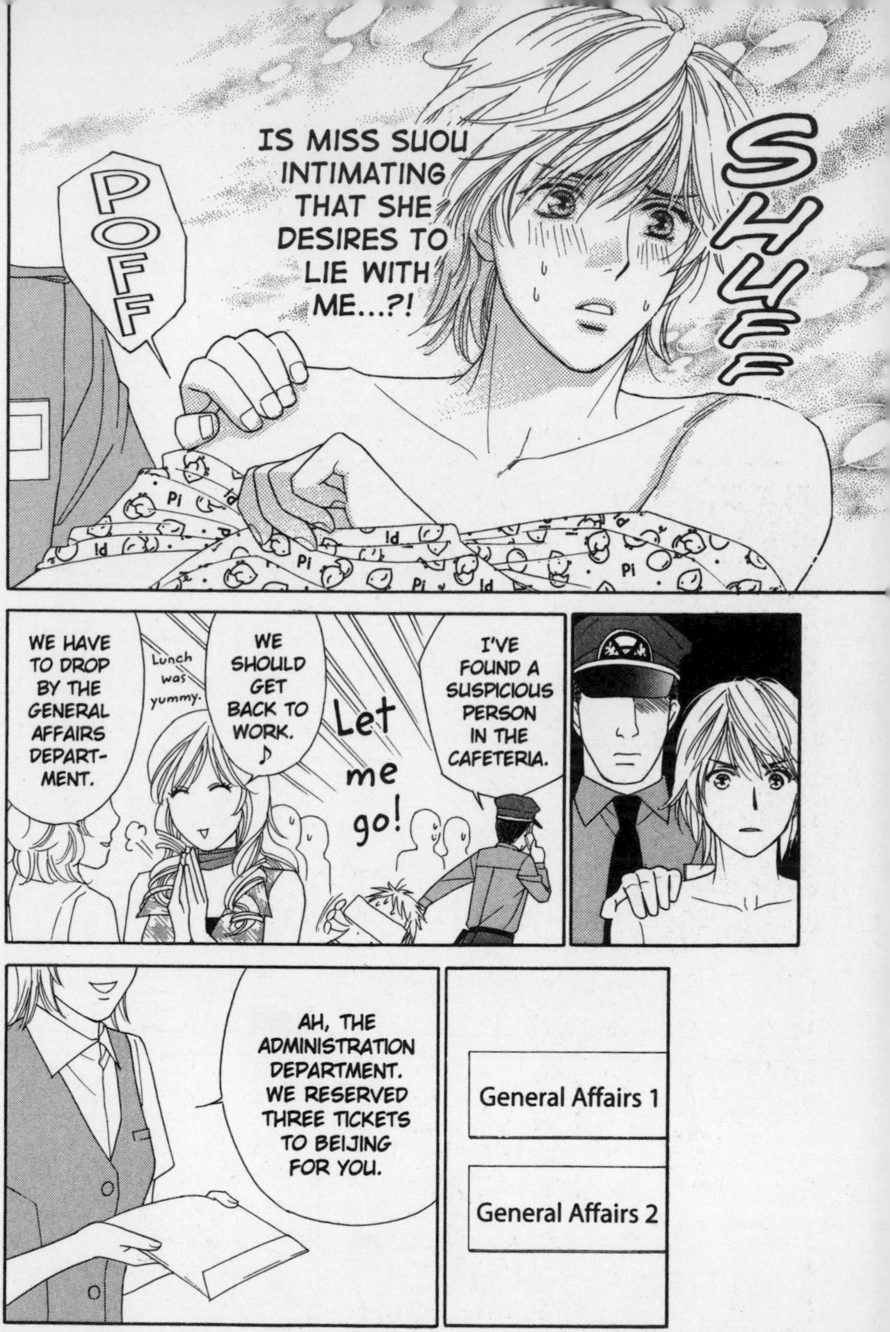
SHUFF
IS MISS SUOU INTIMATING THAT SHE DESIRES TO LIE WITH ME...?!
POFF
Pi
I'VE FOUND A SUSPICIOUS PERSON IN THE CAFETERIA.
Let me go!
WE SHOULD GET BACK TO WORK. ♪
Lunch was yummy.
WE HAVE TO DROP BY THE GENERAL AFFAIRS DEPARTMENT.
General Affairs 1
General Affairs 2
AH, THE ADMINISTRATION DEPARTMENT. WE RESERVED THREE TICKETS TO BEIJING FOR YOU.

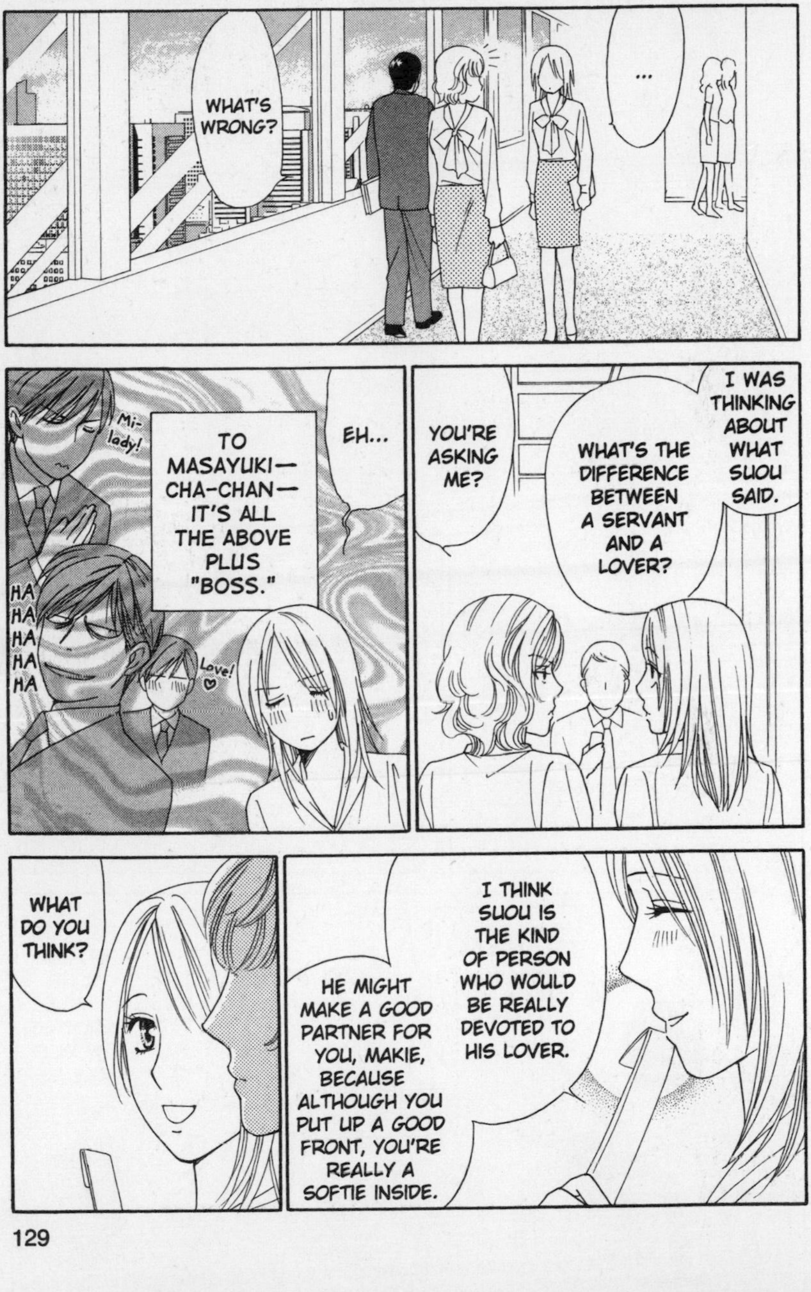
...
WHAT'S WRONG?
I WAS THINKING ABOUT WHAT SUOU SAID.
WHAT'S THE DIFFERENCE BETWEEN A SERVANT AND A LOVER?
YOU'RE ASKING ME?
EH...
TO MASAYUKI—CHA-CHAN—IT'S ALL THE ABOVE PLUS "BOSS."
Mi-lady!
HA HA HA HA HA
Love!
I THINK SUOU IS THE KIND OF PERSON WHO WOULD BE REALLY DEVOTED TO HIS LOVER.
HE MIGHT MAKE A GOOD PARTNER FOR YOU, MAKIE, BECAUSE ALTHOUGH YOU PUT UP A GOOD FRONT, YOU'RE REALLY A SOFTIE INSIDE.
WHAT DO YOU THINK?

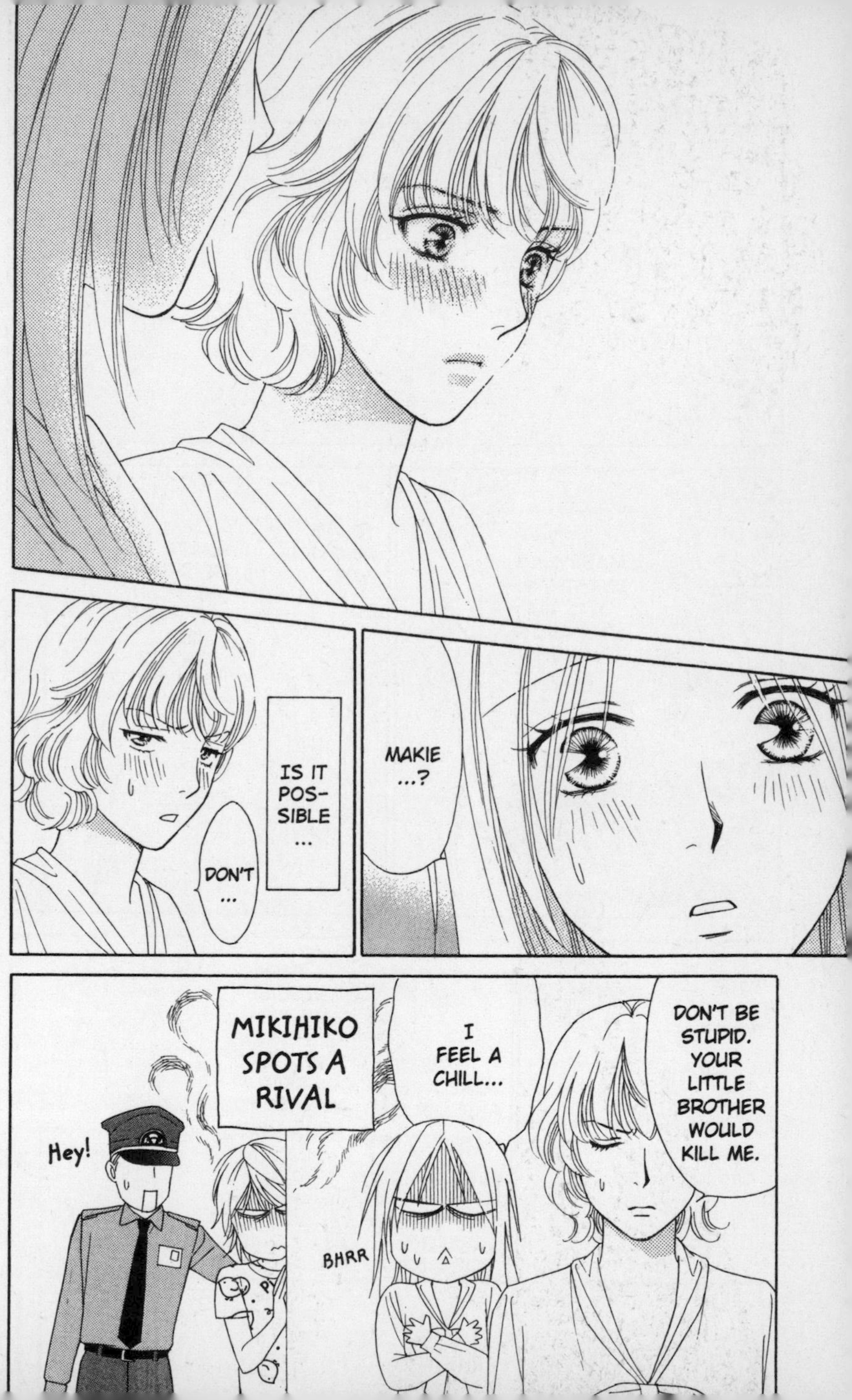
MAKIE ...?
IS IT POS-SIBLE ...
DON'T ...
DON'T BE STUPID. YOUR LITTLE BROTHER WOULD KILL ME.
I FEEL A CHILL...
BHRR
MIKIHIKO SPOTS A RIVAL
Hey!

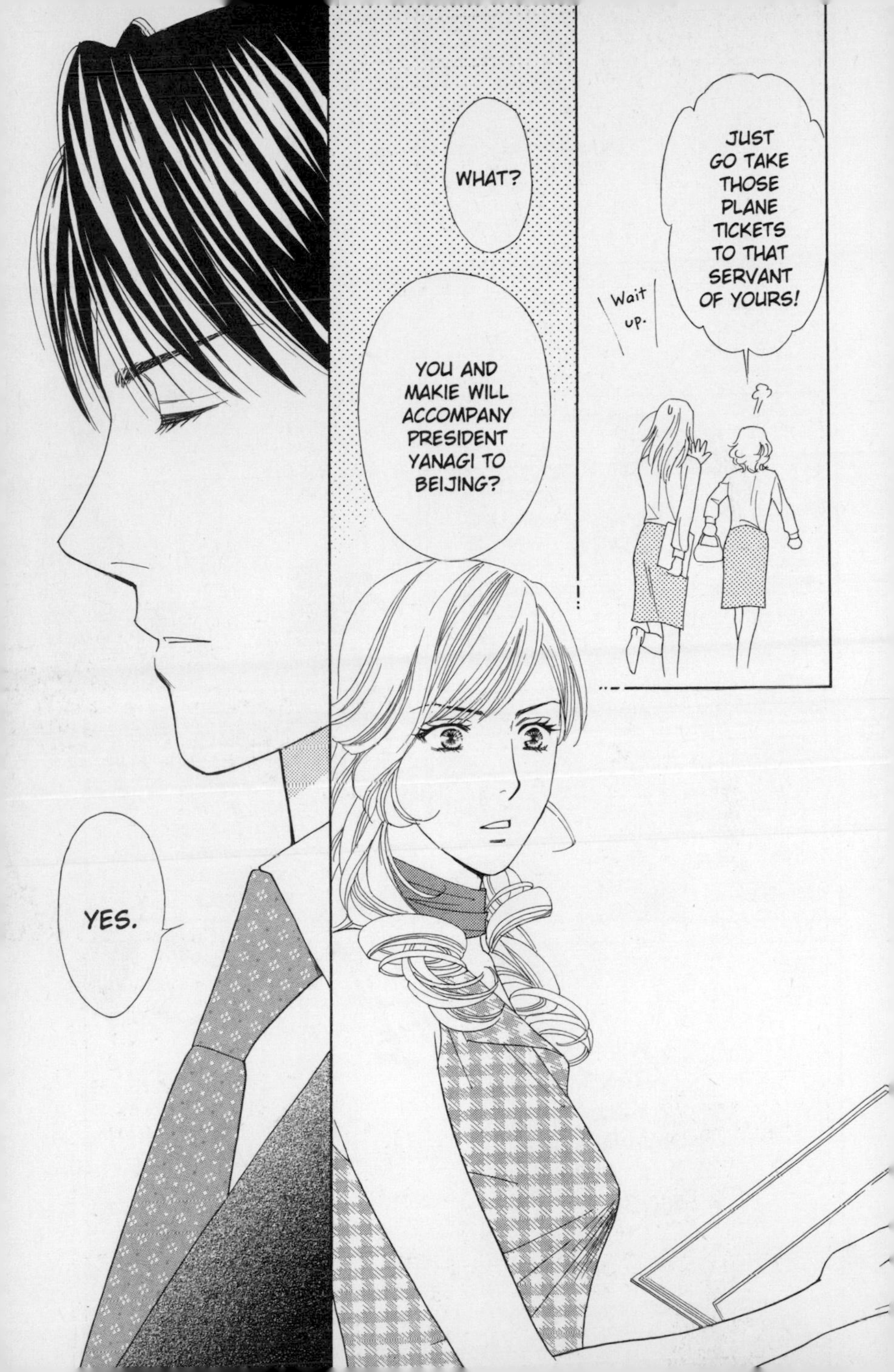
JUST GO TAKE THOSE PLANE TICKETS TO THAT SERVANT OF YOURS!
Wait up.
WHAT?
YOU AND MAKIE WILL ACCOMPANY PRESIDENT YANAGI TO BEIJING?
YES.

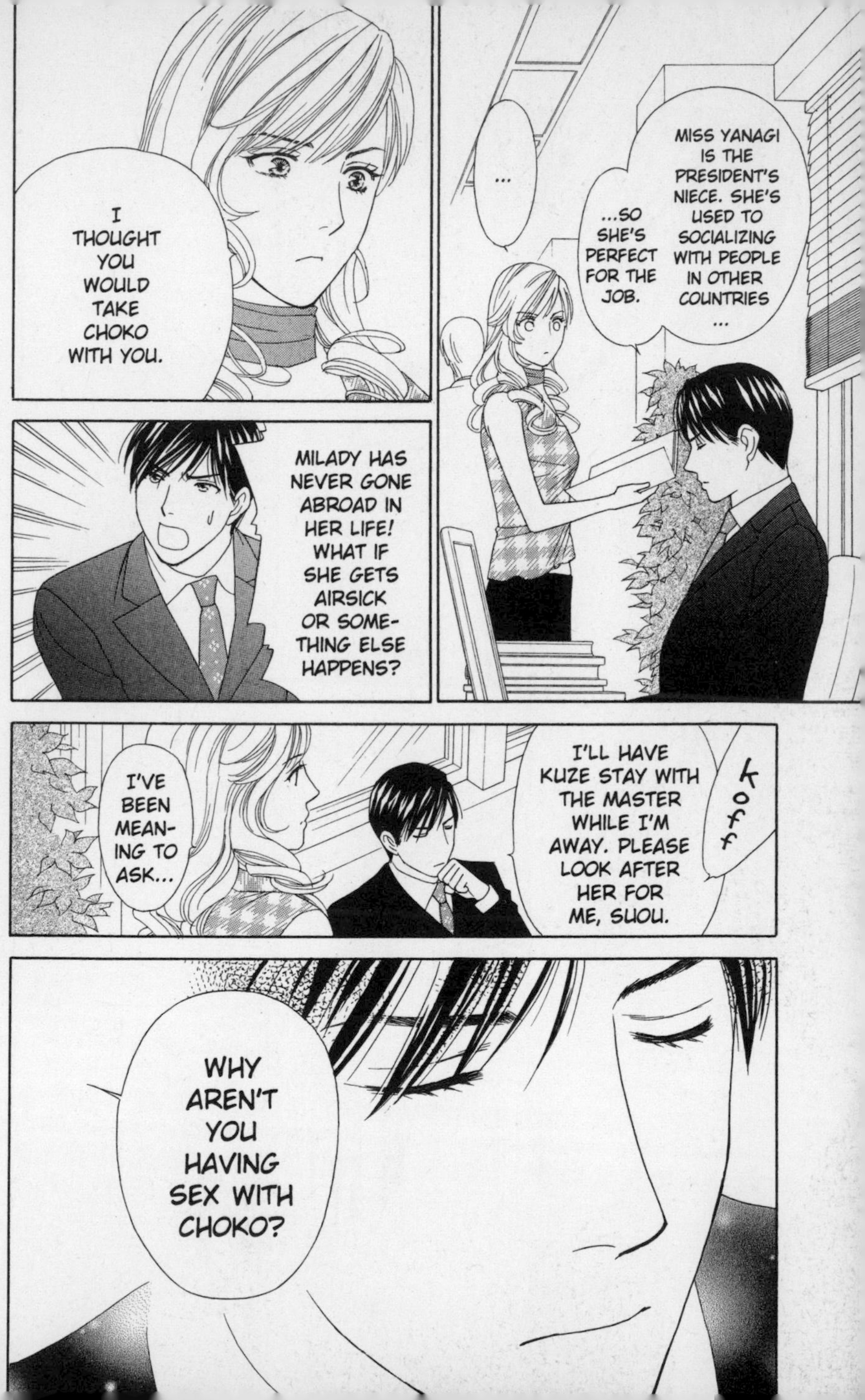
MISS YANAGI IS THE PRESIDENT'S NIECE. SHE'S USED TO SOCIALIZING WITH PEOPLE IN OTHER COUNTRIES ...
...SO SHE'S PERFECT FOR THE JOB.
...
I THOUGHT YOU WOULD TAKE CHOKO WITH YOU.
MILADY HAS NEVER GONE ABROAD IN HER LIFE! WHAT IF SHE GETS AIRSICK OR SOME-THING ELSE HAPPENS?
koff
I'LL HAVE KUZE STAY WITH THE MASTER WHILE I'M AWAY. PLEASE LOOK AFTER HER FOR ME, SUOU.
I'VE BEEN MEAN-ING TO ASK...
WHY AREN'T YOU HAVING SEX WITH CHOKO?

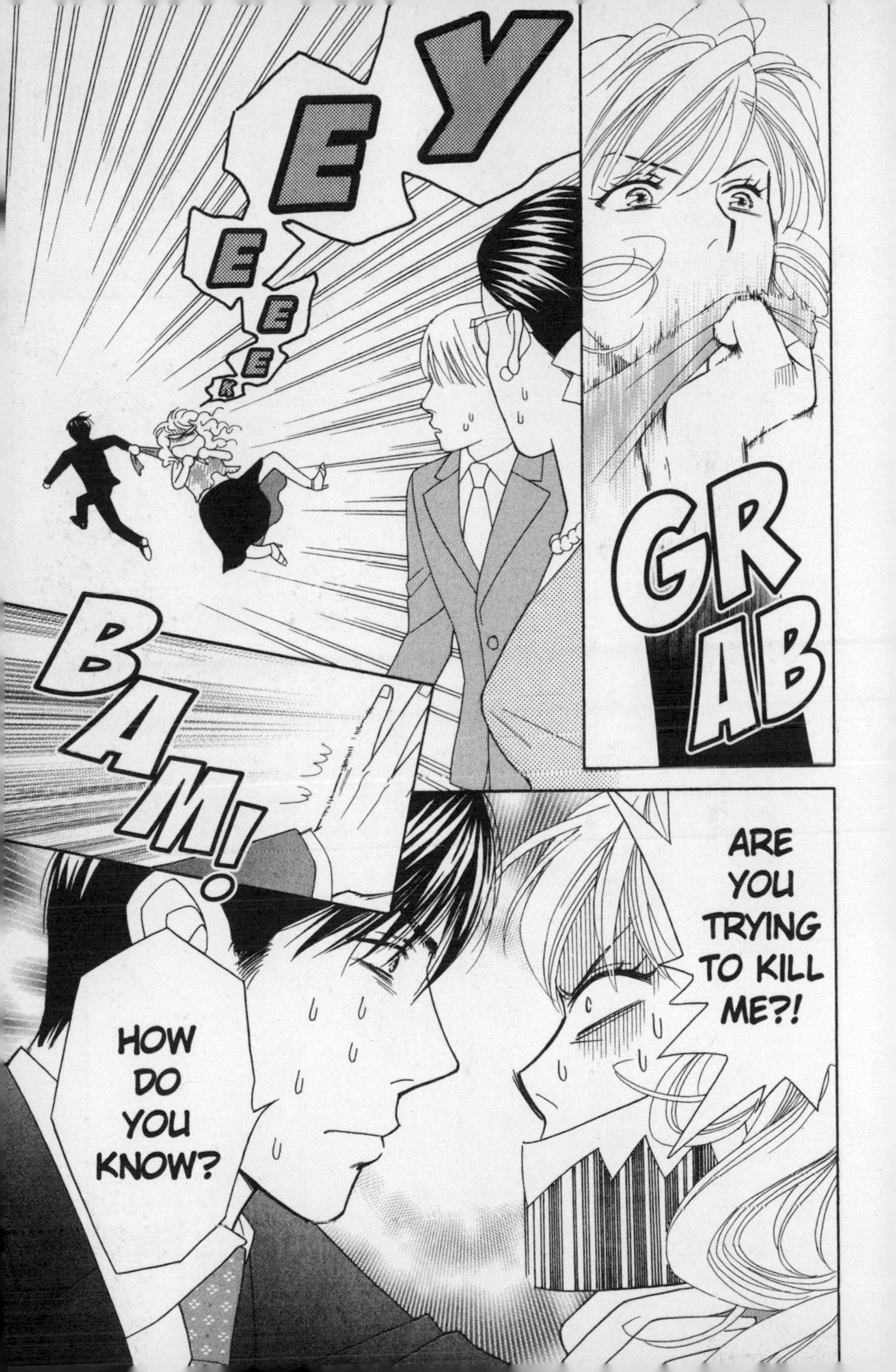

GRAB
YEEEEK
BAM!
ARE YOU TRYING TO KILL ME?!
HOW DO YOU KNOW?

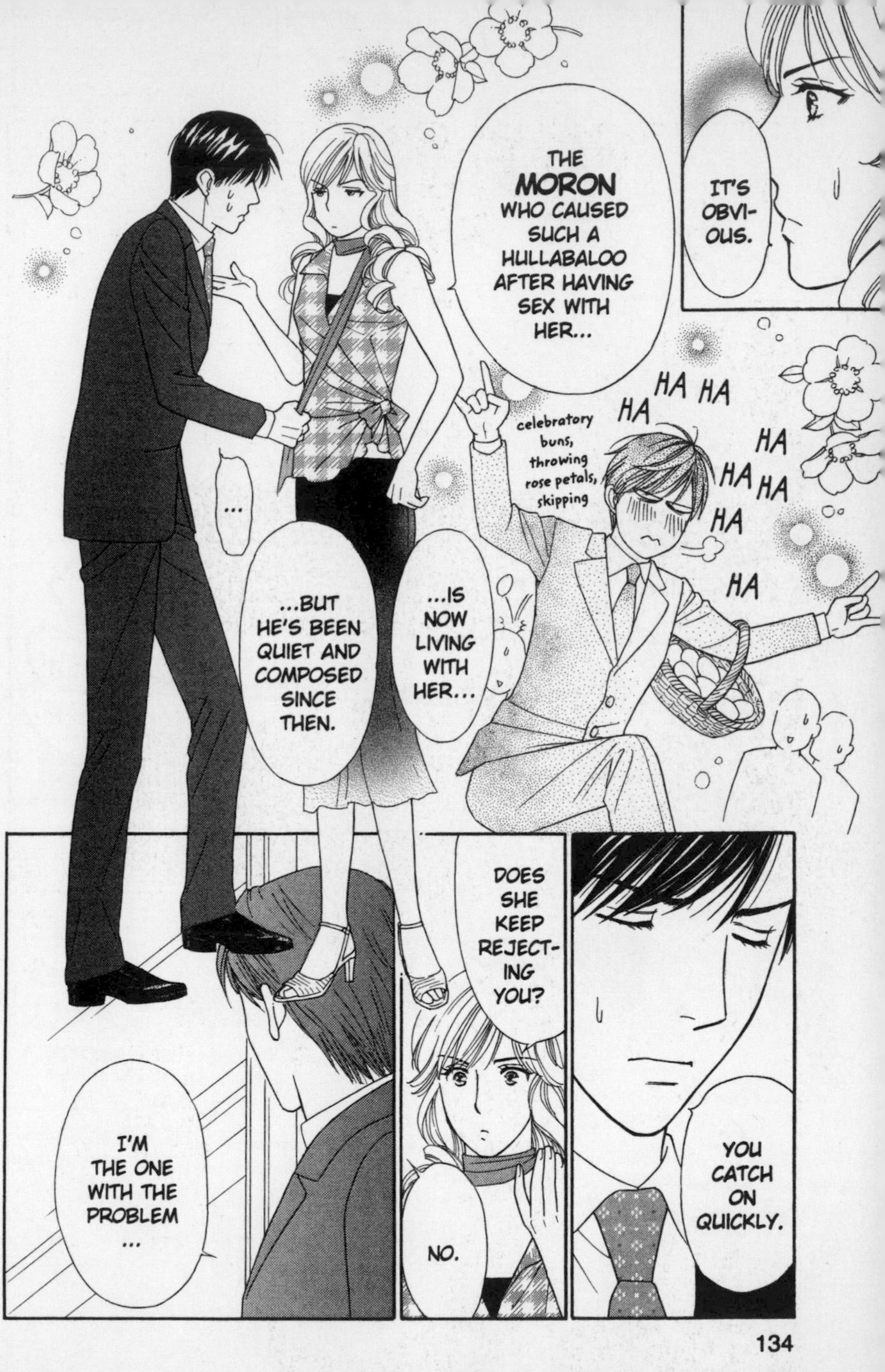
IT'S OBVIOUS.
THE MORON WHO CAUSED SUCH A HULLABALOO AFTER HAVING SEX WITH HER...
HA HA HA
HA HA
HA HA HA
HA
celebratory buns, throwing rose petals, skipping
...IS NOW LIVING WITH HER...
...BUT HE'S BEEN QUIET AND COMPOSED SINCE THEN.
...
YOU CATCH ON QUICKLY.
DOES SHE KEEP REJECTING YOU?
NO.
I'M THE ONE WITH THE PROBLEM...

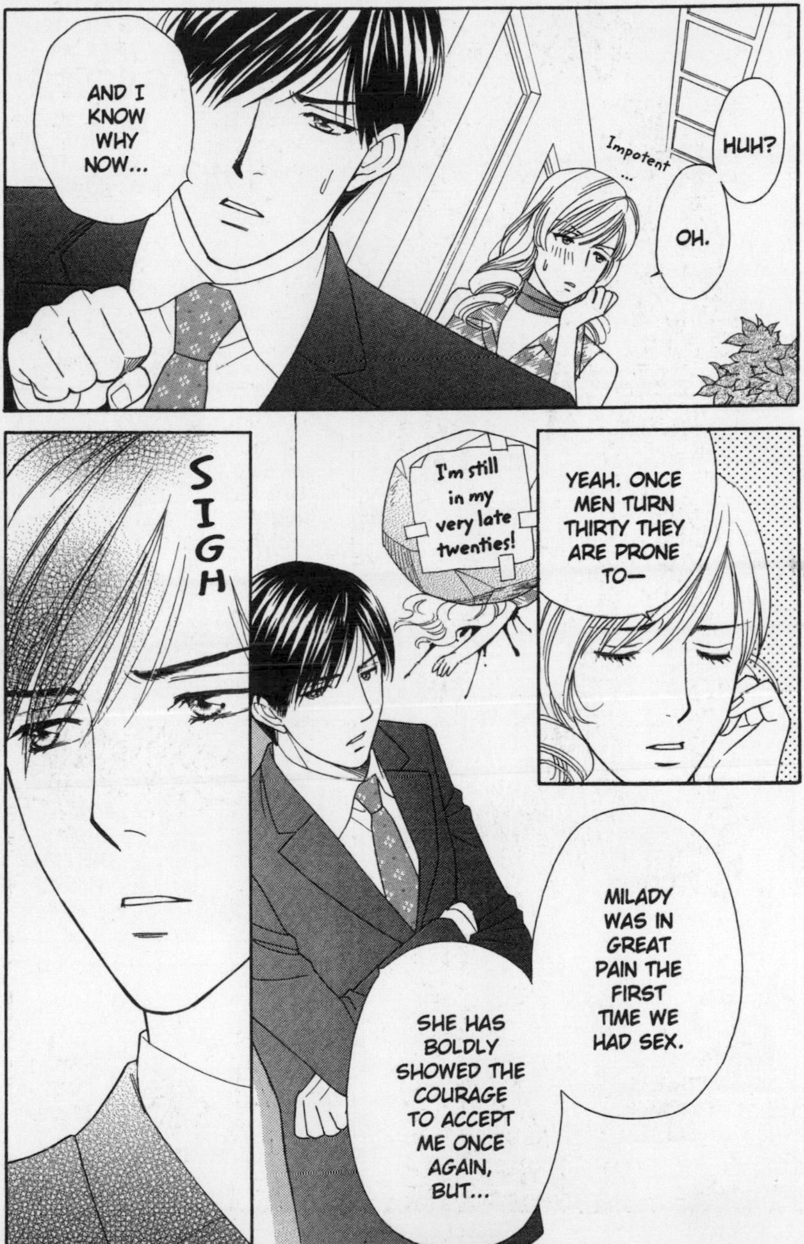

HUH?
Impotent...
OH.
AND I KNOW WHY NOW...
YEAH. ONCE MEN TURN THIRTY THEY ARE PRONE TO—
I'm still in my very late twenties!
MILADY WAS IN GREAT PAIN THE FIRST TIME WE HAD SEX.
SHE HAS BOLDLY SHOWED THE COURAGE TO ACCEPT ME ONCE AGAIN, BUT...
SIGH

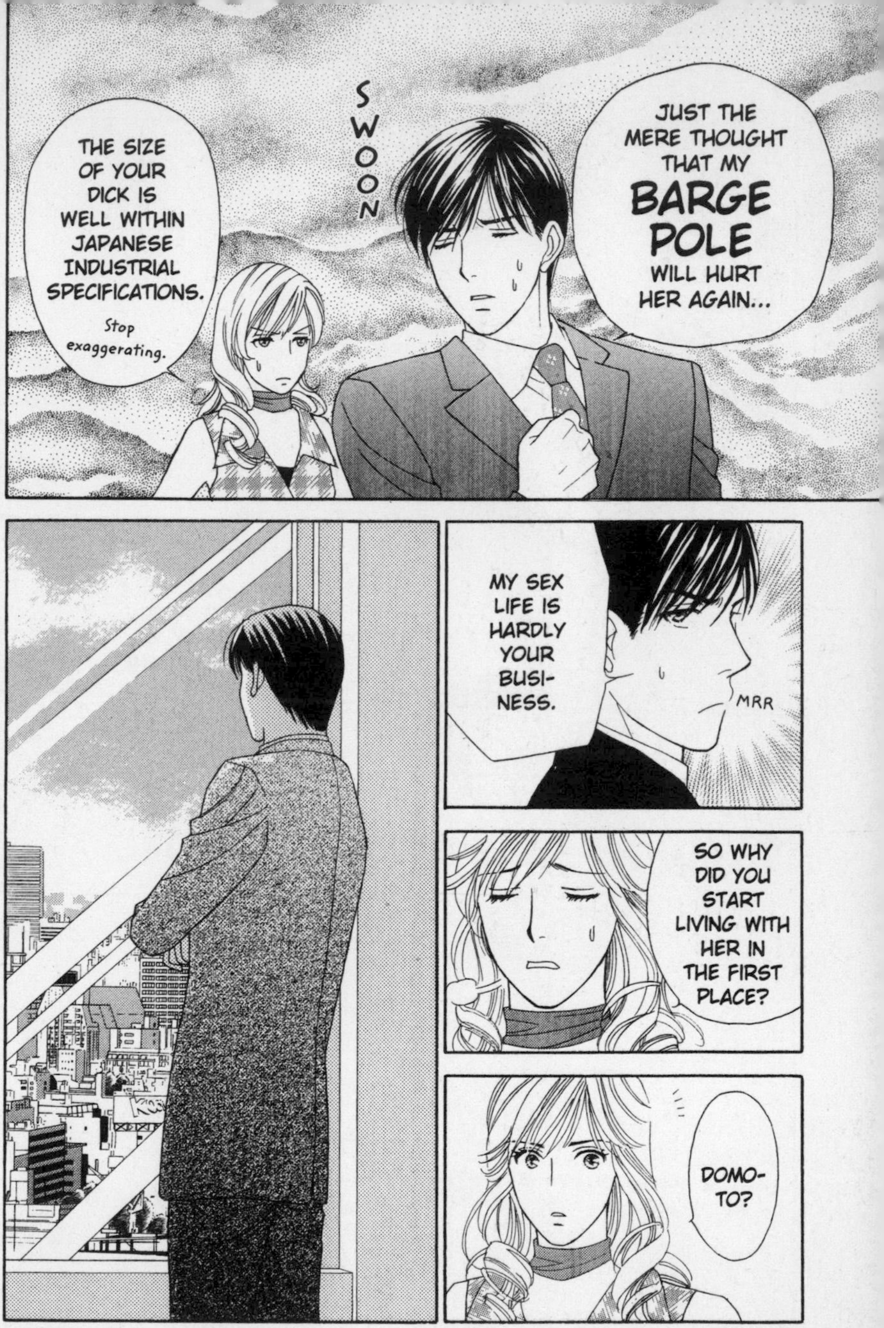
JUST THE MERE THOUGHT THAT MY **BARGE POLE** WILL HURT HER AGAIN...
SWOON
THE SIZE OF YOUR DICK IS WELL WITHIN JAPANESE INDUSTRIAL SPECIFICATIONS.
Stop exaggerating.
MY SEX LIFE IS HARDLY YOUR BUSI-NESS.
MRR
SO WHY DID YOU START LIVING WITH HER IN THE FIRST PLACE?
DOMO-TO?

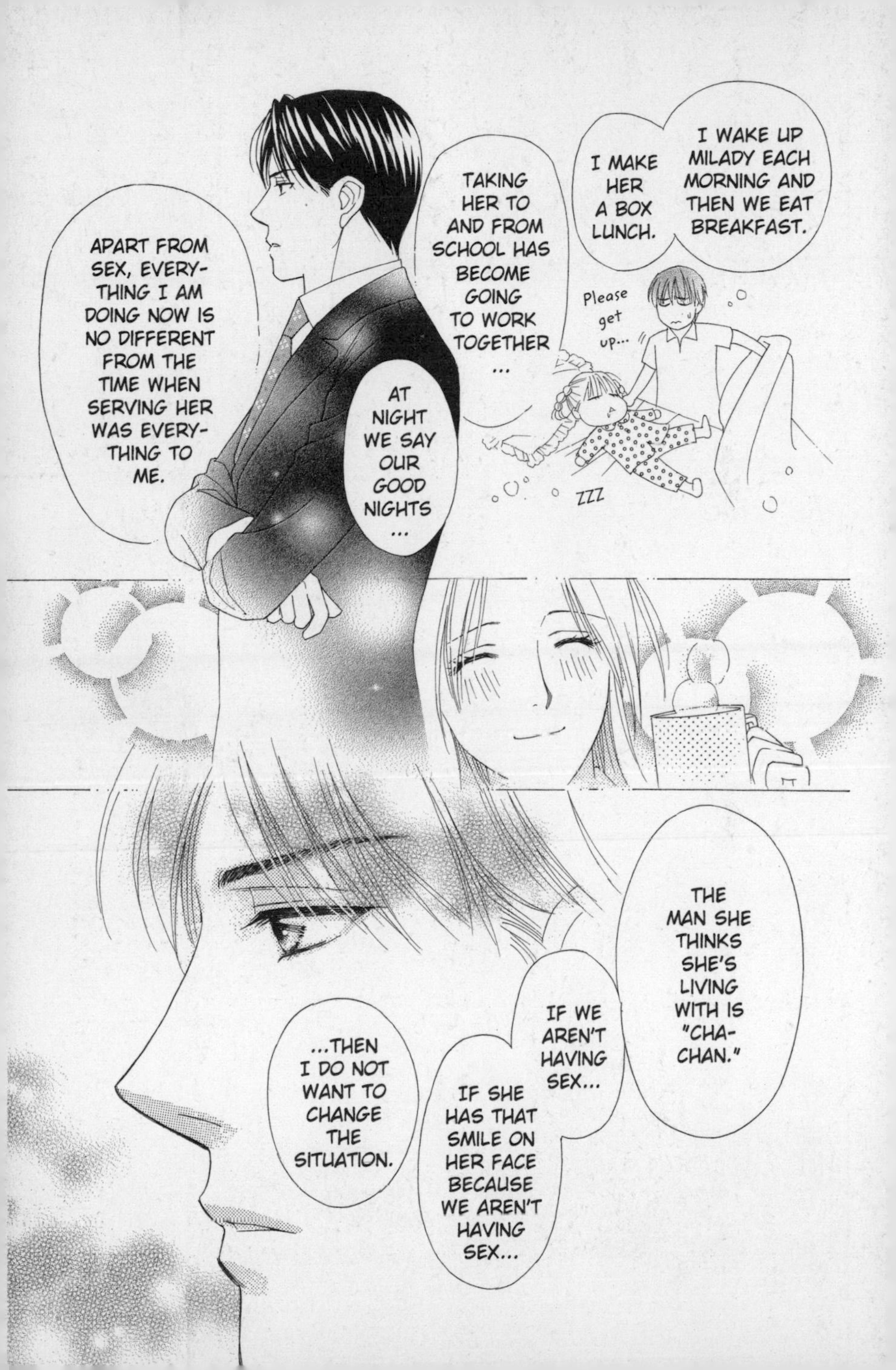
I WAKE UP MILADY EACH MORNING AND THEN WE EAT BREAKFAST.
I MAKE HER A BOX LUNCH.
Please get up...
ZZZ
TAKING HER TO AND FROM SCHOOL HAS BECOME GOING TO WORK TOGETHER ...
AT NIGHT WE SAY OUR GOOD NIGHTS ...
APART FROM SEX, EVERY-THING I AM DOING NOW IS NO DIFFERENT FROM THE TIME WHEN SERVING HER WAS EVERY-THING TO ME.
THE MAN SHE THINKS SHE'S LIVING WITH IS "CHA-CHAN."
IF WE AREN'T HAVING SEX...
IF SHE HAS THAT SMILE ON HER FACE BECAUSE WE AREN'T HAVING SEX...
...THEN I DO NOT WANT TO CHANGE THE SITUATION.

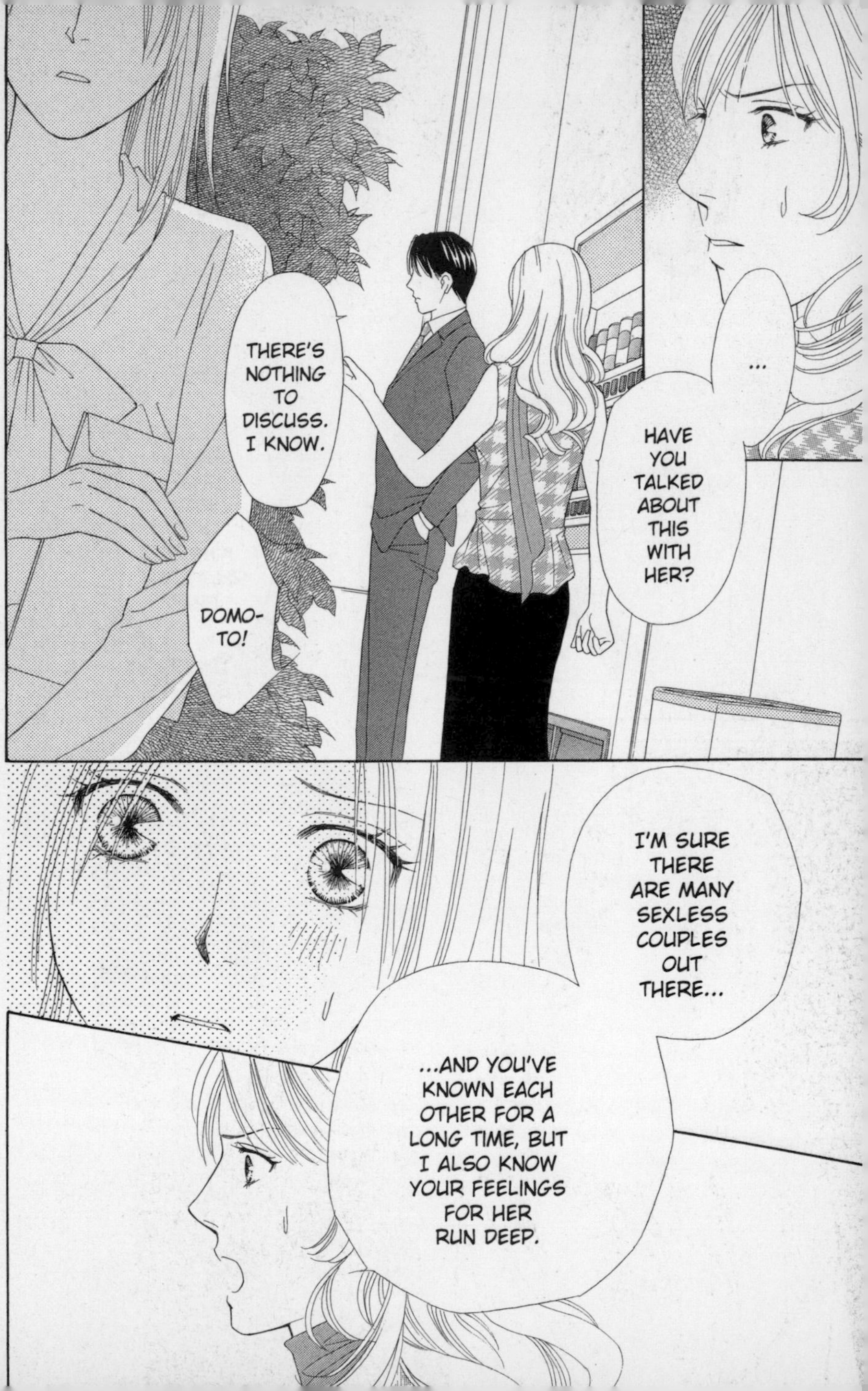
...
HAVE YOU TALKED ABOUT THIS WITH HER?
THERE'S NOTHING TO DISCUSS. I KNOW.
DOMOTO!
I'M SURE THERE ARE MANY SEXLESS COUPLES OUT THERE...
...AND YOU'VE KNOWN EACH OTHER FOR A LONG TIME, BUT I ALSO KNOW YOUR FEELINGS FOR HER RUN DEEP.

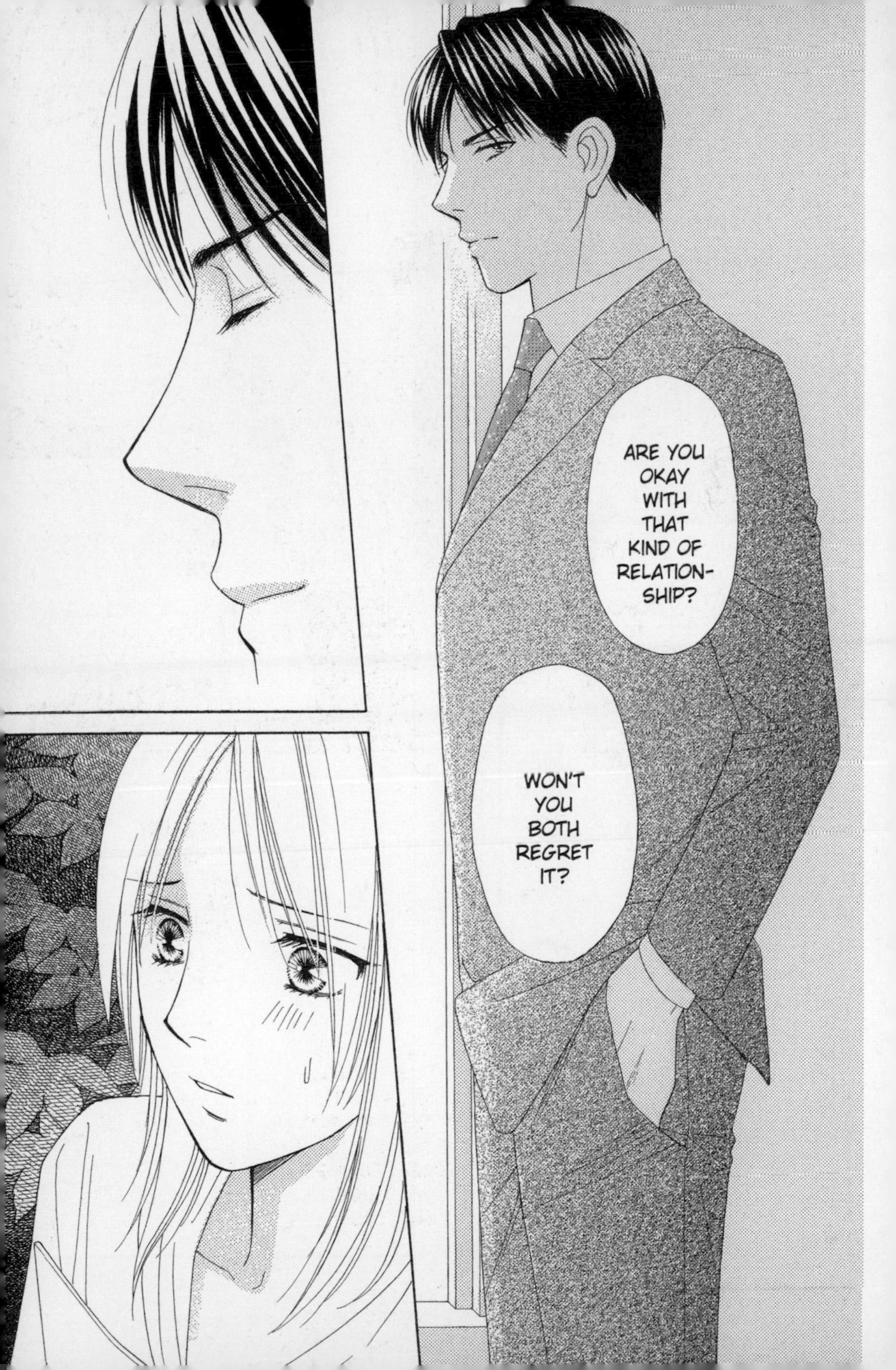
ARE YOU OKAY WITH THAT KIND OF RELATION-SHIP?
WON'T YOU BOTH REGRET IT?

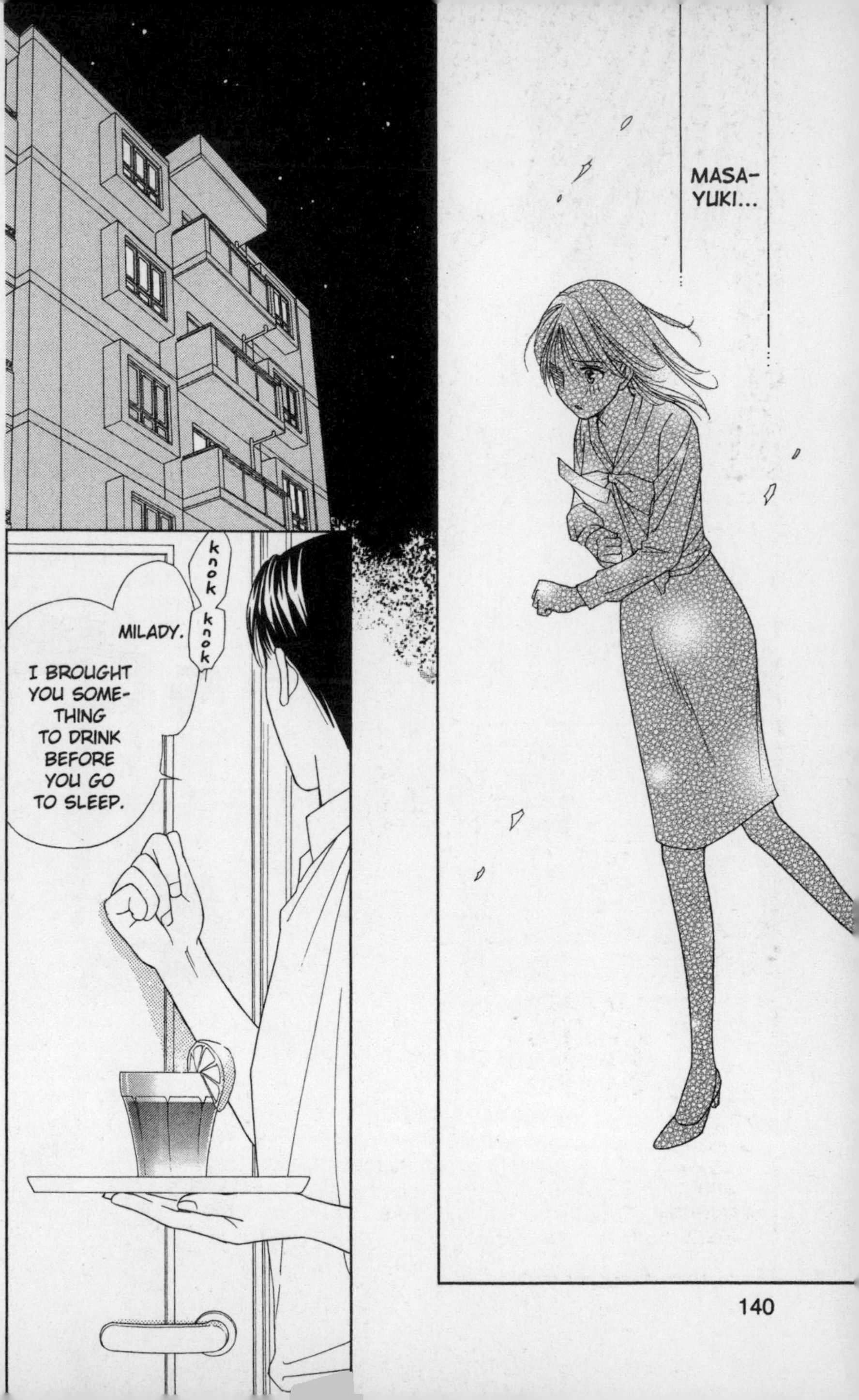
MASA-YUKI...
knok knok
MILADY.
I BROUGHT YOU SOMETHING TO DRINK BEFORE YOU GO TO SLEEP.

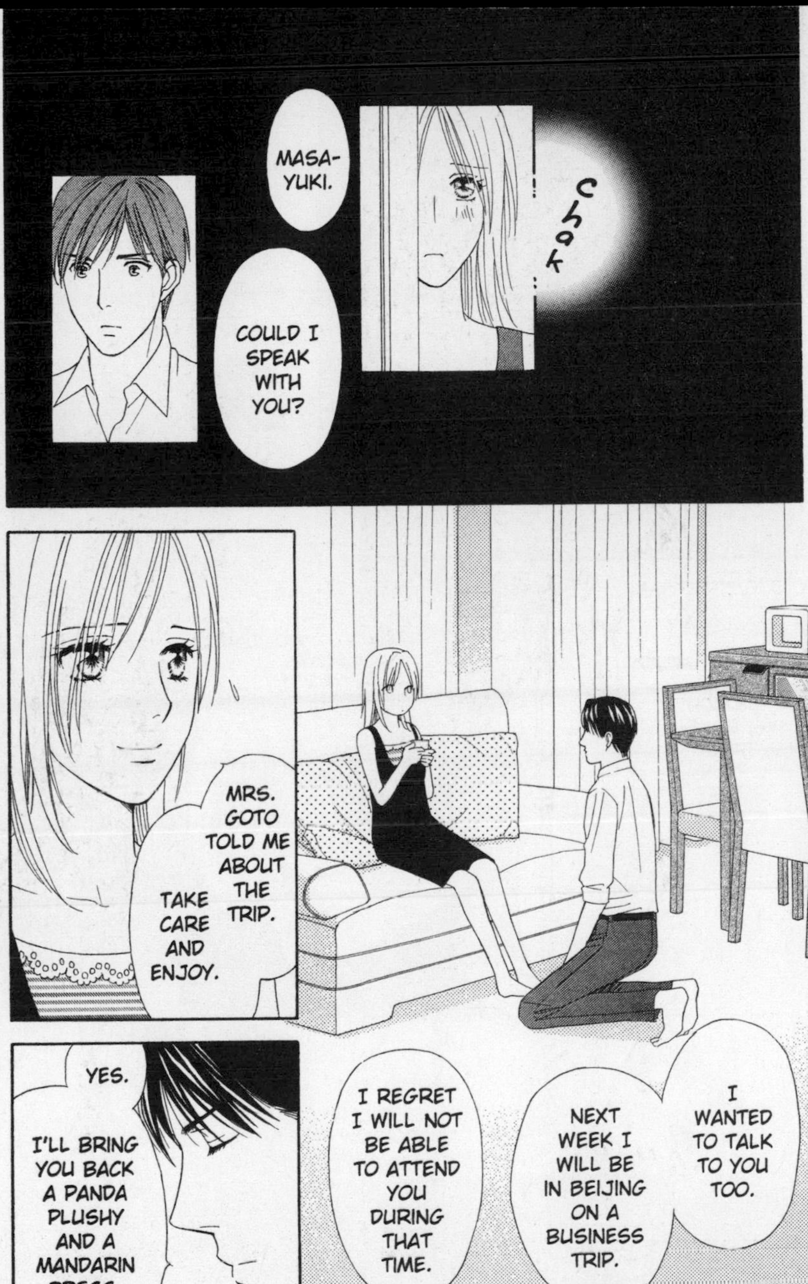
Chak
MASA-YUKI.
COULD I SPEAK WITH YOU?
I WANTED TO TALK TO YOU TOO.
NEXT WEEK I WILL BE IN BEIJING ON A BUSINESS TRIP.
I REGRET I WILL NOT BE ABLE TO ATTEND YOU DURING THAT TIME.
MRS. GOTO TOLD ME ABOUT THE TRIP.
TAKE CARE AND ENJOY.
YES.
I'LL BRING YOU BACK A PANDA PLUSHY AND A MANDARIN DRESS.

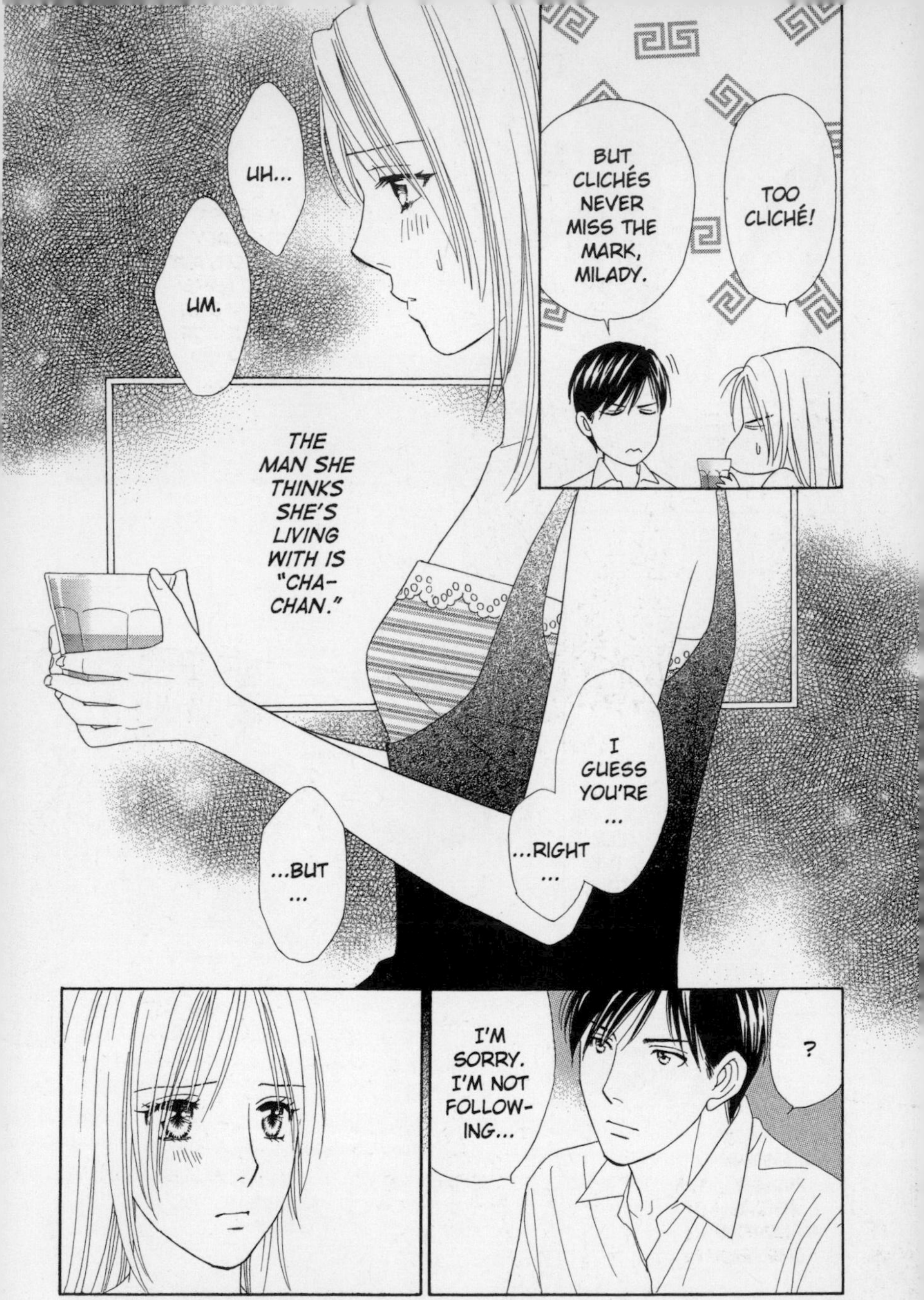
TOO CLICHÉ!
BUT CLICHÉS NEVER MISS THE MARK, MILADY.
UH...
UM.
THE MAN SHE THINKS SHE'S LIVING WITH IS "CHA-CHAN."
I GUESS YOU'RE ...
...RIGHT ...
...BUT ...
?
I'M SORRY. I'M NOT FOLLOWING...

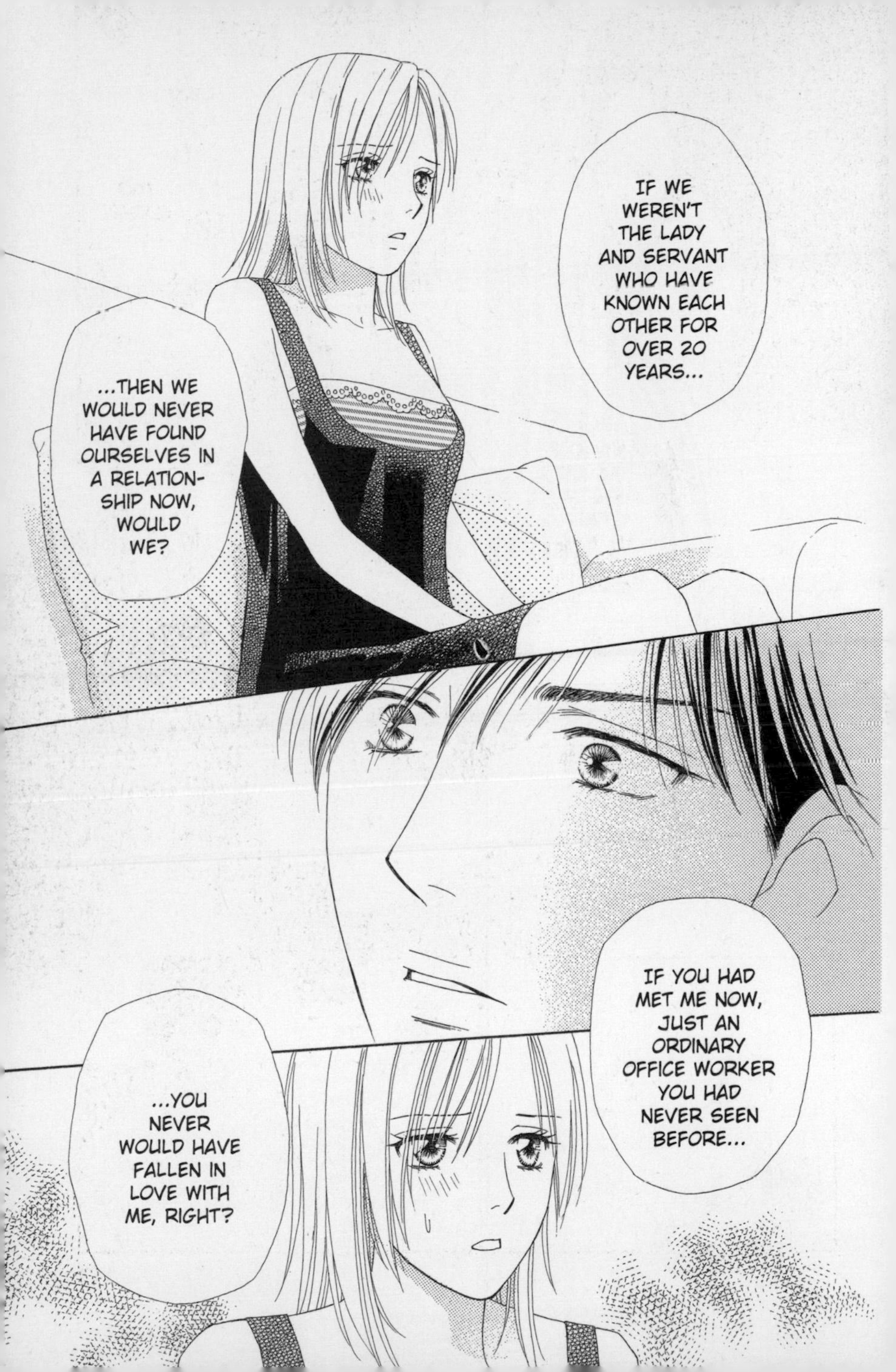
IF WE WEREN'T THE LADY AND SERVANT WHO HAVE KNOWN EACH OTHER FOR OVER 20 YEARS...
...THEN WE WOULD NEVER HAVE FOUND OURSELVES IN A RELATION-SHIP NOW, WOULD WE?
IF YOU HAD MET ME NOW, JUST AN ORDINARY OFFICE WORKER YOU HAD NEVER SEEN BEFORE...
...YOU NEVER WOULD HAVE FALLEN IN LOVE WITH ME, RIGHT?

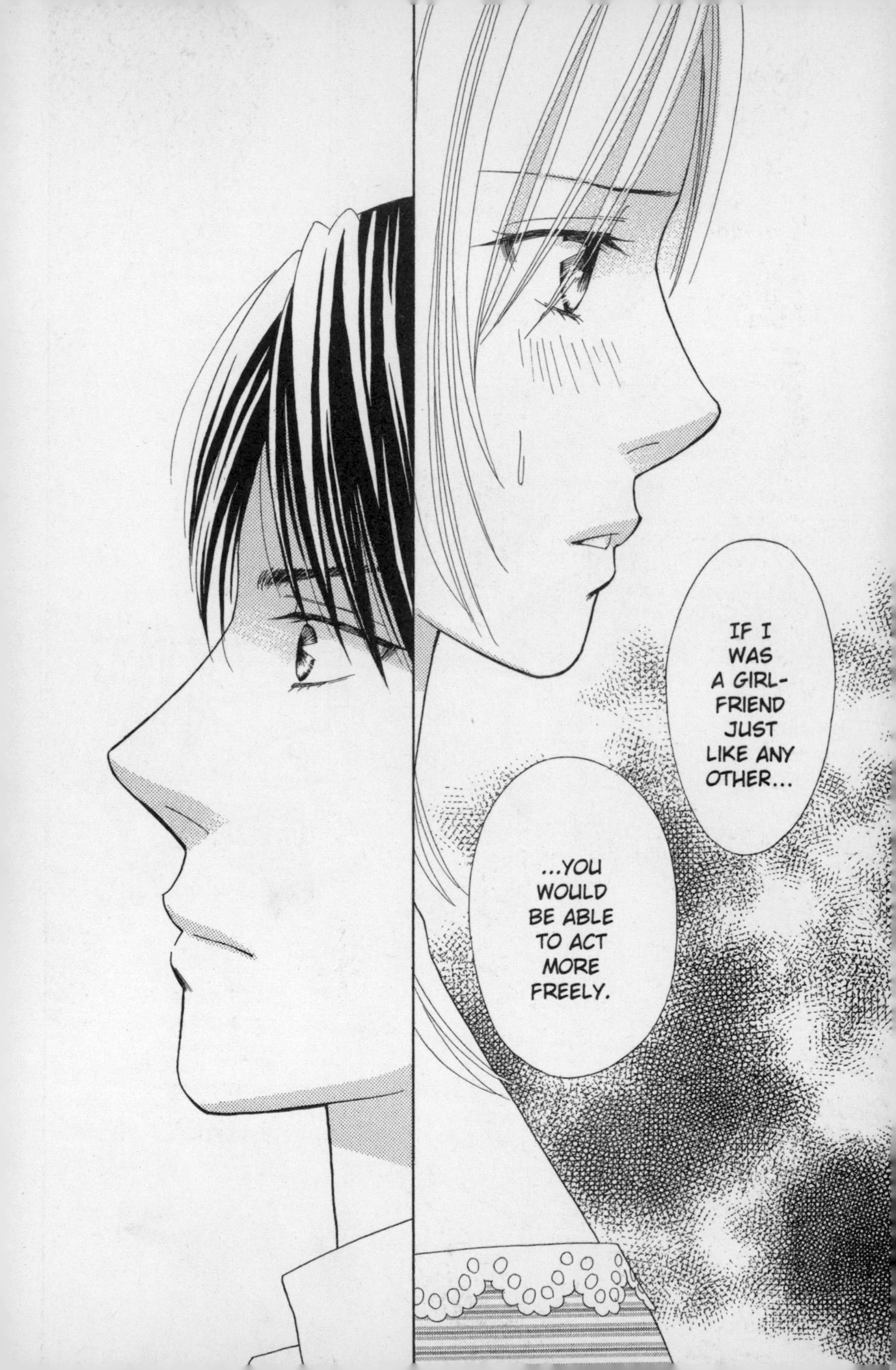
IF I WAS A GIRL-FRIEND JUST LIKE ANY OTHER...
...YOU WOULD BE ABLE TO ACT MORE FREELY.

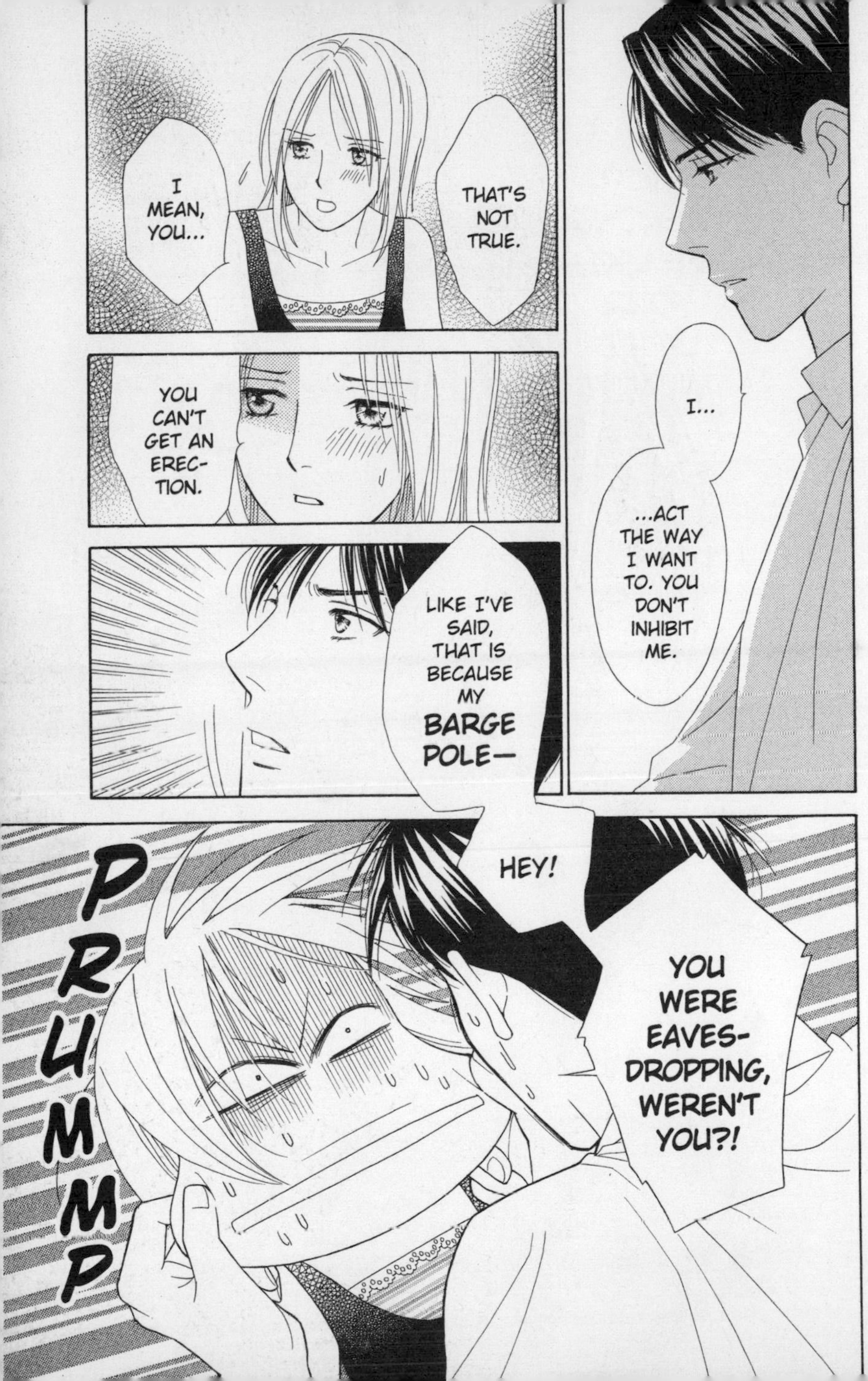
I...
...ACT THE WAY I WANT TO. YOU DON'T INHIBIT ME.
THAT'S NOT TRUE.
I MEAN, YOU...
YOU CAN'T GET AN ERECTION.
LIKE I'VE SAID, THAT IS BECAUSE MY BARGE POLE—
HEY!
YOU WERE EAVESDROPPING, WEREN'T YOU?!
PRUMMP

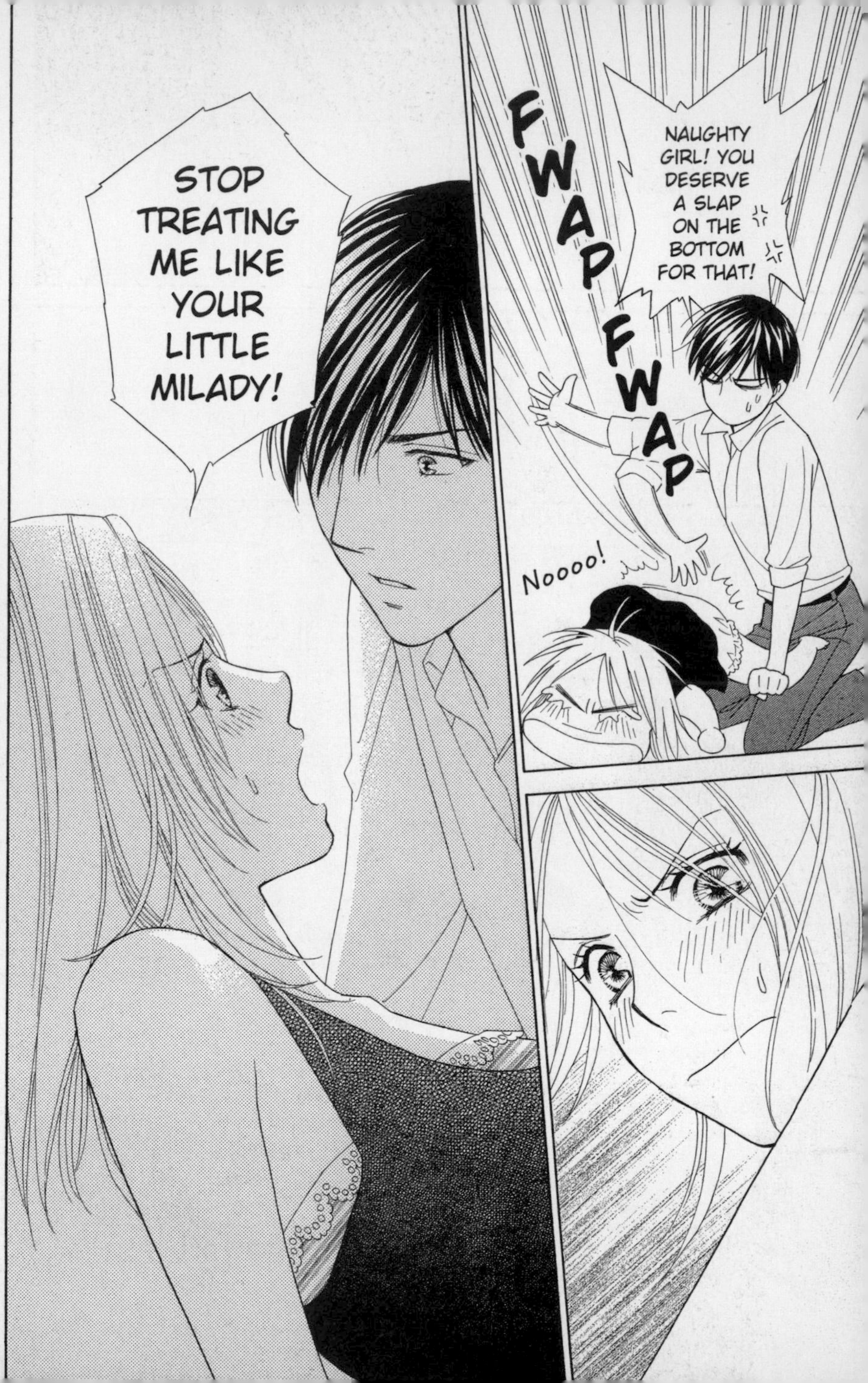
NAUGHTY GIRL! YOU DESERVE A SLAP ON THE BOTTOM FOR THAT!
FWAP
FWAP
FWAP
Noooo!
STOP TREATING ME LIKE YOUR LITTLE MILADY!

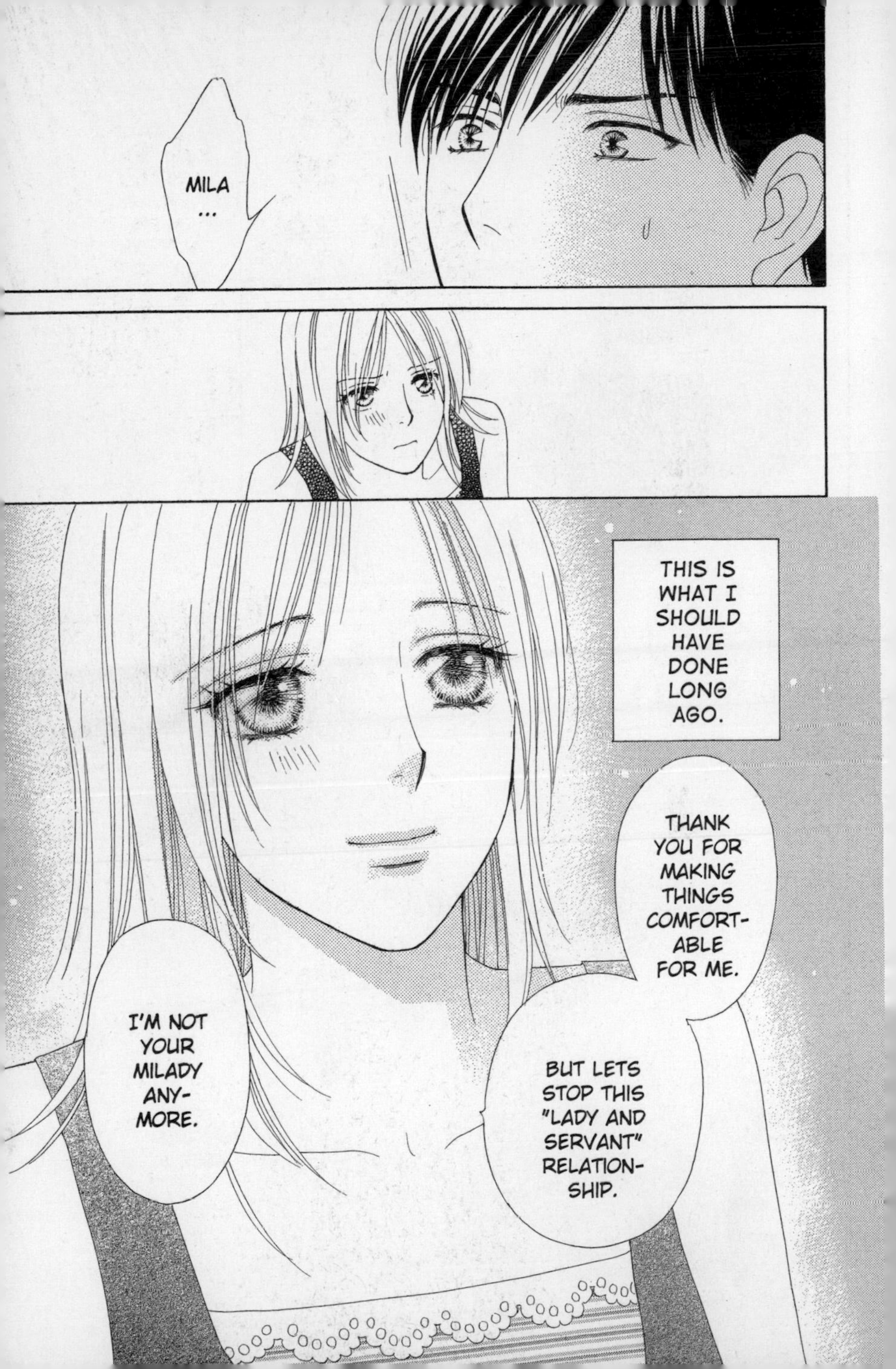
MILA ...
THIS IS WHAT I SHOULD HAVE DONE LONG AGO.
THANK YOU FOR MAKING THINGS COMFORT-ABLE FOR ME.
BUT LETS STOP THIS "LADY AND SERVANT" RELATION-SHIP.
I'M NOT YOUR MILADY ANY-MORE.

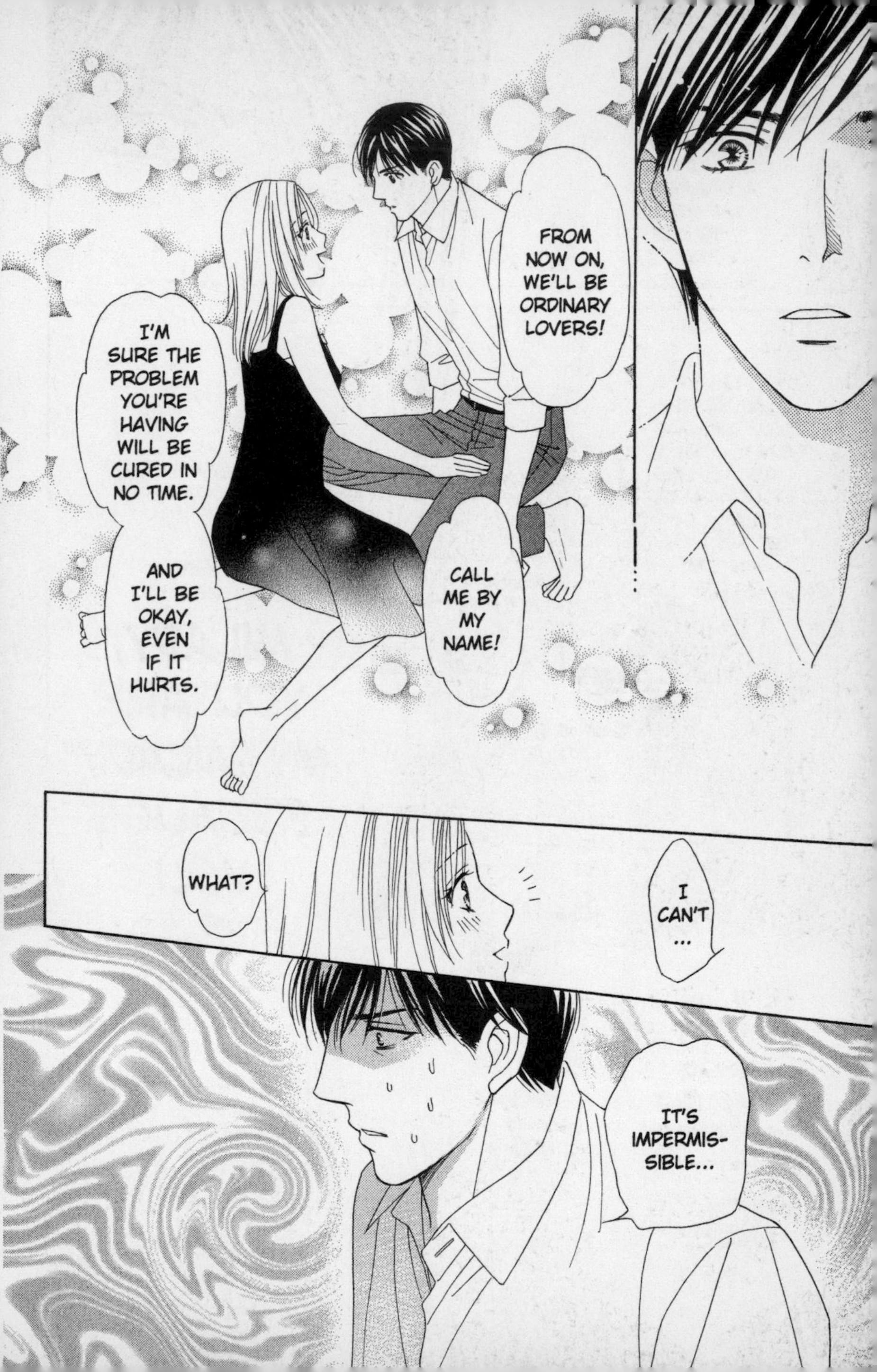
FROM NOW ON, WE'LL BE ORDINARY LOVERS!
CALL ME BY MY NAME!
I'M SURE THE PROBLEM YOU'RE HAVING WILL BE CURED IN NO TIME.
AND I'LL BE OKAY, EVEN IF IT HURTS.
I CAN'T ...
WHAT?
IT'S IMPERMIS-SIBLE...

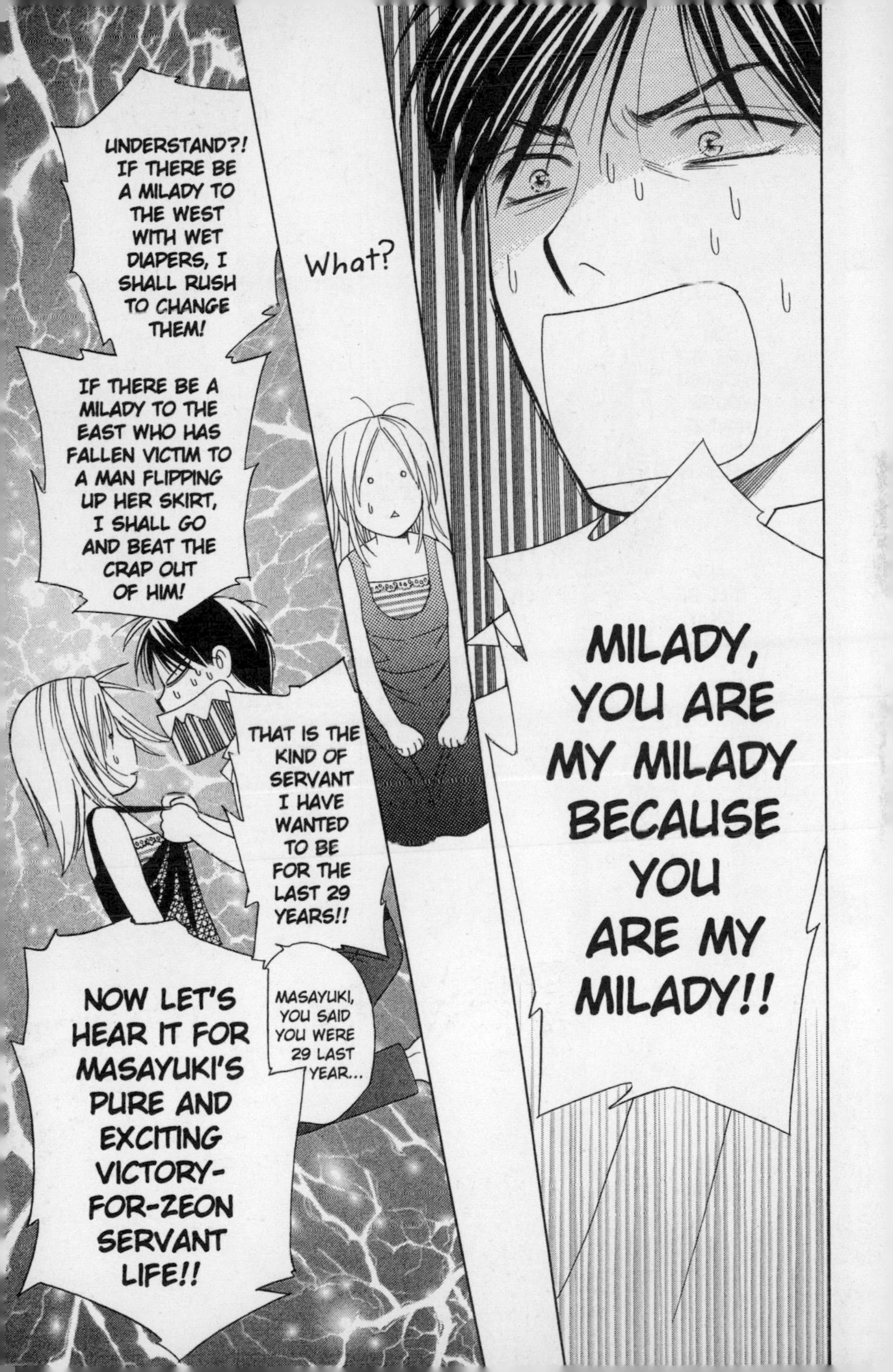
MILADY, YOU ARE MY MILADY BECAUSE YOU ARE MY MILADY!!
What?
UNDERSTAND?! IF THERE BE A MILADY TO THE WEST WITH WET DIAPERS, I SHALL RUSH TO CHANGE THEM!
IF THERE BE A MILADY TO THE EAST WHO HAS FALLEN VICTIM TO A MAN FLIPPING UP HER SKIRT, I SHALL GO AND BEAT THE CRAP OUT OF HIM!
THAT IS THE KIND OF SERVANT I HAVE WANTED TO BE FOR THE LAST 29 YEARS!!
MASAYUKI, YOU SAID YOU WERE 29 LAST YEAR...
NOW LET'S HEAR IT FOR MASAYUKI'S PURE AND EXCITING VICTORY-FOR-ZEON SERVANT LIFE!!

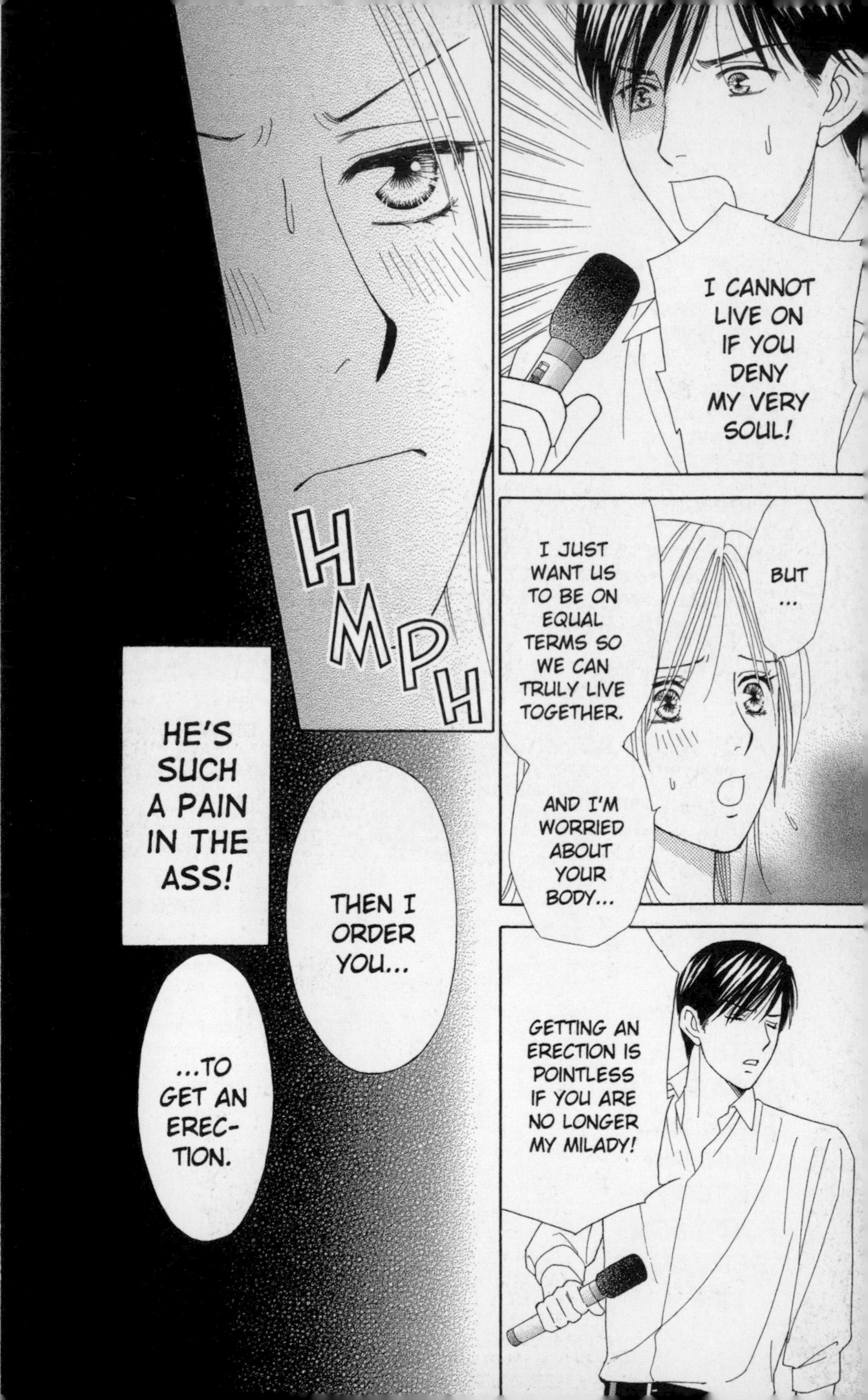
I CANNOT LIVE ON IF YOU DENY MY VERY SOUL!
BUT...
I JUST WANT US TO BE ON EQUAL TERMS SO WE CAN TRULY LIVE TOGETHER.
AND I'M WORRIED ABOUT YOUR BODY...
GETTING AN ERECTION IS POINTLESS IF YOU ARE NO LONGER MY MILADY!
HMPH
HE'S SUCH SUCH A PAIN IN THE ASS!
THEN I ORDER YOU...
...TO GET AN ERECTION.

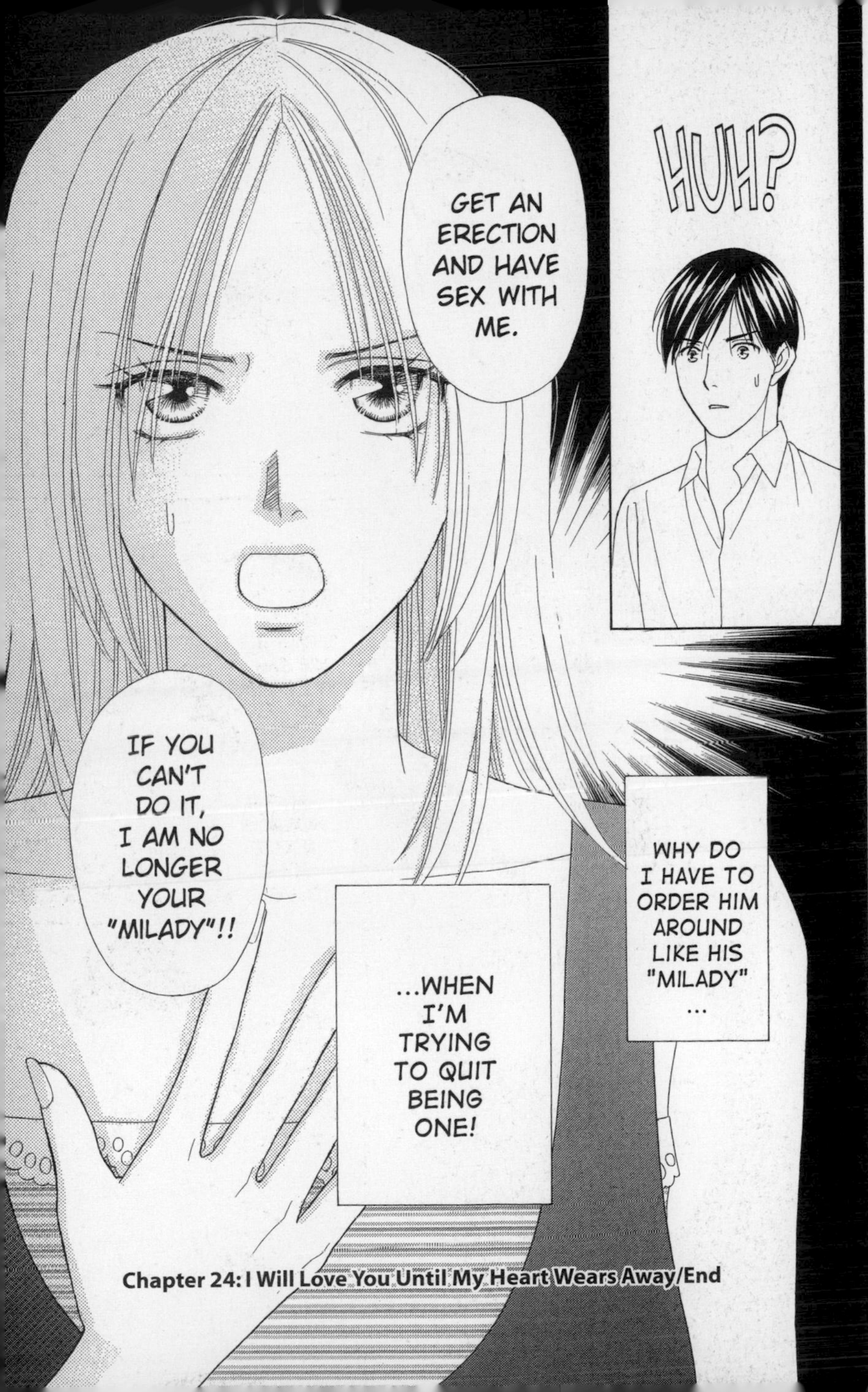
HUH?
GET AN ERECTION AND HAVE SEX WITH ME.
IF YOU CAN'T DO IT, I AM NO LONGER YOUR "MILADY"!!
WHY DO I HAVE TO ORDER HIM AROUND LIKE HIS "MILADY" ...
...WHEN I'M TRYING TO QUIT BEING ONE!

Chapter 24: I Will Love You Until My Heart Wears Away/End

Sorry about that...

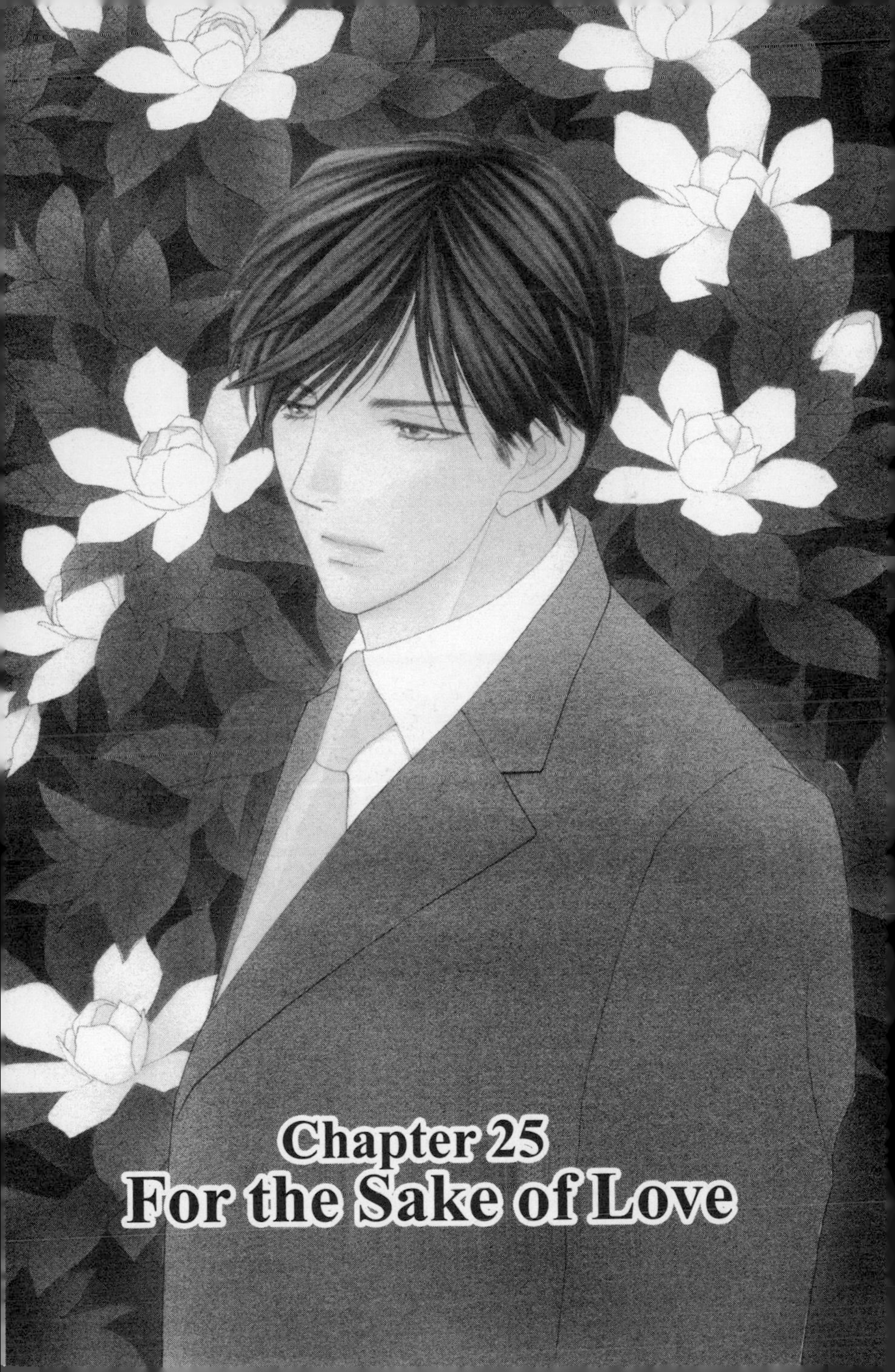

Chapter 25
For the Sake of Love

I said I was sorry...

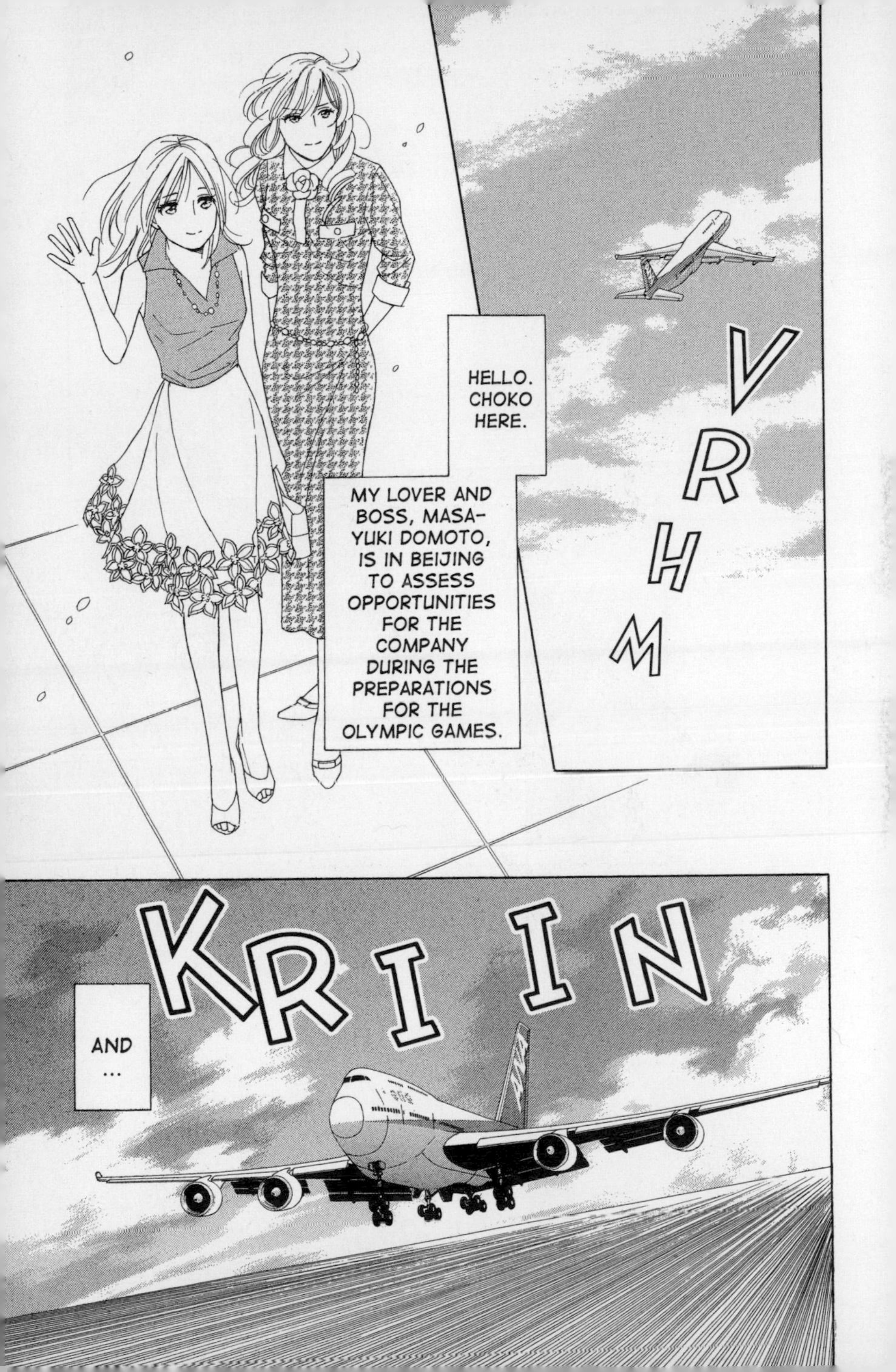
VRHM
HELLO. CHOKO HERE.
MY LOVER AND BOSS, MASA-YUKI DOMOTO, IS IN BEIJING TO ASSESS OPPORTUNITIES FOR THE COMPANY DURING THE PREPARATIONS FOR THE OLYMPIC GAMES.
KRIIN
AND ...

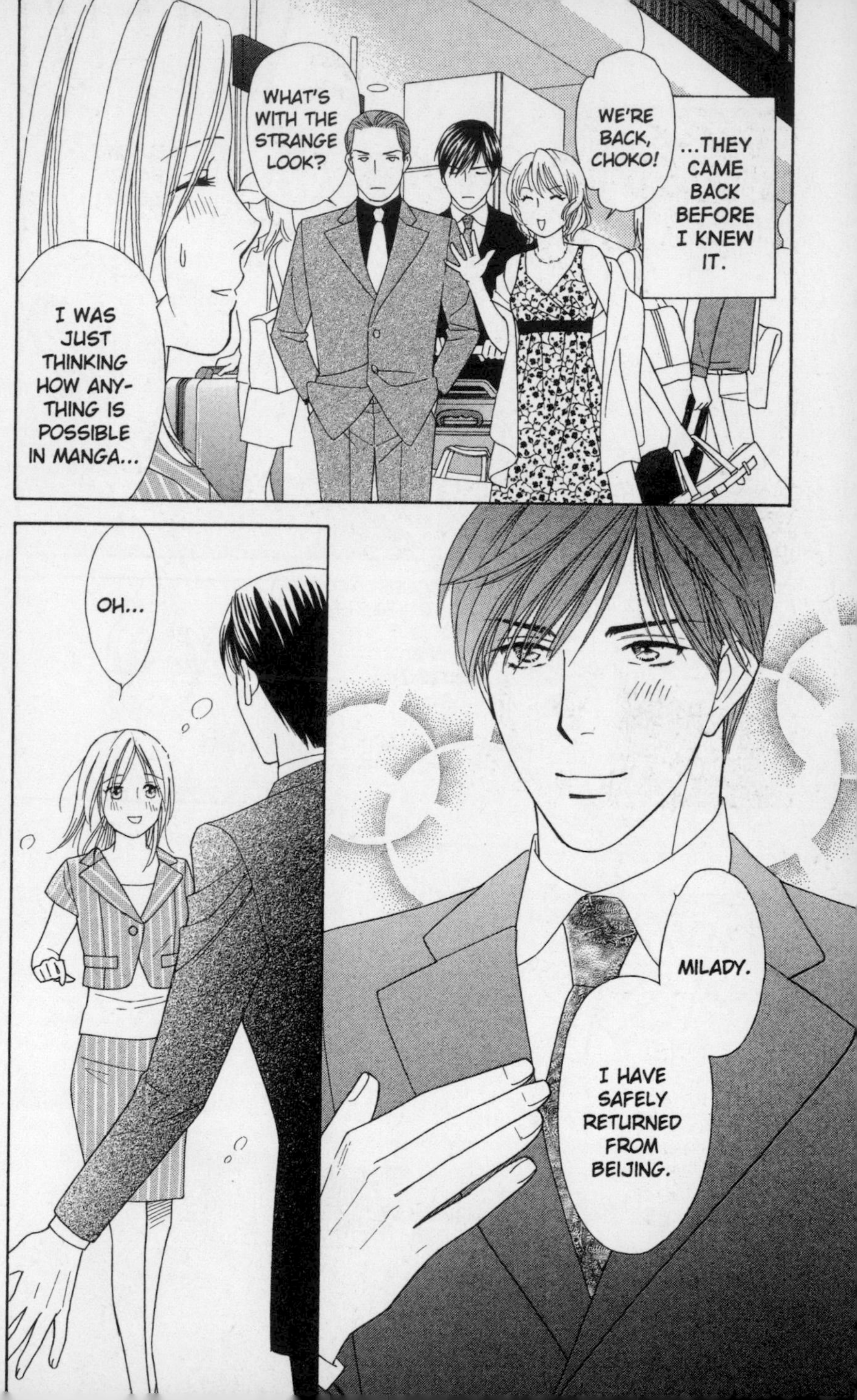
...THEY CAME BACK BEFORE I KNEW IT.
WE'RE BACK, CHOKO!
WHAT'S WITH THE STRANGE LOOK?
I WAS JUST THINKING HOW ANY-THING IS POSSIBLE IN MANGA...
MILADY.
I HAVE SAFELY RETURNED FROM BEIJING.
OH...

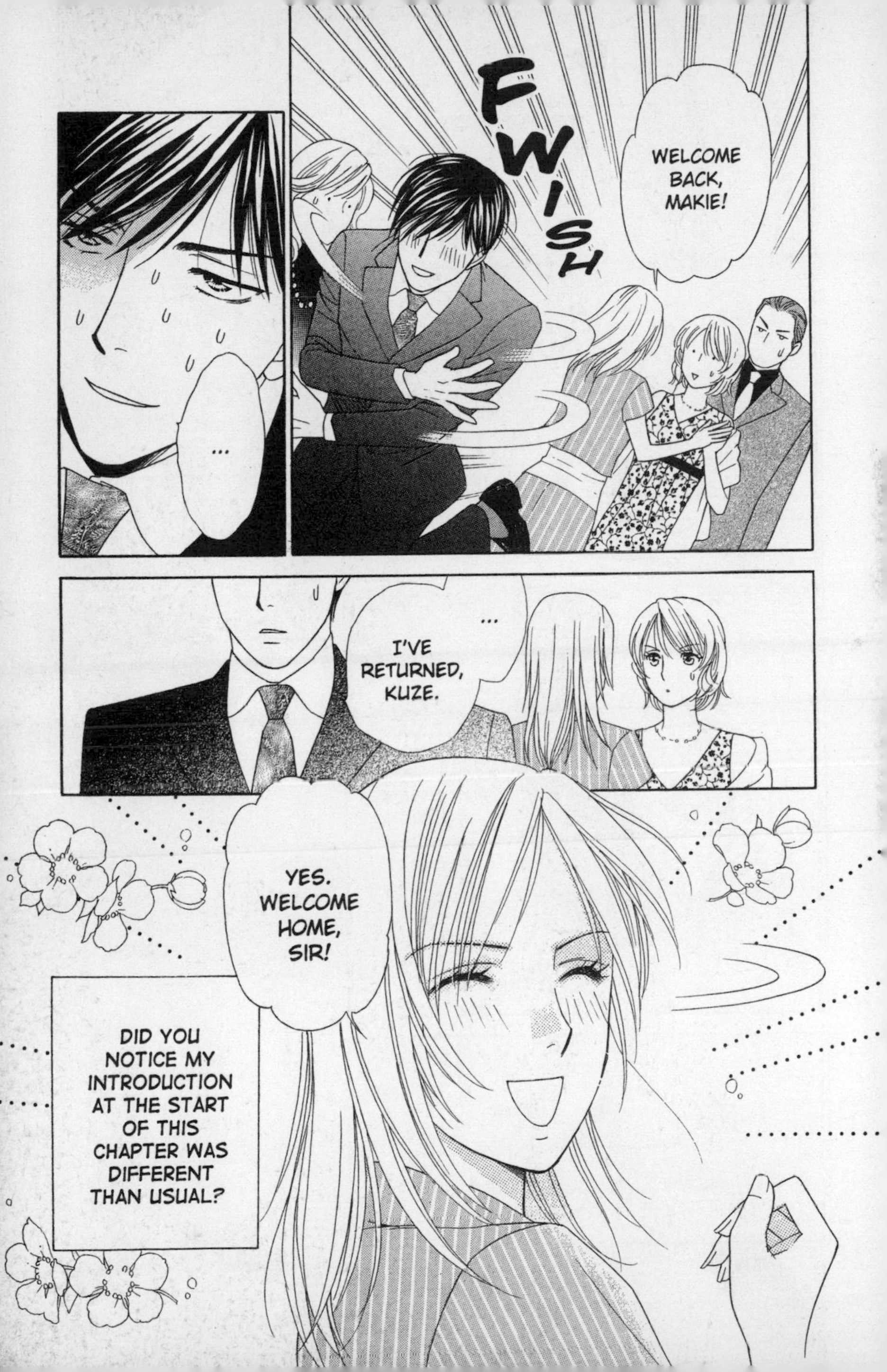
FWISH
WELCOME BACK, MAKIE!
...
...
I'VE RETURNED, KUZE.
YES. WELCOME HOME, SIR!
DID YOU NOTICE MY INTRODUCTION AT THE START OF THIS CHAPTER WAS DIFFERENT THAN USUAL?

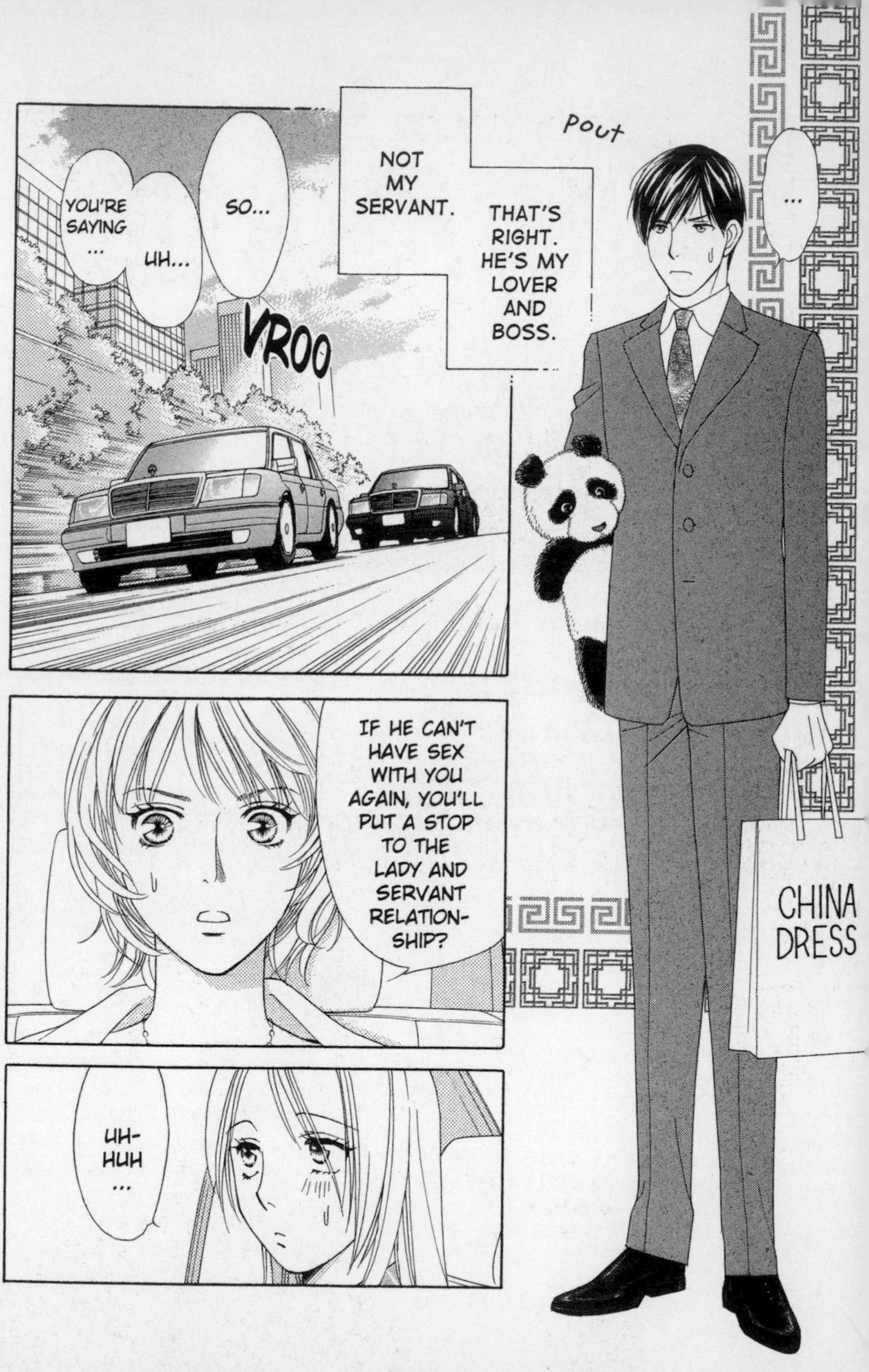
Pout
...
SO...
UH...
YOU'RE SAYING ...
NOT MY SERVANT.
THAT'S RIGHT. HE'S MY LOVER AND BOSS.
VROO
IF HE CAN'T HAVE SEX WITH YOU AGAIN, YOU'LL PUT A STOP TO THE LADY AND SERVANT RELATION-SHIP?
UH-HUH ...
CHINA DRESS

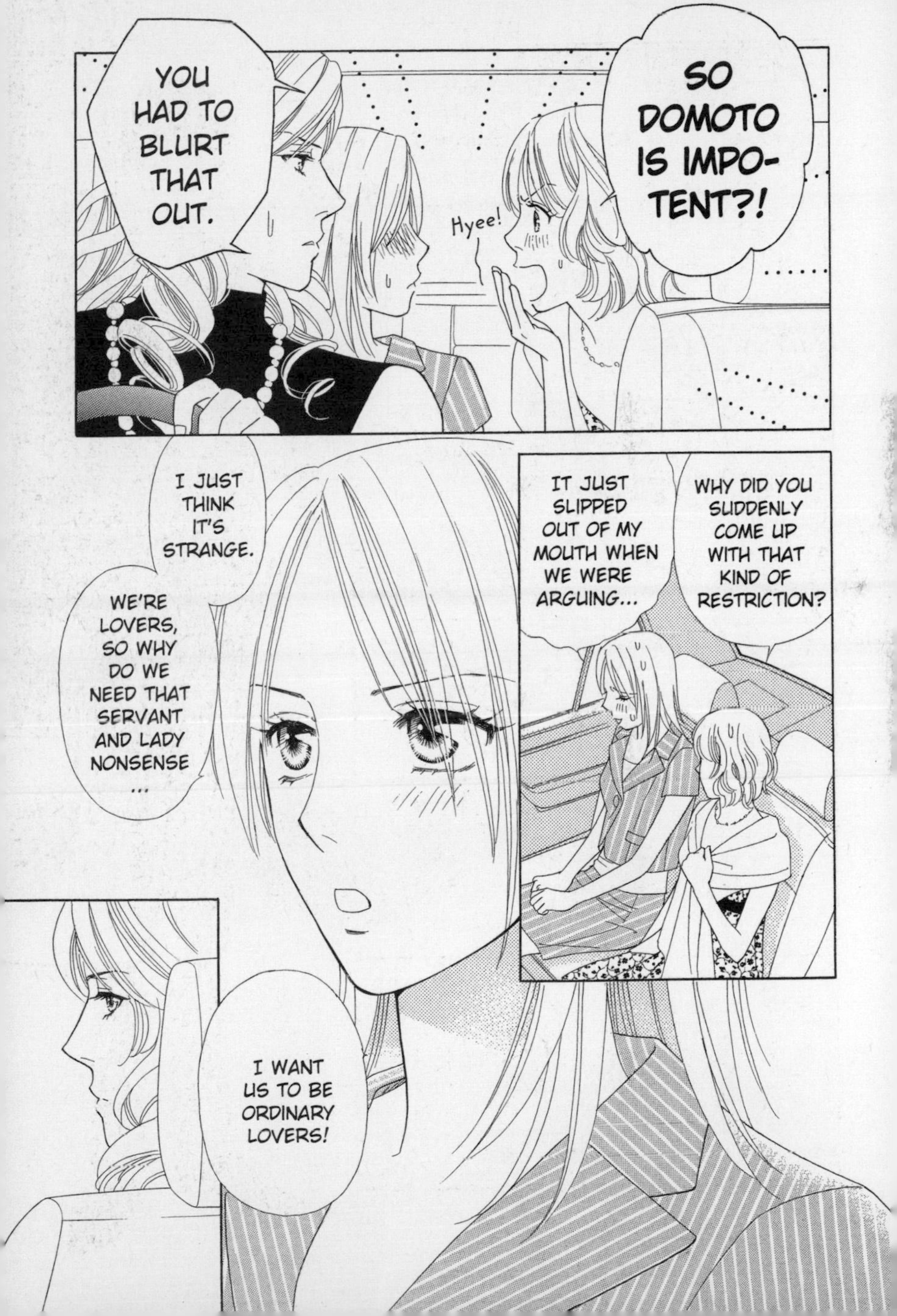
SO DOMOTO IS IMPO-TENT?!
Hyee!
YOU HAD TO BLURT THAT OUT.
WHY DID YOU SUDDENLY COME UP WITH THAT KIND OF RESTRICTION?
IT JUST SLIPPED OUT OF MY MOUTH WHEN WE WERE ARGUING...
I JUST THINK IT'S STRANGE.
WE'RE LOVERS, SO WHY DO WE NEED THAT SERVANT AND LADY NONSENSE ...
I WANT US TO BE ORDINARY LOVERS!

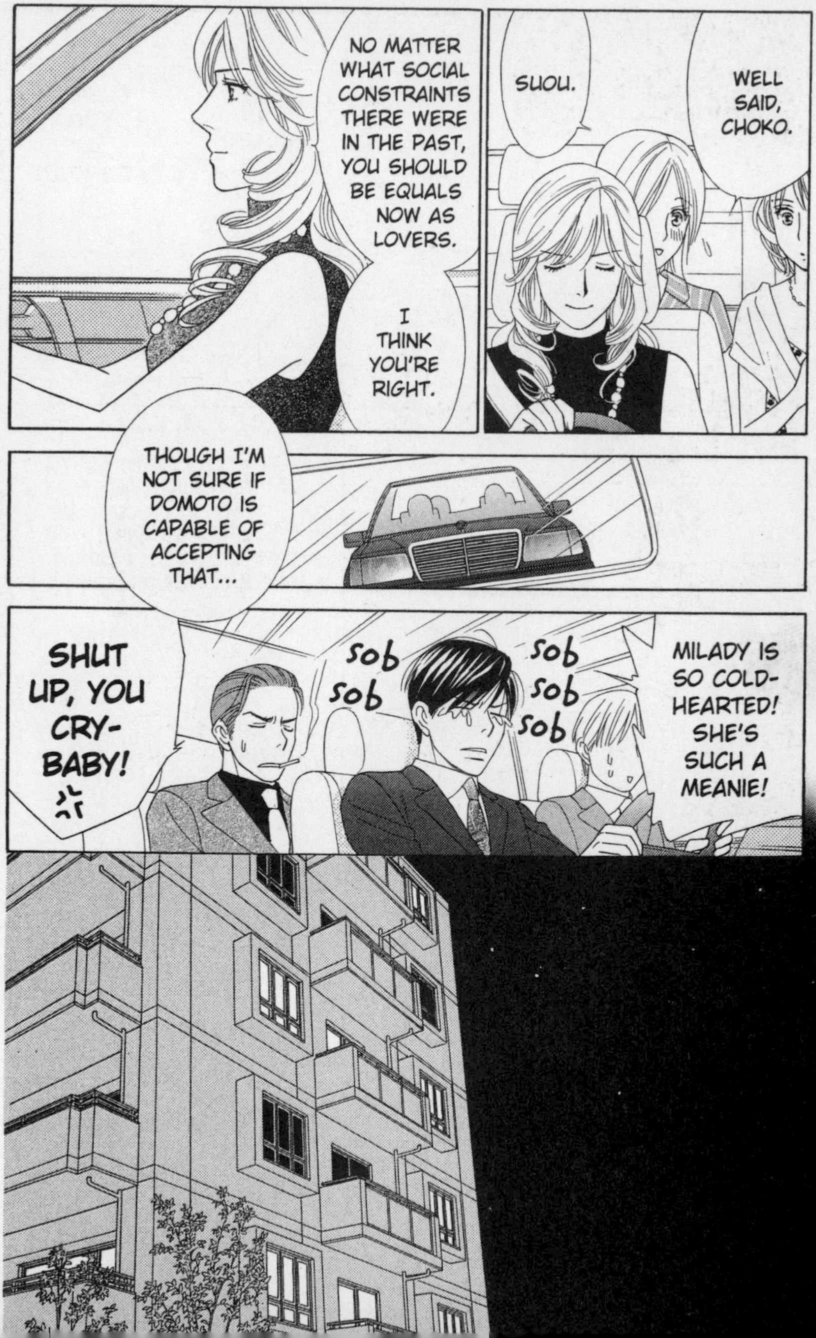
WELL SAID, CHOKO.
SUOU.
NO MATTER WHAT SOCIAL CONSTRAINTS THERE WERE IN THE PAST, YOU SHOULD BE EQUALS NOW AS LOVERS.
I THINK YOU'RE RIGHT.
THOUGH I'M NOT SURE IF DOMOTO IS CAPABLE OF ACCEPTING THAT...
MILADY IS SO COLD-HEARTED! SHE'S SUCH A MEANIE!
sob sob sob
sob sob
SHUT UP, YOU CRY-BABY!

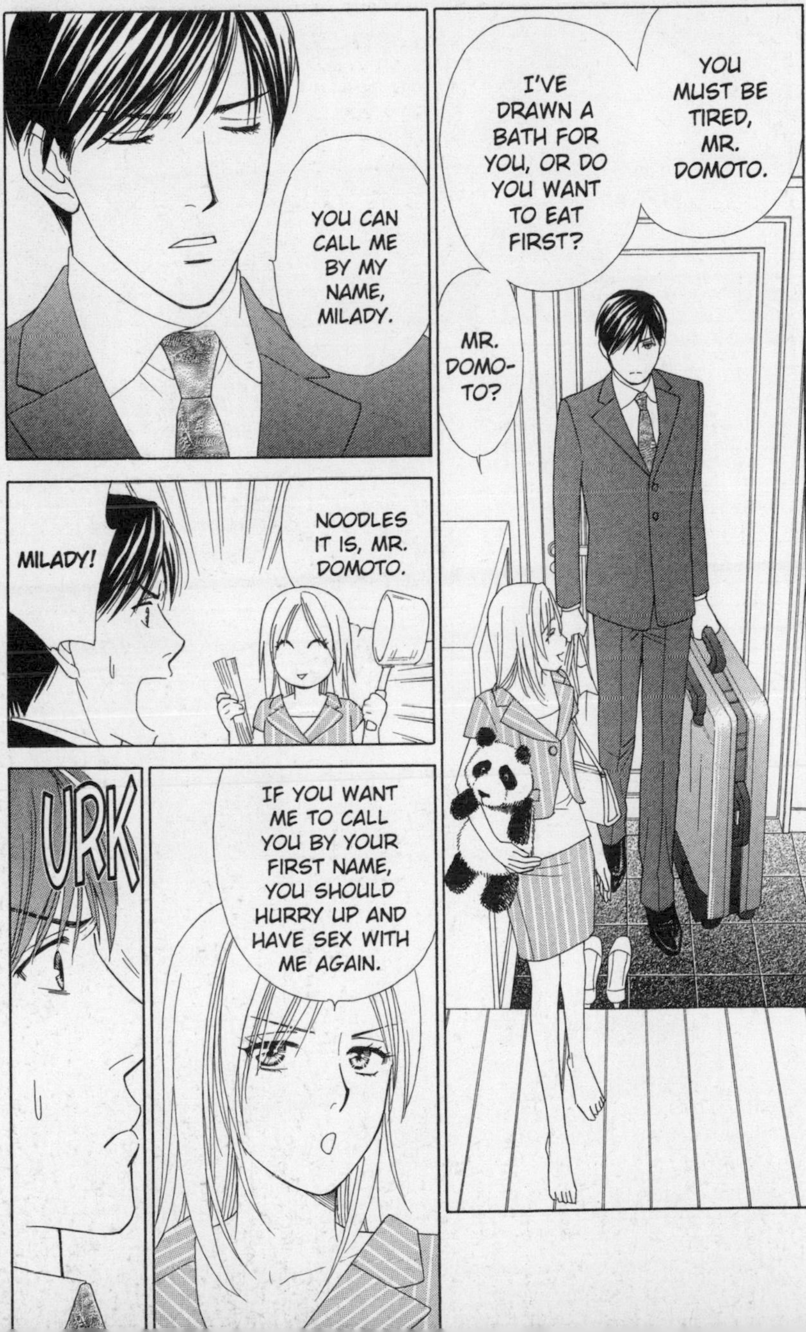
YOU MUST BE TIRED, MR. DOMOTO.
I'VE DRAWN A BATH FOR YOU, OR DO YOU WANT TO EAT FIRST?
MR. DOMO-TO?
YOU CAN CALL ME BY MY NAME, MILADY.
NOODLES IT IS, MR. DOMOTO.
MILADY!
IF YOU WANT ME TO CALL YOU BY YOUR FIRST NAME, YOU SHOULD HURRY UP AND HAVE SEX WITH ME AGAIN.
URK

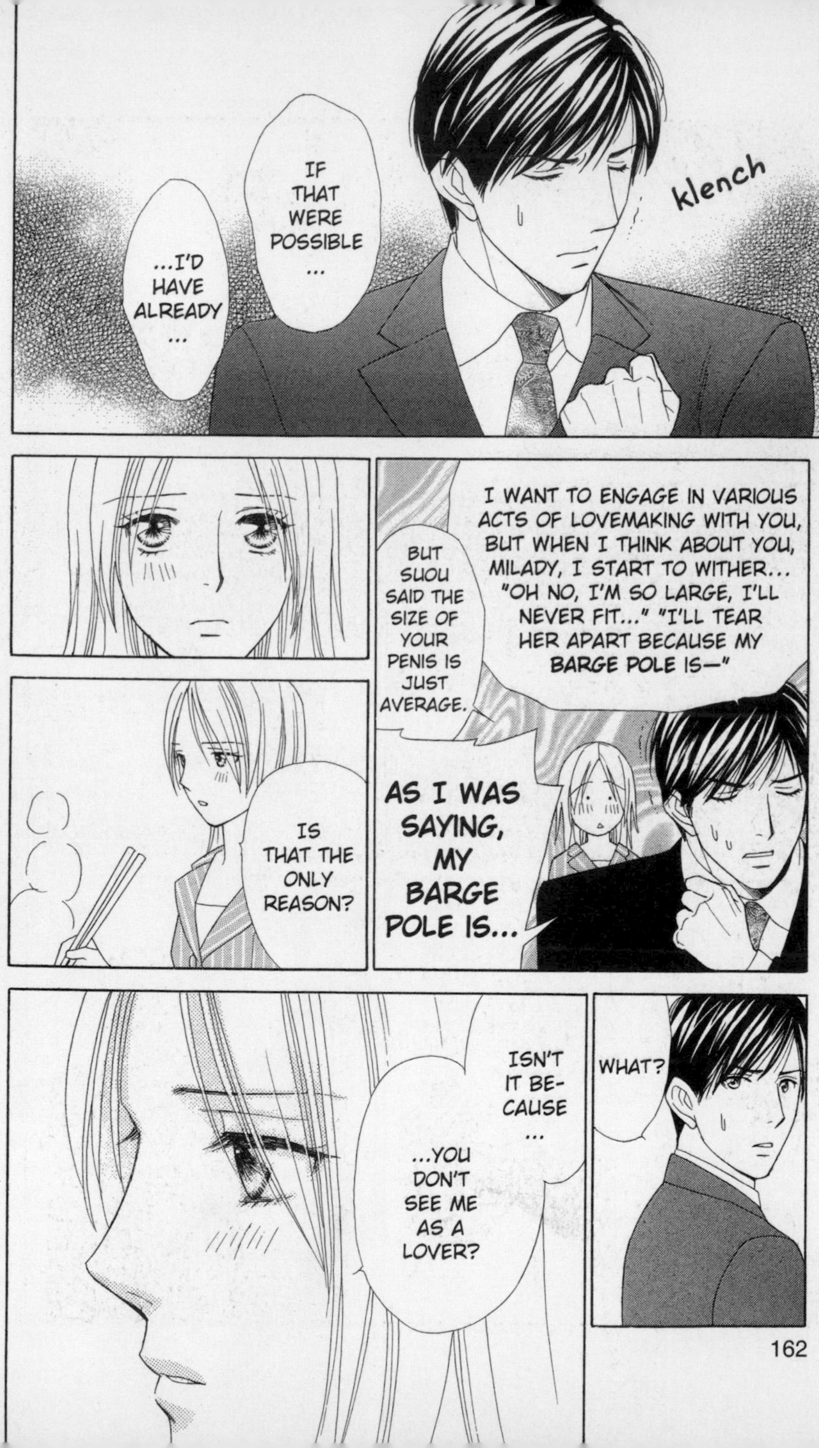
klench
IF THAT WERE POSSIBLE...
...I'D HAVE ALREADY...
I WANT TO ENGAGE IN VARIOUS ACTS OF LOVEMAKING WITH YOU, BUT WHEN I THINK ABOUT YOU, MILADY, I START TO WITHER... "OH NO, I'M SO LARGE, I'LL NEVER FIT..." "I'LL TEAR HER APART BECAUSE MY BARGE POLE IS—"
BUT SUOU SAID THE SIZE OF YOUR PENIS IS JUST AVERAGE.
AS I WAS SAYING, MY BARGE POLE IS...
IS THAT THE ONLY REASON?
WHAT?
ISN'T IT BE-CAUSE...
...YOU DON'T SEE ME AS A LOVER?

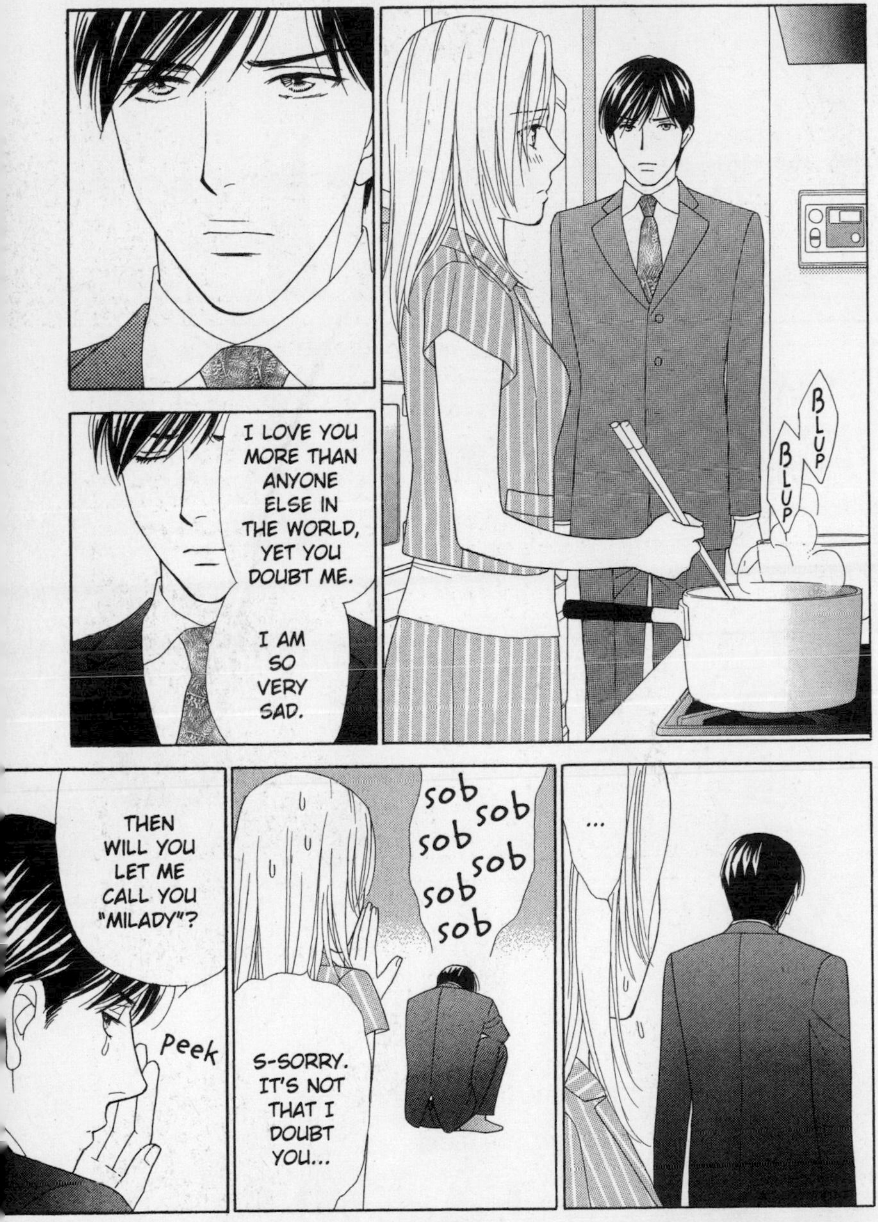
BLUP
BLUP
I LOVE YOU MORE THAN ANYONE ELSE IN THE WORLD, YET YOU DOUBT ME.
I AM SO VERY SAD.
...
sob sob sob sob sob sob
S-SORRY. IT'S NOT THAT I DOUBT YOU...
THEN WILL YOU LET ME CALL YOU "MILADY"?
Peek

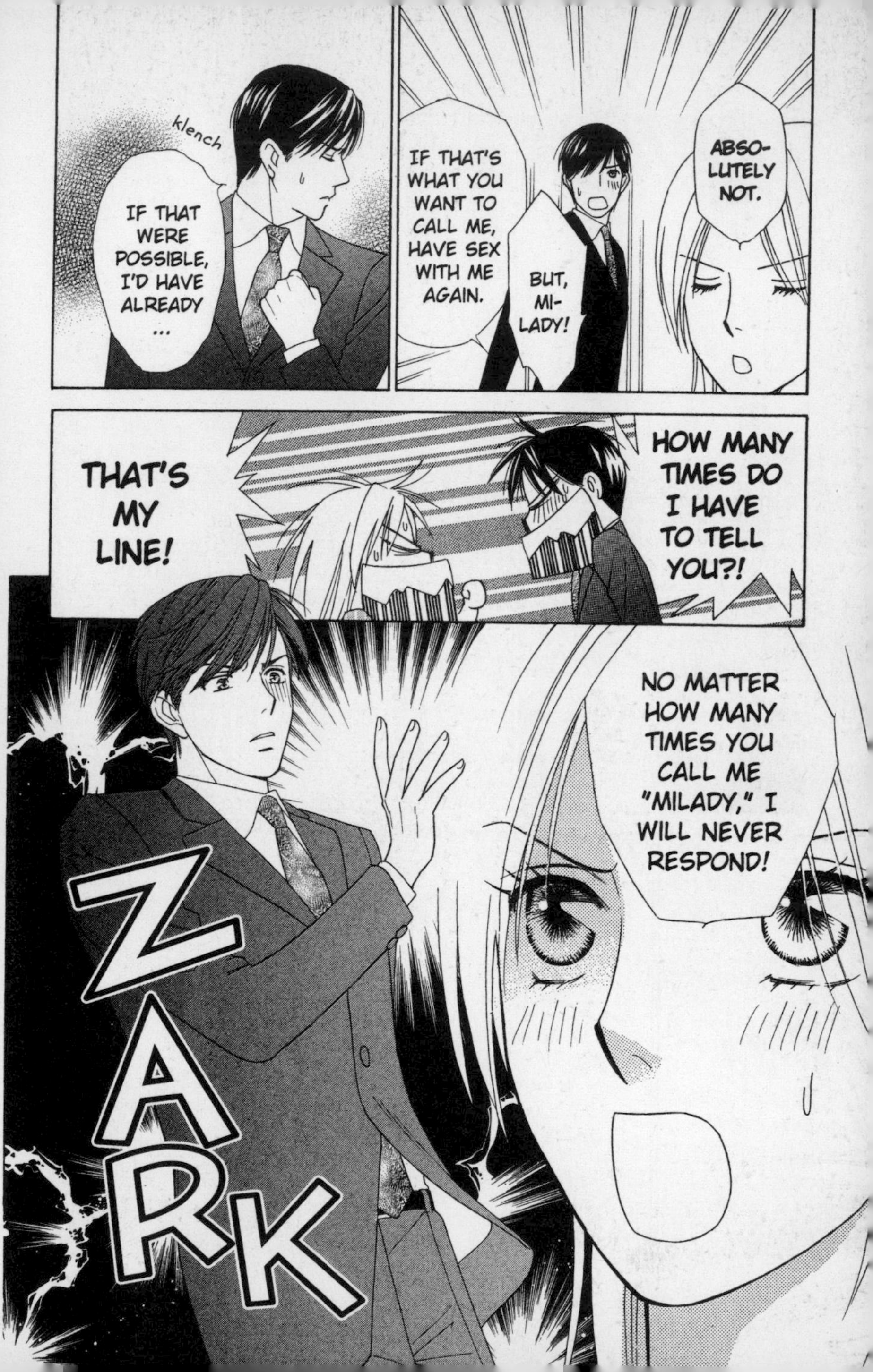
ABSO-LUTELY NOT.
BUT, MI-LADY!
IF THAT'S WHAT YOU WANT TO CALL ME, HAVE SEX WITH ME AGAIN.
klench
IF THAT WERE POSSIBLE, I'D HAVE ALREADY ...
HOW MANY TIMES DO I HAVE TO TELL YOU?!
THAT'S MY LINE!
NO MATTER HOW MANY TIMES YOU CALL ME "MILADY," I WILL NEVER RESPOND!
ZARK

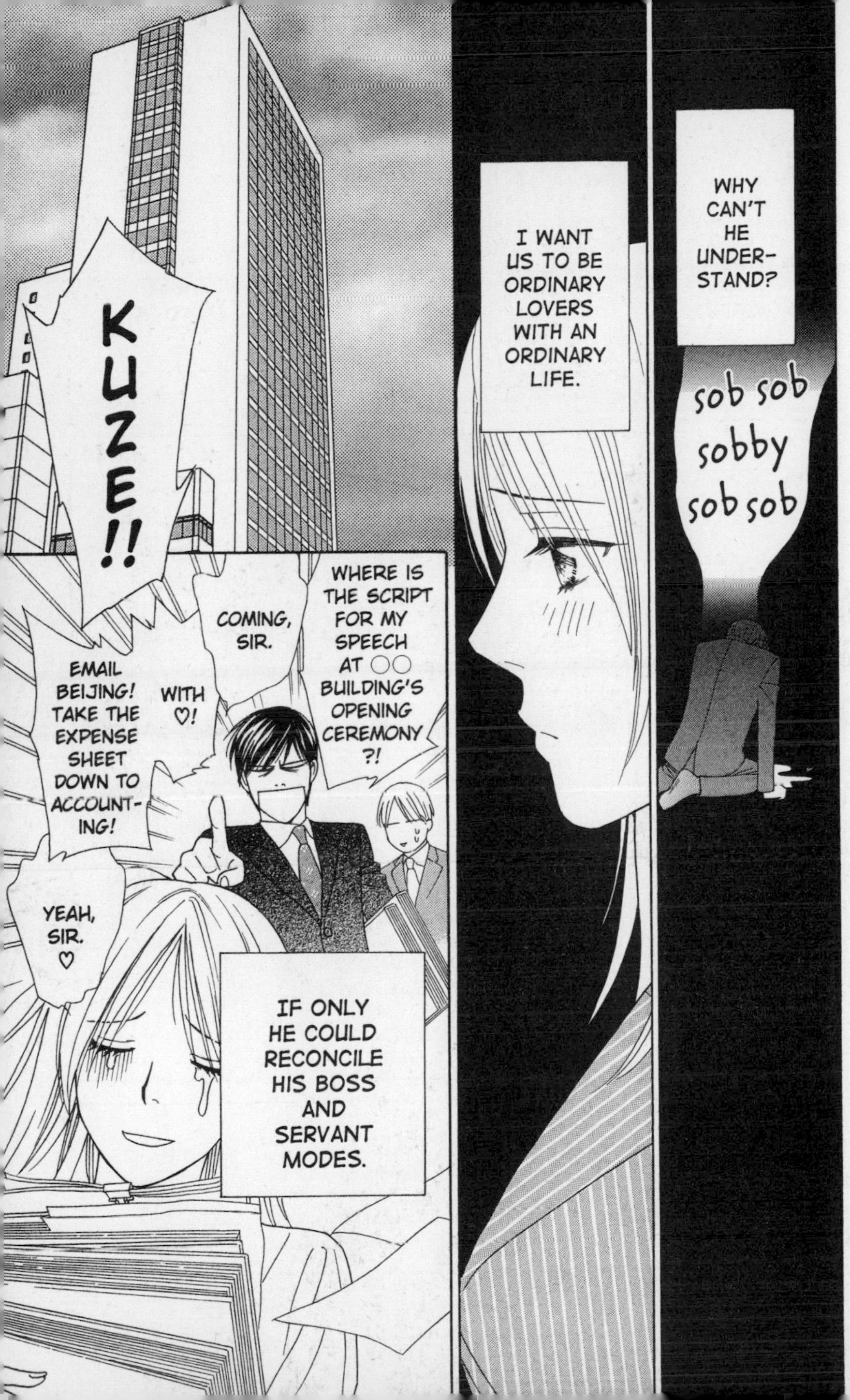
WHY CAN'T HE UNDERSTAND?
sob sob sobby sob sob
I WANT US TO BE ORDINARY LOVERS WITH AN ORDINARY LIFE.
KUZE!!
WHERE IS THE SCRIPT FOR MY SPEECH AT ○○ BUILDING'S OPENING CEREMONY ?!
COMING, SIR.
WITH ♡!
EMAIL BEIJING! TAKE THE EXPENSE SHEET DOWN TO ACCOUNTING!
YEAH, SIR. ♡
IF ONLY HE COULD RECONCILE HIS BOSS AND SERVANT MODES.

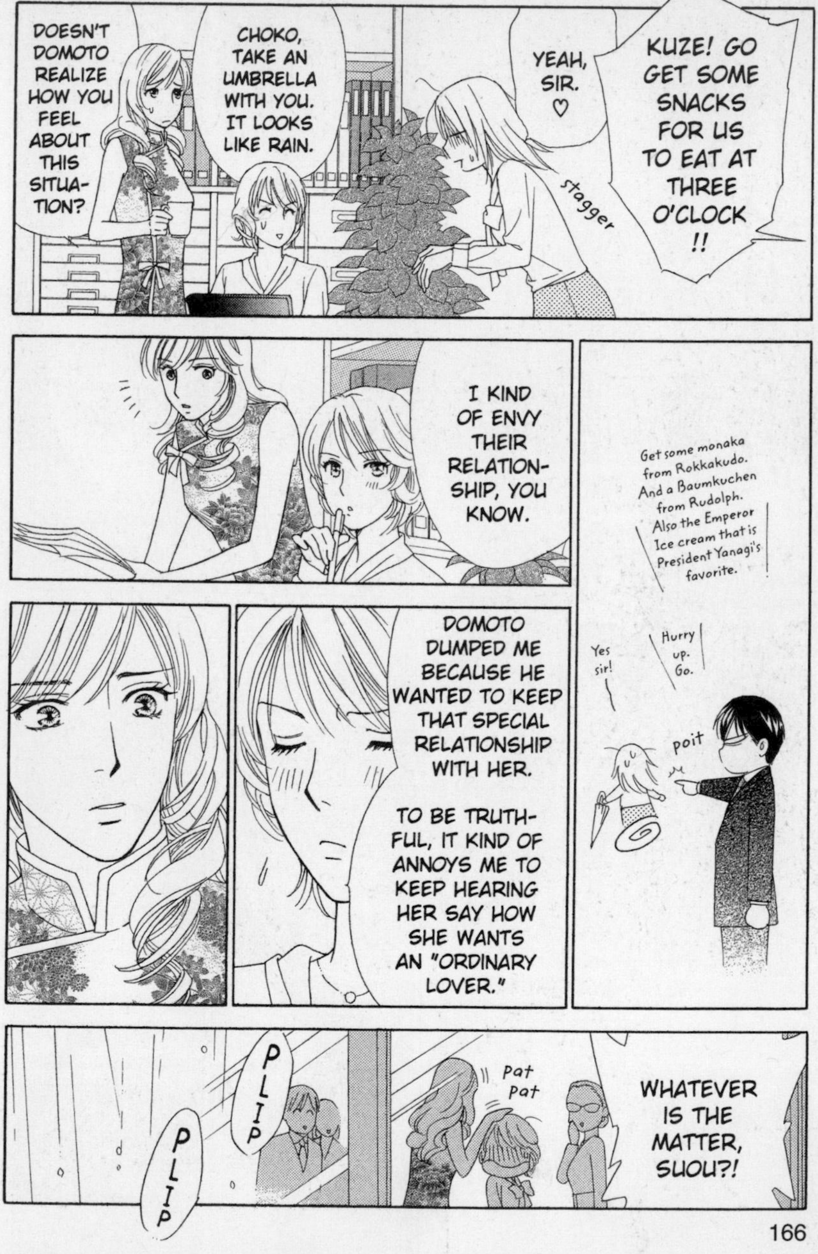
KUZE! GO GET SOME SNACKS FOR US TO EAT AT THREE O'CLOCK!!
YEAH, SIR. ♡
stagger
CHOKO, TAKE AN UMBRELLA WITH YOU. IT LOOKS LIKE RAIN.
DOESN'T DOMOTO REALIZE HOW YOU FEEL ABOUT THIS SITUATION?
Get some monaka from Rokkakudo. And a Baumkuchen from Rudolph. Also the Emperor Ice cream that is President Yanagi's favorite.
Hurry up. Go.
Yes sir!
poit
I KIND OF ENVY THEIR RELATIONSHIP, YOU KNOW.
DOMOTO DUMPED ME BECAUSE HE WANTED TO KEEP THAT SPECIAL RELATIONSHIP WITH HER.
TO BE TRUTHFUL, IT KIND OF ANNOYS ME TO KEEP HEARING HER SAY HOW SHE WANTS AN "ORDINARY LOVER."
WHATEVER IS THE MATTER, SUOU?!
Pat Pat
PLIP
PLIP

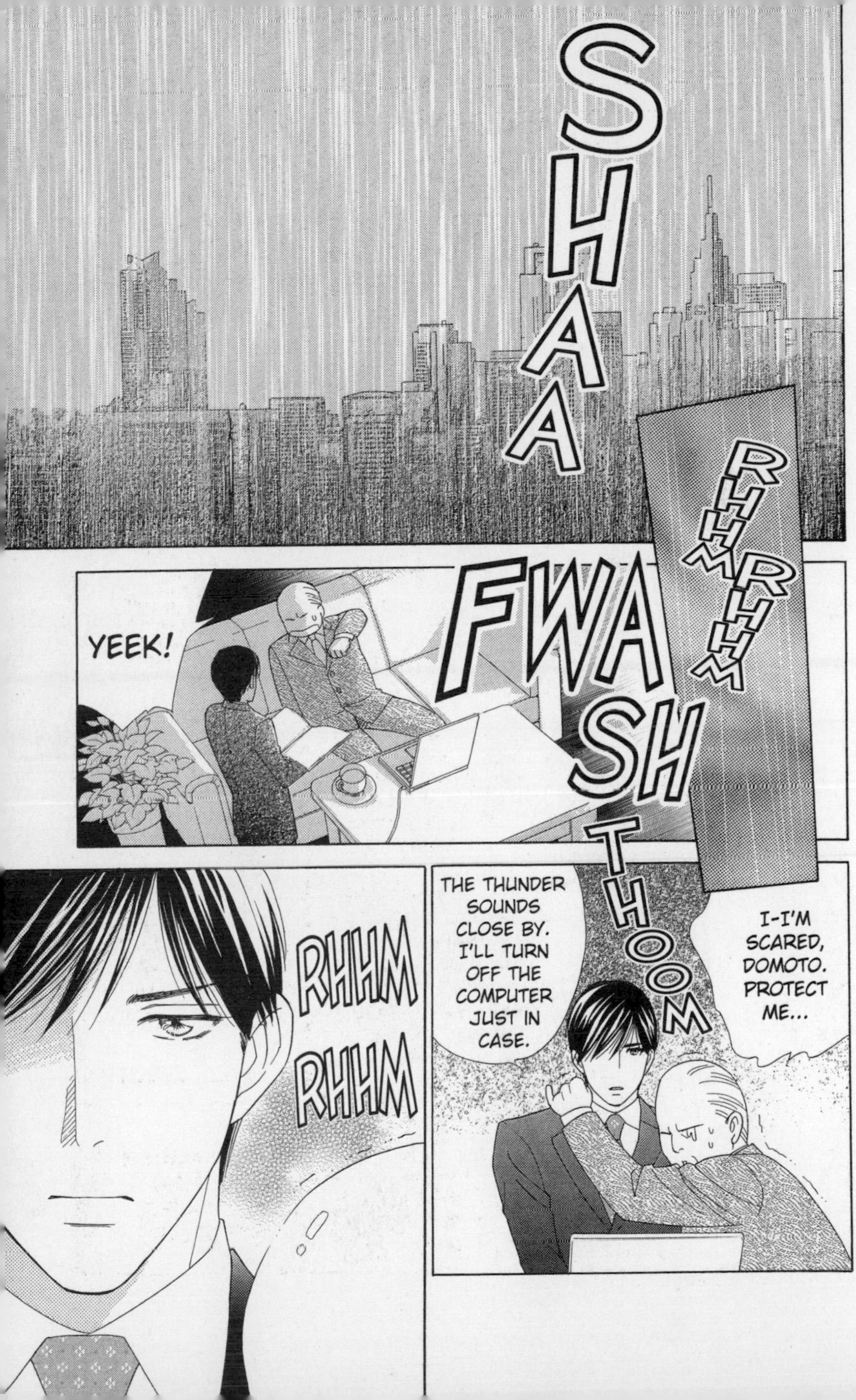
SHAA
RHHM RHHM
FWASH
YEEK!
THOOM
I-I'M SCARED, DOMOTO. PROTECT ME...
THE THUNDER SOUNDS CLOSE BY. I'LL TURN OFF THE COMPUTER JUST IN CASE.
RHHM RHHM

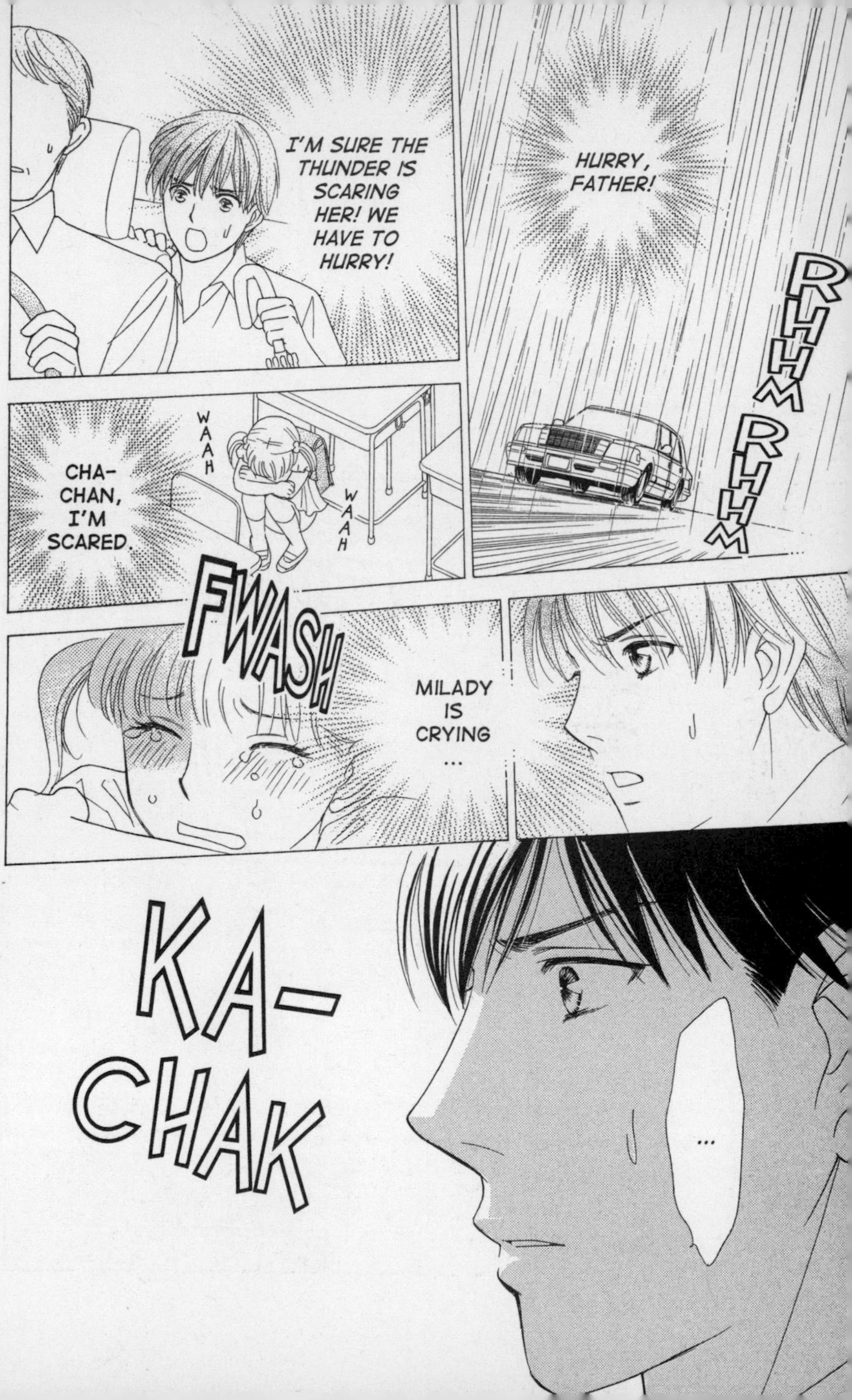

HURRY, FATHER!
RHHM RHHM
I'M SURE THE THUNDER IS SCARING HER! WE HAVE TO HURRY!
WAAH WAAH
CHA-CHAN, I'M SCARED.
FWASH
MILADY IS CRYING ...
...
KA-CHAK

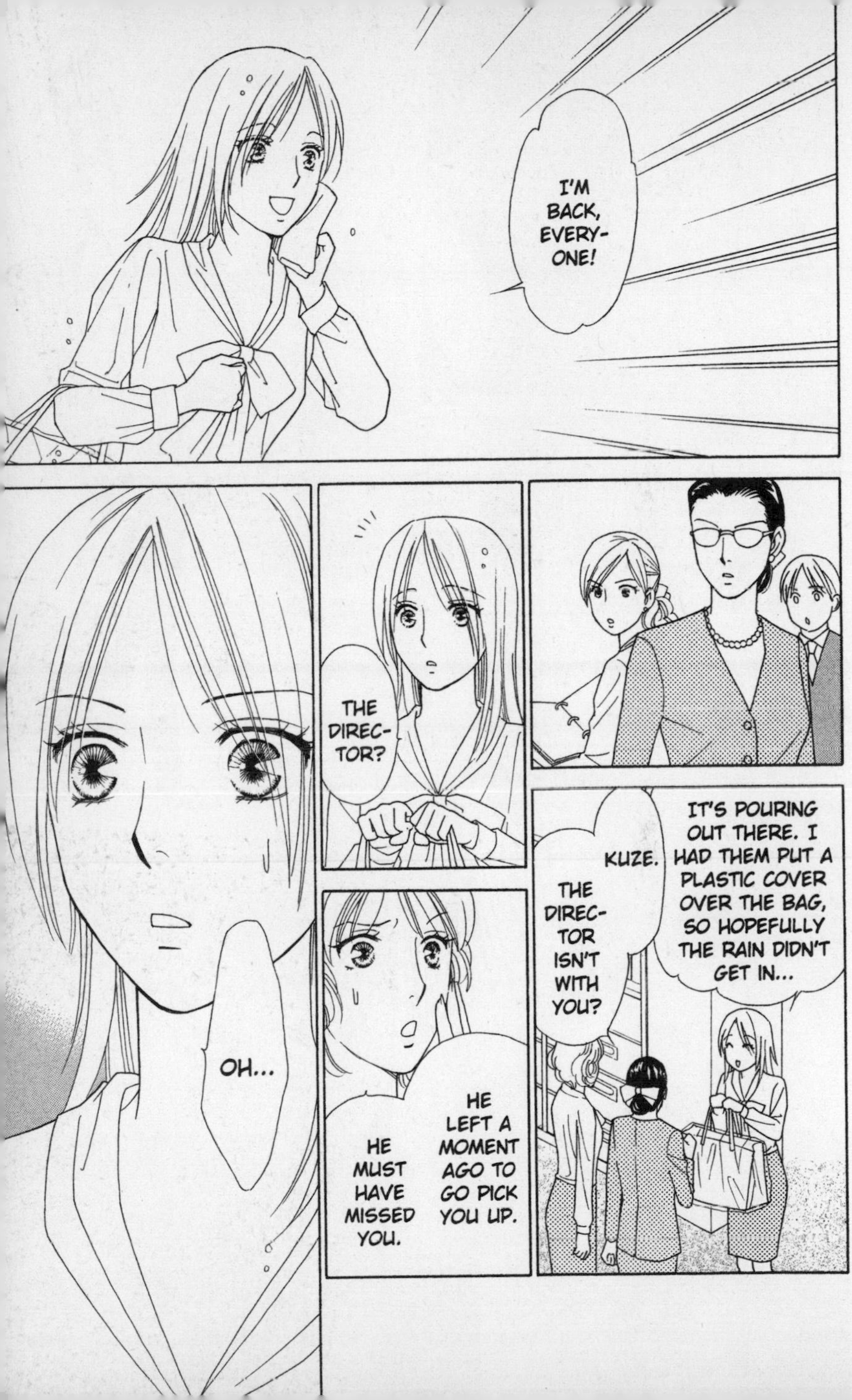
I'M BACK, EVERY-ONE!
THE DIREC-TOR?
IT'S POURING OUT THERE. I HAD THEM PUT A PLASTIC COVER OVER THE BAG, SO HOPEFULLY THE RAIN DIDN'T GET IN...
KUZE. THE DIREC-TOR ISN'T WITH YOU?
HE LEFT A MOMENT AGO TO GO PICK YOU UP.
HE MUST HAVE MISSED YOU.
OH...

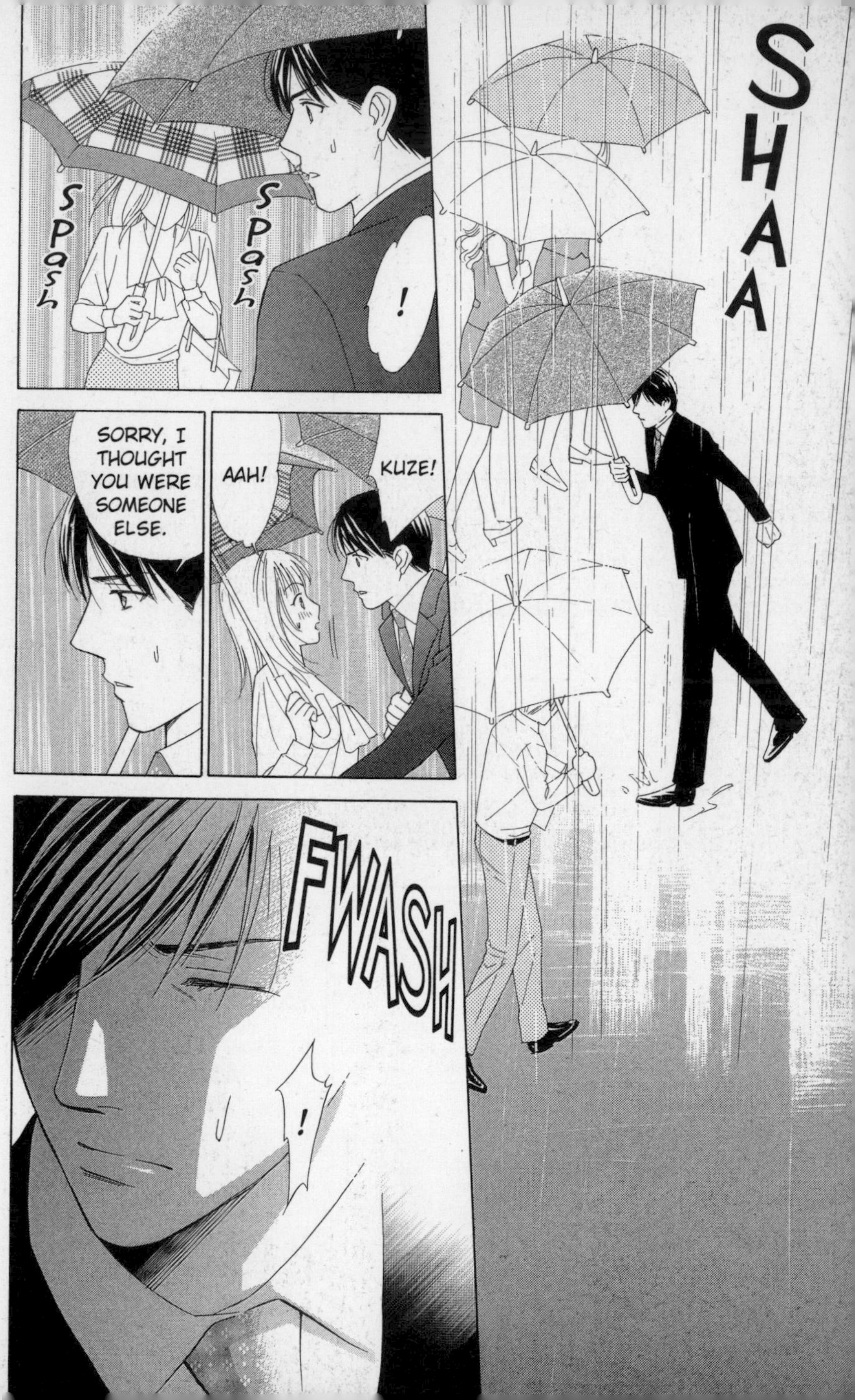
SHAA
Spash
Spash
!
KUZE!
AAH!
SORRY, I THOUGHT YOU WERE SOMEONE ELSE.
FWASH
!

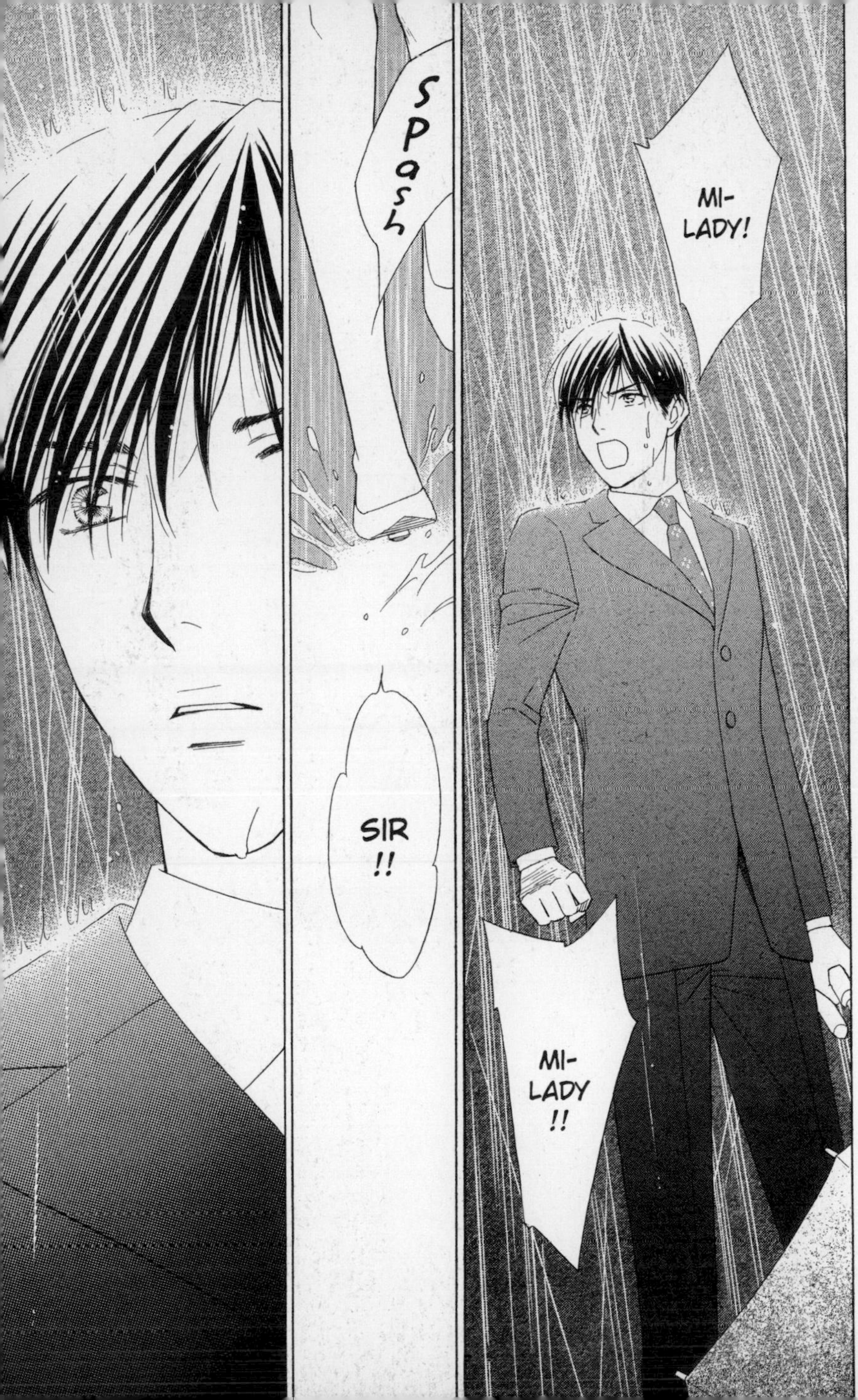
MI-LADY!
MI-LADY!!
Spash
SIR!!

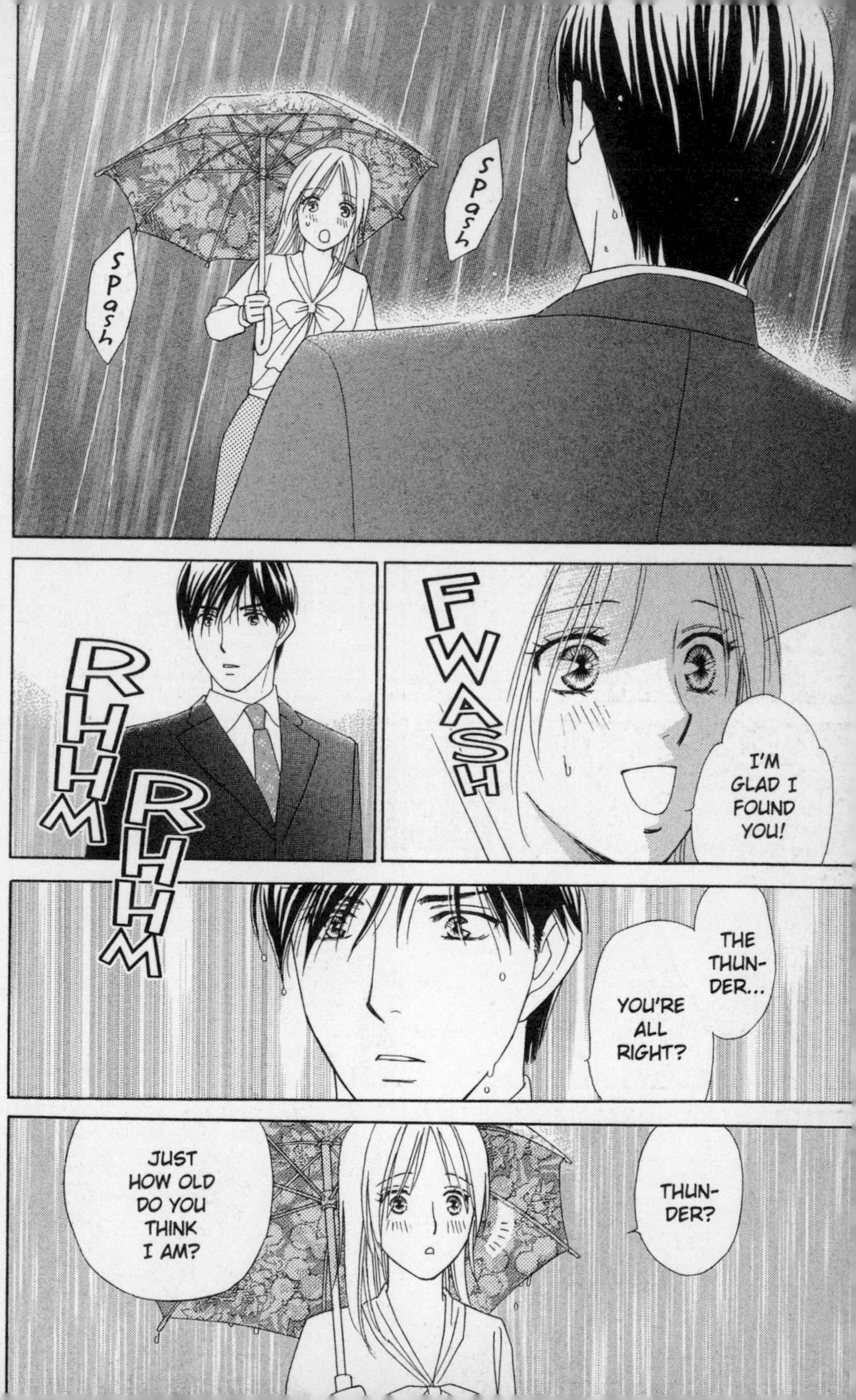
Spash
Spash
FWASH
I'M GLAD I FOUND YOU!
RHHM RHHM
THE THUN-DER...
YOU'RE ALL RIGHT?
THUN-DER?
JUST HOW OLD DO YOU THINK I AM?

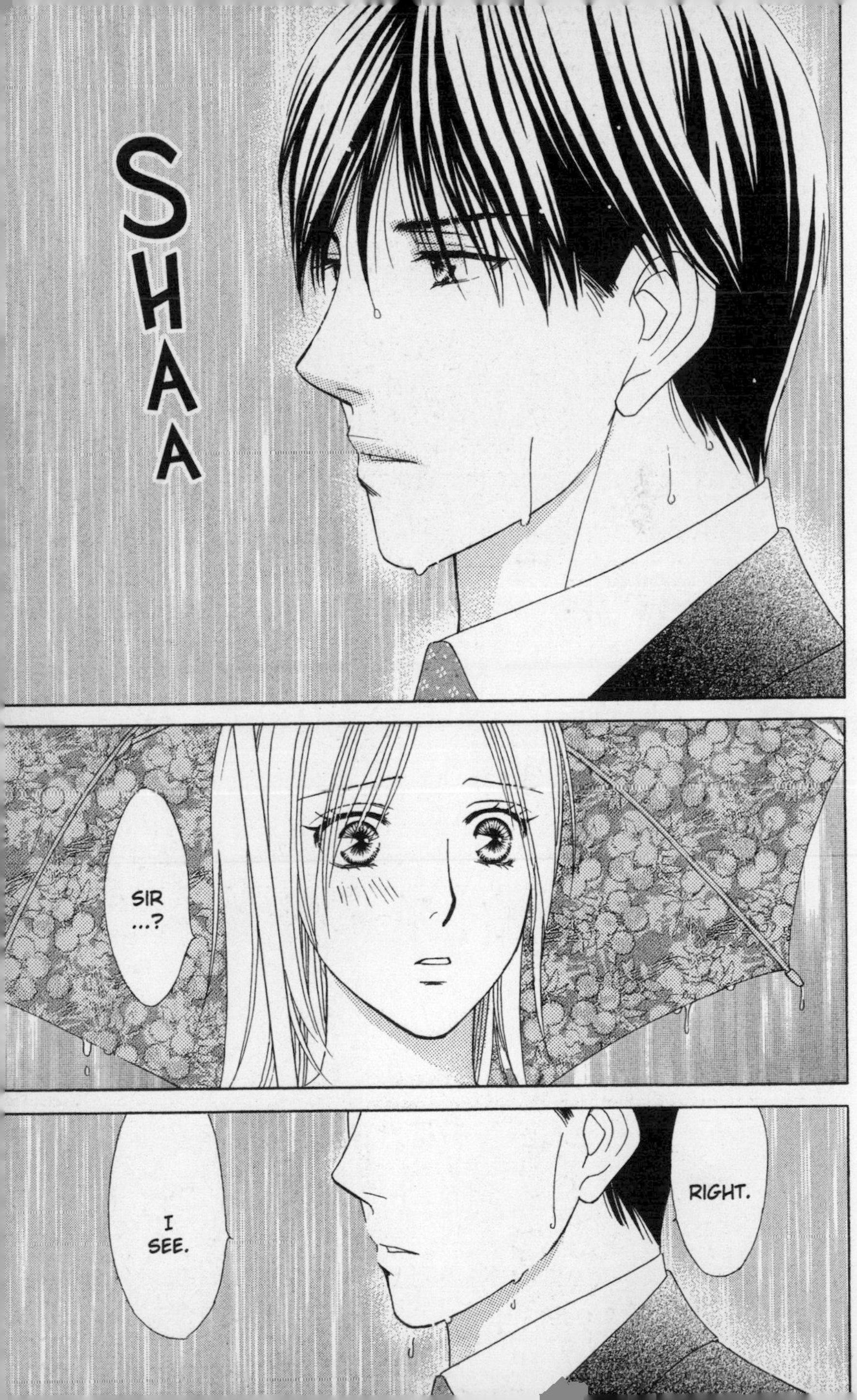
SHAA
SIR ...?
RIGHT.
I SEE.

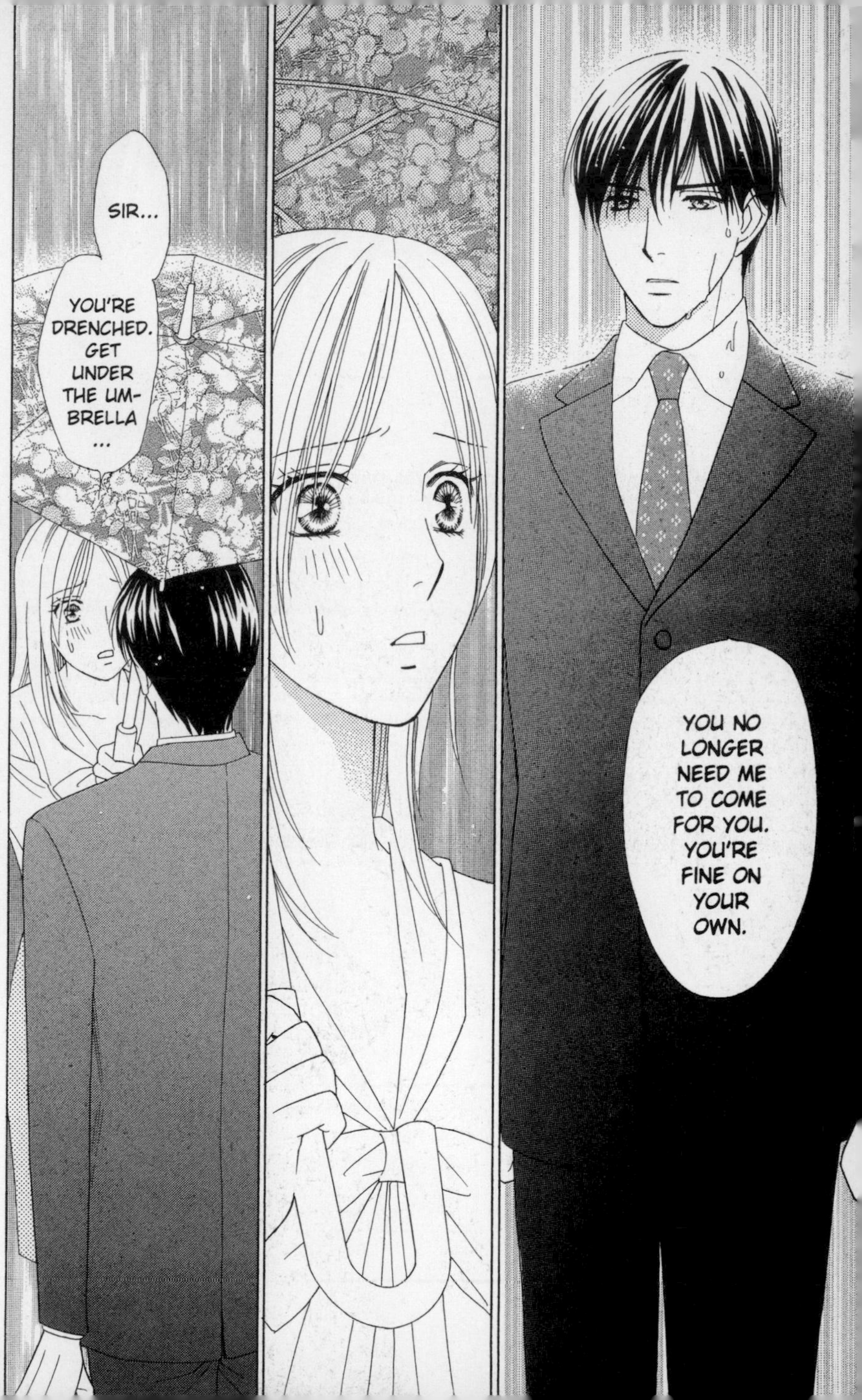
YOU NO LONGER NEED ME TO COME FOR YOU. YOU'RE FINE ON YOUR OWN.
SIR...
YOU'RE DRENCHED. GET UNDER THE UM-BRELLA ...

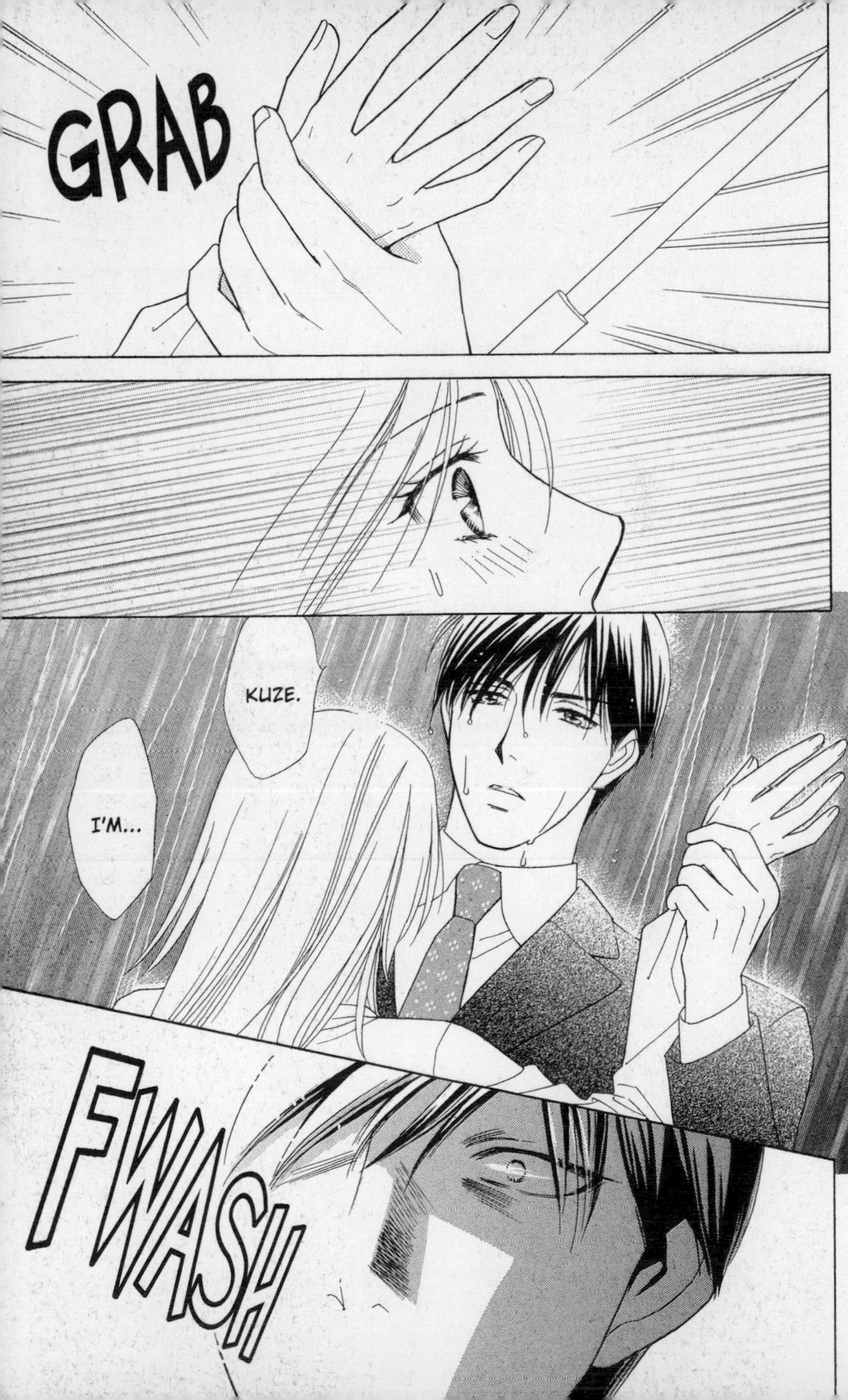
GRAB
KUZE.
I'M...
FWASH

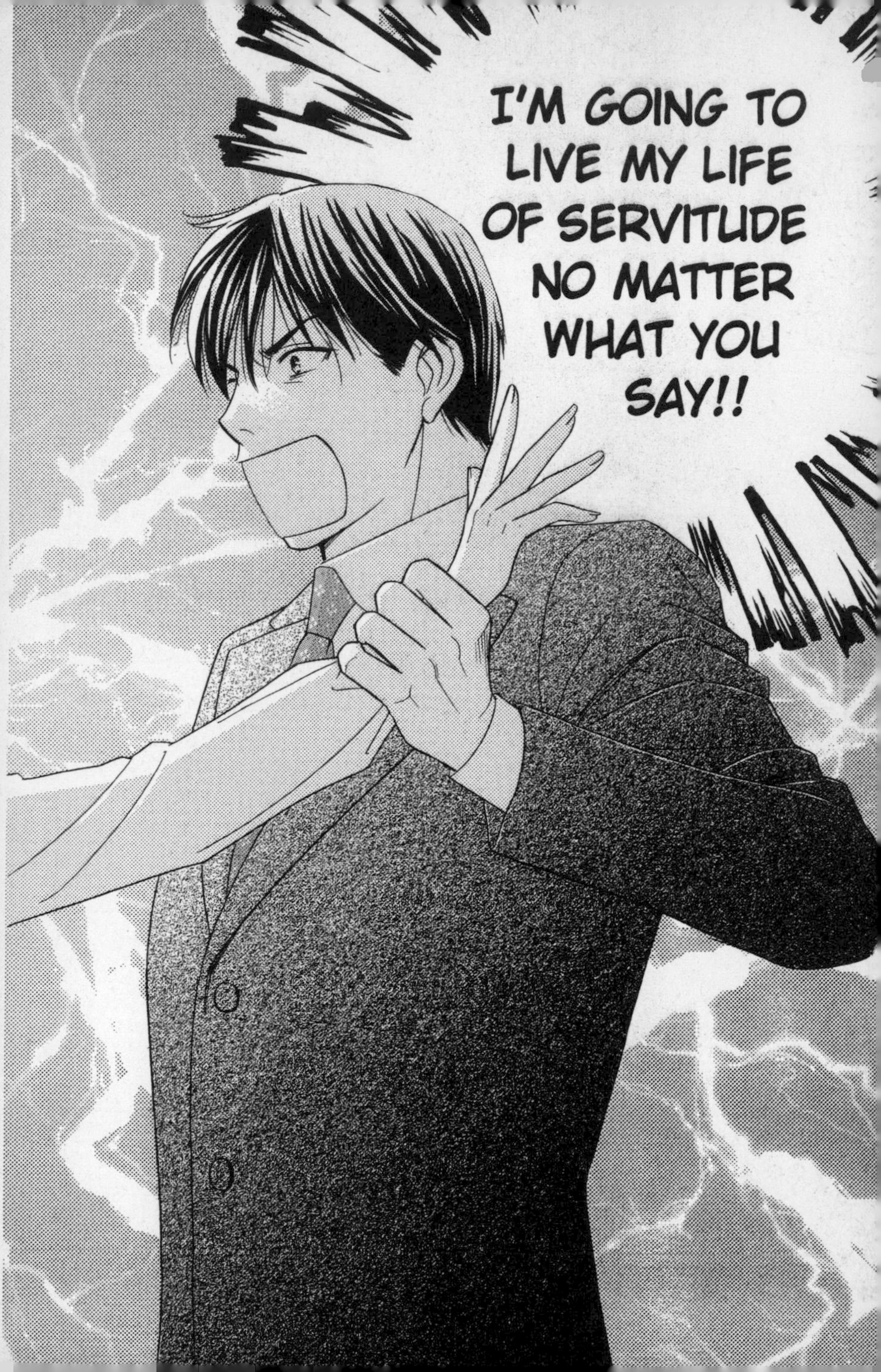
I'M GOING TO LIVE MY LIFE OF SERVITUDE NO MATTER WHAT YOU SAY!!

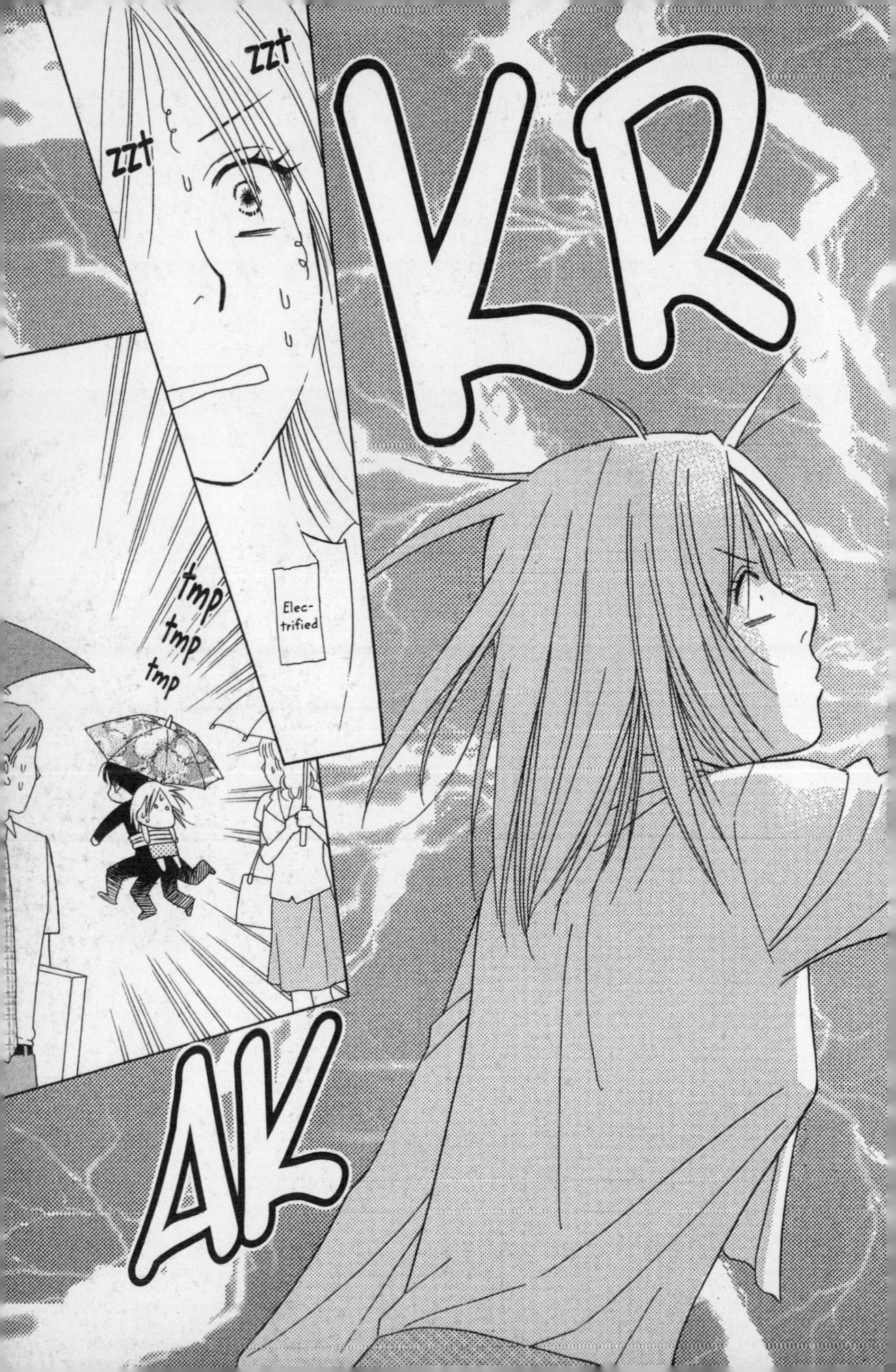
KR
AK
zzt
zzt
Elec-
trified
tmp
tmp
tmp

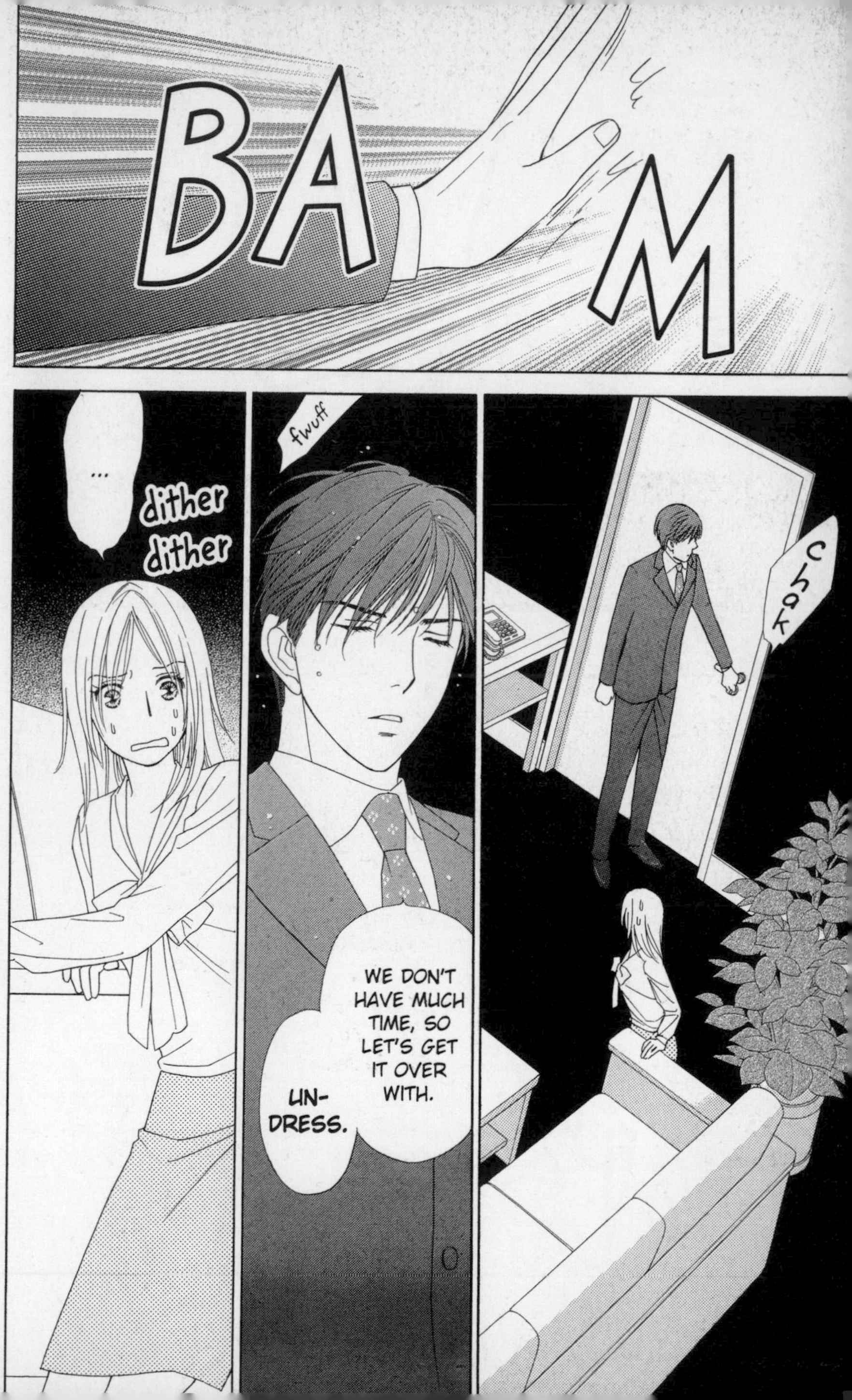
BAM
chak
fwuff
WE DON'T HAVE MUCH TIME, SO LET'S GET IT OVER WITH.
UN-DRESS.
...
dither dither

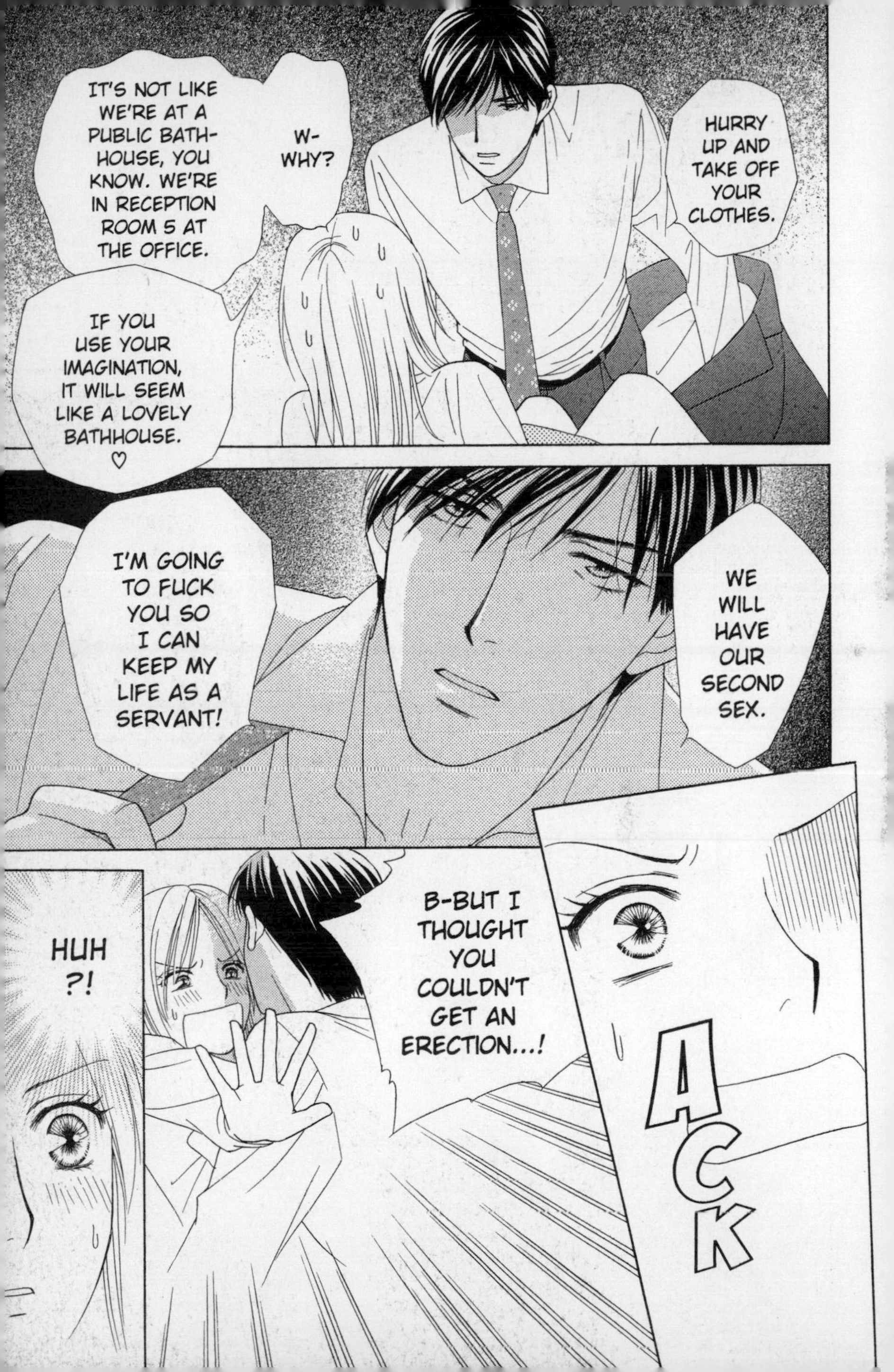
HURRY UP AND TAKE OFF YOUR CLOTHES.
W-WHY?
IT'S NOT LIKE WE'RE AT A PUBLIC BATH-HOUSE, YOU KNOW. WE'RE IN RECEPTION ROOM 5 AT THE OFFICE.
IF YOU USE YOUR IMAGINATION, IT WILL SEEM LIKE A LOVELY BATHHOUSE. ♡
WE WILL HAVE OUR SECOND SEX.
I'M GOING TO FUCK YOU SO I CAN KEEP MY LIFE AS A SERVANT!
B-BUT I THOUGHT YOU COULDN'T GET AN ERECTION...!
ACK
HUH ?!

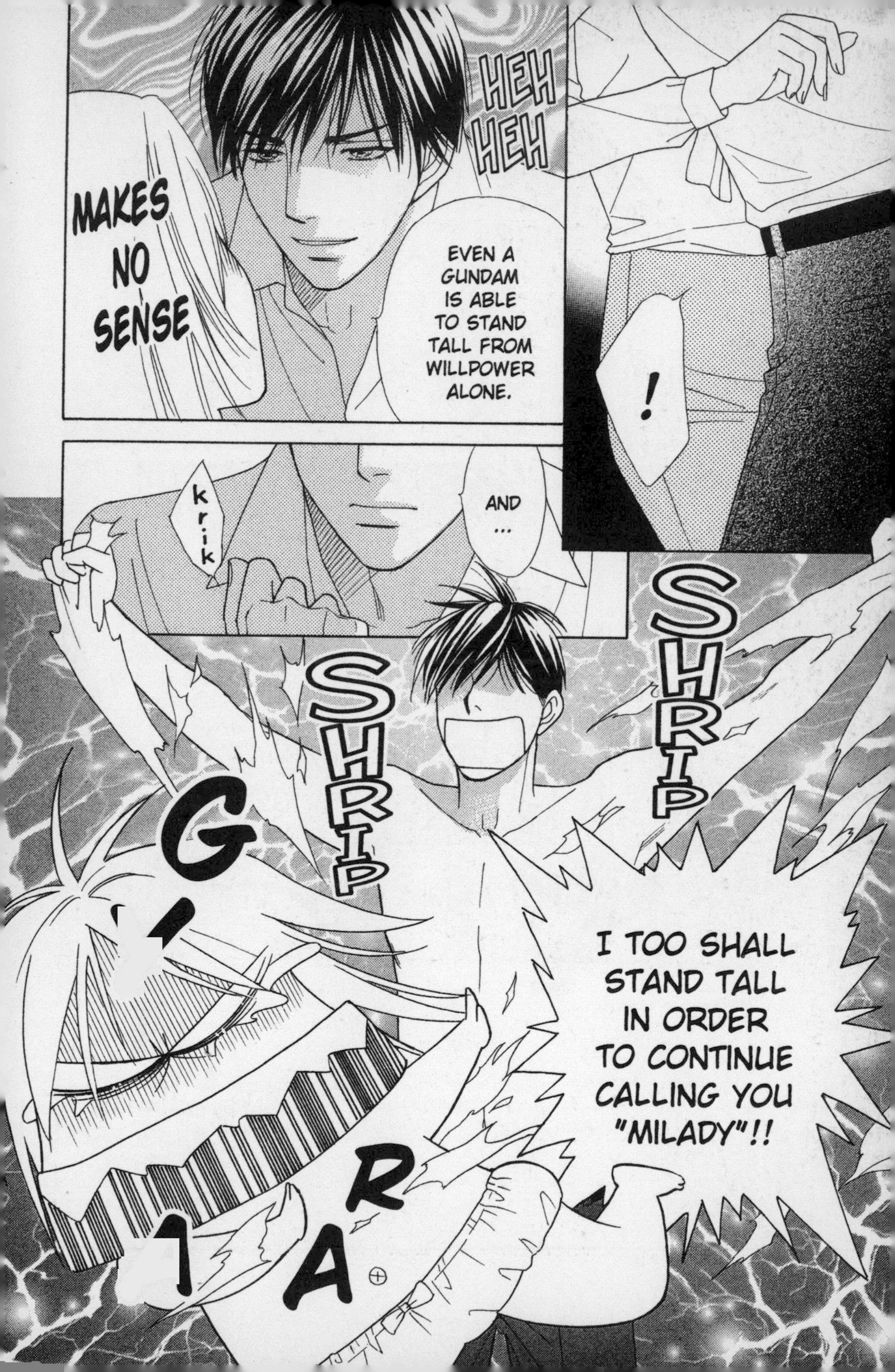
!
HEH HEH
EVEN A GUNDAM IS ABLE TO STAND TALL FROM WILLPOWER ALONE.
MAKES NO SENSE
AND ...
krik
SHRIP
SHRIP
I TOO SHALL STAND TALL IN ORDER TO CONTINUE CALLING YOU "MILADY"!!
GIRA

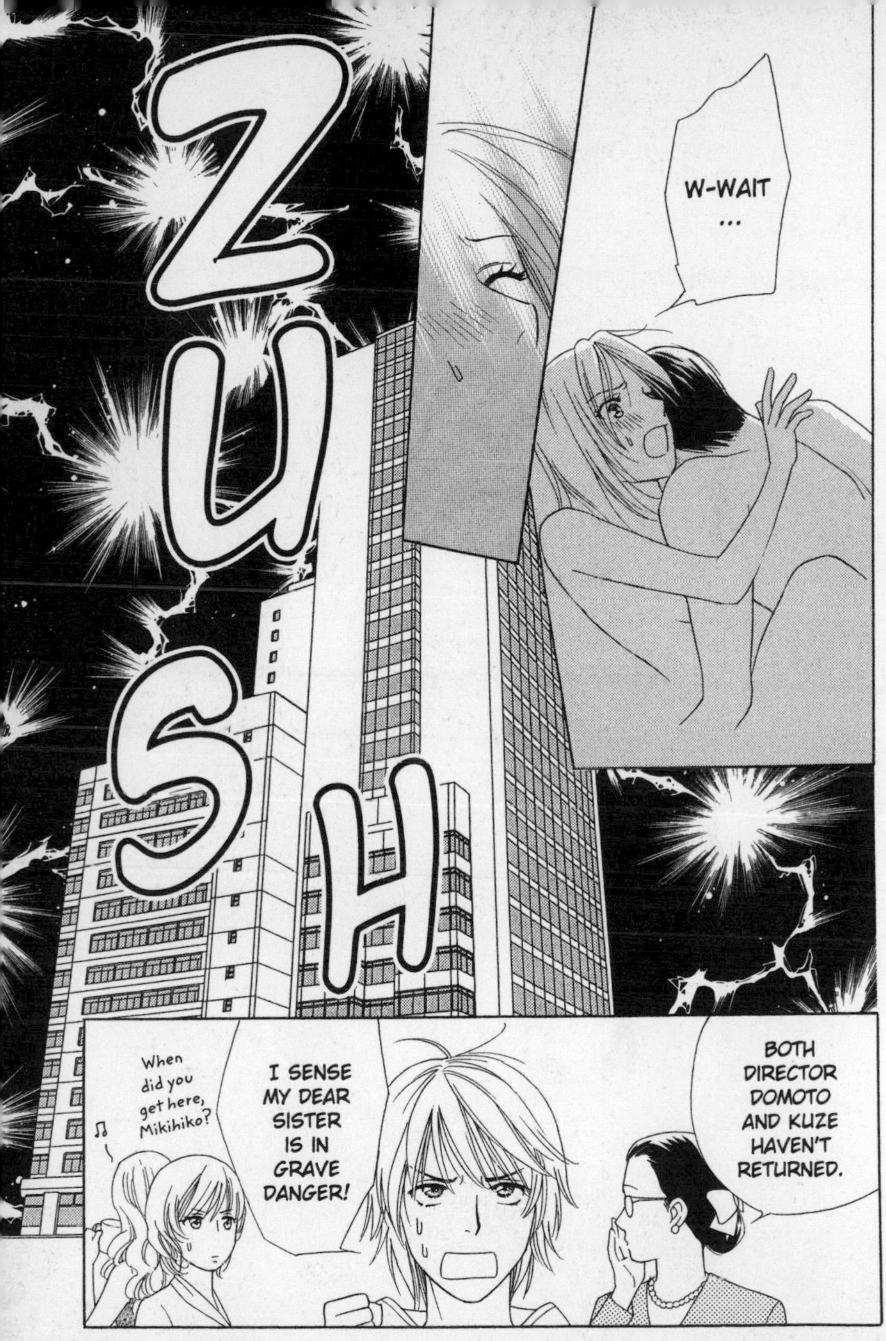
W-WAIT
...
ZUSH
BOTH DIRECTOR DOMOTO AND KUZE HAVEN'T RETURNED.
I SENSE MY DEAR SISTER IS IN GRAVE DANGER!
When did you get here, Mikihiko? ♫

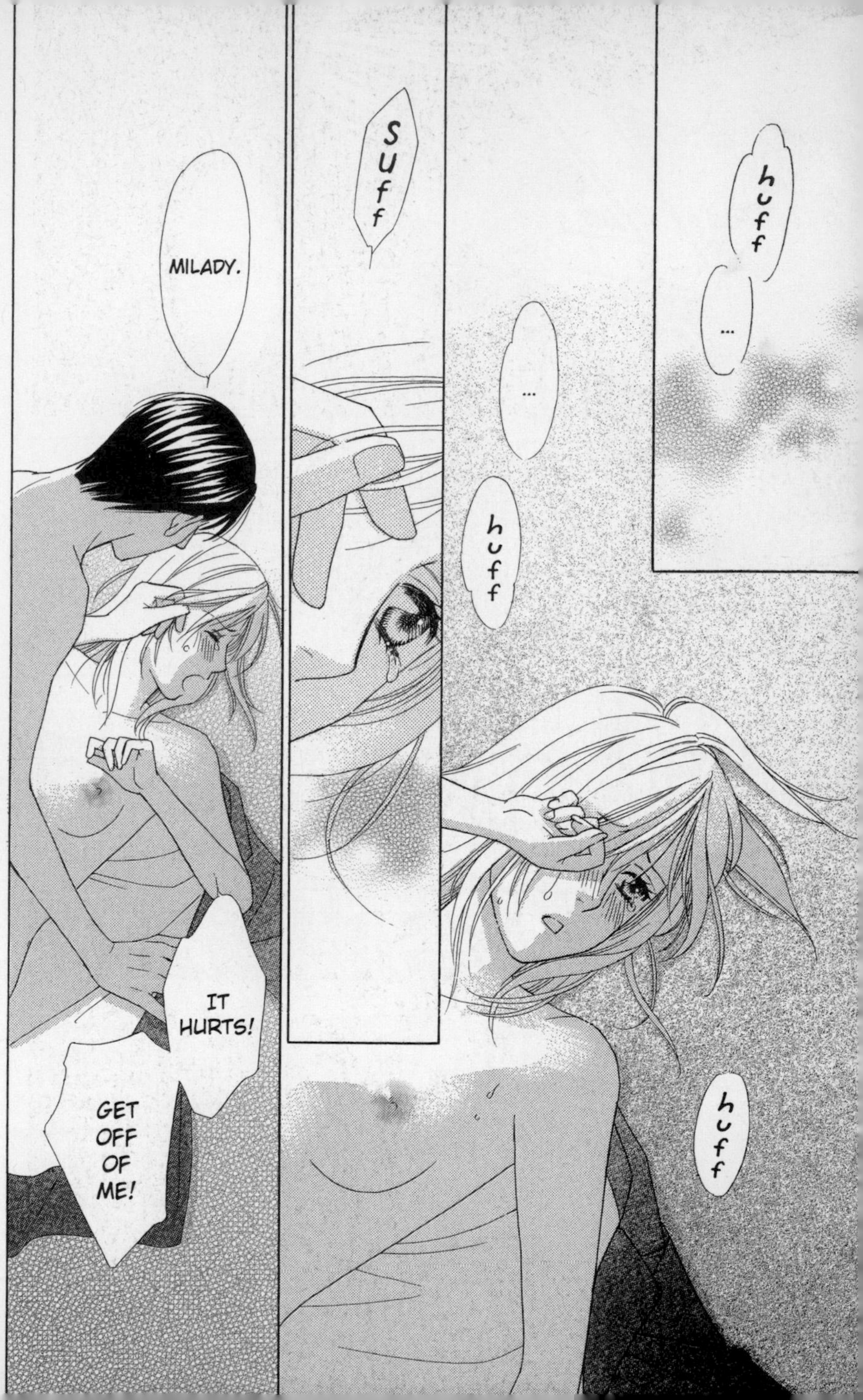
huff
...
...
huff
huff
suff
MILADY.
IT HURTS!
GET OFF OF ME!

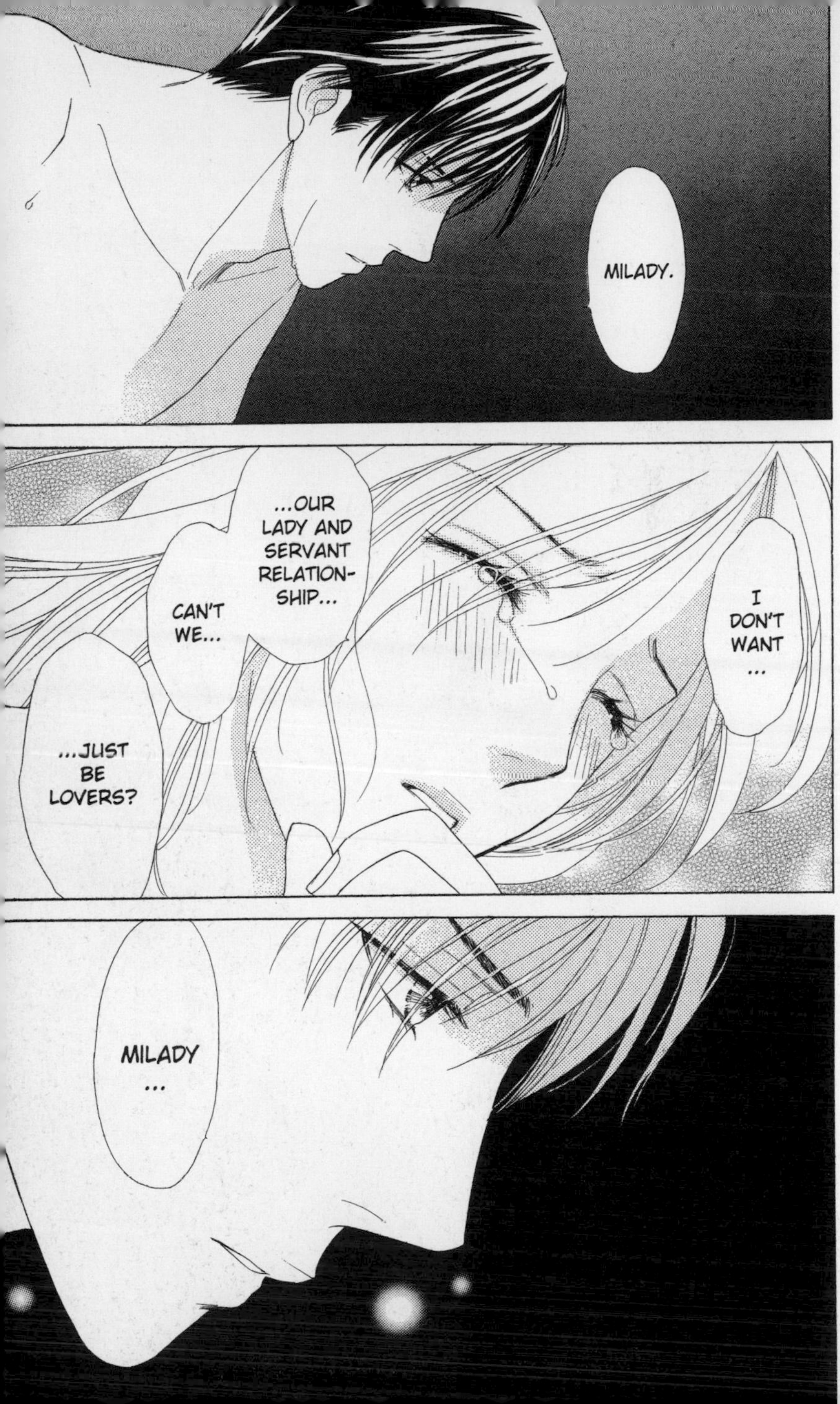
MILADY.
I DON'T WANT ...
...OUR LADY AND SERVANT RELATION-SHIP...
CAN'T WE...
...JUST BE LOVERS?
MILADY ...

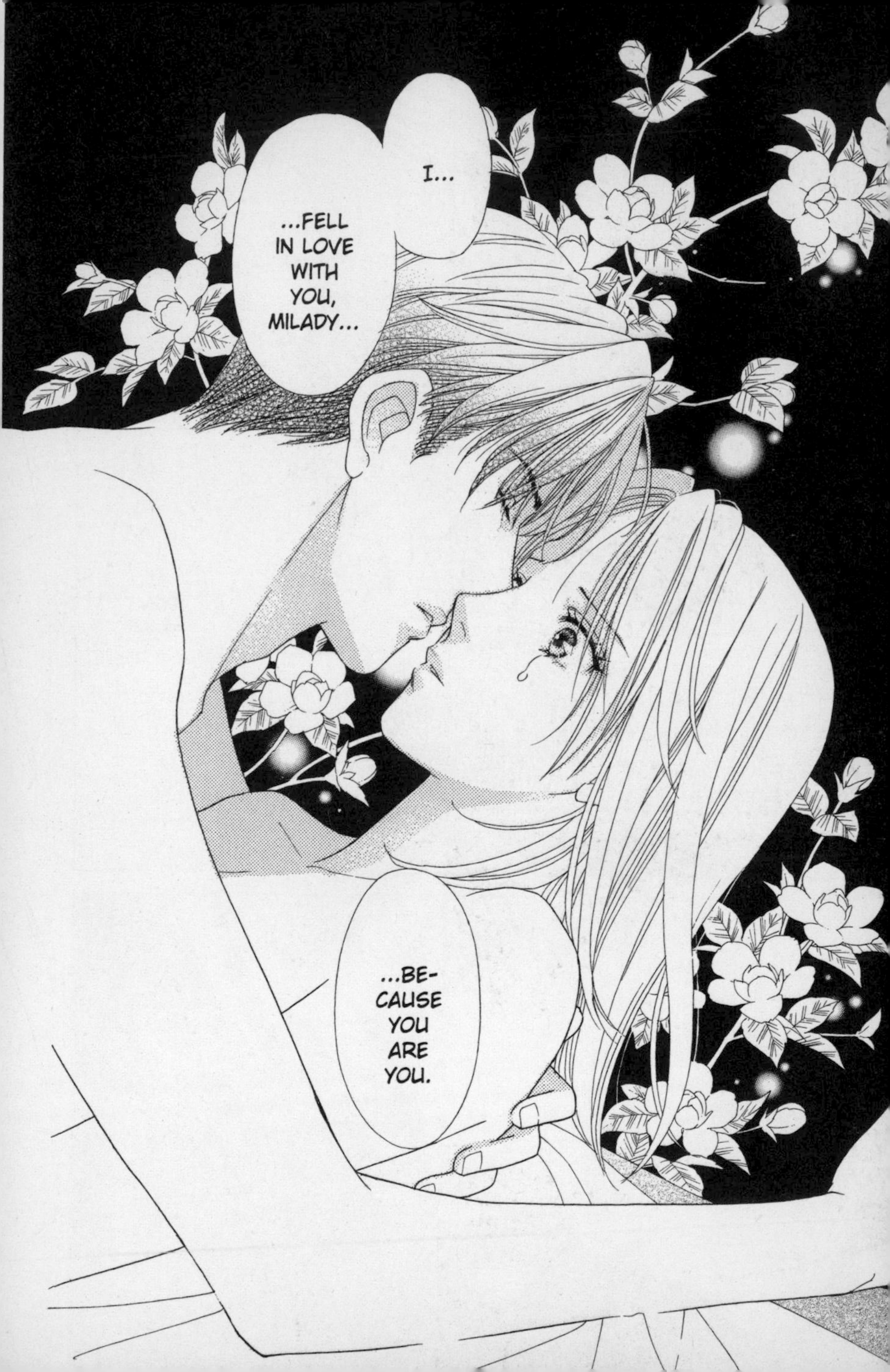
I... ...FELL IN LOVE WITH YOU, MILADY...
...BE-CAUSE YOU ARE YOU.

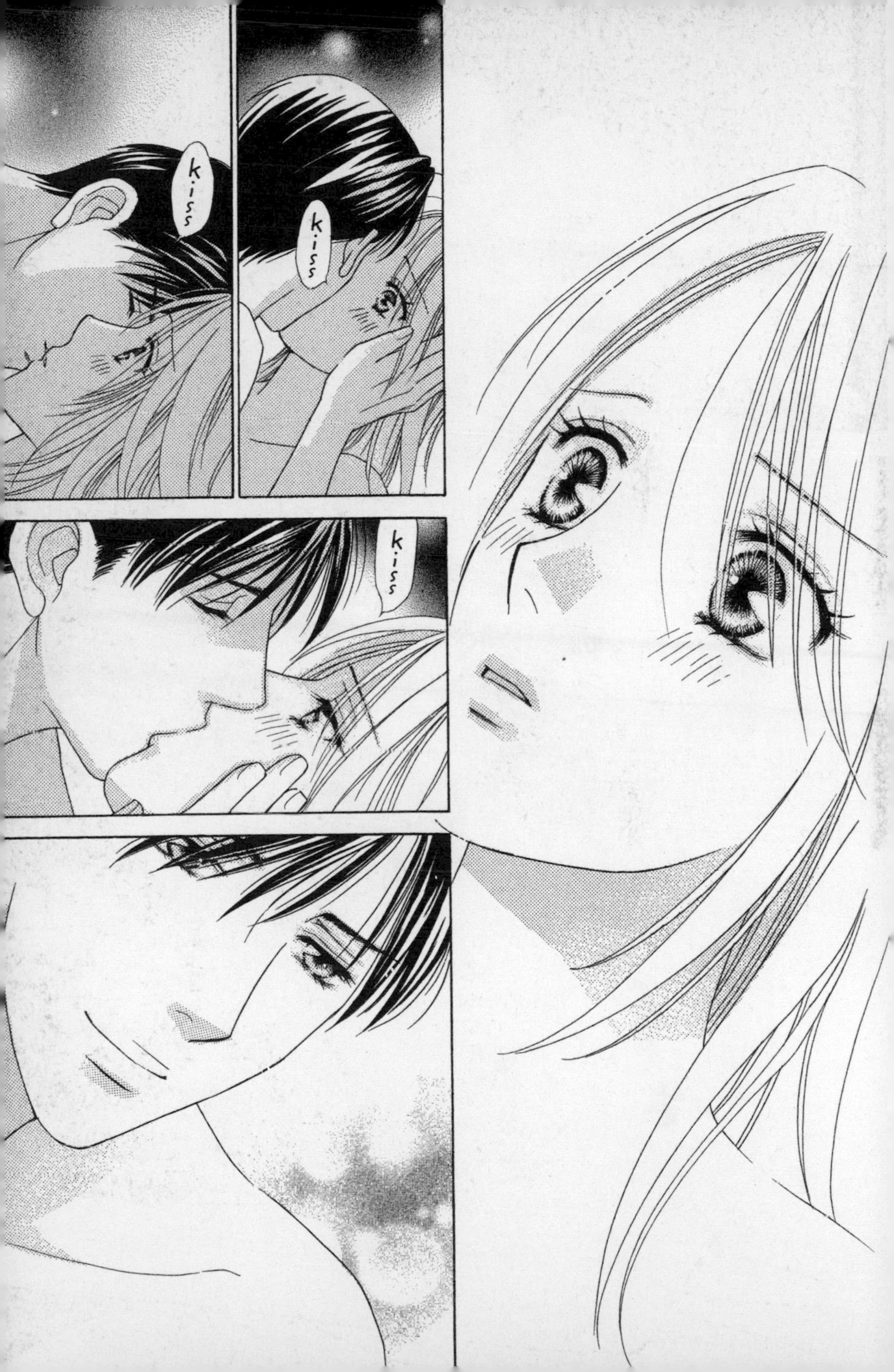
kiss
kiss
kiss

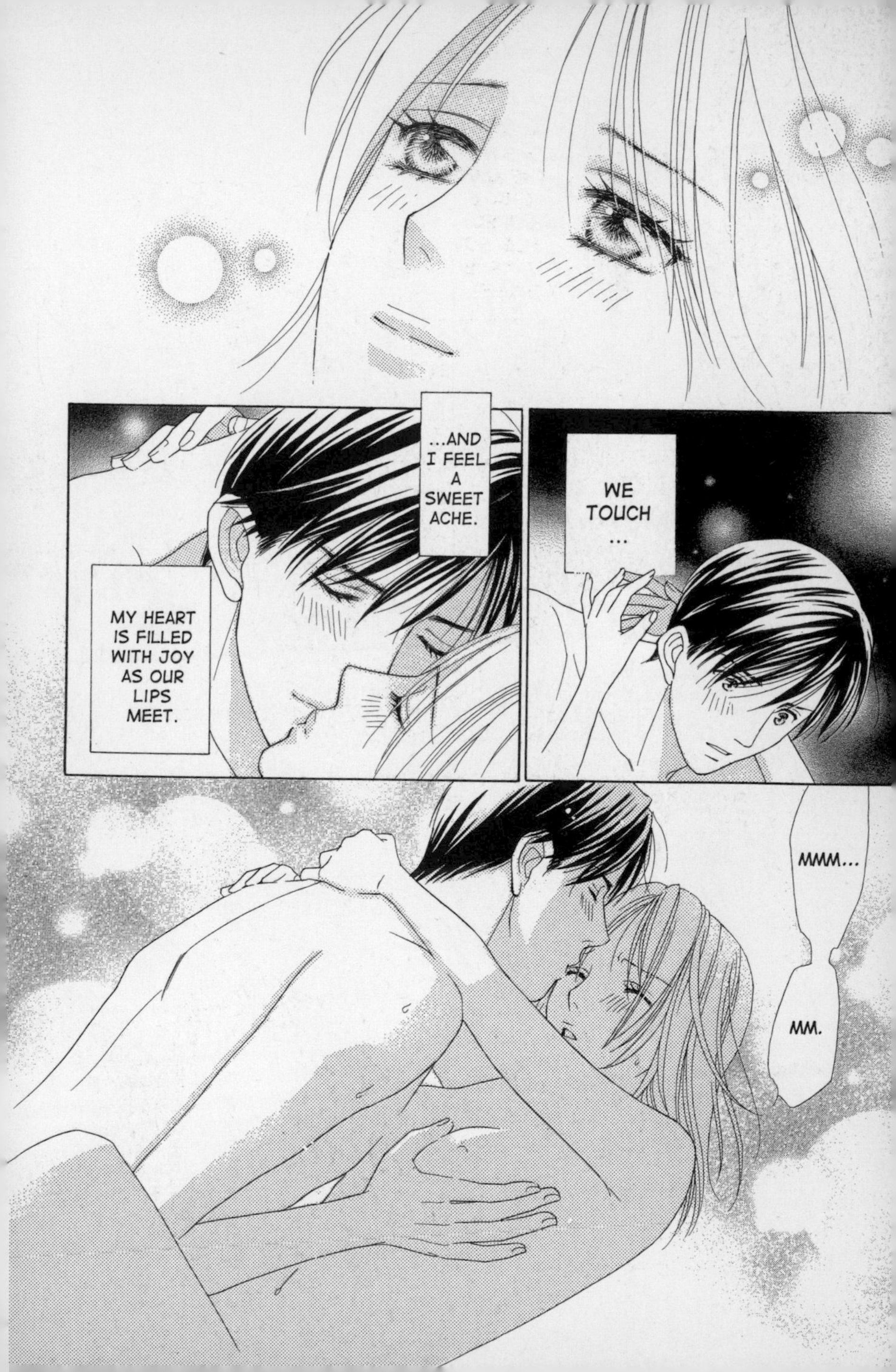
WE TOUCH ...
...AND I FEEL A SWEET ACHE.
MY HEART IS FILLED WITH JOY AS OUR LIPS MEET.
MMM...
MM.

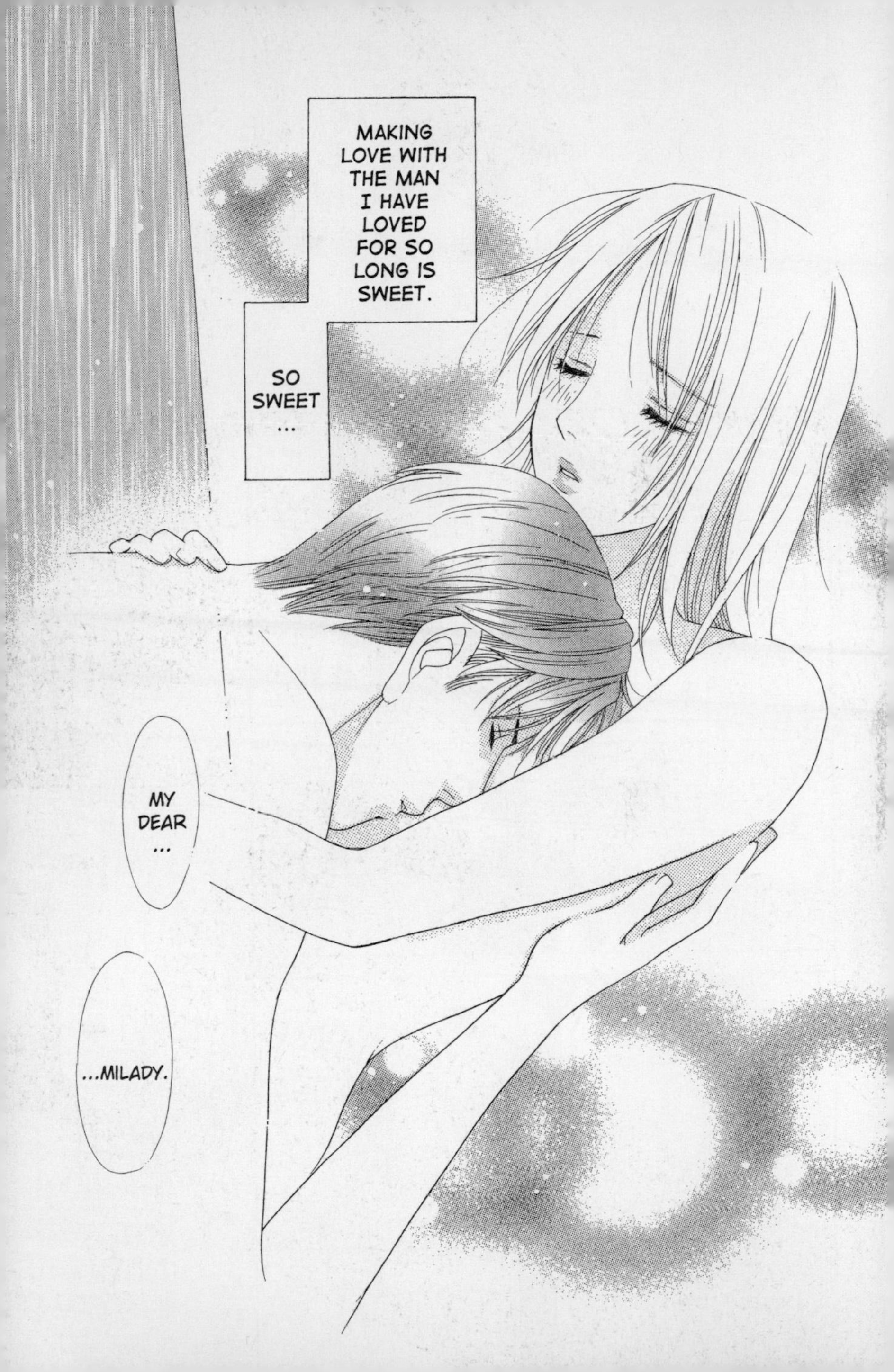
MAKING LOVE WITH THE MAN I HAVE LOVED FOR SO LONG IS SWEET.
SO SWEET ...
MY DEAR ...
...MILADY.

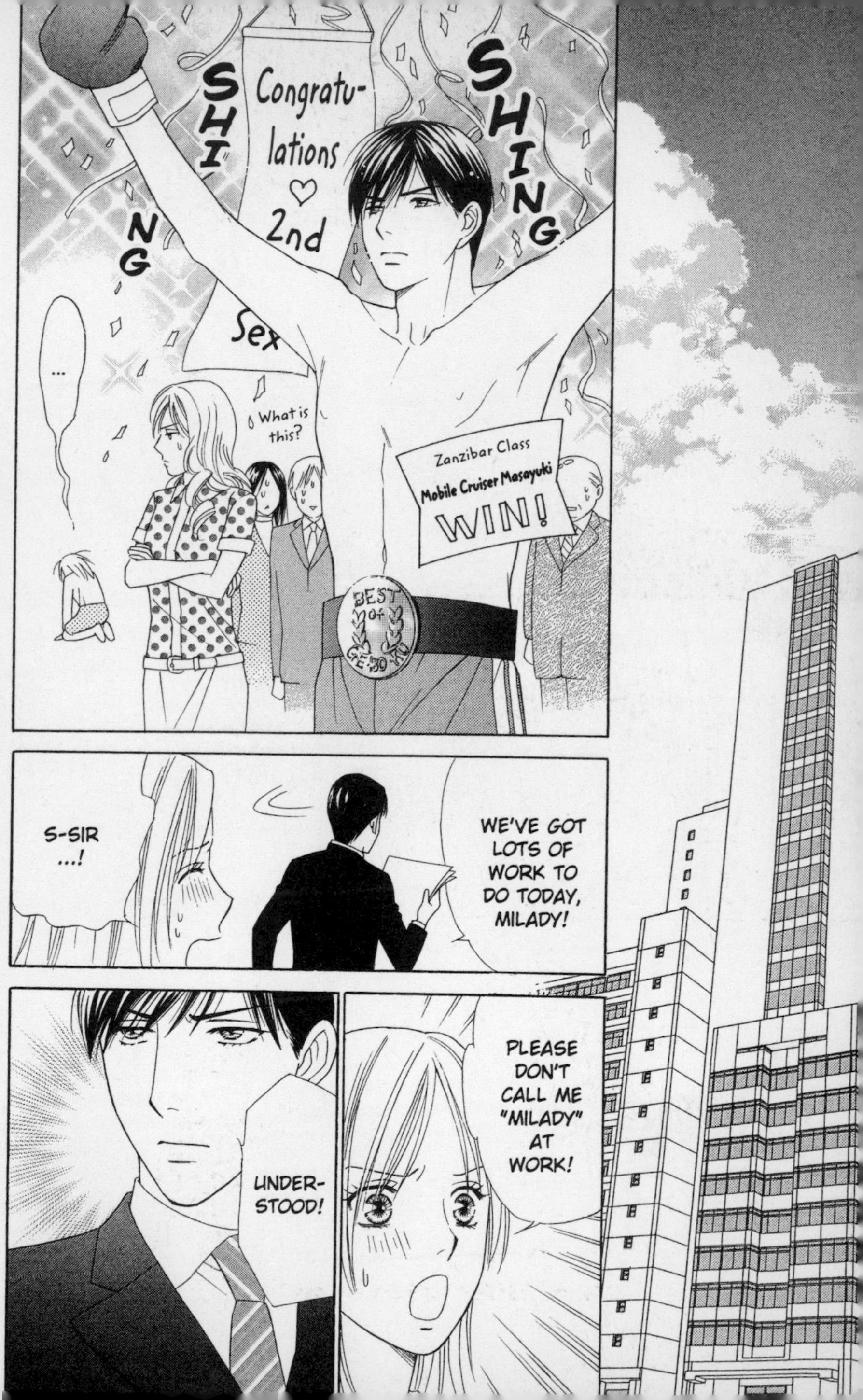
SHING
Congratu-
lations ♡
2nd
Sex
SHING
Zanzibar Class
Mobile Cruiser Masayuki
WIN!
What is this?
...
WE'VE GOT LOTS OF WORK TO DO TODAY, MILADY!
S-SIR ...!
PLEASE DON'T CALL ME "MILADY" AT WORK!
UNDER-STOOD!

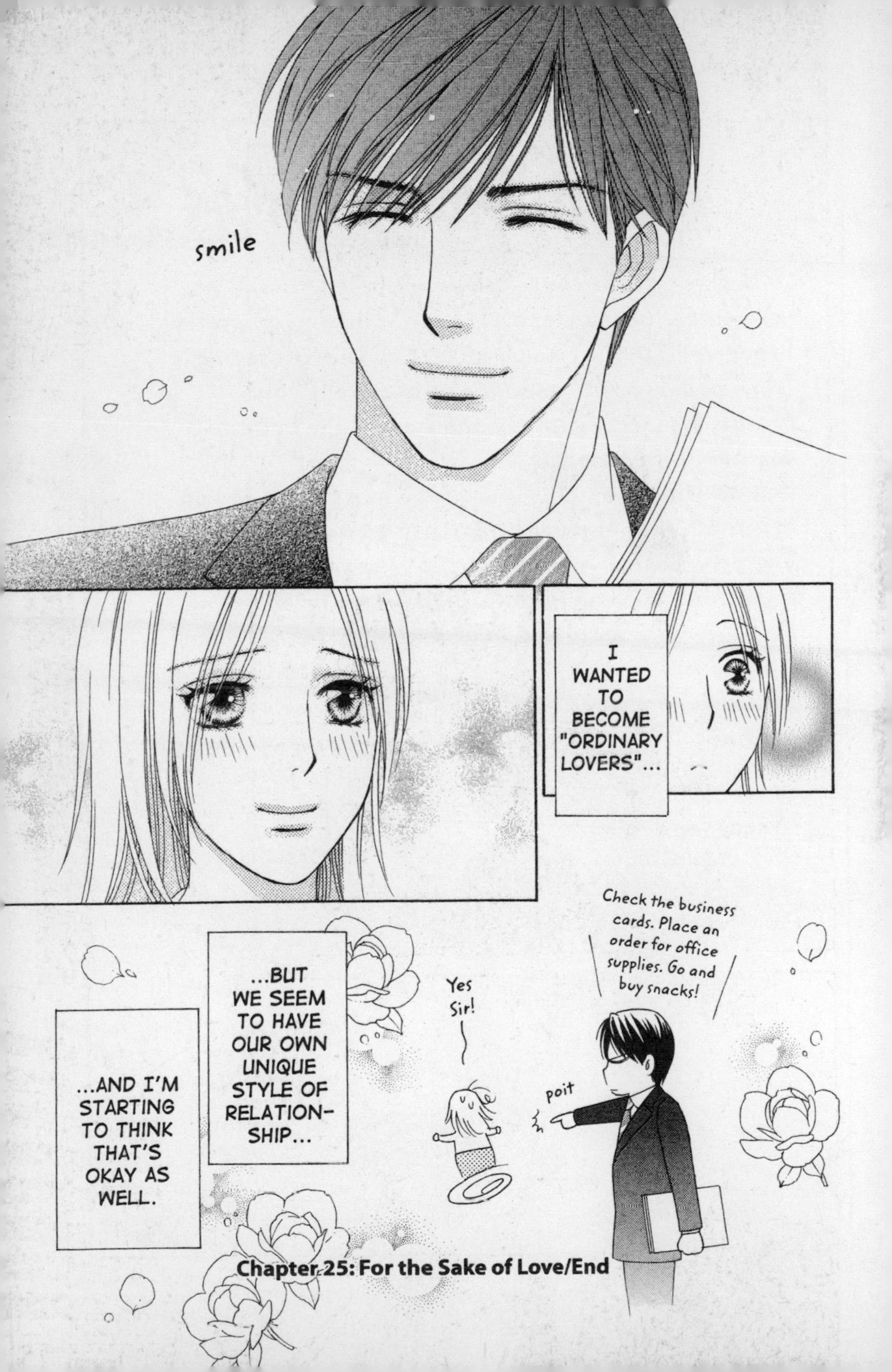
smile
I WANTED TO BECOME "ORDINARY LOVERS"...
Check the business cards. Place an order for office supplies. Go and buy snacks!
Yes Sir!
poit
...BUT WE SEEM TO HAVE OUR OWN UNIQUE STYLE OF RELATION-SHIP...
...AND I'M STARTING TO THINK THAT'S OKAY AS WELL.
Chapter 25: For the Sake of Love/End

FROM THE AUTHOR

So this was *Butterflies, Flowers* volume 5. Thank you very much for reading it. Aaaah!! I'm sorry, I'm sorry! I received tons of angry letters and emails saying, "How could you?!" and "You're so cruel!!" about Masayuki's circumstance, and I can't apologize to you about it enough. υυ

He's an otaku, he's girly and to top it off he ended up like that...so there was **nothing good about him!!** I'm sorry, I'm sorry. I promise that Masayuki will do something to clean his tarnished image in volume 6. He'll probably become cooler and a tad more decent... I think... υυ

Please don't give up on me, and I hope you will all continue to support me. Please send in your comments and complaints.

Nancy Thistlethwaite, Editor
VIZ Media, LLC
295 Bay Street
San Francisco, CA 94133

吉原 由起
Yuki Yoshihara

HMPH

You know, I really think there's no reason to keep calling those new versions "Gundam" series...

Butterflies, Flowers

Notes

Page 52: In Japan, *Ooka Echizen* is a tv drama featuring Ooka Tadasuke, who was a Japanese samurai and magistrate in the Edo period.

Page 121: In Japanese folklore, if you don't cover up your bellybutton during a thunderstorm, the god of thunder will steal it.

Page 180: The first episode of *Mobile Suit Gundam* is called *"Gundam Daichi ni Tatsu!!"* or "Gundam Rising."

About the Author

Yuki Yoshihara was born in
Tokyo on February 11. She
wanted to become a mangaka
since elementary school and
debuted in 1988 with *Chanel
no Sasayaki*. She is the author
of numerous series including
Darling wa Namamono ni Tsuki
and *Itadakimasu*. Yoshihara's
favorite band is the Pet Shop
Boys, and she keeps her TV
tuned to the Mystery Channel.

BUTTERFLIES, FLOWERS
Vol. 5
Shojo Beat Edition

STORY AND ART BY
YUKI YOSHIHARA

© 2006 Yuki YOSHIHARA/Shogakukan
All rights reserved.
Original Japanese edition "CHOU YO HANA YO"
published by SHOGAKUKAN Inc.

Adaptation/Nancy Thistlethwaite
Translation/Tetsuichiro Miyaki
Touch-up Art & Lettering/Freeman Wong
Cover Design/Hidemi Sahara
Interior Design/Yuki Ameda
Editor/Nancy Thistlethwaite

Printed in the U.S.A.

Published by VIZ Media, LLC
P.O. Box 77010
San Francisco, CA 94107

10 9 8 7 6 5 4 3 2 1
First printing, December 2010

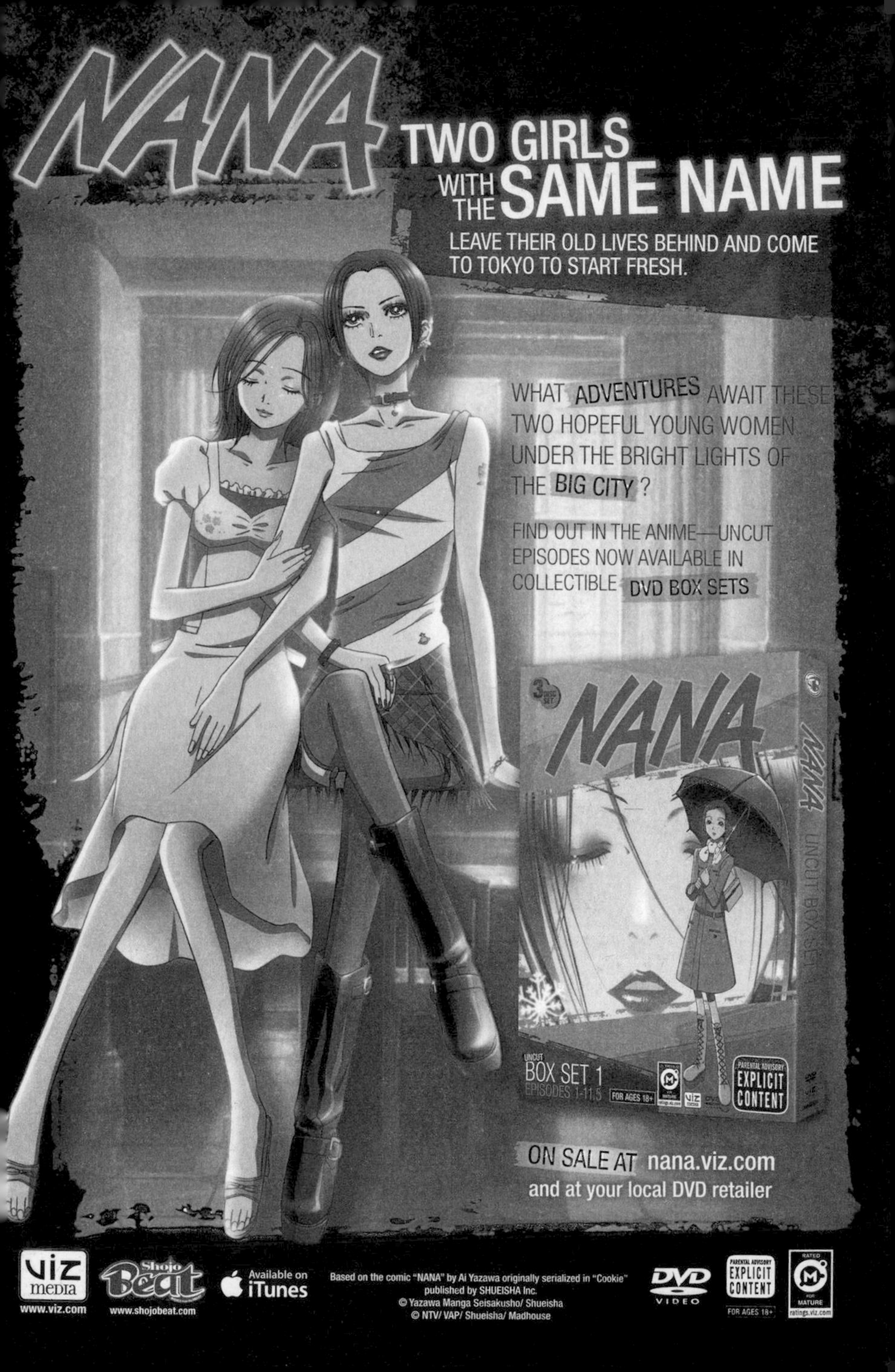

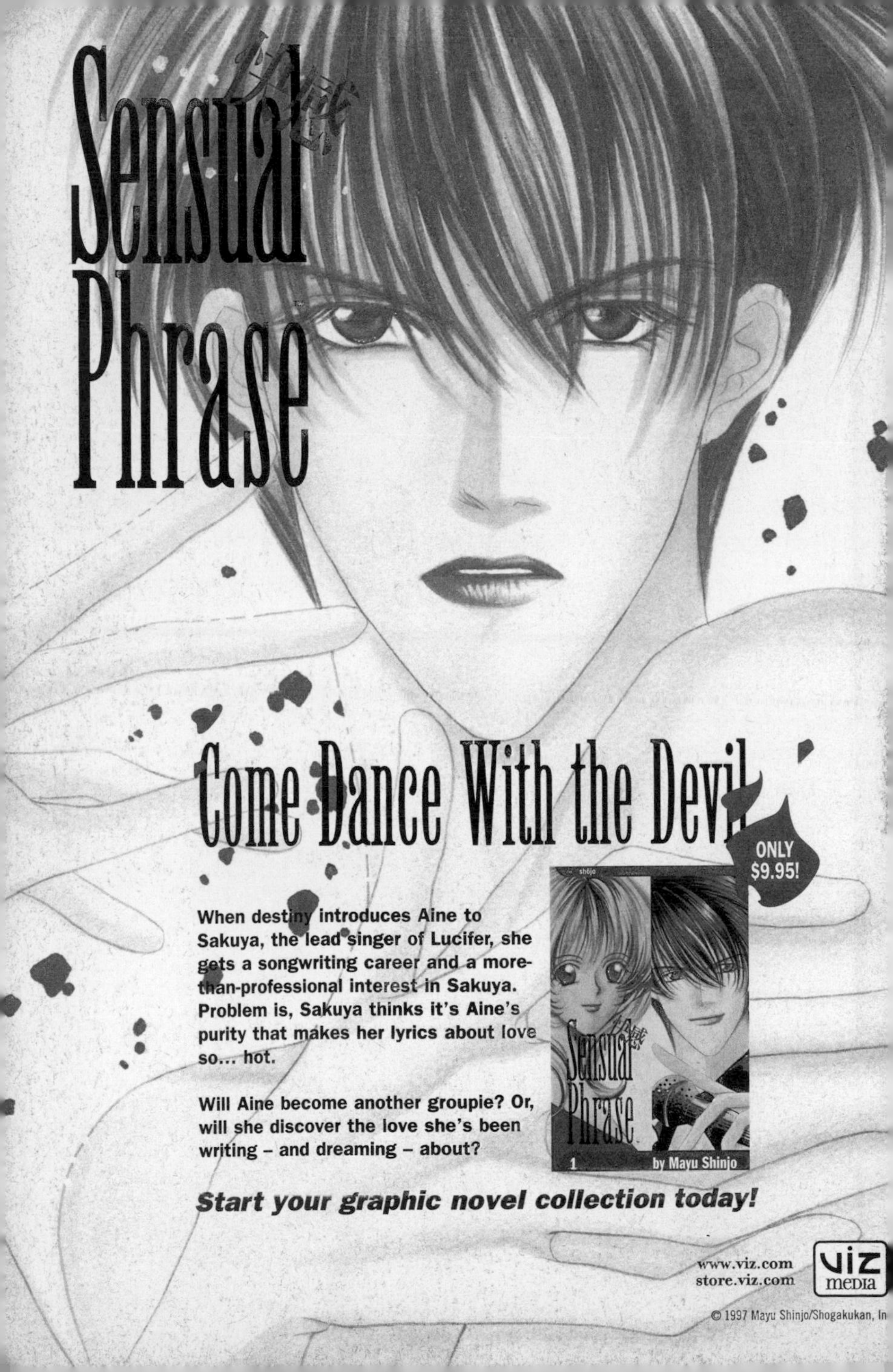
Sensual Phrase™
Come Dance With the Devil
ONLY $9.95!
shôjo
Sensual Phrase
1
by Mayu Shinjo
When destiny introduces Aine to Sakuya, the lead singer of Lucifer, she gets a songwriting career and a more-than-professional interest in Sakuya. Problem is, Sakuya thinks it's Aine's purity that makes her lyrics about love so... hot.
Will Aine become another groupie? Or, will she discover the love she's been writing – and dreaming – about?
Start your graphic novel collection today!
www.viz.com
store.viz.com
VIZ MEDIA
© 1997 Mayu Shinjo/Shogakukan, In

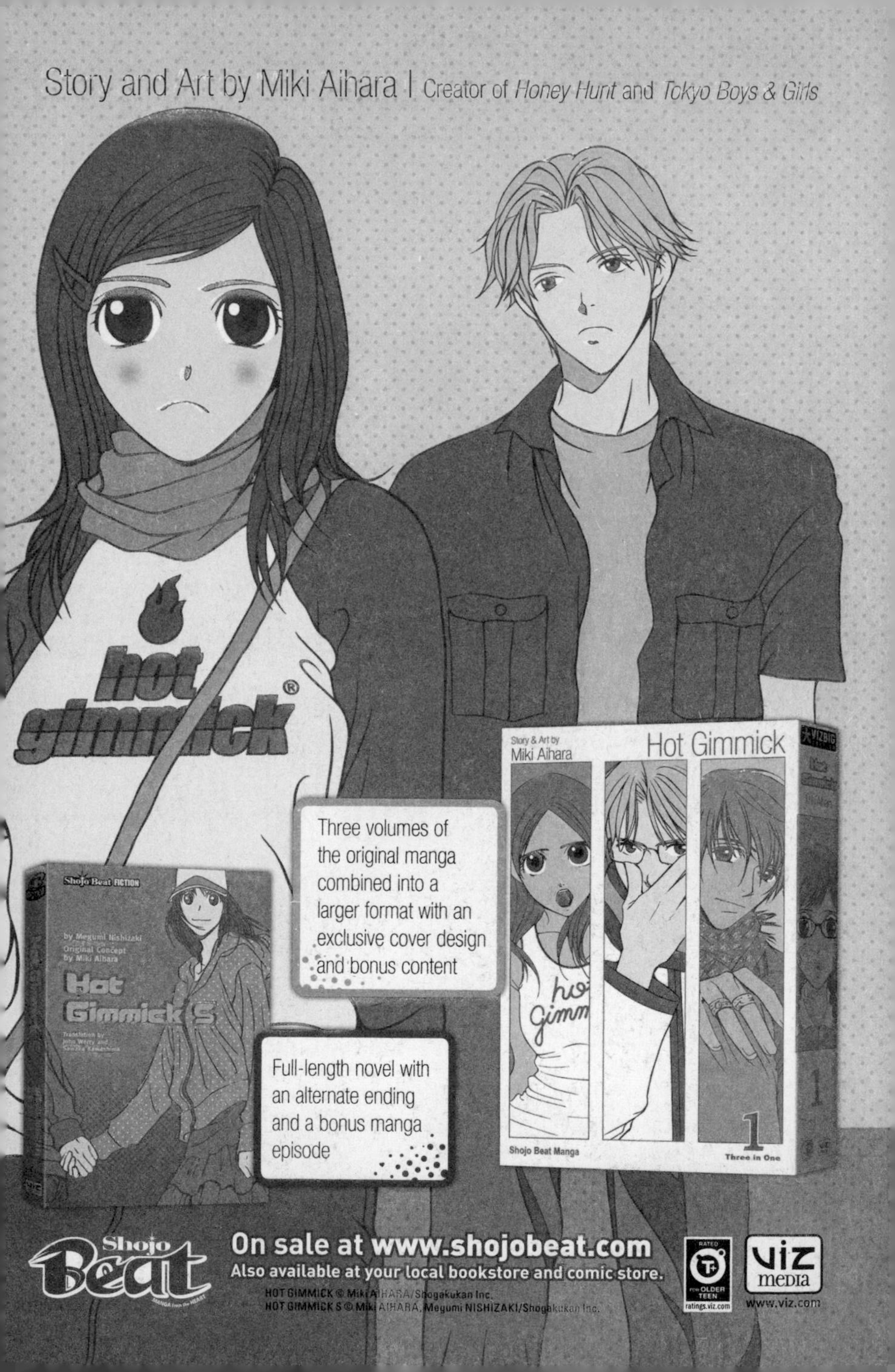
Story and Art by Miki Aihara | Creator of *Honey Hunt* and *Tokyo Boys & Girls*
hot gimmick®
Story & Art by Miki Aihara
Hot Gimmick
Shojo Beat Manga
1
Three in One
Three volumes of the original manga combined into a larger format with an exclusive cover design and bonus content
Shojo Beat FICTION
by Megumi Nishizaki
Original Concept by Miki Aihara
Hot Gimmick S
Full-length novel with an alternate ending and a bonus manga episode
Shojo Beat
On sale at www.shojobeat.com
Also available at your local bookstore and comic store.
HOT GIMMICK © Miki AIHARA/Shogakukan Inc.
HOT GIMMICK S © Miki AIHARA, Megumi NISHIZAKI/Shogakukan Inc.
RATED T+ FOR OLDER TEEN
ratings.viz.com
VIZ MEDIA
www.viz.com

Hot Gimmick

If you think being a teenager is hard, be glad your name isn't Hatsumi Narita

With scandals that would make any gossip girl blush and more triangles than you can throw a geometry book at, this girl may never figure out the game of love!

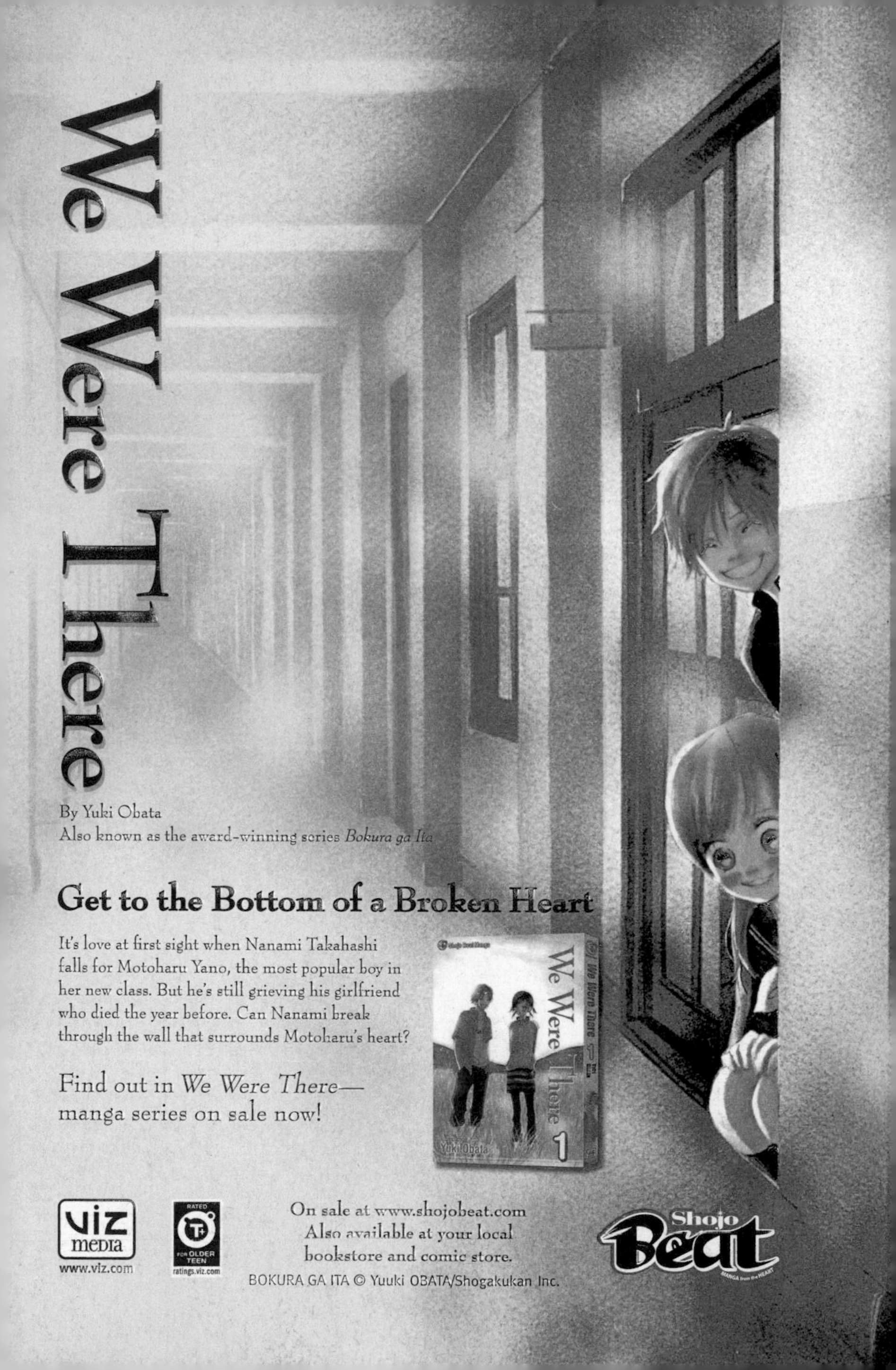